OXFORD WORLD'S CLASSICS

TWELVE PLAYS

ANTON CHEKHOV was born in 1860 in south Russia, the son of a poor grocer. At the age of 19 he followed his family to Moscow, where he studied medicine and helped to support the household by writing comic sketches for popular magazines. By 1888 he was publishing in the prestigious literary monthlies of Moscow and St Petersburg: a sign that he had already attained maturity as a writer of serious fiction. During the next fifteen years he wrote the short stories—fifty or more of them—which form his chief claim to world pre-eminence in the genre and are his main achievement as a writer. His plays are almost equally important, especially during his last years. He was closely associated with the Moscow Art Theatre and married its leading lady, Olga Knipper. In 1898 he was forced to move to Yalta, where he wrote his two greatest plays, *Three Sisters* and *The Cherry Orchard*. The première of the latter took place on his forty-fourth birthday. Chekhov died six months later, on 2 July 1904.

RONALD HINGLEY, Emeritus Fellow of St Antony's College, Oxford, edited and translated The Oxford Chekhov (9 volumes), and is the author of *A Life of Anton Chekhov* (also published by Oxford University Press). He is the translator of several volumes of Chekhov stories in Oxford World's Classics: *The Russian Master and Other Stories*, *Ward Number Six and Other Stories*, and *The Princess and Other Stories*, and his other translation of Chekhov's drama for Oxford World's Classics is *Five Plays*.

OXFORD WORLD'S CLASSICS

For almost 100 years Oxford World's Classics have brought
readers closer to the world's great literature. Now with over 700
titles—from the 4,000-year-old myths of Mesopotamia to the
twentieth century's greatest novels—the series makes available
lesser-known as well as celebrated writing.

The pocket-sized hardbacks of the early years contained
introductions by Virginia Woolf, T. S. Eliot, Graham Greene,
and other literary figures which enriched the experience of reading.
Today the series is recognized for its fine scholarship and
reliability in texts that span world literature, drama and poetry,
religion, philosophy and politics. Each edition includes perceptive
commentary and essential background information to meet the
changing needs of readers.

OXFORD WORLD'S CLASSICS

——

ANTON CHEKHOV

Twelve Plays

——

Translated with an Introduction and Notes by
RONALD HINGLEY

OXFORD
UNIVERSITY PRESS

OXFORD
UNIVERSITY PRESS

Great Clarendon Street, Oxford OX2 6DP

Oxford University Press is a department of the University of Oxford.
It furthers the University's objective of excellence in research, scholarship,
and education by publishing worldwide in

Oxford New York

Athens Auckland Bangkok Bogotá Buenos Aires Calcutta
Cape Town Chennai Dar es Salaam Delhi Florence Hong Kong Istanbul
Karachi Kuala Lumpur Madrid Melbourne Mexico City Mumbai
Nairobi Paris São Paulo Singapore Taipei Tokyo Toronto Warsaw

with associated companies in Berlin Ibadan

Oxford is a registered trade mark of Oxford University Press
in the UK and in certain other countries

Published in the United States
by Oxford University Press Inc., New York

Translation and editorial material © Ronald Hingley 1964, 1967, 1968
Introduction © Ronald Hingley 1992
Chronology © Oxford University Press 1984
Select Bibliography © Patrick Miles 1998

This selection first issued as a World's Classics paperback 1992
Reissued as an Oxford World's Classics paperback 1999

British Library Cataloguing in Publication Data

Data available

Library of Congress Cataloging in Publication Data

Chekhov, Anton Pavlovich, 1860–1904.
[Plays. English. Selections]
Twelve plays / Anton Chekhov ; translated with an introduction and
notes by Ronald Hingley.
p. cm.—(Oxford world's classics)
Translated from the Russian.
Includes bibliographical references.
1. Chekhov, Anton Pavlovich, 1860–1904—Translations into English.
2. One-act plays, Russian—Translations into English. I. Hingley,
Ronald. II. Title. III. Title: 12 plays. IV. Series.
PG3456.A19H5 1992 891.72'3—dc20 91–20381

ISBN 0–19–283674–9

3 5 7 9 10 8 6 4 2

Printed in Great Britain by
Cox & Wyman Ltd.
Reading, Berkshire

CONTENTS

INTRODUCTION

THIS is the seventh volume of Chekhov to appear in the World's Classics. It completes the issue in paperback of translations first brought out in the hardback critical edition *The Oxford Chekhov* (1964–80). With the present *Twelve Plays* and the previously published *Five Plays* the World's Classics now embrace the entire corpus of Chekhov's drama. Five further volumes contain the whole of his mature prose fiction.[1]

No one could pretend that the twelve very mixed items in this volume deserve as prominent a place in the repertoire as is claimed by the Five Plays, including as those do three masterpieces of startling originality (*Uncle Vanya*, *Three Sisters*, and *The Cherry Orchard*), as well as the intriguingly transitional *Seagull* and the far from negligible *Ivanov*. However, each drama in the present dozen has a fascination of its own. They may be minor works, but they are the minor works of a major writer.

The most frequently staged material in this volume, and perhaps the most stageworthy, is to be found among the short plays with which it begins, and consists of the five farces *The Bear*, *The Proposal*, *A Tragic Role*, *The Wedding*, and *The Anniversary*, together with the farcical monologue *Smoking is Bad for You*. The farces are commonly called 'vaudevilles' because that is the name which Chekhov himself gave them. Their pace, verve, and exuberance, expressed in vibrant and richly comic dialogue, have made them favourites with audiences all over the world. They reveal a Chekhov who will astound those reared exclusively on the 'haunting lyricism' of literary cliché. There is no room in them for that celebrated 'minor key', those inevitable 'pastel shades'. Here, in the vaudevilles, is a full-blooded, free-swinging dramatist who specializes in the overdone effect. He thus appears as the very

---

[1] By 'mature fiction' are understood all the short stories—three dozen in all—which first appeared between March 1888 and Chekhov's death in July 1904. Variant versions and detailed accounts of individual works (their origins, biographical involvements, textual history, reception, etc.) have been omitted from the World's Classics volumes, but readers may care to know that such information is to be found in *The Oxford Chekhov*.

opposite of the tentative, laconic, creatively understated Chekhov of the mature four-acters. Now, the high-profile, relatively immature Chekhov of the Twelve Plays is, of course, less important than the low-profile, mature Chekhov of the Five. It is the latter who rightly remains the favourite of theatre-goers and readers, having triumphed over all the mawkish clichés thrown at him by critics and reviewers. But he is barely represented at all in the present collection.

The vaudevilles all belong (with some reservations affecting the date of *Smoking is Bad for You*) to the years 1888–91, which happen to be the first four years of Chekhov's maturity as a writer of short stories. This phase started with the publication, in early 1888, of a story, *The Steppe*, which was at once recognized as strikingly superior to the vast assortment of his earlier-published sketches and stories. Not a few of these had, as it happens, been broadly farcical along the lines of the vaudevilles, and they had been written for fun or money—certainly not, most of them, with any exalted artistic aim. Much of this early short-story material had appeared over the pseudonym 'Antosha Chekhonte', and consisted in its most scurrilous manifestations of uproarious drivel mocking shrill mothers-in-law, gibbering dotards, tottering drunkards, preposterous cuckolds, and the like. By 1888 this sort of thing had long been on the way out. Serious work was taking its place, and with the publication of *The Steppe* the farcical vein virtually disappeared from Chekhov's non-dramatic output.

It is a curious fact that Chekhov continued to exploit such farcical material in drama by starting to write his vaudevilles at the very time when he purged almost every trace of such bubbling absurdities from his non-dramatic prose. This exploitation involved more than mere style, atmosphere, and technique, for three of the vaudevilles are adapted from specific earlier-published short stories by Chekhov himself. *A Tragic Role* is a dramatized version of the story *One among Many* (1887). *The Wedding* is taken from *A Wedding with a General* (1884), but also contains themes from two other stories. *The Anniversary* derives from *A Defenceless Creature* (1887).

The vaudevilles are improvements as well as adaptations. While using what is basically the same material Chekhov sent his three dramatized short stories to the stage with a sharper cutting edge, having honed them into the sparkling brilliance which they share with the three farces lacking short-story counterparts: *The Bear*, *The Proposal*, and *Smoking is Bad for You*. The last-mentioned is a comic monologue with a particularly complex history. The version translated here first appeared in 1903, by which time it was the sixth recension in a series of extensively reshaped drafts dating back to 1886.

In creating stage farces of unusual brilliance, Chekhov leans heavily on the theme of mutual misunderstanding, stressing the inability of human beings to communicate with each other. This, in a very different way, also happens to be a prominent feature of his later, more serious drama, where the realization is infinitely less broad and rumbustious. Here, in the farces, he parades a grotesque gaggle of cackling weirdos—stupid, self-seeking, and grasping in the ultimate degree. Comically absurd as the male characters are, the women are if anything more so. Another feature is a harping on physical disorders: heart attacks, fainting, various violent aches and pains. All in all this is an effervescent mixture giving off a powerful, sometimes pungent, exhalation of laughing gas.

The vaudevilles were a success on the stage from the beginning. They were also lucrative, which was why Chekhov once remarked: 'When I've written myself out I'm going to write vaudevilles and live on them. I think I could write about a hundred of them every year. Vaudeville subjects gush out of me like oil from the wells of Baku.'[2] The vaudevilles are indeed a superb realization of their particular genre, and one might regret that Chekhov wrote only half a dozen; a hundred a year, though, might have taxed the theatre's capacity to absorb them.

In addition to the six completed farces Chekhov's short plays include four other items. Among these *The Night before the Trial* is yet another vaudeville, but was left incomplete. *On the High Road* and *Swan Song* are further dramatic adaptations of previously published Chekhov stories. Here the material is poignant rather than farcical, and the overall impact is less than that of the vaudevilles. Perhaps these two 'tear-jerkers' could be—conceivably they have been—successfully brought off on

[2] Letter to A. S. Suvorin, 23 Dec. 1888.

the stage. But it would require a pathos-purveying and bathos-skirting actor of genius to play a Bortsov or a Svetlovidov triumphantly. Finally, *Tatyana Repin* is less a play for the stage than a private joke in dramatic form between Chekhov and his close friend the publisher A. S. Suvorin; it is included here as a curio and for the sake of completeness.

From the ten short plays we now turn to the two four-acters which constitute the remainder of this volume. Each occupies a significant position in the evolution of Chekhov's art, and in the case of *The Wood-Demon* this partly derives from its close relationship with the later masterpiece *Uncle Vanya*. The earlier play is too different from the later to be considered a mere draft version, but it certainly served as a quarry from which the masonry for a great deal of the later play was taken. About half the characters and about half the dialogue, much of it in long continuous blocks, was transferred from the one to the other, and so adroitly is the old material dovetailed into new material that we indisputably have two different plays here: not two versions of the same play.

As might be expected, *The Wood-Demon* has affinities with the early Chekhov such as are absent in *Uncle Vanya*. The tone of the earlier play is lighter, but echoes of the all-out slapstick of the vaudevilles are muted. *The Wood-Demon* also seems to incorporate a moralizing urge, reminding one of the miscued story *Lights* (1888) and of certain earlier stories in which Chekhov, for whatever reason, set himself to propagate the moral lessons preached by his older contemporary Leo Tolstoy: a distillation, much in vogue in the period, of the Christian ethic as that bearded sage interpreted it. In *The Wood-Demon* the Tolstoyan–Christian virtues of repentance, charity, and commitment to a good cause are by implication commended in the person of Michael Khrushchov. The eager, energetic, impulsive Khrushchov also seems to represent a half-hearted attempt by Chekhov to create a 'positive character'— an occupational obsession of Russian writers from which he luckily soon freed himself. Then again, to take another 'moral' element in *The Wood-Demon*, the beauteous Helen Serebryakov seems to be held out for approval because she has 'sacrificed herself' to her elderly, gout-ridden husband.

This moralizing concern, which Tolstoy could successfully

infuse into so much of his later fiction, was to prove a stumbling-block to Chekhov. It did not suit his muse at all—indeed, it was through *The Wood-Demon* and the various moralizing short stories that he discovered this. Nor was the conventionally 'happy ending' of *The Wood-Demon* in the least consistent with Chekhov's art as it eventually developed: witness the relentlessly downbeat denouement of *Uncle Vanya*, and of so many among his later plays and stories. The value of *The Wood-Demon* to Chekhov was that of an experiment which succeeded only because it helped to teach him what he should not be doing. But it would be a pity to regard the play as no more than that. It has its own special charm if sensitively staged.

Of all the items in this volume *Platonov* least accords with any conceivable stereotype of Chekhov's work. Laconic it most definitely is not, for it sprawls over enough pages to accommodate about three of the mature four-act plays. As for Chekhov the master of hints, half-statements, and pregnant silences, he will be sought in vain in this, his first serious attempt to establish himself as a dramatist. *Platonov* was never designed as a farce, though a cynic might be tempted to claim that some of its scenes could be played as such. As for on-stage 'action', which the mature Chekhov so notoriously tended to keep out of his plays, *Platonov* positively revels in it. Full-blooded quarrels, savage denunciations, passionate avowals of love and hatred—these follow each other in rapid succession. At their mildest the characters are repeatedly found telling each other to vacate the premises or hold their tongues, and otherwise indulging in the 'hard-hitting dialogue' beloved of a later age's television dramatists. The play contains two attempted suicides, an attempted knifing, and the off-stage lynching of a horse-thief by incensed peasants. It ends when the hero is murdered by one of a group of women who fall violently in love–hate with him. A far cry, all this, from Uncle Vanya's low-key self-pity, from the ineffectual urges of the Three Sisters and their brother, from the ditherings of the Cherry Orchard's proprietors.

It is as if the young Chekhov had decided on a spectacular act of self-purgation by disgorging into a single mega-play all the paraphernalia of traditional theatricality which he was later to abandon when he found his true originality as a dramatist. *Platonov* therefore has much to say to those who wish to examine the roots of his art. The evidence of the young author's literary power is impressive, and it is significant that he could only learn to apply that power so successfully at a later stage through having misapplied it on so grand a scale in youth.

Platonov is one of Chekhov's earliest extant works. If its origins do not go back to his schooldays, which they may, the play had probably been completed by the end of his second year as a medical student at Moscow University, that is in 1881. He tried to have it staged, submitting it to M. N. Yermolova, a prominent Muscovite Thespian of the period; but was unsuccessful. After that it disappears from the record until its discovery among the author's papers after his death in 1904. It was published posthumously in 1923. The very title *Platonov*—appropriate enough, since it is the name of the sexually irresistible village schoolmaster who appears on practically every page—is not that of Chekhov, who left his play nameless, but has been adopted by the common consent of editors.

Bizarre though *Platonov* may seem, both in its textual history and in its text, it provides valuable evidence on Chekhov's attitude to his art at the outset of his career. It shows, for example, how seriously he took dramatic writing, as opposed to short-story writing, at so early a stage in his literary evolution. He, who was simultaneously publishing light-hearted trivia in the comic press, adopted a very different attitude when it came to writing for the stage. Here his intentions were entirely serious. What he still lacked was the technique to express such seriousness effectively, and to give it his own inimitable twist.

Platonov offers the Chekhov addict compulsive reading. But it was written to be staged, not read. And staged it frequently has been over the years, beginning with German and Czech performances in the 1920s. Since then various abridgements and adaptations—necessary, since a performance rivalling Wagner's *Ring* in length is neither possible nor desirable—have served to keep alive the memory of this least Chekhovian, but in some ways most tantalizing, of Chekhov's plays.

The present volume completes the publication of my work on

Chekhov in the World's Classics. It marks the culmination of efforts dissipated over the years since 1947, when I began to research the first of my two biographies. This Introduction may therefore turn out to be the last which it will have been my pleasant duty to provide. That might be just as well, since there is a limit to the number of such essays which can usefully come from the same pen, and this happens to be the six-teenth—no less—of my prefatory ramblings on the great Anton Pavlovich. In any case this seems a suitable opportunity to thank the Oxford University Press most cordially for its professional expertise, unfailing support and kindness to me straddling several decades and editors, while above all saluting its signal loyalty to the Russian Master. No English-language publisher has done more for Chekhov than the Press.

RONALD HINGLEY
Oxford, 1991

SELECT BIBLIOGRAPHY

Biography and Autobiography

Heim, Michael Henry (trans.), and Karlinsky, Simon (ed.), *Letters of Anton Chekhov* (New York, 1973).

Hingley, Ronald, *A Life of Chekhov* (Oxford, 1989).

Rayfield, Donald, *Anton Chekhov: A Life* (London, 1997).

Bibliography

Lantz, Kenneth, *Anton Chekhov, A Reference Guide to Literature* (Boston, 1985).

Background

Bruford, W. H., *Chekhov and His Russia* (London, 1948).

Tulloch, John, *Chekhov: A Structuralist Study* (London, 1980).

Criticism

Clyman, Toby W. (ed.), *A Chekhov Companion* (Westport, Conn., 1985).

Emeljanow, Victor, *Chekhov: The Critical Heritage* (London, 1981).

Gottlieb, Vera, *Chekhov and the Vaudeville* (Cambridge, 1982).

Magarshack, David, *Chekhov the Dramatist* (New York, 1952).

Pitcher, Harvey, *The Chekhov Play: A New Interpretation* (London, 1973).

Rayfield, Donald, *Chekhov's 'Uncle Vania', and 'The Wood Demon'* (London, 1995).

Senelick, Laurence, *Anton Chekhov* (London, 1985).

—— *The Chekhov Theatre: A Century of the Plays in Performance* (Cambridge, 1997).

Worrall, Nick (ed.), *File on Chekhov* (London, 1986).

Further Reading in Oxford World's Classics

Five Plays, translated and edited by Ronald Hingley (*Ivanov*; *The Seagull*; *Uncle Vanya*; *Three Sisters*; *The Cherry Orchard*).

Early Stories, translated and edited by Patrick Miles and Harvey Pitcher.

The Steppe, and Other Stories, translated and edited by Ronald Hingley.

Ward Number Six and Other Stories, translated and edited by Ronald Hingley.

A CHRONOLOGY OF
ANTON CHEKHOV

All dates are given old style.

1860	16 or 17 January. Born in Taganrog, a port on the Sea of Azov in south Russia
1876	His father goes bankrupt. The family moves to Moscow, leaving Anton to finish his schooling.
1879	Joins family and enrols in the Medical Faculty of Moscow University.
1880	Begins to contribute to *Strekoza* ('Dragonfly'), a St Petersburg comic weekly.
1882	Starts to write short stories and a gossip column for *Oskolki* ('Splinters') and to depend on writing for an income.
1884	Graduates in medicine. Shows early symptoms of tuberculosis.
1885–6	Contributes to *Peterburgskaya gazeta* ('St Petersburg Gazette') and *Novoye vremya* ('New Time').
1886	March. Letter from D. V. Grigorovich encourages him to take writing seriously. First collection of stories: *Motley Stories*.
1887	Literary reputation grows fast. Second collection of stories: *In the Twilight*. 19 November. First Moscow performance of *Ivanov*: mixed reception.
1888	First publication (*The Steppe*) in a serious literary journal, *Severny vestnik* ('The Northern Herald').
1889	31 January. First St Petersburg performance of *Ivanov*: widely and favourably reviewed. June. Death of brother Nicholas from tuberculosis.
1890	April–December. Crosses Siberia to visit the penal settlement on Sakhalin Island. Returns via Hong Kong, Singapore, and Ceylon.
1891	First trip to western Europe: Italy and France.
1892	March. Moves with family to small country estate at Melikhovo, 50 miles south of Moscow.
1895	First meeting with Tolstoy.

1896   17 October. First—disastrous—performance of *The Seagull* in St Petersburg.

1897   Suffers severe haemorrhage.

1897–8   Winters in France. Champions Zola's defence of Dreyfus.

1898   Beginning of collaboration with the newly founded Moscow Art Theatre. Meets Olga Knipper. Spends the winter in Yalta, where he meets Gorky.

            17 December. First Moscow Art Theatre performance of *The Seagull*: successful.

1899   Completes the building of a house in Yalta, where he settles with mother and sister.

            26 October. First performance by Moscow Art Theatres of *Uncle Vanya* (written ?1896).

1899–1901 First collected edition of his works (10 volumes).

1901   31 January. *Three Sisters* first performed.
            25 May. Marries Olga Knipper.

1904   17 January. First performance of *The Cherry Orchard*.
            2 July. Dies in Badenweiler, Germany.

ON THE HIGH ROAD

[*На большой дороге*]

A DRAMATIC STUDY IN ONE ACT

(1885)

CHARACTERS

TIKHON YEVSTIGNEYEV, keeper of an inn on the high road

SIMON BORTSOV, a ruined landowner

MARY, his wife

SAVVA, an old pilgrim

NAZAROVNA ⎱ pious old women
YEFIMOVNA ⎰

FEDYA, a factory worker who is passing through

YEGOR MERIK, a tramp

KUZMA, a traveller

A POSTMAN

DENIS, a coachman

Pilgrims, drovers, travellers, etc

The action takes place in south Russia

TIKHON's inn. Right, the bar; shelves containing bottles. At the back of the stage, a door opening on the road, with a dirty red lantern hanging above it on the outside. The floor and benches by the walls are jammed with pilgrims and travellers. Many are sleeping in a sitting position for lack of room. It is late at night. As the curtain rises there is a clap of thunder, and a flash of lightning is seen through the open door.

SCENE I

[TIKHON is behind the bar. FEDYA is sprawled on one of the benches, quietly playing an accordion. Near him sits BORTSOV in shabby summer clothes. SAVVA, NAZAROVNA and YEFIMOVNA have settled on the floor near the benches.]

YEFIMOVNA [to NAZAROVNA]. Give the old man a shove, dear. He ain't long for this world, I reckon.

NAZAROVNA [pulling the edge of SAVVA's coat off his face]. Good Christian sir, be you alive or be you dead?

SAVVA. What—me dead? I'm alive, I am. [Raising himself on one elbow.] Cover my legs, old thing. That's right. A bit more on the right side. That's right. Bless you.

NAZAROVNA [covering SAVVA's legs]. Go to sleep, dearie.

SAVVA. Sleep? How can I? If only I had the patience to bear this agony, I could do without sleep. A sinner deserves no peace. What's that noise, my dear?

NAZAROVNA. Thunder, by God's grace. There's a howling wind and the rain's fair lashing down, beating on the roof and windows like it was peas from the pod. Hear it? The floodgates of heaven are opened. [Thunder.] Holy saints above us!

FEDYA. All that roaring, thundering, crashing—when will it ever end? Boom, boom—like the roar of the forest. Boom, boom! Like a dog's howling, the wind is. [Hunches himself up.] It's cold. My clothes are sopping wet and the door's wide open. [Plays softly.] My accordion's soaked, friends, there's no tunes left in it, or I'd let you have a proper basinful—fair take your breath away, it would! Great stuff! Quadrilles, polkas, say, or your Russian song and dance—I can do 'em all.

When I was waiter at the Grand Hotel in town, I never saved no money, but when it came to the accordion, I really knew my stuff. I play the guitar too.

VOICE FROM THE CORNER. A foolish man talks foolish talk.

FEDYA. Fool yourself! [*Pause.*]

NAZAROVNA [*to* SAVVA]. You should be lying in the warm now, dearie, and warming your poor leg. [*Pause.*] Old man, good Christian sir. [*Nudges* SAVVA.] Not a-dying, are you?

FEDYA. Better have a drop of vodka, grandpa. That'll put fire in your belly, it will, and ease your heart a bit. Here, have some.

NAZAROVNA. Less of the fancy talk, young man. The old fellow may be passing away, a-repenting of his sins, and you carry on like this, you and your accordion. Leave the music alone, you saucy creature.

FEDYA. Why are *you* bothering him then? He's proper poorly, and you—. Women's foolishness, this is. He can't speak harshly to you, him being a holy man. Pretty pleased with yourself, ain't you, because he listens to a ninny like you? Sleep on, granddad, don't you listen to her. Let her chatter away and to hell with her. A woman's tongue's like the devil's broom, it sweeps the wise and cunning out of the house. Let her go to hell. [*Throws up his arms.*] Hey, you're thin as a rake, grandpa. Not half you are—just like a dead skelington, with no life in you. Are you really dying?

SAVVA. Why should I die? God grant I don't die before my time. I'll have a bad turn, and then, God willing, I'll get up. The Blessed Virgin will see I don't die in foreign parts, I'll die at home.

FEDYA. Do you come from far?

SAVVA. I'm a Vologda man, a humble citizen of that town.

FEDYA. Where's Vologda?

TIKHON. T'other side of Moscow, in the Province of——

FEDYA. Phew, you have come a way, granddad. Done it all on foot, have you?

SAVVA. I have, lad. I've been to the shrine of St. Tikhon and I'm on my way to the Holy Mountains. Then, God willing, I'll go to Odessa. They say you can get a cheap passage from there to Jerusalem. Twenty-one roubles it costs, 'tis said.

FEDYA. Ever been in Moscow?

SAVVA. That I have! Half a dozen times.

FEDYA. Decent town, is it? [*Lights a cigarette.*] Worth-while?

SAVVA. There's plenty of holy shrines, boy. And where there's lots of shrines it's always worth-while.

BORTSOV [*goes up to the bar and speaks to* TIKHON]. Once again, for Christ's sake give me a drink.

FEDYA. The great thing is, a town should be clean. If it's dusty they should water the place, and if it's muddy they should clean it up. There should be tall houses, a theatre, police and cab-drivers, er—. I've lived in towns myself, I know what's what.

BORTSOV. Just a glass, just this little one. Chalk it up, I'll pay.

TIKHON. That's enough of that.

BORTSOV. Oh come on! Please!

TIKHON. You clear off!

BORTSOV. You don't understand me. Get this into your head, you clod, if there's one drop of grey matter in your country bumpkin's skull: it's not me that's asking—it's my guts, to put it in your yokel language. It's my illness that's asking, can't you see?

TIKHON. There's nothing *to* see. Go away.

BORTSOV. Look, if I don't get a drink now, see, if I don't satisfy my craving, I may do something awful. God knows what I may not do. You've seen lots of drunks since you started keeping a pub, you swine, surely you know what they're like by now! They're ill! Chain 'em up, beat 'em, stab 'em if you like—but let 'em have their vodka. Look, I'm asking you humbly! Please! I'm demeaning myself, my God, I am.

TIKHON. Let's have the money and you'll get your vodka.

BORTSOV. Where can I get money? It's all gone on drink, the whole damn lot. So what can I give you? All I have left is my overcoat, but that I can't give you because I have nothing on underneath. How about my cap. [*Takes off his cap and gives it to* TIKHON.]

TIKHON [*examining the cap*]. H'm. There's caps and caps. This one's like a sieve.

FEDYA [*laughs*]. It's a proper gentleman's cap, one to walk down the street in and take off to the young ladies. 'I say, what ho! How do you do?'

TIKHON [*gives the cap back to* BORTSOV]. I wouldn't take that filthy thing as a gift.

BORTSOV. Well, if you don't like it, give me a drink on tick. I'll be coming back from town and I'll bring you your five copecks, and may it choke you. Yes, choke you—may it stick in your throat! [*Coughs.*] I loathe you.

TIKHON [*banging his fist on the counter*]. Can't you leave me alone? Who do you think you are? Some kind of a crook? What brought you here?

BORTSOV. I want a drink. It's not me that wants it, it's my illness, see?

TIKHON. Don't aggravate me, or you'll find yourself getting some fresh air double quick!

BORTSOV. What can I do? [*Leaves the bar.*] What can I do? [*Reflects.*]

YEFIMOVNA. It's the devil tempting you. You take no notice, guv'nor. That's the Evil One a-whispering 'drink, drink, drink!' But you answer back: 'No, no, no!' Then he'll leave you be.

FEDYA. There's a ruddy great banging in your brain-pan, I'll bet, and your insides ain't feeling too good either. [*Roars with laughter.*] You're a funny one, sir. Lie down and sleep. No point in flapping round the place like a ruddy great scarecrow, this ain't no kitchen garden.

BORTSOV [*angrily*]. Shut up! No one asked your opinion, jackass.

FEDYA. You keep a civil tongue in your head! I know your sort— as if there weren't enough tramps like you on the high road! As for me being a jackass, when I fetch you one over the ear-hole you won't half roar—the storm won't be in it! Jackass yourself! Low scum! [*Pause.*] Bastard.

NAZAROVNA. The good old man may be praying and giving up his soul to God, while these blackguards are quarrelling and swearing. You should be ashamed of yourselves.

FEDYA. Stop snivelling, you old frump. Them as comes in taverns must put up with tavern ways.

BORTSOV. What am I to do? What can I do? How can I make him see? What more eloquence do I need? [*To* TIKHON.] This makes my blood run cold. Dear old Tikhon! [*Weeps.*] Tikhon, please.

SAVVA [*groans*]. There's a shooting pain in my leg, like a bullet of fire. Old woman——

YEFIMOVNA. What is it, dearie?

SAVVA. Who's that crying?

YEFIMOVNA. The squire.

SAVVA. Ask the squire to shed a tear for me, so I may die in Vologda. Tears can make a prayer work wonders.

BORTSOV. I'm not praying, granddad. And these aren't tears either— it's my heart's blood running out. [*Sits down by* SAVVA's *feet.*] Heart's blood, I tell you. Anyway, this is a bit beyond you, a bit outside your dim horizons, old boy. You're a benighted lot.

SAVVA. But where are those who can see the light?

BORTSOV. There are some bright enough to understand, granddad.

SAVVA. There are for sure, son. The saints had the light, they under- stood all sorrows. No need to explain, they'd just understand. They can tell from the look in your eyes. And when they understand you, it's such a comfort, you might never have been troubled—it goes away like magic.

FEDYA. Have you really seen the saints?

SAVVA. I have, lad. It takes all sorts to make a world. There are sinners and there are the servants of the Lord.

BORTSOV. I can't make sense of this. [*Quickly gets up.*] Talk must make sense, but what sense is there in me at the moment? I just have an instinct, a thirst! [*Hurries to the bar.*] Tikhon, take my coat, do you hear? [*Makes to take his coat off.*] My overcoat——

TIKHON. What have you got underneath? [*Looks under* BORTSOV's *overcoat.*] Your bare skin? Keep it, I won't have it. I won't take a sin upon my soul.

[MERIK *comes in.*]

SCENE II

[The above and MERIK.*]*

BORTSOV. Very well, I'll take the sin upon *my* soul. Agreed?

MERIK *[silently takes off his outer coat and stands there wearing a jerkin; he has an axe at his belt].* There's them as feels the cold, but the bear and the homeless wanderer are always too hot. Fair sweating, I am. *[Puts the axe on the floor and takes off his jerkin.]* While you drag one foot out of the mud, you sweat a bucketful, and by the time one foot's free t'other's got stuck.

YEFIMOVNA. Quite right. Is it raining less, son?

MERIK *[with a glance at* YEFIMOVNA*].* I don't bandy words with women. *[Pause.]*

BORTSOV *[to* TIKHON*].* I'll take the sin upon myself, do you hear?

TIKHON. I don't want to hear, leave me alone.

MERIK. It's so dark—like as if the sky had a coat of tar. You can't see your nose in front of you, and the rain whips your face like it was a real old blizzard. *[Takes his clothes and axe in his arms.]*

FEDYA. It's a nice day for crime, ain't it? Even wild animals take cover, but you jokers are in your element.

MERIK. Who said that?

FEDYA. Take a look. Not blind, are you?

MERIK. I'll chalk that up to you. *[Goes up to* TIKHON.*]* Hallo there, you with the face! Or don't you know me?

TIKHON. Expect me to know all you drunken vagabonds? Reckon I'd need a dozen sets of eyes for that.

MERIK. Well, have a look. *[Pause.]*

TIKHON. But I do recognize you, I declare—I know you by your eyes. *[Shakes hands.]* Andrew Polikarpov, ain't it?

MERIK. It was, but now it's Yegor Merik, I'd say.

TIKHON. How come?

MERIK. Whatever label God gives me, that's my name. I've been Merik for a couple of months. *[Thunder.]* Ger! Thunder away, you don't scare me. *[Looks round him.]* No bloodhounds about?

TIKHON. Bloodhounds? Midges and gnats, more like! They're a soft lot. The bloodhounds will be snoring in their feather-beds, I reckon. [*Loudly.*] Watch your pockets, friends, and your clothes too, if you care about 'em. This is a bad man. He'll rob you.

MERIK. Let 'em look to their money if they have any, but clothes I won't touch, I've no use for 'em.

TIKHON. Where the devil are you heading for?

MERIK. The Kuban District.

TIKHON. Are you now!

FEDYA. The Kuban? Really? [*Sits up.*] That's wonderful country, lads, it's a land beyond your wildest dreams. Fine open country! There's no end of birds, they say, and game and all kind of beasts, and the grass, by God, grows all year round. The folks are real friendly like, and they've more land than they know what to do with. They say the government will let you have three hundred acres a head—or so a soldier was telling me t'other day. What luck, God damn me!

MERIK. Luck? Luck walks behind your back, you don't see it. Bite your elbow and you may glimpse it. It's all foolishness. [*Looks at the benches and people.*] You might be a chain-gang having a night off. Hallo there, down-and-outs!

YEFIMOVNA [*to* MERIK]. What vicious eyes you have! You have the devil inside you, boy. Don't look at us.

MERIK. What cheer, my beggarly chums!

YEFIMOVNA. Turn away. [*Pushes* SAVVA.] Savva dear, a bad man's looking at us. He'll hurt you, dearie. [*To* MERIK.] Turn away, you snake, I tell you.

SAVVA. He won't harm you, old woman, never fear. God won't let him.

MERIK. Hallo there, friends! [*Shrugs his shoulders.*] They don't speak. Not asleep, are you, you clumsy oafs? Why won't you speak?

YEFIMOVNA. Turn those great eyes away. And turn away from your satanic pride.

MERIK. Shut up, you old bitch! I wanted to give you a word of kindness and good cheer in your misery, there's no satanic pride in that. You're huddled up in the cold like a lot of flies—so I felt sorry for you and wanted to say a kind word and comfort you in your wretchedness, but you all turn your ugly mugs away. Ah well, a fat lot I care! [*Goes up to* FEDYA.] And where might you come from?

FEDYA. From these parts—the Khamonyev brickworks.

MERIK. Get up, will you?

FEDYA [*sitting up*]. What's that?

MERIK. Get up, man. Get right up, I want that place.

FEDYA. Oh, so this is *your* place, is it?

MERIK. Yes. You go and lie on the floor.

FEDYA. Out of my way, you tramp! You don't scare me.

MERIK. Quite a lively lad! Now you clear off and don't argue, you fool, or you'll be sorry.

TIKHON [*to* FEDYA]. Don't cross him, boy. Let him have his way and to hell with him.

FEDYA. What right have you got? Rolls his great fish eyes at me and thinks I'm scared. [*Gathers up his belongings in his arms and goes and makes a bed on the floor.*] Blast you! [*Lies down and pulls the clothing over his head.*]

MERIK [*makes his bed on the bench*]. Well, you don't know much about devils if you think I'm one. They're not like me. [*Lies down and puts the axe by his side.*] Lie there, little axe—let me cover up your handle.

TIKHON. Where did you get that axe?

MERIK. Stole it, I did, and now I seem stuck with the blasted thing— it seems a pity to throw it away, and I've nowhere to put it. It's like a wife you've got sick of, it is. [*Covers himself up.*] Devils aren't like me, lad.

FEDYA [*poking his head out from under his coat*]. Then what are they like?

MERIK. They're like steam or your breath. If you blow [*blows*]— they're like that. You can't see 'em.

VOICE [*from the corner*]. If you sit under a harrow, you'll see 'em.

MERIK. I've sat under one and seen none. That's an old wives' tale. Devils, pixies, ghosts—you can't see 'em. Our eyes ain't made to see everything. When I was a boy, I used to go into the forest at night, specially to see the pixies. I'd yell for a pixy at the top of my voice, and keep my eyes skinned. I'd see all sorts of funny things, but no pixies. Then I'd go to a churchyard of a night to look for ghosts— but that was all old wives' tales too. I saw various animals, but as for anything to scare me—nothing doing. The eye ain't made that way.

VOICE [*from the corner*]. Don't say that, it does happen. A peasant was gutting a pig in our village. He's cutting out the tripes when out pops one of 'em.

SAVVA [*sitting up*]. Don't talk of the devil, lads! It's a sin, dear boys.

MERIK. Aha, the old greybeard! Mr. Skelington! [*Laughs.*] No need for us to go to no churchyard, we've got our own ghosts crawling out of the woodwork to tell ùs where we get off! Sinful, he calls it. It's not for you to lay down the law—you and your stupid ideas! You're an ignorant, benighted lot. [*Lights his pipe.*] My father was a peasant and liked laying down the law too, at times. He steals a sack of apples from the priest one night and brings it to us with a sermon: 'Mind you kids don't scoff them apples before Harvest Festival, because that's a sin.' That's you all over—you won't speak the devil's name, but you can behave like devils incarnate. Take this old cow, for instance. [*Points to* YEFIMOVNA.] She saw me as the devil, but I'll bet she's sold her own soul to the devil half a dozen times over, on account of her woman's foolishness.

YEFIMOVNA. Ugh! May the power of the Cross be with us! [*Buries her face in her hands.*] Savva, dear.

TIKHON. Why try to scare us? Think you're clever, don't you? [*The door bangs in the wind.*] Christ, what a wind!

MERIK [*stretches*]. Oh, for a chance to show my strength! [*The door bangs in the wind.*] I'd like to match my strength with yon wind! It can't pull the door off, but for two pins I'd rip this whole inn up by the roots! [*Gets up and lies down again.*] Oh, I'm fed up.

NAZAROVNA. Say a prayer, you monster! Can't you stop fidgeting?

YEFIMOVNA. Leave him alone, blast him. He's looking at us again. [*To* MERIK.] Don't stare, bad man! Them eyes! He looks like Satan at his prayers!

SAVVA. Let him look, good women. Say a prayer and the evil eye can't touch you.

BORTSOV. Oh, I can't stand it, it's more than I can bear. [*Goes to the bar.*] Look here, Tikhon, for the last time, please—give me half a glass!

TIKHON [*shakes his head*]. Then where's the money?

BORTSOV. Oh God, I've told you once, haven't I? It's all gone on drink. Where do you think I can get any? It won't break you, will it, if you let me have a drop of vodka on tick? A glass of vodka hardly costs you anything, but it will save me from torture—torture, I tell you! I'm not just fussing, this is real suffering, can't you see?

TIKHON. Go and tell someone else about it, not me. Go and beg from these good Christian people—let them treat you if they like. Beggars get bread from me, nothing else.

BORTSOV. *You* take the poor creatures' money—I can't, I'm sorry. It's not my job to rob them, and I won't do it, see? [*Bangs his fist on the bar.*] I won't do it! [*Pause.*] Eh, wait a minute. [*Turns to the pilgrims.*] It's an idea, friends, I must say. Give me five copecks. My guts needs it, I'm ill.

FEDYA. So we're to stand you a drink, you dirty twister? How about a glass of water?

BORTSOV. The depths I've sunk to! Never mind, I don't want it—it was a joke.

MERIK. You'll get nothing from him, Squire, he's too stingy—we all know that. Wait a minute—I had five copecks somewhere about. We'll have a glass between us. [*Rummages in his pockets.*] Hell, it must be somewhere. I thought I heard a jingling in my pocket t'other day. No, I've nothing. Nothing doing, old man—it's just your bad luck. [*Pause.*]

BORTSOV. I must have a drink or I'll do something violent, I might kill myself. Oh God, what can I do? [*Looks out through the door.*] Shall I go away? Shall I go off into the blue—the black, rather?

MERIK. Why don't you preach at him, you pious old women! And you, Tikhon, why don't you kick him out? He hasn't paid for his night's lodging, has he? Get rid of him, chuck him out on his ear! People are that cruel nowadays, there's no gentleness and kindness in them. A lot of brutes, they are! If they see a drowning man, they shout: 'Go on then—drown. We've no time to watch—we've got our work to do.' As for throwing him a rope, not a chance! Ropes cost money.

SAVVA. Don't you be so hard on people, good sir.

MERIK. Shut up, you old horror! You're a savage lot! Monsters! Treacherous scum! [*To* TIKHON.] Come here and take my boots off! Jump to it!

TIKHON. I say, he has gone off the deep end! [*Laughs.*] Proper terror, aren't you?

MERIK. Come here, I tell you. And look sharp. [*Pause.*] Do you hear me? I'm not talking to thin air, am I? [*Gets up.*]

TIKHON. All right, all right—that'll do.

MERIK. I want you to pull my boots off, you vampire—the boots of a beggar and tramp.

TIKHON. Come on, come on—don't be so bad-tempered. Come and have a drink. Come on.

MERIK. What did I say I wanted, friends? A free vodka or my boots pulled off? Didn't I make myself clear, didn't I put it straight? [*To* TIKHON.] So you didn't catch what I said? I'll give you a minute— you'll catch it then all right.

[*This causes some stir among the pilgrims and travellers, who get up and look at* TIKHON *and* MERIK *in silent expectation.*]

TIKHON. What the hell brought you here! [*Comes out from the bar.*] Quite fancy yourself, don't you? Ah well, I'd better, I suppose. [*Takes off* MERIK's *boots.*] You treacherous scum!

MERIK. That's right. And put them side by side. That's right. Now clear off.

TIKHON [*after taking off the boots, goes behind the bar*]. Think you're very clever, don't you? Any more of your tricks and you'll be out of this place on your neck, I'm telling you! [*To* BORTSOV, *who comes up to him.*] You again?

BORTSOV. Look, I've got something in gold I might let you have. All right then, if you like, I'll give you——

TIKHON. Why are you shaking? Talk sense.

BORTSOV. It's a rotten, low thing to do, but there's nothing for it. It's a dirty trick I have in mind, but then my mind's none too sound— any court would acquit me. Take it, but on this condition: return it to me when I get back from town. I give it before witnesses. Now witness this, all of you. [*Gets a gold locket from an inside pocket.*] Here. I ought to take the picture out, but I've nowhere to put it, I'm wet through. Come on, take the lot—the picture too! But one thing: don't, er, put your fingers on the face. Please. I was rude to you, my dear fellow, and silly, but forgive me and don't finger it. I don't want your eyes looking at the face. [*Gives* TIKHON *the locket.*]

TIKHON [*examines the locket*]. A stolen watch. All right then, have your drink. [*Pours some vodka.*] Put that inside you!

BORTSOV. Only don't you, er, touch—. [*Drinks slowly with shuddering pauses.*]

TIKHON [*opens the locket*]. I see—a lady. Where did you pick up a bit of stuff like that?

MERIK. Show it here. [*Gets up and goes to the bar.*] Give me a look.

TIKHON [*pushes his hand away*]. What do you think you're doing? Look at it while I hold it.

FEDYA [*gets up and goes to* TIKHON]. Let's have a look.

[*The pilgrims and travellers go up to the bar from various directions and form a group.*]

MERIK [*firmly clasps in both his hands* TIKHON's *hand which holds the locket, and looks at the portrait in silence; pause*]. Handsome little devil! A lady and all——

FEDYA. Not half—. Look at those cheeks and eyes! Move your fingers out a bit, I can't see. Hair down to the waist. It's just like she was alive and going to speak. [*Pause.*]

MERIK. That's the road to ruin for a weak man. Once saddled with a woman like that [*gives a gesture of despair*]—and you're dished!

KUZMA [*off-stage*]. Whoa! Stop, you stupid creature!

[*Enter* KUZMA.]

SCENE III

[*The above and* KUZMA.]

KUZMA [*comes in*]. 'The inn, a place where one and all
            Who use this road are bound to call.'
Yes, you may drive past your dear old father in broad daylight without seeing him, but an inn—that you can spot a hundred miles off in the dark. Out of my way, all true believers! You there! [*Bangs a coin on the bar.*] A glass of real madeira. And make it snappy!

FEDYA. Hey, you seem in one hell of a hurry!

TIKHON. Don't wave your arms, you'll knock something over.

KUZMA. What are arms for but to wave? What are you so scared of, you ruddy wilting lilies? A spot of rain, poor dears? [*Drinks.*]

YEFIMOVNA. It's enough to scare anyone, good sir, to be caught on the road on a night like this. We're well off these days, praise the

Lord, with plenty of villages and farms on the way, so you've somewhere to shelter from the weather. But in the old days things was past praying for. Seventy miles you might travel, and not see a single twig, let alone a village or farm. You had to sleep rough.

KUZMA. How long have you been knocking round, old girl?

YEFIMOVNA. I'm past seventy, sir.

KUZMA. Seventy! You'll soon be in your second childhood then. [*Looks at* BORTSOV.] What queer fish is this? [*Stares at* BORTSOV.] A gentleman, eh?

    [BORTSOV *recognizes* KUZMA, *goes into a corner, embarrassed, and sits on a bench.*]

KUZMA. Mr. Bortsov, is it you—yes or no? What are you doing in this dump? This is no place for you, surely.

BORTSOV. Hold your tongue.

MERIK [*to* KUZMA]. Who is he?

KUZMA. A most unhappy man. [*Walks nervously up and down by the bar.*] Eh? In a low dive—I ask you! In rags! Drunk! Oh, this has given me quite a turn, it has that! [*To* MERIK, *in a half whisper.*] This is the guv'nor, our landlord—Mr. Simon Bortsov, Esquire. See what a state he's in? He looks like nothing on earth! That's what the drink does for you. Fill me up, will you? [*Drinks.*] I come from his village, Bortsovka—you may have heard of it, it's about a hundred and fifty miles from here, in the Yergov District. We were his father's serfs. It's a rotten shame.

MERIK. Was he rich?

KUZMA. Oh yes, he was a big man.

MERIK. Squandered his father's money, did he?

KUZMA. No, it was sheer bad luck, man. He was a grand gentleman— rich, never the worse for drink. [*To* TIKHON.] You must have seen him yourself at times, I reckon, driving past the inn on his way to town. He had proper squire's horses—real nippy, they were—and a carriage with springs, all high-class stuff. He kept five troikas, man. I remember him crossing by the Mikishkin ferry hereabouts five years ago, and tossing them a rouble instead of five copecks. 'No time to wait for change,' says he. Not bad, eh?

MERIK. He must have gone out of his mind then.

KUZMA. He still seems to have his wits about him. It all came from being so feeble. And spoilt. The great thing is, it was all woman's work, lads. The poor man falls in love with a girl in town, fancies she's the loveliest thing in creation. She ain't no fairy princess, but he loves her like she was, see? She was a young lady, though, not a loose woman or anything like that, but a giddy little thing. Oh, she was proper flighty, she was—screwing her eyes up and laughing and all that. No sense, she had. The gentry like that kind—think they're real clever, when none of us peasants would give 'em house room. Well, the squire takes a fancy to her, and it's all up with him. He starts carrying on with her, and one thing leads to another and so on, with them going boating all night and playing pianos and that.

BORTSOV. Don't tell them, Kuzma. What's the point? What business is it of theirs, how I've lived?

KUZMA. Sorry, sir, I've only told them a bit of it. I've had my say, and that's all they'll hear. I told them that bit because I was upset like, oh, very upset I was. Come on, fill it up. [*Drinks.*]

MERIK [*in a half-whisper*]. And did she love him?

KUZMA [*in a half-whisper which gradually turns into ordinary speech*]. Well, what do you think? It's not as if the squire was just anyone! What—her not fall in love, and him with his couple of thousand acres and money to burn! And he was that respectable, too— dignified and well-behaved, like—and well in with the nobs. Like this. [*Takes* MERIK's *hand.*] 'Oh, I say, what ho! Cheerio! Oh, do come in!' Well, one night I'm walking through the squire's garden —and, brother, what a garden! Miles and miles of it. I'm walking along quietly, keeping my eyes open, and there they are sitting on a bench [*makes the sound of a kiss*], a-kissin' of each other. He kisses her once and she kisses him twice, the little bitch. He takes her little white hand, and she blushes and snuggles up to him, drat 'er! 'I love you, Simon,' says she. And Simon goes about like a lunatic, boasting how happy he is, being a bit weak in the head, like. Gives a rouble here and two roubles there. Gives me money to buy a horse. Lets everyone off their debts, he's so pleased with hisself.

BORTSOV. Oh—why go into all this? These people have no feelings. It's painful, can't you see?

KUZMA. I've not said much, sir. They keep on at me. Why not tell them a bit? All right then, I won't if it makes you angry. I won't. I don't give a damn for 'em.

[*The noise of mail-coach bells is heard.*]

FEDYA. Don't yell, tell it quietly.

KUZMA. I *am* telling it quietly. Can I help it if he wants me to stop? There's no more to tell, anyway. They got married and that was that. Pour a glass for good old Kuzma! [*Drinks.*] I don't like drunkenness. Just as the ladies and gentlemen are going to sit down to the wedding breakfast, she ups and rushes off in a carriage. [*In a whisper.*] Dashes off to town to a lawyer-fellow who's her lover. How do you like that, eh? She certainly picked her moment! Killing's too good for her, I'd say.

MERIK [*pensively*]. I see. And what happened next?

KUZMA. He goes clean off his rocker. He went on the booze, as you see, and he's never looked back since, they say. First it was little ones, now he's got to pink elephants. Still loves her, he does. Look how he loves her. He's walking all the way to town now just to have a peep at her, I reckon. Then he'll come back.

[*The mail-coach drives up to the inn. The* POSTMAN *comes in and has a drink.*]

TIKHON. The mail's late today.

[*The* POSTMAN *pays and goes out without speaking. The coach drives off with bells jingling.*]

VOICE [*from the corner*]. Just the weather for a mail robbery—it would be dead easy.

MERIK. I've been around for thirty-five years and never robbed the mail yet. [*Pause.*] Now it's gone and I'm too late. Too late I am.

KUZMA. Feel like a sniff at Siberia, do you?

MERIK. Not everyone gets caught. Anyway, I wouldn't mind. [*Abruptly.*] And what happened next?

KUZMA. You mean to this poor fellow?

MERIK. Why, who else?

KUZMA. Well, friends, the next thing that helped to ruin him was his brother-in-law, his sister's husband. He takes it into his head to back this brother-in-law, a bank loan to the tune of thirty thousand. The brother-in-law's a regular shark—the swine knows which side his bread's buttered on, of course, and he don't bat an eyelid. Borrows the money, but don't feel obliged to pay it back. So the master pays up all thirty thousand. [*Sighs.*] A fool and his money are soon parted. His wife has children by this lawyer-man, Brother-in-law buys an estate near Poltava, and our friend crawls round like an idiot from one low dive to another a-moaning and a-groaning to the likes of us: 'I've lost my faith, friends. I don't trust no one now!' Sheer weakness, I call it. We've all got our troubles nagging at us, but that don't mean we have to drown 'em in drink, do it? Take our village elder, now. His wife entertains the schoolmaster in broad daylight and spends her husband's money on booze, while her old man goes round with a grin on his face. He has got a bit thin, though.

TIKHON [*sighs*]. It depends how much strength God gives you.

KUZMA. Some are stronger than others, I grant you. Well, how much? [*Pays.*] Take my hard-earned cash. Good-bye, boys. Good night and pleasant dreams. It's time I was off. I'm fetching a midwife from hospital for the missus. Poor woman must be tired of waiting and wet through. [*Runs out.*]

TIKHON [*after a pause*]. Hey, you—what's your name? Come and have a drink, poor fellow. [*Pours one out.*]

BORTSOV [*comes up hesitantly to the bar and drinks*]. So I owe you for two glasses.

TIKHON. Owe me? Rubbish! Drink up and forget it. Drown your sorrows.

FEDYA. Have one on me too, Squire! Ah well! [*Throws a five-copeck piece on the bar.*] You die if you drink and you die if you don't. Life's all right without vodka—still, vodka does put a bit of life in you, by golly! Grief ain't grief when you've a drink inside you. Swill it down!

BORTSOV. Phew, hot stuff that!

MERIK. Give it here! [*Takes the locket from TIKHON and examines the portrait.*] I see. Ran away on her wedding day. Quite a girl!

VOICE [*from the corner*]. Give him another, Tikhon. Let him have one on me.

MERIK [*bangs the locket on the floor violently*]. Blast her!

[*Goes quickly to his place and lies down, face to the wall. General consternation.*]

BORTSOV. What's that? What's going on? [*Picks up the locket.*] How dare you, you swine? What right have you to do that? [*Tearfully.*] Want me to break your neck, you clumsy lout?

TIKHON. Don't be angry, Squire. It ain't made of glass, it's not broken. Have another, and sleep it off. [*Pours another glass.*] I'm tired of all your talk, and it's long past closing-time. [*Goes and shuts the outer door.*]

BORTSOV [*drinks*]. How dare he? The idiot! [*To* MERIK.] Know what you are? An idiot! A jackass!

SAVVA. Won't you please curb your tongues? Why make such a row, good friends? Let folk sleep.

TIKHON. Lie down, lie down. That will do. [*Goes behind the bar and locks the till.*] It's bedtime.

FEDYA. It is that. [*Lies down.*] Happy dreams, boys.

MERIK [*stands up and spreads a fur coat on the bench*]. Come and lie down, Squire.

TIKHON. But where will you sleep?

MERIK. Anywhere, I don't mind the floor. [*Spreads his coat on the floor.*] I don't care. [*Puts his axe by his side.*] The floor's agony to him, being used to silk and soft bedding and such.

TIKHON [*to* BORTSOV]. Lie down, sir. Don't look at that there picture any more. [*Puts out the candle.*] Forget her!

BORTSOV [*staggering*]. Where shall I lie?

TIKHON. In the tramp's place. He wants you to have it, didn't you hear?

BORTSOV [*goes to the bench*]. I, er—I'm drunk. What's this? I'm to lie here, am I?

TIKHON. Yes, here, don't be afraid—lie down. [*Stretches out on the bar.*]

BORTSOV [*lies down*]. I'm drunk. My head's going round. [*Opens the locket.*] Have you a bit of candle? [*Pause.*] You're a funny girl, Mary, looking out of the frame and laughing at me. [*Laughs.*] I'm drunk—you shouldn't laugh at a drunkard. But don't you take no notice, as the man says in the play. You love the poor old soak.

FEDYA. How the wind howls—scares you, don't it?

BORTSOV [*laughs*]. You are a funny girl! Why twist and turn like that? I can't catch you.

MERIK. He's raving. He's been looking at that portrait too long. [*Laughs.*] What a business! Brainy gents have invented machines and medicines galore, but what about a cure for the female sex? No one ain't had the brains to invent that. They try to cure every illness, but one thing's never even crossed their minds: there's more men comes a cropper over a bit of skirt than from any illness. They're sly and cruel, women are, they're out for what they can get. And they ain't got no sense. The old woman torments her son's wife, and the girl herself never stops trying to do her husband down. And so it goes on.

TIKHON. Women have led him such a dance, he's still dizzy.

MERIK. I ain't the only one. Men have been suffering since time began. And why is it that women and the devil always go together in fairy-tales and songs? That ain't no accident, believe you me. It's more than half true, it is. [*Pause.*] There's the squire making a fool of himself, but what about me turning tramp and leaving my father and mother? That wasn't too clever either.

FEDYA. Women's doing, eh?

MERIK. Same as the squire here. I went round like I was mad or bewitched—boasted how happy I was. It was like being on fire day and night, but when the time came my eyes was opened. It weren't love, it were all a fraud.

FEDYA. What did you do to her?

MERIK. None of your business. [*Pause.*] Think I killed her, eh? My arms ain't that long. Killed her? Felt sorry for her, more like! 'Live and be happy,' I tells her. 'Only don't let me set eyes on you, and may I forget you, you treacherous bitch.'

[*A knock on the door.*]

TIKHON. Who the devil's that? Who's there? [*A knock.*] Who's knocking? [*Gets up and goes to the door.*] Who's knocking? Move on, we're locked up.

DENIS [*off-stage, on the other side of the door*]. Let us in, Tikhon, for goodness' sake. A spring's gone in the carriage. Help me, please. I only want a bit of rope to tie it up and I'll get by somehow.

TIKHON. Who is it then?

DENIS [*off-stage*]. A lady from town on her way to Varsonofyevo, with only three miles to go. Help us, please!

TIKHON. Go and tell your lady—for ten roubles she'll have her rope and we'll mend the spring.

DENIS [*off-stage*]. Are you mad? Ten roubles! You must be crazy! Glad to see folks in trouble, are you?

TIKHON. Have it your own way. You can take it or leave it.

DENIS [*off-stage*]. Oh, all right then, wait. [*Pause.*] The lady says yes.

TIKHON. Come in then. [*Opens the door and lets* DENIS *in.*]

SCENE IV

[*The above and* DENIS.]

DENIS. Hallo, friends. Well, let's have the rope. Hurry up. Who'll come and help, boys? We'll make it worth your while.

TIKHON. Never mind that. Let 'em snore, we'll manage between us.

DENIS. Phew, I'm dead beat, what with the cold and mud and being soaked to the skin. Another thing—have you a room for the lady to warm herself? The carriage is down on one side and she can't sit there.

TIKHON. What—a room is it now? She can get warm in here if she's cold, we'll find space for her. [*Goes up to* BORTSOV *and clears the space next to him.*] Get up there. You can doss down on the floor for an hour while the lady's getting warm. [*To* BORTSOV.] Get up a moment, please, sir. And sit for a bit. [BORTSOV *sits up.*] There's a place for you.

[DENIS *goes out.*]

FEDYA. So we've a visitor now, blast her! Now we won't get a wink till daybreak.

TIKHON. I'm sorry I didn't ask fifteen roubles, she'd have paid it. [*Stands before the door expectantly.*] Be on your best behaviour, all of you, and no bad language.

[*Enter* MARY *followed by* DENIS.]

SCENE V

[The above, MARY *and* DENIS.]

TIKHON [*bows*]. Come in, lady. This is a humble place, fit for peasants and black beetles. But don't you be put out.

MARY. I can't see a thing here. Where do I go?

TIKHON. This way, lady. [*Takes her to the seat next to* BORTSOV.] This way, please. [*Blows on the seat.*] I've no separate room, sorry, but don't worry, lady—they're nice, quiet folk.

MARY [*sits down next to* BORTSOV]. I say, isn't it stuffy! Can't we at least have the door open?

TIKHON. Very well, lady. [*Runs and opens the door wide.*]

MERIK. Folks are freezing and they must have the door wide open. [*Gets up and slams it.*] Who does she think she is! [*Lies down.*]

TIKHON. I'm sorry, lady, this is a kind of village idiot, like. But don't be frightened, he won't do no harm. Only I can't manage this for ten roubles, missus—sorry. I can do it for fifteen if you like.

MARY. Very well, but be quick.

TIKHON. This minute. It'll only take a jiffy. [*Brings out some ropes from under the bar.*] This very instant. [*Pause.*]

BORTSOV [*stares at* MARY]. Mary. Mary——

MARY [*looking at* BORTSOV]. What is it now?

BORTSOV. Mary—is it you? Where have you come from?

[MARY *recognizes* BORTSOV, *shrieks and jumps away into the middle of the room.*]

BORTSOV [*follows her*]. Mary, it's me. Me. [*Roars with laughter.*] My wife! Mary! But where am I? Let's have some light, you there!

MARY. Leave me alone. You must be lying, it isn't you, it can't be! [*Buries her face in her hands.*] This is some silly trick.

BORTSOV. Her voice, the way she moves! Mary, it's me. I won't be, er, drunk in a moment. My head's going round. My God! Just a moment, nothing makes any sense. [*Shouts.*] My wife! [*Falls at her feet and sobs. A group gathers round the couple.*]

MARY. Go away from me. [*To* DENIS.] We're leaving, Denis, I can't stay here.

MERIK [*jumps up and stares at her face*]. The portrait! [*Clutches her arm.*] It's her! Hey, all of you—it's the squire's wife!

MARY. Leave me alone, you lout. [*Tries to tear her hand away.*] Don't just stand there, Denis. [DENIS *and* TIKHON *run up to her and seize* MERIK *under the arms.*] This is a den of thieves. You let go my arm. I'm not scared. Go away!

MERIK. Wait a moment and I'll let you go. I want a word with you, to make you understand, so wait a minute. [*Turns to* TIKHON *and* DENIS.] Go away, and take your filthy hands off of me! I'm not letting her go till I've had my say. Just wait a minute. [*Bangs his forehead with his fist.*] God, I'm so stupid—can't think what I want to say.

MARY [*pulls her arm away*]. Go away, you're all drunk. We're leaving, Denis. [*Makes for the door.*]

MERIK [*blocks her way*]. You might spare him a glance. At least say one kind word to him, in God's name!

MARY. Take this maniac away!

MERIK. Then the curse of hell be on you, blast you!

[*Swings his axe: A frightful commotion. Everyone jumps up noisily. Shouts of horror.* SAVVA *stands between* MERIK *and* MARY. DENIS *shoves* MERIK *violently to one side and carries his mistress out of the inn. Then all stand rooted to the spot. A long pause.*]

BORTSOV [*clutches the air with his hands*]. Mary. Where are you, Mary?

NAZAROVNA. My God, my God, you've made my heart bleed, you murderers. What a dreadful night!

MERIK [*dropping the hand which holds the axe*]. Did I kill her or not?

TIKHON. You're in the clear, praise the Lord.

MERIK. I didn't kill her, so—. [*Staggers to his place.*] So I'm not to die through a stolen axe. [*Falls on his coat and sobs.*] I'm so fed up, so damn miserable—aren't you sorry for me, all of you?

CURTAIN

SWAN SONG

(CALCHAS)

[*Лебединая песня (Калхас)*]

A DRAMATIC STUDY IN ONE ACT

(1887–1888)

CHARACTERS

VASILY SVETLOVIDOV, a comic actor, aged 68

NIKITA, a prompter, an old man

The action takes place at night on the stage of a provincial theatre after a performance

The empty stage of a second-class provincial theatre. Right, a row of roughly-made unpainted doors leading to the dressing-rooms. The left and the back of the stage are cluttered up with litter and rubbish. There is an overturned stool in mid-stage. Night. Dark.

SCENE I

[SVETLOVIDOV, *in the stage costume of Calchas, comes out of a dressing-room carrying a candle, and roars with laughter.*]

SVETLOVIDOV. This is the limit, it really is too much—falling asleep in my dressing-room! The play ended hours ago, the audience went home—and there's me snoring away without a care in the world. Oh, you silly old man—you are a bad lad, old boy. Got so pickled, you dozed off in your chair! Very clever! Congratulations, old boy. [*Shouts.*] George! George, curse you! Peter! They're asleep, damn them, blast them and may they rot in hell! George! [*Picks up the stool, sits on it and puts a candle on the floor.*] And answer came there none— apart from the echo, that is. I tipped George and Peter three roubles each today for looking after me, and by now they must be sunk without trace. They've left. And the bastards must have locked up the theatre. [*Twists his head about.*] Ugh, I'm drunk. God, the booze I knocked back in honour of my benefit night! I feel as if I'd been kippered, my mouth's like the bottom of a parrot's cage. Disgusting! [*Pause.*] And stupid! The old codger gets drunk, but what has he to celebrate? He hasn't the foggiest! God, I've got back-ache, the old head-piece is splitting, I'm shivering all over, and I have this dark, cold feeling, as if I was in a cellar. If you won't spare your health, you might at least remember you're too old for this caper, you silly old so-and-so. [*Pause.*] Old age—whether you try to wriggle out of it or make the best of it or just act the fool, the fact is your life's over. Sixty-eight years down the drain, damn it! Gone with the wind! The cup's drained, there's just a bit left at the bottom: the dregs. That's the way of it, that's how it is, old man. Like it or not, it's time you rehearsed for the part you play in your coffin. Good old death's only just round the corner. [*Looks in front of him.*] I say, I've been on the stage for forty-five years, but this must be the first time I've seen a theatre in the middle of the night, the very first time. You know, it's weird, damn it. [*Goes up to the footlights.*] Can't see a thing. Well, I can just make out the prompter's box and that other box over there—the one with the letter on it—and that music-stand. The rest is darkness, a bottomless black pit like a tomb: the haunt of Death itself. Brrr! It's cold, there's a piercing draught from the auditorium. Just the place to call up spirits! It's eerie, blast it, it sends shudders down my spine. [*Shouts.*] George! Peter! Hell, where are you? But why do I talk of hell, God help me? Oh, why can't you stop drinking and using bad language, for God's sake, seeing you're old and it's time you were pushing up the daisies? At sixty-eight people go to church, they get ready to die, but you—. Oh Lord, you and your bad language and your drunken gargoyle's face and this damfool costume! What a sight! I'll go and change quickly. It's all so eerie. Why, if I stayed here all night, I'd die of fright at this rate. [*Makes for his dressing-room. At that moment* NIKITA, *wearing a white dressing-gown, appears from the furthest dressing-room at the back of the stage.*]

SCENE II

SVETLOVIDOV [*seeing* NIKITA, *gives a terrified shriek and staggers back*]. Who are you? What are you after? Who do you want? [*Stamps.*] Who are you?

NIKITA. It's me, sir.

SVETLOVIDOV. Who's me?

NIKITA [*slowly approaching him*]. It's me. Nikita, the prompter. It's me, Mr. Svetlovidov, sir.

SVETLOVIDOV [*collapses helplessly on the stool, breathes hard and shudders all over*]. God, who is it? Is it you—you, Nikita? W-w-what are you doing here?

NIKITA. I always spend the night here in the dressing-rooms, sir, only please don't tell the manager. I've nowhere else to sleep, and that's God's truth.

SVETLOVIDOV. So it's you, Nikita. Hell, I had sixteen curtain-calls, three bunches of flowers and a lot of other things—they were all quite carried away, but no one bothered to wake the old soak up and take him home. I'm old, Nikita. Sixty-eight, I am. I'm ill. I feel faint and weary. [*Leans over the prompter's hand and weeps.*] Don't leave me, Nikita. I'm old and weak and I've got to die. I'm frightened, so terribly frightened.

NIKITA [*gently and respectfully*]. It's time you went home, Mr. Svetlovidov, sir.

SVETLOVIDOV. I won't go. I haven't got any home—haven't got one, I tell you.

NIKITA. Goodness me, the gentleman's forgotten where he lives!

SVETLOVIDOV. I don't want to go to that place, I tell you. I'm on my own there, I haven't anyone, Nikita—no old woman, no children, neither kith nor kin. I'm as lonely as the wind on the heath. There will be no one to remember me when I die. I'm frightened all alone. There's no one to comfort me, to make a fuss of me and put me to bed when I'm drunk. Where do I belong? Who needs me? Who loves me? No one loves me, Nikita.

NIKITA [*through tears*]. Your audiences love you, Mr. Svetlovidov.

SVETLOVIDOV. The audience has left and gone to bed, and it's forgotten the old clown. No, nobody needs me, no one loves me. I've neither wife nor children.

NIKITA. Then you've nothing to worry about.

SVETLOVIDOV. I'm a man, aren't I? I'm alive. I have blood, not water, flowing in my veins. I'm a gentleman, Nikita, I'm well connected, and I was in the army before landing up in this dump. I was a gunner. And a fine, dashing, gallant, high-spirited young officer I was. Ye gods, what's happened to all that? And what an actor I became, eh, Nikita? [*Hoists himself up and leans on the prompter's arm.*] What's become of it all, where have those days gone to? God, I just looked into this black pit and it all came back to me! It's swallowed forty-five years of my life, this pit has—and what a life! Looking into it now, I see everything down to the last detail as plain as I see your face. To be gay, young, confident, fiery! And the love of women! Women, Nikita!

NIKITA. It's time you were in bed and asleep, Mr. Svetlovidov, sir.

SVETLOVIDOV. When I was a young actor and just getting into my stride, there was a girl who loved me for my acting, I remember. She was elegant, graceful as a young poplar, innocent, unspoilt. And she seemed all ablaze like the sun on a May morning. Those blue eyes, that magic smile could banish the darkest night. The ocean waves dash themselves against the cliffs, but against the waves of her hair the very cliffs, icebergs and snow avalanches might dash themselves to no avail. I remember standing before her as I stand before you now. She was looking lovelier than ever, and she gave me a look I shan't forget even in the grave. There was a kind of soft, deep, velvety caress about it, and all the dazzle of youth. Drunk with joy, I fall on my knees and beg her to make me happy. [*Continues in a broken voice.*] And she—she tells me to leave the stage. Leave the stage, see? She could love an actor, but be an actor's wife? Never! I remember how I acted that same night. It was a vulgar, slapstick part, and I could feel the scales fall from my eyes as I played it. I saw then that there's no such thing as 'sacred art', that the whole thing's just a phoney racket—saw myself a slave, a toy for people's idle moments, a buffoon, a man of straw. It was then I took the public's measure. Applause, bouquets, wild enthusiasm—I've never believed in 'em since. Yes, Nikita, these people cheer me, they pay a rouble for my photograph, but to them I'm a stranger, I'm just so much dirt—an old whore, practically! They scrape up acquaintance with me to make themselves feel important, but not one would sink to letting me marry his sister or daughter. I don't trust 'em. [*Sinks on to the stool.*] Don't trust 'em.

NIKITA. You look like nothing on earth, Mr. Svetlovidov, sir—you've even scared me. Have a heart and let me take you home, sir.

SVETLOVIDOV. Then my eyes were opened, but the vision cost me dear, Nikita. After that affair—with the girl—I began drifting aimlessly, living from hand to mouth with no thought for the morrow. I took cheap, slapstick parts and hammed them. I was a corrupting influence. But I'd been a true artist, you know, I was really good! I buried my talent, cheapened it. I spoke in an affected voice, I lost my dignity as a human being. This black pit swallowed me up and gobbled me down. I never felt like this before. But when I woke up tonight, I looked back—and I've sixty-eight years behind me. I've only just seen what old age means. The show is over. [*Sobs.*] You can ring down the curtain!

NIKITA. Mr. Svetlovidov, sir. I say, really, old man. Do calm yourself, sir. Oh goodness me! [*Shouts.*] Peter! George!

SVETLOVIDOV. And what flair, what power, what a delivery! The wealth of feeling and grace, the gamut of emotions here in this breast [*beats his breast*]—you simply can't imagine! I feel like choking. Listen, old man—wait, let me get my breath. Here's something from *Boris Godunov*:

> 'Ivan the Terrible pronounced me son.
> And from the grave his spirit named me Dmitry;
> He stirred the peoples to revolt for me
> And destined Godunov to die my victim.
> I am Tsarevich. But enough! 'Tis shame
> To cringe before a haughty Polish beauty!'

Not bad, eh? [*Eagerly.*] Wait, here's something from *King Lear*. There's a black sky, see, and rain, with thunder growling and lightning whipping across the heavens, and he says:

> 'Blow, winds, and crack your cheeks! rage! blow!
> You cataracts and hurricanoes, spout
> Till you have drench'd our steeples, drown'd the cocks!
> You sulphurous and thought-executing fires,
> Vaunt-couriers to oak-cleaving thunderbolts,
> Singe my white head! And thou, all-shaking thunder,
> Strike flat the thick rotundity o' the world!
> Crack nature's moulds, all germens spill at once
> That make ingrateful man!'

[*Impatiently.*] Quick, the Fool's cue! [*Stamps.*] The Fool's cue and quick about it! I'm in a hurry.

NIKITA [*playing the part of the Fool*]. 'O nuncle, court holy-water in a dry house is better than this rain-water out o' door. Good nuncle, in, and ask thy daughters' blessing; here's a night pities neither wise man nor fool.'

SVETLOVIDOV. 'Rumble thy bellyfull! Spit, fire! spout, rain!
> Nor rain, wind, thunder, fire, are my daughters:
> I tax not you, you elements, with unkindness;
> I never gave you kingdom, called you children.'

What power, what genius, what an artist! Now for something else— something else to bring back old times. Let's take something [*gives a peal of happy laughter*] from *Hamlet*. All right—I commence! But what shall I do? Ah, I know. [*Playing Hamlet.*] 'O! the recorders: let me see one.' [*To* NIKITA.] 'Why do you go about as if you would drive me into a toil?'

NIKITA. 'O! my lord, if my duty be too bold, my love is too unmannerly.'

SVETLOVIDOV. 'I do not well understand that. Will you play upon this pipe?'

NIKITA. 'My Lord, I cannot.'

SVETLOVIDOV. 'I pray you.'

NIKITA. 'Believe me, I cannot.'

SVETLOVIDOV. 'I do beseech you.'

NIKITA. 'I know no touch of it, my lord.'

SVETLOVIDOV. ''Tis as easy as lying; govern these ventages with your finger and thumb, give it breath with your mouth, and it will discourse most eloquent music.'

NIKITA. 'I have not the skill.'

SVETLOVIDOV. 'Why, look you now, how unworthy a thing you make of me. You would play upon me; you would seem to know my stops; you would pluck out the heart of my mystery. Do you think I am easier to be played on than a pipe? Call me what instrument you will, though you can fret me, you cannot play upon me.' [*Roars with laughter and claps.*] Bravo! Encore! Bravo! Not much old age about that, was there, damn it? There's no such thing as old age, that's a lot of nonsense. I feel strength pulsing in every vein—why, this is youth, zest, the spice of life! If you're good enough, Nikita, being old doesn't count. Think I'm crazy, eh? Gone off my head, have I? Wait, let me pull myself together. Good Lord above us! Now, listen to this—how tender and subtle. Ah, the music of it! Shush, be quiet!

> 'O silent night in old Ukraine!
> The stars are bright, clear is the sky.
> All drowsy is the heavy air
> And silver poplars faintly sigh.'

[*There is the sound of doors being opened.*] What's that?

NIKITA. It must be George and Peter. You're good, Mr. Svetlovidov, a great actor!

SVETLOVIDOV [*shouts in the direction of the noise*]. This way, lads! [*To* NIKITA.] Let's go and change. There's no such thing as old age, that's all stuff and nonsense. [*Roars with happy laughter.*] So why the tears? Why so down in the mouth, you dear, silly fellow? Now this won't do, it really won't. Really, old chap, you mustn't look like that—what good does it do? There, there. [*Embraces him with tears in his eyes.*] You mustn't cry. Where art and genius are, there's no room for old age, loneliness and illness—why, death itself loses half its sting. [*Weeps.*] Ah well, Nikita, we've made our last bow. I'm no great actor, just a squeezed lemon, a miserable nonentity, a rusty old nail. And you're just an old stage hack, a prompter. Come on. [*They start to move off.*] I'm no real good—in a serious play I could just about manage a member of Fortinbras's suite, and for that I'm too old. Ah, well. Remember that bit of *Othello*, Nikita?

> 'Farewell the tranquil mind; farewell content!
> Farewell the plumed troop and the big wars
> That make ambition virtue! O, farewell!
> Farewell the neighing steed, and the shrill trump,
> The spirit-stirring drum, the ear-piercing fife,
> The royal banner, and all quality,
> Pride, pomp, and circumstance of glorious war!'

NIKITA. Terrific! Great stuff!

SVETLOVIDOV. Or take this:

> 'Away from Moscow! Never to return!
> I'll flee the place with not a backward glance,
> And scour the globe for some forgotten corner
> To nurse my wounded heart in. Get my coach!'

> [*Goes out with* NIKITA.]

THE CURTAIN SLOWLY FALLS

THE BEAR

[*Медведь*]

A FARCE IN ONE ACT

(1888)

(Dedicated to N. N. Solovtsov)

CHARACTERS

MRS. HELEN POPOV, a young widow with dimpled cheeks, a landowner

GREGORY SMIRNOV, a landowner in early middle age

LUKE, Mrs. Popov's old manservant

The action takes place in the drawing-room of Mrs. Popov's country house

SCENE I

[MRS. POPOV, *in deep mourning, with her eyes fixed on a snapshot,* and LUKE.]

LUKE. This won't do, madam, you're just making your life a misery. Cook's out with the maid picking fruit, every living creature's happy and even our cat knows how to enjoy herself—she's parading round the yard trying to pick up a bird or two. But here you are cooped up inside all day like you was in a convent cell—you never have a good time. Yes, it's true. Nigh on twelve months it is since you last set foot outdoors.

MRS. POPOV. And I'm never going out again, why should I? My life's finished. He lies in his grave, I've buried myself inside these four walls—we're both dead.

LUKE. There you go again! I don't like to hear such talk, I don't. Your husband died and that was that—God's will be done and may he rest in peace. You've shed a few tears and that'll do, it's time to call it a day—you can't spend your whole life a-moaning and a-groaning. The same thing happened to me once, when my old woman died, but what did I do? I grieved a bit, shed a tear or two for a month or so and that's all she's getting. Catch me wearing sackcloth and ashes for the rest of my days, it'd be more than the old girl was worth! [*Sighs.*] You've neglected all the neighbours—won't go and see them or have them in the house. We never get out and about, lurking here like dirty great spiders, saving your presence. The mice have been at my livery too. And it's not for any lack of nice people either—the county's full of 'em, see. There's the regiment stationed at Ryblovo and them officers are a fair treat, a proper sight for sore eyes they are. They have a dance in camp of a Friday and the brass band plays most days. This ain't right, missus. You're young, and pretty as a picture with that peaches-and-cream look, so make the most of it. Them looks won't last for ever, you know. If you wait another ten years to come out of your shell and lead them officers a dance, you'll find it's too late.

MRS. POPOV [*decisively*]. Never talk to me like that again, please. When Nicholas died my life lost all meaning, as you know. You may think I'm alive, but I'm not really. I swore to wear this mourning and shun society till my dying day, do you hear? Let his departed spirit see how I love him! Yes, I realize you know what went on—that he was often mean to me, cruel and, er, unfaithful even, but I'll be true to the grave and show him how much I can love. And he'll find me in the next world just as I was before he died.

LUKE. Don't talk like that—walk round the garden instead. Or else have Toby or Giant harnessed and go and see the neighbours.

MRS. POPOV. Oh dear! [*Weeps.*]

LUKE. Missus! Madam! What's the matter? For heaven's sake!

MRS. POPOV. He was so fond of Toby—always drove him when he went over to the Korchagins' place and the Vlasovs'. He drove so well too! And he looked so graceful when he pulled hard on the reins, remember? Oh Toby, Toby! See he gets an extra bag of oats today.

LUKE. Very good, madam.

[*A loud ring.*]

MRS. POPOV [*shudders*]. Who is it? Tell them I'm not at home.

LUKE. Very well, madam. [*Goes out.*]

SCENE II

[MRS. POPOV, *alone.*]

MRS. POPOV [*looking at the snapshot*]. Now you shall see how I can love and forgive, Nicholas. My love will only fade when I fade away myself, when this poor heart stops beating. [*Laughs, through tears.*] Well, aren't you ashamed of yourself? I'm your good, faithful little wifie, I've locked myself up and I'll be faithful to the grave, while you—aren't you ashamed, you naughty boy? You deceived me and you used to make scenes and leave me alone for weeks on end.

SCENE III

[MRS. POPOV *and* LUKE.]

LUKE [*comes in, agitatedly*]. Someone's asking for you, madam. Wants to see you——

MRS. POPOV. Then I hope you told them I haven't received visitors since the day my husband died.

LUKE. I did, but he wouldn't listen—his business is very urgent, he says.

MRS. POPOV. *I am not at home!*

LUKE. So I told him, but he just swears and barges straight in, drat him. He's waiting in the dining-room.

MRS. POPOV [*irritatedly*]. All right, ask him in here then. Aren't people rude?

[LUKE *goes out.*]

MRS. POPOV. Oh, aren't they all a bore? What do they want with me, why must they disturb my peace? [*Sighs.*] Yes, I see I really shall have to get me to a nunnery. [*Reflects.*] I'll take the veil, that's it.

SCENE IV

[MRS. POPOV, LUKE *and* SMIRNOV.]

SMIRNOV [*coming in, to* LUKE]. You're a fool, my talkative friend. An ass. [*Seeing* MRS. POPOV, *with dignity.*] May I introduce myself, madam? Gregory Smirnov, landed gentleman and lieutenant of artillery retired. I'm obliged to trouble you on most urgent business.

MRS. POPOV [*not holding out her hand*]. What do you require?

SMIRNOV. I had the honour to know your late husband. He died owing me twelve hundred roubles—I have his two IOUs. Now I've some interest due to the land-bank tomorrow, madam, so may I trouble you to let me have the money today?

MRS. POPOV. Twelve hundred roubles—. How did my husband come to owe you that?

SMIRNOV. He used to buy his oats from me.

MRS. POPOV [*sighing, to* LUKE]. Oh yes—Luke, don't forget to see Toby has his extra bag of oats. [LUKE *goes out. To* SMIRNOV.] Of course I'll pay if Nicholas owed you something, but I've nothing on me today, sorry. My manager will be back from town the day after tomorrow and I'll get him to pay you whatever it is then, but for the time being I can't oblige. Besides, it's precisely seven months today since my husband died and I am in no fit state to discuss money.

SMIRNOV. Well, I'll be in a fit state to go bust with a capital B if I can't pay that interest tomorrow. They'll have the bailiffs in on me.

MRS. POPOV. You'll get your money the day after tomorrow.

SMIRNOV. I don't want it the day after tomorrow, I want it now.

MRS. POPOV. I can't pay you now, sorry.

SMIRNOV. And I can't wait till the day after tomorrow.

MRS. POPOV. Can I help it if I've no money today?

SMIRNOV. So you can't pay then?

MRS. POPOV. Exactly.

SMIRNOV. I see. And that's your last word, is it?

MRS. POPOV. It is.

SMIRNOV. Your last word? You really mean it?

MRS. POPOV. I do.

SMIRNOV [*sarcastic*]. Then I'm greatly obliged to you, I'll put it in my diary! [*Shrugs.*] And people expect me to be cool and collected! I met the local excise man on my way here just now. 'My dear Smirnov,' says he, 'why are you always losing your temper?' But how can I help it, I ask you? I'm in desperate need of money! Yesterday morning I left home at crack of dawn. I call on everyone who owes me money, but not a soul forks out. I'm dog-tired. I spend the night in some God-awful place—by the vodka barrel in a Jewish pot-house. Then I fetch up here, fifty miles from home, hoping to see the colour of my money, only to be fobbed off with this 'no fit state' stuff! How *can* I keep my temper?

MRS. POPOV. I thought I'd made myself clear. You can have your money when my manager gets back from town.

SMIRNOV. It's not your manager I'm after, it's you. What the blazes, pardon my language, do I want with your manager?

MRS. POPOV. I'm sorry, my dear man, but I'm not accustomed to these peculiar expressions and to this tone. I have closed my ears. [*Hurries out.*]

SCENE V

[SMIRNOV, *alone.*]

SMIRNOV. Well, what price that! 'In no fit state'! Her husband died seven months ago, if you please! Now have I got my interest to pay or not? I want a straight answer—yes or no? All right, your husband's dead, you're in no fit state and so on and so forth, and your blasted manager's hopped it. But what am I supposed to do? Fly away from my creditors by balloon, I take it! Or go and bash the old brain-box against a brick wall? I call on Gruzdev—not at home. Yaroshevich is in hiding. I have a real old slanging-match with Kuritsyn and almost chuck him out of the window. Mazutov has the belly-ache, and this creature's 'in no fit state'. Not one of the swine will pay. This is what comes of being too nice to them and behaving like some snivelling no-hoper or old woman. It doesn't pay to wear kid gloves with this lot! All right, just you wait—I'll give you something to remember me by! You don't make a monkey out of me, blast you! I'm staying here—going to stick around till she coughs up. Pah! I feel well and truly riled today. I'm shaking like a leaf, I'm so furious—choking I am. Phew, my God, I really think I'm going to pass out! [*Shouts.*] Hey, you there!

SCENE VI

[SMIRNOV *and* LUKE.]

LUKE [*comes in*]. What is it?

SMIRNOV. Bring me some kvass or water, will you?

[LUKE *goes out.*]

SMIRNOV. What a mentality, though! You need money so bad you could shoot yourself, but she won't pay, being 'in no fit state to discuss money', if you please! There's female logic for you and no mistake! That's why I don't like talking to women. Never have. Talk to a woman—why, I'd rather sit on top of a powder magazine! Pah! It makes my flesh creep, I'm so fed up with her, her and that great trailing dress! Poetic creatures they call 'em! Why, the very sight of one gives me cramp in both legs, I get so aggravated.

SCENE VII

[SMIRNOV *and* LUKE.]

LUKE [*comes in and serves some water*]. Madam's unwell and won't see anyone.

SMIRNOV. You clear out!

[LUKE *goes out.*]

SMIRNOV. 'Unwell and won't see anyone.' All right then, don't! I'm staying put, chum, and I don't budge one inch till you unbelt. Be ill for a week and I'll stay a week, make it a year and a year I'll stay. I'll have my rights, lady! As for your black dress and dimples, you don't catch me that way—we know all about those dimples! [*Shouts through the window.*] Unhitch, Simon, we're here for some time— I'm staying put. Tell the stable people to give my horses oats. And you've got that animal tangled in the reins again, you great oaf! [*Imitates him.*] 'I don't care.' I'll give you don't care! [*Moves away from the window.*] How ghastly—it's unbearably hot, no one will pay up, I had a bad night, and now here's this female with her long black dress and her states. I've got a headache. How about a glass of vodka? That might be an idea. [*Shouts.*] Hey, you there!

LUKE [*comes in*]. What is it?

SMIRNOV. Bring me a glass of vodka.

[*LUKE goes out.*]

SMIRNOV. Phew! [*Sits down and looks himself over.*] A fine specimen I am, I must say—dust all over me, my boots dirty, unwashed, hair unbrushed, straw on my waistcoat. I bet the little woman took me for a burglar. [*Yawns.*] It's not exactly polite to turn up in a drawing-room in this rig! Well, anyway, I'm not a guest here, I'm collecting money. And there's no such thing as correct wear for the well-dressed creditor.

LUKE [*comes in and gives him the vodka*]. This is a liberty, sir.

SMIRNOV [*angrily*]. What!

LUKE. I, er, it's all right, I just——

SMIRNOV. Who do you think you're talking to? You hold your tongue!

LUKE [*aside*]. Now we'll never get rid of him, botheration take it! It's an ill wind brought him along.

[*LUKE goes out.*]

SMIRNOV. Oh, I'm so furious! I could pulverize the whole world, I'm in such a rage. I feel quite ill. [*Shouts.*] Hey, you there!

SCENE VIII

[MRS. POPOV and SMIRNOV.]

MRS. POPOV [*comes in, with downcast eyes*]. Sir, in my solitude I have grown unaccustomed to the sound of human speech, and I can't stand shouting. I must urgently request you not to disturb my peace.

SMIRNOV. Pay up and I'll go.

MRS. POPOV. As I've already stated quite plainly, I've no ready cash. Wait till the day after tomorrow.

SMIRNOV. I've also had the honour of stating quite plainly that I need the money today, not the day after tomorrow. If you won't pay up now, I'll have to put my head in a gas-oven tomorrow.

MRS. POPOV. Can I help it if I've no cash in hand? This is all rather odd.

SMIRNOV. So you won't pay up now, eh?

MRS. POPOV. I can't.

SMIRNOV. In that case I'm not budging, I'll stick around here till I do get my money. [*Sits down.*] You'll pay the day after tomorrow, you say? Very well, then I'll sit here like this till the day after tomorrow. I'll just stay put exactly as I am. [*Jumps up.*] I ask you—have I got that interest to pay tomorrow or haven't I? Think I'm trying to be funny, do you?

MRS. POPOV. Kindly don't raise your voice at me, sir—we're not in the stables.

SMIRNOV. I'm not discussing stables, I'm asking whether my interest falls due tomorrow. Yes or no?

MRS. POPOV. You don't know how to treat a lady.

SMIRNOV. Oh yes I do.

MRS. POPOV. Oh no you don't. You're a rude, ill-bred person. Nice men don't talk to ladies like that.

SMIRNOV. Now, this *is* a surprise! How do you want me to talk then? In French, I suppose? [*In an angry, simpering voice.*] *Madame, je voo pree.* You won't pay me—how perfectly delightful. Oh, *pardong*, I'm sure—sorry you were troubled! Now isn't the weather divine today? And that black dress looks too, too charming! [*Bows and scrapes.*]

MRS. POPOV. That's silly. And not very clever.

SMIRNOV [*mimics her*]. 'Silly, not very clever.' I don't know how to treat a lady, don't I? Madam, I've seen more women in my time than you have house-sparrows. I've fought three duels over women. There have been twenty-one women in my life. Twelve times it was me broke it off, the other nine got in first. Oh yes! Time was I made an ass of myself, slobbered, mooned around, bowed and scraped and practically crawled on my belly. I loved, I suffered, I sighed at the moon, I languished, I melted, I grew cold. I loved passionately, madly, in every conceivable fashion, damn me, bur-bling nineteen to the dozen about women's emancipation and wasting half my substance on the tender passion. But now—no thank you very much! I can't be fooled any more, I've had enough. Black eyes, passionate looks, crimson lips, dimpled cheeks, moonlight, 'Whispers, passion's bated breathing'—I don't give a tinker's cuss for the lot now, lady. Present company excepted, all women, large or small, are simpering, mincing, gossipy creatures. They're great haters. They're eyebrow-deep in lies. They're futile, they're trivial, they're cruel, they're outrageously illogical. And as for having any-thing upstairs [*taps his forehead*]—I'm sorry to be so blunt, but the very birds in the trees can run rings round your average blue-stocking. Take any one of these poetical creations. Oh, she's all froth and fluff, she is, she's half divine, she sends you into a million raptures. But you take a peep inside her mind, and what do you see? A common or garden crocodile! [*Clutches the back of a chair, which cracks and breaks.*] And yet this crocodile somehow thinks its great life-work, privilege and monopoly is the tender passion—that's what really gets me! But damn and blast it, and crucify me upside down on that wall if I'm wrong—does a woman know how to love any living creature apart from lap-dogs? Her love gets no further than snivelling and slobbering. The man suffers and makes sacrifices, while she just twitches the train of her dress and tries to get him squirming under her thumb, that's what her love adds up to! You must know what women are like, seeing you've the rotten luck to be one. Tell me frankly, did you ever see a sincere, faithful, true woman? You know you didn't. Only the old and ugly ones are true and faithful. You'll never find a constant woman, not in a month of Sundays you won't, not once in a blue moon!

MRS. POPOV. Well, I like that! Then who is true and faithful in love to your way of thinking? Not men by any chance?

SMIRNOV. Yes, madam. Men.

MRS. POPOV. *Men!* [*Gives a bitter laugh.*] Men true and faithful in love! That's rich, I must say. [*Vehemently.*] What right have you to talk like that? Men true and faithful! If it comes to that, the best man I've ever known was my late husband, I may say. I loved him passionately, with all my heart as only an intelligent young woman can. I gave him my youth, my happiness, my life, my possessions. I lived only for him. I worshipped him as an idol. And—what do you think? This best of men was shamelessly deceiving me all along the line! After his death I found a drawer in his desk full of love letters, and when he was alive—oh, what a frightful memory!—he used to leave me on my own for weeks on end, he carried on with other girls before my very eyes, he was unfaithful to me, he spent my money like water, and he joked about my feelings for him. But I loved him all the same, and I've been faithful to him. What's more, I'm still faithful and true now that he's dead. I've buried myself alive inside these four walls and I shall go round in these widow's weeds till my dying day.

SMIRNOV [*with a contemptuous laugh*]. Widow's weeds! Who do you take me for? As if I didn't know why you wear this fancy dress and bury yourself indoors! Why, it sticks out a mile! Mysterious and romantic, isn't it? Some army cadet or hack poet may pass by your garden, look up at your windows and think: 'There dwells Tamara, the mysterious princess, the one who buried herself alive from love of her husband.' Who do you think you're fooling?

MRS. POPOV [*flaring up*]. *What!* You dare to take that line with me!

SMIRNOV. Buries herself alive—but doesn't forget to powder her nose!

MRS. POPOV. You dare adopt that tone!

SMIRNOV. Don't you raise your voice to me, madam, I'm not one of your servants. Let me call a spade a spade. Not being a woman, I'm used to saying what I think. So stop shouting, pray.

MRS. POPOV. It's you who are shouting, not me. Leave me alone, would you mind?

SMIRNOV. Pay up, and I'll go.

MRS. POPOV. You'll get nothing out of me.

SMIRNOV. Oh yes I shall.

MRS. POPOV. Just to be awkward, you won't get one single copeck. And you can leave me alone.

SMIRNOV. Not having the pleasure of being your husband or fiancé, I'll trouble you not to make a scene. [*Sits down.*] I don't like it.

MRS. POPOV [*choking with rage*]. Do I see you sitting down?

SMIRNOV. You most certainly do.

MRS. POPOV. Would you mind leaving?

SMIRNOV. Give me my money. [*Aside.*] Oh, I'm in such a rage! Furious I am!

MRS. POPOV. I've no desire to bandy words with cads, sir. Kindly clear off! [*Pause.*] Well, are you going or aren't you?

SMIRNOV. No.

MRS. POPOV. No?

SMIRNOV. No!

MRS. POPOV. Very well then! [*Rings.*]

SCENE IX

[*The above and* LUKE.]

MRS. POPOV. Show this gentleman out, Luke.

LUKE [*goes up to* SMIRNOV]. Be so good as to leave, sir, when you're told, sir. No point in——

SMIRNOV [*jumping up*]. You hold your tongue! Who do you think you're talking to? I'll carve you up in little pieces.

LUKE [*clutching at his heart*]. Heavens and saints above us! [*Falls into an armchair.*] Oh, I feel something terrible—fair took my breath away, it did.

MRS. POPOV. But where's Dasha? Dasha! [*Shouts.*] Dasha! Pelageya! Dasha! [*Rings.*]

LUKE. Oh, they've all gone fruit-picking. There's no one in the house. I feel faint. Fetch water.

MRS. POPOV. Be so good as to clear out!

SMIRNOV. Couldn't you be a bit more polite?

MRS. POPOV [*clenching her fists and stamping*]. You uncouth oaf! You have the manners of a bear! Think you own the place? Monster!

SMIRNOV. What! You say that again!

MRS. POPOV. I called you an ill-mannered oaf, a monster!

SMIRNOV [*advancing on her*]. Look here, what right have you to insult me?

MRS. POPOV. All right, I'm insulting you. So what? Think I'm afraid of you?

SMIRNOV. Just because you look all romantic, you can get away with anything—is that your idea? This is duelling talk!

LUKE. Heavens and saints above us! Water!

SMIRNOV. Pistols at dawn!

MRS. POPOV. Just because you have big fists and the lungs of an ox you needn't think I'm scared, see? Think you own the place, don't you!

SMIRNOV. We'll shoot it out! No one calls me names and gets away with it, weaker sex or no weaker sex.

MRS. POPOV [*trying to shout him down*]. You coarse lout!

SMIRNOV. Why should it only be us men who answer for our insults? It's high time we dropped that silly idea. If women want equality, let them damn well have equality! I challenge you, madam!

MRS. POPOV. Want to shoot it out, eh? Very well.

SMIRNOV. This very instant!

MRS. POPOV. Most certainly! My husband left some pistols, I'll fetch them instantly. [*Moves hurriedly off and comes back.*] I'll enjoy putting a bullet through that thick skull, damn your infernal cheek! [*Goes out.*]

SMIRNOV. I'll pot her like a sitting bird. I'm not one of your sentimental young puppies. She'll get no chivalry from me!

LUKE. Kind sir! [*Kneels.*] Grant me a favour, pity an old man and leave this place. First you frighten us out of our wits, now you want to fight a duel.

SMIRNOV [*not listening*]. A duel! There's true women's emancipation for you! That evens up the sexes with a vengeance! I'll knock her off as a matter of principle. But what a woman! [*Mimics her.*] 'Damn your infernal cheek! I'll put a bullet through that thick skull.' Not bad, eh? Flushed all over, flashing eyes, accepts my challenge! You know, I've never seen such a woman in my life.

LUKE. Go away, sir, and I'll say prayers for you till the day I die.

SMIRNOV. There's a regular woman for you, something I do appreciate! A proper woman—not some namby-pamby, wishy-washy female, but a really red-hot bit of stuff, a regular pistol-packing little spitfire. A pity to kill her, really.

LUKE [*weeps*]. Kind sir—do leave. Please!

SMIRNOV. I definitely like her. Definitely! Never mind her dimples, I like her. I wouldn't mind letting her off what she owes me, actually. And I don't feel angry any more. Wonderful woman!

SCENE X

[*The above and* MRS. POPOV.]

MRS. POPOV [*comes in with the pistols*]. Here are the pistols. But before we start would you mind showing me how to fire them? I've never had a pistol in my hands before.

LUKE. Lord help us! Mercy on us! I'll go and find the gardener and coachman. What have we done to deserve this? [*Goes out.*]

SMIRNOV [*examining the pistols*]. Now, there are several types of pistol. There are Mortimer's special duelling pistols with percussion caps. Now, yours here are Smith and Wessons, triple action with extractor, centre-fired. They're fine weapons, worth a cool ninety roubles the pair. Now, you hold a revolver like this. [*Aside.*] What eyes, what eyes! She's hot stuff all right!

MRS. POPOV. Like this?

SMIRNOV. Yes, that's right. Then you raise the hammer and take aim like this. Hold your head back a bit, stretch your arm out properly. Right. And then with this finger you press this little gadget and that's it. But the great thing is—don't get excited and do take your time about aiming. Try and see your hand doesn't shake.

MRS. POPOV. All right. We can't very well shoot indoors, let's go in the garden.

SMIRNOV. Very well. But I warn you, I'm firing in the air.

MRS. POPOV. Oh, this is the limit! Why?

SMIRNOV. Because, because—. That's my business.

MRS. POPOV. Got cold feet, eh? I see. Now don't shilly-shally, sir.

Kindly follow me. I shan't rest till I've put a bullet through your brains, damn you. Got the wind up, have you?

SMIRNOV. Yes.

MRS. POPOV. That's a lie. Why won't you fight?

SMIRNOV. Because, er, because you, er, I like you.

MRS. POPOV [*with a vicious laugh*]. He likes me! He dares to say he likes me! [*Points to the door.*] I won't detain you.

SMIRNOV [*puts down the revolver without speaking, picks up his peaked cap and moves off; near the door he stops and for about half a minute the two look at each other without speaking; then he speaks, going up to her hesitantly*]. Listen. Are you still angry? I'm absolutely furious myself, but you must see—how can I put it? The fact is that, er, it's this way, actually—. [*Shouts.*] Anyway, can I help it if I like you? [*Clutches the back of a chair, which cracks and breaks.*] Damn fragile stuff, furniture! I like you! Do you understand? I, er, I'm almost in love.

MRS. POPOV. Keep away from me, I loathe you.

SMIRNOV. God, what a woman! Never saw the like of it in all my born days. I'm sunk! Without trace! Trapped like a mouse!

MRS. POPOV. Get back or I shoot.

SMIRNOV. Shoot away. I'd die happily with those marvellous eyes looking at me, that's what you can't see—die by that dear little velvet hand. Oh, I'm crazy! Think it over and make your mind up now, because once I leave this place we shan't see each other again. So make your mind up. I'm a gentleman and a man of honour, I've ten thousand a year, I can put a bullet through a coin in mid air and I keep a good stable. Be my wife.

MRS. POPOV [*indignantly brandishes the revolver*]. A duel! We'll shoot it out!

SMIRNOV. I'm out of my mind! Nothing makes any sense. [*Shouts.*] Hey, you there—water!

MRS. POPOV [*shouts*]. We'll shoot it out!

SMIRNOV. I've lost my head, fallen for her like some damfool boy! [*Clutches her hand. She shrieks with pain.*] I love you! [*Kneels.*] I love you as I never loved any of my twenty-one other women—twelve times it was me broke it off, the other nine got in first. But I never loved anyone as much as you. I've gone all sloppy, soft and sentimental. Kneeling like an imbecile, offering my hand! Disgraceful! Scandalous! I haven't been in love for five years, I swore not to, and here I am crashing head over heels, hook, line and sinker! I offer you my hand. Take it or leave it. [*Gets up and hurries to the door.*]

MRS. POPOV. Just a moment.

SMIRNOV [*stops*]. What is it?

MRS. POPOV. Oh, never mind, just go away. But wait. No, go, go away. I hate you. Or no—don't go away. Oh, if you knew how furious I am! [*Throws the revolver on the table.*] My fingers are numb from holding this beastly thing. [*Tears a handkerchief in her anger.*] Why are you hanging about? Clear out!

SMIRNOV. Good-bye.

MRS. POPOV. Yes, yes, go away! [*Shouts.*] Where are you going? Stop. Oh, go away then. I'm so furious! Don't you come near me, I tell you.

SMIRNOV [*going up to her*]. I'm so fed up with myself! Falling in love like a schoolboy! Kneeling down! It's enough to give you the willies! [*Rudely.*] I love you! Oh, it's just what the doctor ordered, this is! There's my interest due in tomorrow, haymaking's upon us— and *you* have to come along! [*Takes her by the waist.*] I'll never forgive myself.

MRS. POPOV. Go away! You take your hands off me! I, er, hate you! We'll sh-shoot it out!

[*A prolonged kiss.*]

SCENE XI

[*The above,* LUKE *with an axe, the gardener with a rake, the coachman with a pitchfork and some workmen with sundry sticks and staves.*]

LUKE [*seeing the couple kissing*]. Mercy on us! [*Pause.*]

MRS. POPOV. [*lowering her eyes*]. Luke, tell them in the stables—Toby gets no oats today.

CURTAIN

THE PROPOSAL

[*Предложение*]

A FARCE IN ONE ACT

(1888–1889)

CHARACTERS

STEPHEN CHUBUKOV, a landowner

NATASHA, his daughter, aged 25

IVAN LOMOV, a landowning neighbour of Chubukov's, hefty and well-nourished, but a hypochondriac

The action takes place in the drawing-room of Chubukov's country-house

SCENE I

[CHUBUKOV *and* LOMOV; *the latter comes in wearing evening dress and white gloves.*]

CHUBUKOV [*going to meet him*]. Why, it's Ivan Lomov—or do my eyes deceive me, old boy? Delighted. [*Shakes hands.*] I say, old bean, this is a surprise! How *are* you?

LOMOV. All right, thanks. And how might you be?

CHUBUKOV. Not so bad, dear boy. Good of you to ask and so on. Now, you simply must sit down. Never neglect the neighbours, old bean—what? But why so formal, old boy—the tails, the gloves and so on? Not going anywhere, are you, dear man?

LOMOV. Only coming here, my dear Chubukov.

CHUBUKOV. Then why the tails, my dear fellow? Why make such a great thing of it?

LOMOV. Well, look, the point is—. [*Takes his arm.*] I came to ask a favour, my dear Chubukov, if it's not too much bother. I have had the privilege of enlisting your help more than once, and you've always, as it were—but I'm so nervous, sorry. I'll drink some water, my dear Chubukov. [*Drinks water.*]

CHUBUKOV [*aside*]. He's come to borrow money. Well, there's nothing doing! [*To him.*] What's the matter, my dear fellow?

LOMOV. Well, you see, my chear Dubukov—my dear Chubukov, I mean, sorry—that's to say, I'm terribly jumpy, as you see. In fact only you can help me, though I don't deserve it, of course and, er, have no claims on you either.

CHUBUKOV. Now don't muck about with it, old bean. Let's have it. Well?

LOMOV. Certainly, this instant. The fact is, I'm here to ask for the hand of your daughter Natasha.

CHUBUKOV [*delightedly*]. My dear Lomov! Say that again, old horse, I didn't quite catch it.

LOMOV. I have the honour to ask——

CHUBUKOV [*interrupting him*]. My dear old boy! I'm delighted and so on, er, and so forth—what? [*Embraces and kisses him.*] I've long wanted it, it's always been my wish. [*Sheds a tear.*] I've always loved you as a son, dear boy. May you both live happily ever after and so on. As for me, I've always wanted—. But why do I stand around like a blithering idiot? I'm tickled pink, I really am! Oh, I most cordially—. I'll go and call Natasha and so forth.

LOMOV [*very touched*]. My dear Chubukov, what do you think—can I count on a favourable response?

CHUBUKOV. What—her turn down a good-looking young fellow like you! Not likely! I bet she's crazy about you and so on. One moment. [*Goes out.*]

SCENE II

[LOMOV, *alone.*]

LOMOV. I feel cold, I'm shaking like a leaf. Make up your mind, that's the great thing. If you keep chewing things over, dithering on the brink, arguing the toss and waiting for your ideal woman or true love to come along, you'll never get hitched up. Brrr! I'm cold. Natasha's a good housewife. She's not bad-looking and she's an educated girl—what more can you ask? But I'm so jumpy, my ears have started buzzing. [*Drinks water.*] And get married I must. In the first place, I'm thirty-five years old—a critical age, so to speak. Secondly, I should lead a proper, regular life. I've heart trouble and constant palpitations, I'm irritable and nervous as a kitten. See how my lips are trembling now? See my right eyelid twitch? But my nights are the worst thing. No sooner do I get in bed and start dozing off than I have a sort of shooting pain in my left side. It goes right through my shoulder and head. Out I leap like a lunatic, walk about a bit, then lie down again—but the moment I start dropping off I get this pain in my side again. And it happens twenty times over.

SCENE III

[NATASHA *and* LOMOV.]

NATASHA [*comes in*]. Oh, it's you. That's funny, Father said it was a dealer collecting some goods or something. Good morning, Mr. Lomov.

LOMOV. And good morning to you, my dear Miss Chubukov.

NATASHA. Excuse my apron, I'm not dressed for visitors. We've been shelling peas—we're going to dry them. Why haven't you been over for so long? Do sit down. [*They sit.*] Will you have lunch?

LOMOV. Thanks, I've already had some.

NATASHA. Or a smoke? Here are some matches. It's lovely weather, but it rained so hard yesterday—the men were idle all day. How much hay have you cut? I've been rather greedy, you know—I mowed all mine, and now I'm none too happy in case it rots. I should have hung on. But what's this I see? Evening dress, it seems. That *is* a surprise! Going dancing or something? You're looking well, by the way—but why on earth go round in that get-up?

LOMOV [*agitated*]. Well, you see, my dear Miss Chubukov. The fact is, I've decided to ask you to—er, lend me your ears. You're bound to be surprised—angry, even. But I—. [*Aside.*] I feel terribly cold.

NATASHA. What's up then? [*Pause.*] Well?

LOMOV. I'll try to cut it short. Miss Chubukov, you are aware that I have long been privileged to know your family—since I was a boy, in fact. My dear departed aunt and her husband—from whom, as you are cognizant, I inherited the estate—always entertained the deepest respect for your father and dear departed mother. We Lomovs and Chubukovs have always been on the friendliest terms— you might say we've been pretty thick. And what's more, as you are also aware, we own closely adjoining properties. You may recall that my land at Oxpen Field is right next to your birch copse.

NATASHA. Sorry to butt in, but you refer to Oxpen Field as 'yours'? Surely you're not serious!

LOMOV. I am, madam.

NATASHA. Well, I like that! Oxpen Field is ours, it isn't yours.

LOMOV. You're wrong, my dear Miss Chubukov, that's my land.

NATASHA. This is news to me. How can it be yours?

LOMOV. How? What do you mean? I'm talking about Oxpen Field, that wedge of land between your birch copse and Burnt Swamp.

NATASHA. That's right. It's our land.

LOMOV. No, you're mistaken, my dear Miss Chubukov. It's mine.

NATASHA. Oh, come off it, Mr. Lomov. How long has it been yours?

LOMOV. How long? As long as I can remember—it's always been ours.

NATASHA. I say, this really is a bit steep!

LOMOV. But you have only to look at the deeds, my dear Miss Chubukov. Oxpen Field once *was* in dispute, I grant you, but it's mine now—that's common knowledge, and no argument about it. If I may explain, my aunt's grandmother made over that field rent free to your father's grandfather's labourers for their indefinite use in return for firing her bricks. Now, your great-grandfather's people used the place rent free for forty years or so, and came to look on it as their own. Then when the government land settlement was brought out——

NATASHA. No, that's all wrong. My grandfather and great-grandfather both claimed the land up to Burnt Swamp as theirs. So Oxpen Field was ours. Why argue? That's what I can't see. This is really rather aggravating.

LOMOV. I'll show you the deeds, Miss Chubukov.

NATASHA. Oh, you must be joking or having me on. This *is* a nice surprise! You own land for nearly three hundred years, then someone ups and tells you it's not yours! Mr. Lomov, I'm sorry, but I simply can't believe my ears. I don't mind about the field—it's only the odd twelve acres, worth the odd three hundred roubles. But it's so unfair—that's what infuriates me. I can't stand unfairness, I don't care what you say.

LOMOV. Do hear me out, please! With due respect, your great-grandfather's people baked bricks for my aunt's grandmother, as I've already told you. Now, my aunt's grandmother wanted to do them a favour——

NATASHA. Grandfather, grandmother, aunt—it makes no sense to me. The field's ours, and that's that.

LOMOV. It's mine.

NATASHA. It's ours! Argue till the cows come home, put on tail-coats by the dozen for all I care—it'll still be ours, ours, ours! I'm not after your property, but I don't propose losing mine either, and I don't care what you think!

LOMOV. My dear Miss Chubukov, it's not that I need that field—it's the principle of the thing. If you want it, have it. Take it as a gift.

NATASHA. But it's mine to give *you* if I want—it's my property. This is odd, to put it mildly. We always thought you such a good neighbour and friend, Mr. Lomov. We lent you our threshing-machine last year, and couldn't get our own threshing done till November in consequence. We might be gipsies, the way you treat us. Making me a present of my own property! I'm sorry, but that's not exactly neighbourly of you. In fact, if you ask me, it's sheer howling cheek.

LOMOV. So I'm trying to pinch your land now, am I? It's not my habit, madam, to grab land that isn't mine, and I won't have anyone say it is! [*Quickly goes to the carafe and drinks some water.*] Oxpen Field belongs to me.

NATASHA. That's a lie, it's ours.

LOMOV. It's mine.

NATASHA. That's a lie and I'll nail it! I'll send my men to cut that field this very day.

LOMOV. What do you say?

NATASHA. My men will be out on that field today!

LOMOV. Too right, they'll be out! Out on their ear!

NATASHA. You'd never dare.

LOMOV [*clutches his heart*]. Oxpen Field belongs to me, do you hear? It's mine!

NATASHA. Kindly stop shouting. By all means yell yourself blue in the face when you're in your own home, but I'll thank you to keep a civil tongue in your head in this house.

LOMOV. Madam, if I hadn't got these awful, agonizing palpitations and this throbbing in my temples, I'd give you a piece of my mind! [*Shouts.*] Oxpen Field belongs to me.

NATASHA. To us, you mean!

LOMOV. It's mine!

NATASHA. It's ours!

LOMOV. Mine!

SCENE IV

[*The above and* CHUBUKOV.]

CHUBUKOV [*coming in*]. What's going on, what's all the row in aid of?

NATASHA. Father, who owns Oxpen Field? Would you mind telling this gentleman? Is it his or ours?

CHUBUKOV [*to* LOMOV]. That field's ours, old cock!

LOMOV. Now look here, Chubukov, how can it be? You at least might show some sense! My aunt's grandmother made over that field to your grandfather's farm-labourers rent free on a temporary basis. Those villagers had the use of the land for forty years and came to think of it as theirs, but when the settlement came out——

CHUBUKOV. Now hang on, dear man, you forget one thing. That field was in dispute and so forth even in those days—and that's why the villagers paid your grandmother no rent and so on. But now it belongs to us, every dog in the district knows that, what? You can't have seen the plans.

LOMOV. It's mine and I'll prove it.

CHUBUKOV. Oh no you won't, my dear good boy.

LOMOV. Oh yes, I will.

CHUBUKOV. No need to shout, old bean. Shouting won't prove anything, what? I'm not after your property, but I don't propose losing mine, either. Why on earth should I? If it comes to that, old sausage, if you're set on disputing the field and so on, I'd rather give it to the villagers than you. So there.

LOMOV. This makes no sense to me. What right have you to give other people's property away?

CHUBUKOV. Permit me to be the best judge of that. Now, look here, young feller-me-lad—I'm not used to being spoken to like this, what? I'm twice your age, boy, and I'll thank you to talk to me without getting hot under the collar and so forth.

LOMOV. Oh, really, you must take me for a fool. You're pulling my leg. You say my land's yours, then you expect me to keep my temper and talk things over amicably. I call this downright unneighbourly, Chubukov. You're not a neighbour, you're a thorough-going shark!

CHUBUKOV. I *beg* your pardon! What did you say?

NATASHA. Father, send the men out to mow that field this very instant!

CHUBUKOV [*to* LOMOV]. What was it you said, sir?

NATASHA. Oxpen Field's ours and I won't let it go, I won't, I won't!

LOMOV. We'll see about that! I'll have the law on you!

CHUBUKOV. You will, will you? Then go right ahead, sir, and so forth, go ahead and sue, sir! Oh, I know your sort! Just what you're angling for and so on, isn't it—a court case, what? Quite the legal eagle, aren't you? Your whole family's always been litigation-mad, every last one of 'em!

LOMOV. I'll thank you not to insult my family. We Lomovs have always been honest, we've none of us been had up for embezzlement like your precious uncle.

CHUBUKOV. The Lomovs have always been mad as hatters!

NATASHA. Yes! All of you! Mad!

CHUBUKOV. Your grandfather drank like a fish, and your younger Aunt What's-her-name—Nastasya—ran off with an architect and so on.

LOMOV. And your mother was a cripple. [*Clutches his heart.*] There's that shooting pain in my side, and a sort of blow on the head. Heavens alive! Water!

CHUBUKOV. Your father gambled and ate like a pig!

NATASHA. Your aunt was a most frightful busybody!

LOMOV. My left leg's gone to sleep. And you're a very slippery customer. Oh my heart! And it's common knowledge that at election time you bri—. I'm seeing stars. Where's my hat?

NATASHA. What a rotten, beastly, filthy thing to say.

CHUBUKOV. You're a thoroughly nasty, cantankerous, hypocritical piece of work, what? Yes, sir!

LOMOV. Ah, there's my hat. My heart—. Which way do I go? Where's the door? Oh, I think I'm dying. I can hardly drag one foot after another. [*Moves to the door.*]

CHUBUKOV [*after him*]. You need never set either of those feet in my house again, sir.

NATASHA. Go ahead and sue, we'll see what happens.

[LOMOV *goes out staggering.*]

SCENE V

[CHUBUKOV *and* NATASHA.]

CHUBUKOV. Oh, blast it! [*Walks up and down in agitation.*]

NATASHA. The rotten cad! So much for trusting the dear neighbours!

CHUBUKOV. Scruffy swine!

NATASHA. He's an out-and-out monster! Pinches your land and then has the cheek to swear at you!

CHUBUKOV. And this monstrosity, this blundering oaf, has the immortal rind to come here with his proposal and so on, what? A proposal! I ask you!

NATASHA. A proposal, did you say?

CHUBUKOV. Not half I did! He came here to propose to you!

NATASHA. Propose? To me? Then why didn't you say so before?

CHUBUKOV. That's why he dolled himself up in tails. Damn popinjay! Twerp!

NATASHA. Me? Propose to me? Oh! [*Falls in an armchair and groans.*] Bring him back! Bring him back! Bring him back, I tell you!

CHUBUKOV. Bring who back?

NATASHA. Hurry up, be quick, I feel faint. Bring him back. [*Has hysterics.*]

CHUBUKOV. What's this? What do you want? [*Clutches his head.*] Oh, misery! I might as well go and boil my head! I'm fed up with them!

NATASHA. I'm dying. Bring him back!

CHUBUKOV. Phew! All right then. No need to howl. [*Runs out.*]

NATASHA [*alone, groans*]. What have we done! Bring him, bring him back!

CHUBUKOV [*runs in*]. He'll be here in a moment and so on, damn him! Phew! You talk to him—I don't feel like it, what?

NATASHA [*groans*]. Bring him back!

CHUBUKOV [*shouts*]. He's coming, I tell you.

> 'My fate, ye gods, is just too bad—
> To be a grown-up daughter's dad!'

I'll cut my throat, I'll make a point of it. We've sworn at the man, insulted him and kicked him out of the house. And it was all your doing.

NATASHA. It was *not*, it was yours!

CHUBUKOV. So now it's my fault, what?

[LOMOV *appears in the doorway*.]

CHUBUKOV. All right, now you talk to him. [*Goes out*.]

SCENE VI

[NATASHA *and* LOMOV.]

LOMOV [*comes in, exhausted*]. My heart's fairly thumping away, my leg's gone to sleep and there's this pain in my side——

NATASHA. I'm sorry we got a bit excited, Mr. Lomov. I've just remembered—Oxpen Field really does belong to you.

LOMOV. My heart's fairly thumping away. That field's mine. I've a nervous tic in both eyes.

NATASHA. The field *is* yours, certainly. Do sit down. [*They sit*.] We were mistaken.

LOMOV. This is a question of principle. It's not the land I mind about, it's the principle of the thing.

NATASHA. Just so, the principle. Now let's change the subject.

LOMOV. Especially as I can prove it. My aunt's grandmother gave your father's grandfather's villagers——

NATASHA. All right, that'll do. [*Aside*.] I don't know how to start. [*To him*.] Thinking of going shooting soon?

LOMOV. Yes, I'm thinking of starting on the woodcock after the harvest, my dear Miss Chubukov. I say, have you heard? What awful bad luck! You know my dog Tracker? He's gone lame.

NATASHA. Oh, I am sorry. How did it happen?

LOMOV. I don't know. Either it must be a sprain, or the other dogs bit him. [*Sighs*.] My best dog, to say nothing of what he set me back!

Do you know, I gave Mironov a hundred and twenty-five roubles for him?

NATASHA. Then you were had, Mr. Lomov.

LOMOV. He came very cheap if you ask me—he's a splendid dog.

NATASHA. Father only gave eighty-five roubles for Rover. And Rover's a jolly sight better dog than Tracker, you'll agree.

LOMOV. Rover better than Tracker! Oh, come off it! [*Laughs.*] Rover a better dog than Tracker!

NATASHA. Of course he is. Rover's young, it's true, and not yet in his prime. But you could search the best kennels in the county without finding a nippier animal, or one with better points.

LOMOV. I am sorry, Miss Chubukov, but you forget he has a short lower jaw, and a dog like that can't grip.

NATASHA. Oh, can't he! That's news to me!

LOMOV. He has a weak chin, you can take that from me.

NATASHA. Why, have you measured it?

LOMOV. Yes, I have. Naturally he'll do for coursing, but when it comes to retrieving, that's another story.

NATASHA. In the first place, Rover has a good honest coat on him, and a pedigree as long as your arm. As for that mud-coloured, piebald animal of yours, his antecedents are anyone's guess, quite apart from him being ugly as a broken-down old cart-horse.

LOMOV. Old he may be, but I wouldn't swap him for half a dozen Rovers—not on your life! Tracker's a real dog, and Rover—why, it's absurd to argue. The kennels are lousy with Rovers, he'd be dear at twenty-five roubles.

NATASHA. You *are* in an awkward mood today, Mr. Lomov. First you decide our field is yours, now you say Tracker's better than Rover. I dislike people who won't speak their mind. Now, you know perfectly well that Rover's umpteen times better than that—yes, that stupid Tracker. So why say the opposite?

LOMOV. I see you don't credit me with eyes or brains, Miss Chubukov. Well, get it in your head that Rover has a weak chin.

NATASHA. That's not true.

LOMOV. Oh yes it is!

NATASHA [*shouts*]. Oh no it isn't!

LOMOV. Don't you raise your voice at me, madam.

NATASHA. Then don't you talk such utter balderdash! Oh, this is infuriating! It's time that measly Tracker was put out of his misery— and you compare him with Rover!

LOMOV. I can't go on arguing, sorry—it's my heart.

NATASHA. Men who argue most about sport, I've noticed, are always the worst sportsmen.

LOMOV. Will you kindly hold your trap, madam—my heart's breaking in two. [*Shouts.*] You shut up!

NATASHA. I'll do nothing of the sort till you admit Rover's a hundred times better than Tracker.

LOMOV. A hundred times worse, more like! I hope Rover drops dead! Oh, my head, my eye, my shoulder——

NATASHA. That half-wit Tracker doesn't need to drop dead—he's pretty well a walking corpse already.

LOMOV [*weeps*]. Shut up! I'm having a heart attack!

NATASHA. I will *not* shut up!

SCENE VII

[*The above and* CHUBUKOV.]

CHUBUKOV [*comes in*]. What is it this time?

NATASHA. Father, I want an honest answer: which is the better dog, Rover or Tracker?

LOMOV. Will you kindly tell us just one thing, Chubukov: has Rover got a weak chin or hasn't he? Yes or no?

CHUBUKOV. What if he has? As if that mattered! Seeing he's only the best dog in the county and so on.

LOMOV. Tracker's better, and you know it! Be honest!

CHUBUKOV. Keep your shirt on, dear man. Now look here. Tracker has got some good qualities, what? He's a pedigree dog, has firm paws, steep haunches and so forth. But that dog has two serious faults if you want to know, old bean: he's old and he's pug-nosed.

LOMOV. I'm sorry—it's my heart! Let's just look at the facts. You may recall that Tracker was neck and neck with the Count's Swinger on Maruskino Green when Rover was a good half-mile behind.

CHUBUKOV. He dropped back because the Count's huntsman fetched him a crack with his whip.

LOMOV. Serve him right. Hounds are all chasing the fox and Rover has to start worrying a sheep!

CHUBUKOV. That's not true, sir. I've got a bad temper, old boy, and the fact is—let's please stop arguing, what? He hit him because everyone hates the sight of another man's dog. Oh yes they do. Loathe 'em, they do. And you're no one to talk either, sir! The moment you spot a better dog than the wretched Tracker, you always try to start something and, er, so forth—what? I don't forget, you see.

LOMOV. Nor do I, sir.

CHUBUKOV [mimics him]. 'Nor do I, sir.' What is it you don't forget then?

LOMOV. My heart! My leg's gone to sleep. I can't go on.

NATASHA [mimics him]. 'My heart!' Call yourself a sportsman! You should be lying on the kitchen stove squashing black-beetles, not fox-hunting. His heart!

CHUBUKOV. Some sportsman, I must say! With that heart you should stay at home, not bob around in the saddle, what? I wouldn't mind if you hunted properly, but you only turn out to pick quarrels and annoy the hounds and so on. I have a bad temper, so let's change the subject. You're no sportsman, sir—what?

LOMOV. What about you then? You only turn out so you can get in the Count's good books and intrigue against people. Oh, my heart! You're a slippery customer, sir!

CHUBUKOV. What's that, sir? Oh, I am, am I? [Shouts.] Hold your tongue!

LOMOV. You artful old dodger!

CHUBUKOV. Why, you young puppy!

LOMOV. Nasty old fogy! Canting hypocrite!

CHUBUKOV. Shut up, or I'll pot you like a ruddy partridge. And I'll use a dirty gun too, you idle gasbag!

LOMOV. And it's common knowledge that—oh, my heart—your wife

used to beat you. Oh, my leg! My head! I can see stars! I can't
stand up!

CHUBUKOV. And your housekeeper has you eating out of her hand!

LOMOV. Oh, oh! My heart's bursting. My shoulder seems to have
come off—where is the thing? I'm dying. [*Falls into an armchair.*]
Fetch a doctor. [*Faints.*]

CHUBUKOV. Why, you young booby! Hot air merchant! I think
I'm going to faint. [*Drinks water.*] I feel unwell.

NATASHA. Calls himself a sportsman and can't even sit on a horse!
[*To her father.*] Father, what's the matter with him? Father, have a
look. [*Screeches.*] Mr. Lomov! He's dead!

CHUBUKOV. I feel faint. I can't breathe! Give me air!

NATASHA. He's dead. [*Tugs* LOMOV's *sleeve.*] Mr. Lomov, Mr.
Lomov! What have we done? He's dead. [*Falls into an armchair.*]
Fetch a doctor, a doctor! [*Has hysterics.*]

CHUBUKOV. Oh! What's happened? What's the matter?

NATASHA [*groans*]. He's dead! Dead!

CHUBUKOV. Who's dead? [*Glancing at* LOMOV.] My God, you're
right! Water! A doctor! [*Holds a glass to* LOMOV's *mouth.*] Drink!
No, he's not drinking. He must be dead, and so forth. Oh, misery,
misery! Why don't I put a bullet in my brain? Why did I never get
round to cutting my throat? What am I waiting for? Give me a
knife! A pistol! [LOMOV *makes a movement.*] I think he's coming
round. Drink some water! That's right.

LOMOV. I can see stars! There's a sort of mist. Where am I?

CHUBUKOV. Hurry up and get married and—oh, to hell with you!
She says yes. [*Joins their hands.*] She says yes, and so forth. You have
my blessing, and so on. Just leave me in peace, that's all.

LOMOV. Eh? What? [*Raising himself.*] Who?

CHUBUKOV. She says yes. Well, what about it? Kiss each other and—
oh, go to hell!

NATASHA [*groans*]. He's alive. Yes, yes, yes! I agree.

CHUBUKOV. Come on, kiss.

LOMOV. Eh? Who? [*Kisses* NATASHA.] Very nice too. I say, what's
all this about? Oh, I see—. My heart! I'm seeing stars! Miss Chubukov, I'm so happy. [*Kisses her hand.*] My leg's gone to sleep.

NATASHA. I, er, I'm happy too.

CHUBUKOV. Oh, what a weight off my mind! Phew!

NATASHA. Still, you must admit now that Tracker's not a patch on Rover.

LOMOV. Oh yes he is!

NATASHA. Oh no he isn't!

CHUBUKOV. You can see those two are going to live happily ever after! Champagne!

LOMOV. He's better.

NATASHA. He's worse, worse, worse.

CHUBUKOV [*trying to shout them down*]. Champagne, champagne, champagne!

CURTAIN

TATYANA REPIN

[*Татьяна Репина*]

A DRAMA IN ONE ACT

(1889)

(Dedicated to A. S. Suvorin)

CHARACTERS

VERA OLENIN

MRS. KOKOSHKIN

MATVEYEV

SONNENSTEIN

PETER SABININ

KOTELNIKOV

KOKOSHKIN

PATRONNIKOV

VOLGIN, a young officer

A student

A young lady

FATHER IVAN, the cathedral dean, aged 70

FATHERS NICHOLAS and ALEXIS, young priests

Deacon

Acolyte

KUZMA, the cathedral caretaker

Woman in black

The assistant public prosecutor

Actors and actresses

Between six and seven o'clock in the evening. The cathedral. All lamps and candles are burning. The holy gates in front of the chancel are open. Two choirs are taking part: the bishop's choir and the cathedral choir. The church is crowded, close and stuffy. A marriage service is being performed. VERA *and* SABININ *are the bride and groom. The groom is attended by* KOTELNIKOV *and* VOLGIN, *the bride by her student brother and the* ASSISTANT PUBLIC PROSECUTOR. *The entire local intelligentsia is present. Smart dresses. The officiating clergy are:* FATHER IVAN *in a faded high hat;* FATHER NICHOLAS, *who wears a low cap and has a lot of hair; and* FATHER ALEXIS, *who is very young and wears dark glasses. In the rear and somewhat to the right of* FATHER IVAN *stands the tall thin* DEACON *with a book in his hands. The congregation includes the local theatrical company headed by* MATVEYEV.

FATHER IVAN [*reading*]. Remember, O God, the parents who have reared them; for the prayers of parents confirm the foundation of houses. Remember, O Lord our God, thy servants, the paranymphs, who are present at this rejoicing. Remember, O Lord our God, thy servant PETER and thine handmaid VERA, and bless them. Give them fruit of the womb, fair children and unanimity of soul and body. Exalt them as the cedars of Libanus, and as a well-cultured vine. Bestow upon them seed of corn, that, having every sufficiency, they may abound in every work that is good and acceptable unto thee; and let them behold their son's sons as newly planted olive-trees round about their table; and, being accepted before thee, may they shine as the luminaries in heaven unto thee, our Lord. And, together with thee, be glory, might, honour, and worship, to thine unbeginning Father, and to thy life-creating Spirit, now and ever, and to ages of ages.

BISHOP'S CHOIR [*singing*]. Amen.

PATRONNIKOV. It's close in here. What's that medal you've got round your neck, Mr. Sonnenstein?

SONNENSTEIN. It's Belgian. But why such a large congregation? Who let them in, isn't it? Ugh! This is worse than a village bath-house!

PATRONNIKOV. It was the wretched police.

DEACON. Let us pray to the Lord.

CATHEDRAL CHOIR [*singing*]. Lord, have mercy.

FATHER NICHOLAS [*reading*]. O Holy God, who didst form man from the dust, and from his rib didst fashion woman, and yoke her unto him a helpmeet for him, because so it was seemly unto thy majesty for man not to be alone upon the earth; do thou thyself now, O Master, stretch forth thy hand from thy holy dwelling-place, and conjoin this thy servant PETER, and this thine handmaid VERA; for by thee a woman is conjoined unto a man. Yoke them together in unanimity, crown them in one flesh, bestow on them fruit of the womb, and the gain of well-favoured children.

For thine is the might, and thine is the kingdom, and the power, and the glory, of the Father, and of the Son, and of the Holy Ghost, now and ever, and to ages of ages.

CATHEDRAL CHOIR [*singing*], Amen.

YOUNG LADY [*to* SONNENSTEIN]. They're just going to put the crowns on. Look, look!

FATHER IVAN [*taking a crown from the lectern and turning his face to* SABININ]. The servant of God PETER is crowned for the handmaid of God VERA, in the name of the Father, and of the Son, and of the Holy Ghost. Amen. [*Hands the crown to* KOTELNIKOV.]

VOICES IN THE CONGREGATION. 'The best man's just as tall as the groom. He's not much to look at, though. Who is he?' 'That's Kotelnikov. That officer's not up to much either.' 'I say, will you let the lady through.' 'You can't get through here, madam.'

FATHER IVAN [*addresses* VERA]. The handmaid of God VERA is crowned for the servant of God PETER, in the name of the Father, and of the Son, and of the Holy Ghost. [*Hands the crown to the* STUDENT.]

KOTELNIKOV. These crowns are heavy. My hand feels numb already.

VOLGIN. Never mind, I'll take over soon. Who's that stinking of cheap scent? That's what I'd like to know.

ASSISTANT PROSECUTOR. It's Kotelnikov.

KOTELNIKOV. That's a lie.

VOLGIN. Shush!

FATHER IVAN. O Lord our God, crown them with glory and honour.

O Lord our God, crown them with glory and honour. O Lord our God, crown them with glory and honour.

MRS. KOKOSHKIN [*to her husband*]. Doesn't Vera look nice today? I've been admiring her. And she isn't a bit nervous.

KOKOSHKIN. She's used to it. It is her second wedding, after all.

MRS. KOKOSHKIN. Well, that's true enough. [*Sighs.*] I do hope she'll be happy, she has such a kind heart.

ACOLYTE [*coming into the middle of the church*]. The prokimenon of the Epistle, tone viii. Thou hast set upon their heads crowns of precious stones: they asked life of thee, and thou gavest it them.

BISHOP'S CHOIR [*singing*]. Thou hast set upon their heads——

KOTELNIKOV. I wish I could have a smoke.

ACOLYTE. The words of Paul the Apostle.

DEACON. Let us hearken.

ACOLYTE [*intoning in a deep bass*]. Brethren, give thanks always for all things unto God and the Father in the name of our Lord Jesus Christ; submitting yourselves one to another in the fear of God. Wives, submit yourselves unto your own husbands, as unto the Lord. For the husband is the head of the wife, even as Christ is the head of the church: and he is the saviour of the body. Therefore as the church is subject unto Christ, so let the wives be to their own husbands in every thing——

SABININ [*to* KOTELNIKOV]. You're hurting my head with the crown.

KOTELNIKOV. Nonsense, I'm holding it a good six inches above your head.

SABININ. You're squashing my head, I tell you.

ACOLYTE. Husbands, love your wives, even as Christ also loved the church, and gave himself for it; that he might sanctify and cleanse it with the washing of water by the word, that he might present it to himself a glorious church, not having spot, or wrinkle, or any such thing; but that it should be holy and without blemish.

VOLGIN. That's a fine deep voice. [*To* KOTELNIKOV.] Shall I take over?

KOTELNIKOV. I'm not tired yet.

ACOLYTE. So ought men to love their wives as their own bodies. He that loveth his wife loveth himself. For no man ever yet hated his own flesh; but nourisheth and cherisheth it, even as the Lord the church: for we are members of his body, of his flesh, and of his bones. For this cause shall a man leave his father and mother——

SABININ. Hold the crown a bit higher, you're squashing me.

KOTELNIKOV. Rubbish.

ACOLYTE. —and shall be joined unto his wife, and they two shall be one flesh.

KOKOSHKIN. The Governor's here.

MRS. KOKOSHKIN. Where do you see him?

KOKOSHKIN. Over there, standing in front on the right with Mr. Altukhov. He's here unofficially.

MRS. KOKOSHKIN. I see, I see. He's talking to Masha Ganzen. He's crazy about her.

ACOLYTE. This is a great mystery: but I speak concerning Christ and the church. Nevertheless let every one of you in particular so love his wife even as himself; and the wife see that she reverence her husband.

CATHEDRAL CHOIR [singing]. Hallelujah, hallelujah, hallelujah.

VOICES. 'Hear that, Natalya? "Let the wife reverence her husband."' 'Oh, you leave me alone!' [Laughter.] 'Shush! This won't do, you people.'

DEACON. Wisdom, standing, let us hear the Holy Gospel.

FATHER IVAN. Peace be to all.

CATHEDRAL CHOIR [singing]. And to thy spirit.

VOICES. 'Reading the Epistle and the New Testament—how long it all takes! It's time they gave us a rest.' 'You can't breathe in here, I'm going.' 'You won't get through. Wait a bit, it'll be over soon.'

FATHER IVAN. The lesson from the Gospel of Saint John.

ACOLYTE. Let us hearken.

FATHER IVAN [after taking off his tall hat]. At that time there was a marriage in Cana of Galilee; and the mother of Jesus was there: and both Jesus was called, and his disciples, to the marriage. And when they wanted wine, the mother of Jesus saith unto him, They have no wine. Jesus saith unto her, Woman, what have I to do with thee? mine hour is not yet come.

SABININ [*to* KOTELNIKOV]. Will it be over soon?

KOTELNIKOV. I don't know, I'm not well up in these things. I should think it must be.

VOLGIN. The bride and groom still have to make their procession.

FATHER IVAN. His mother saith unto the servants, Whatsoever he saith unto you, do it. And there were set there six waterpots of stone, after the manner of the purifying of the Jews, containing two or three firkins apiece. Jesus saith unto them, Fill the waterpots with water. And they filled them up to the brim. And he saith unto them, Draw out now, and bear unto the governor of the feast——

[*A groan is heard.*]

VOLGIN. *Qu'est-ce que c'est?* Has someone been trodden on?

VOICES. 'Shush! Shush!'

[*A groan.*]

FATHER IVAN. And they bare it. When the ruler of the feast had tasted the water that was made wine, and knew not whence it was: (but the servants which drew the water knew;) the governor of the feast called the bridegroom, and saith unto him——

SABININ [*to* KOTELNIKOV]. Who gave that groan just now?

KOTELNIKOV [*staring at the congregation*]. Something's moving there, a woman in black. She must have been taken ill, they're leading her out.

SABININ [*staring*]. Hold the crown a bit higher.

FATHER IVAN. Every man at the beginning doth set forth good wine; and when men have well drunk, then that which is worse: but thou hast kept the good wine until now. This beginning of miracles did Jesus in Cana of Galilee, and manifested forth his glory; and his disciples believed on him——

VOICE. 'I don't know why they let hysterical women in here.'

BISHOP'S CHOIR [*singing*]. Glory be to thee, O Lord, glory be to thee.

PATRONNIKOV. Stop buzzing like a bee, Sonnenstein. And don't stand with your back to the chancel, it's not done.

SONNENSTEIN. It's the young lady who is buzzing like a bee, not me, tee hee hee!

ACOLYTE. Let us all say with our whole soul, and with our whole mind let us say——

CATHEDRAL CHOIR [*singing*]. Lord have mercy.

DEACON. Lord almighty, God our Father, we pray to thee, do thou listen and have mercy.

VOICES. 'Shush! Be quiet!' 'But I'm being pushed myself.'

CHOIR [*sings*]. Lord, have mercy.

VOICES. 'Be quiet! Shush!' 'Who's that fainted?'

DEACON. Have mercy on us, O Lord, in thy great kindness, we pray thee, do thou listen and have mercy.

CHOIR [*sings three times*]. Lord, have mercy.

DEACON. Let us also pray for our Most Pious Autocratic Great Lord, THE EMPEROR ALEXANDER ALEKSANDROVICH of all Russia, for his power, victory, life, peace, health and salvation. May our Lord God help and succour him in all things and humble all his enemies and foes beneath his feet.

CHOIR [*sings three times*]. Lord, have mercy.

[*A groan. Movement in the crowd.*]

MRS. KOKOSHKIN. What's that? [*To the woman standing next to her.*] My dear, this is intolerable. Why can't they open the doors or something? We'll all die of heat.

VOICES. 'They're trying to take her out, but she won't go.' 'Who is it?' 'Shush!'

DEACON. Let us also pray for his Consort, the Most Pious Lady, THE EMPRESS MARIYA FEODOROVNA.

CHOIR [*sings*]. Lord, have mercy.

DEACON. Let us also pray for His Heir, the Right-believing Lord, THE CESAREVITCH and GRAND DUKE NICHOLAS ALEKSAN- DROVICH and for the whole ruling house.

CHOIR [*sings*]. Lord, have mercy.

SABININ. Oh, my God——

VERA. What is it?

DEACON. Let us also pray for the Most Holy Governing SYNOD and for our most reverend Lord THEOPHILUS, the Bishop of This and That, and all our brothers in Christ.

CHOIR [*sings*]. Lord, have mercy.

VOICES. 'Another woman poisoned herself in the Hotel Europe yesterday.' 'Yes, they say it was some doctor's wife.' 'Why did she do it, do you know?'

DEACON. Let us also pray for all their Christ-loving army.

CHOIR [*sings*]. Lord, have mercy.

VOLGIN. It sounds as if someone's crying. The congregation's behaving disgracefully.

DEACON. Let us also pray for our brethren, priests and monks and all our brothers in Christ.

CHOIR [*sings*]. Lord, have mercy.

MATVEYEV. The choirs are singing well today.

COMIC ACTOR. I wish we could get singers like that, Mr. Matveyev.

MATVEYEV. You don't expect much, do you, funny-face! [*Laughter.*] Shush!

DEACON. Let us also pray for the grace, life, peace, health, happiness and good fortune of the servants of the Lord PETER and VERA.

CHOIR [*sings*]. Lord, have mercy.

DEACON. Let us also pray for the blessed——

VOICE. 'Yes, some doctor's wife—in the hotel.'

DEACON. And for the Most Holy Orthodox Patriarchs of eternal memory——

VOICES. 'That's the fourth one to do a Tatyana Repin and poison herself. How do you explain these poisonings, old man?' 'Sheer neuroticism, what else?' 'Are they copying each other, do you think?'

DEACON. And the Pious Tsars and Right-believing Tsarinas and those who keep this Holy Temple and all fathers and brothers who rest in the Lord——

VOICES. 'Suicide's catching.' 'There are so many neurotic females about these days, it's something awful!' 'Be quiet. And stop moving around.'

DEACON. —Christian people here and everywhere.

VOICE. 'Less shouting, please.'

[*A groan.*]

CHOIR [*sings*]. Lord, have mercy.

VOICES. 'Tatyana's death has poisoned the air. Our ladies have all caught the disease, their grievances have driven them mad.' 'Even the air in church is poisoned. Can you feel the tension?'

DEACON. Let us also pray for those who work fruitfully and do good, labouring, singing and standing, in this holy and reverend temple, awaiting the bounty of thy mighty grace.

CHOIR [*sings*]. Lord, have mercy.

FATHER IVAN. For thou art a merciful God, and lovest mankind, and to thee we ascribe glory—to the Father, and to the Son, and to the Holy Ghost, now and ever, and to ages of ages.

CHOIR [*sings*]. Amen.

SABININ. I say, Kotelnikov.

KOTELNIKOV. What is it?

SABININ. Nothing. Oh God, Tatyana Repin's here. She's here, I tell you!

KOTELNIKOV. You must be crazy.

SABININ. That woman in black—it's her. I recognized her, saw her.

KOTELNIKOV. There's no resemblance. She's just another brunette, that's all.

DEACON. Let us pray unto the Lord.

KOTELNIKOV. Don't whisper, it's bad manners. People are looking at you.

SABININ. For God's sake—I can hardly stand. It's her.

[*A groan.*]

CHOIR. Lord, have mercy.

VOICES. 'Be quiet. Shush! Who's that pushing at the back, you people? Shush!' 'They've taken her behind a pillar.' 'You can't move anywhere for women, they should stay at home.'

SOMEONE [*shouts*]. Be quiet!

FATHER IVAN [*reads*]. O Lord our God, who, in thy saving providence, didst vouchsafe in Cana of Galilee—. [*Looks at the congregation.*]

What people, I must say! [*Continues reading.*]—to declare marriage honourable by thy presence—. [*Raising his voice.*] I must ask you to be quieter. You're interfering with the service. Please don't walk about the church, and don't talk or make a noise, but stand still and pray. That's right. Have fear of the Lord. [*Reads.*] O Lord our God, who, in Thy saving providence, didst vouchsafe in Cana of Galilee to declare marriage honourable by thy presence; do thou now thyself preserve in peace and unanimity thy servants PETER and VERA, whom thou art well pleased should be conjoined to one another: declare their marriage honourable: preserve their bed undefiled: be pleased that their mutual life may be unblameable, and count them worthy to attain unto a ripe old age, keeping thy commandments in a pure heart.

For thou art our God, the God to have mercy and to save, and to thee we ascribe glory, with thine unbeginning Father, and with thine all-holy, and good, and life-creating Spirit, now and ever, and to ages of ages.

BISHOP'S CHOIR [*sings*]. Amen.

SABININ [*to* KOTELNIKOV]. Have the police been told not to let anyone else in the church?

KOTELNIKOV. What do you mean? They're jammed in like sardines already. Be quiet, stop whispering.

SABININ. She—Tatyana's here.

KOTELNIKOV. You're raving. She's dead and buried.

DEACON. Help us, save us, have mercy on us, and keep us, O God, by thy grace.

CATHEDRAL CHOIR [*singing*]. Lord, have mercy.

DEACON. That the whole day may be perfect, holy, peaceful and sinless, we ask the Lord.

CATHEDRAL CHOIR [*singing*]. Vouchsafe, O Lord.

DEACON. An angel of peace, a true teacher, a saviour of our souls and bodies, we ask the Lord.

CHOIR [*sings*]. Vouchsafe, O Lord.

VOICES. 'The deacon looks as if he's going on for ever with his "Have mercy, O Lords" and his "Vouchsafe, O Lords".' 'I'm fed up with standing about.'

DEACON. Pardon and forgiveness of our sins and transgressions we ask the Lord.

CHOIR [*sings*]. Vouchsafe, O Lord.

DEACON. What is good and profitable for our souls, and peace unto the world, we ask the Lord.

A VOICE. 'They're being rowdy again. What awful people!'

CHOIR [*sings*]. Vouchsafe, O Lord.

VERA. Peter, you're shuddering and breathing heavily. Are you going to faint?

SABININ. The woman in black, she—it's our fault.

VERA. What woman?

[*A groan.*]

SABININ. It's Tatyana groaning. I'm trying to pull myself together. Kotelnikov's pressing the crown on my head. Oh, all right—never mind.

DEACON. That the remaining time of our life may end in peace and repentance, we ask the Lord.

CHOIR. Vouchsafe, O Lord.

KOKOSHKIN. Vera's as white as a sheet. Look, there are tears in her eyes, I think. And he—look at him!

MRS. KOKOSHKIN. I told her that people would behave badly. I can't think why she decided to be married here—why didn't she go to a village church?

DEACON. A christian end of our life without sickness or shame, in peace and able to answer at the last judgement of Christ, we ask it.

CHOIR [*sings*]. Vouchsafe, O Lord.

MRS. KOKOSHKIN. We ought to ask Father Ivan to hurry. She looks like death.

VOLGIN. I say, let me take over. [*Takes* KOTELNIKOV's *place.*]

DEACON. Having prayed for the unity of the faith, and the communion of the Holy Ghost both for ourselves and for each other, let us make over our whole lives to Christ our God.

CHOIR [*sings*]. To Thee, O Lord.

SABININ. Pull yourself together, Vera—be like me. Ah, well. The service will soon be over anyway. We'll leave at once. It's her——

VOLGIN. Shush!

FATHER IVAN. And count us worthy, O Master, with boldness to dare without condemnation to call upon thee, our heavenly Father God, and say——

BISHOP'S CHOIR [sings]. Our Father which art in heaven, hallowed be thy name, thy kingdom come——

MATVEYEV [to the actors]. Make way a bit, boys, I want to kneel. [Kneels and bows to the ground.] Thy will be done, in heaven as on earth. Give us this day our daily bread and forgive us our sins——

BISHOP'S CHOIR. Thy will be done, as in heaven—in heaven—our daily bread—daily——

MATVEYEV. Remember, O Lord, thy deceased handmaiden TATYANA and forgive her her sins of commission and omission, and forgive us and have mercy on us——. [Stands up.] It's hot!

BISHOP'S CHOIR. —give us this day and forgive us—and forgive us our trespasses—as we forgive them that trespass against us—us——

VOICE. 'They *are* dragging the thing out, I must say.'

BISHOP'S CHOIR. —and lead us—us not into temptation, but deliver us from e-e-evil.

KOTELNIKOV [to the ASSISTANT PROSECUTOR]. What's bitten the groom? See him trembling?

ASSISTANT PROSECUTOR. What's the matter with him?

KOTELNIKOV. That woman in black who just had hysterics—he thought she was Tatyana. He must be seeing things.

FATHER IVAN. For thine is the kingdom, the power and the glory, Father, Son and Holy Ghost, now and forever, world without end.

CHOIR. Amen.

ASSISTANT PROSECUTOR. Mind he doesn't do something silly.

KOTELNIKOV. He won't break down—not him!

ASSISTANT PROSECUTOR. Yes, it's pretty tough on him.

FATHER IVAN. Peace to all.

CHOIR. And on thy spirit.

DEACON. Bow your heads to the Lord.

CHOIR. To thee, O Lord.

VOICES. 'I think they're going to have the procession now. Shush!' 'Have they had an inquest on the doctor's wife?' 'Not yet. They say her husband left her. And Sabinin abandoned Tatyana, didn't he? That's true, isn't it?' 'Ye-es.' 'I remember the inquest on Miss Repin.'

DEACON. Let us pray to the Lord.

CHOIR. Lord, have mercy.

FATHER IVAN [reads]. O God, who by thy might createst all things, and confirmest the universe, and adornest the crown of all things created by thee; do thou, with thy spiritual blessing, bless also this common cup given for the community of marriage unto them that are conjoined. For blessed is thy name, and glorified thy kingdom, Father, Son and Holy Ghost, now and forever, world without end. [Gives SABININ and VERA wine to drink.]

CHOIR. Amen.

ASSISTANT PROSECUTOR. Mind he doesn't faint.

KOTELNIKOV. He's a rugged brute, he won't break down.

VOICES. 'Stick around, all of you—we'll all go out together. Is Zipunov here?' 'Yes. We must stand round the carriage and hiss for five minutes or so.'

FATHER IVAN. Give me your hands, please. [Ties SABININ's and VERA's hands together with a handkerchief.] Not too tight?

ASSISTANT PROSECUTOR [to the STUDENT]. Give me the crown, boy, and you carry the train.

BISHOP'S CHOIR [sings]. Rejoice, O Esaias, the virgin is with child——

[FATHER IVAN walks round the lectern followed by the bride and groom and their attendants.]

VOICE. 'The student's got tangled up in the train.'

BISHOP'S CHOIR. —and bringeth forth a son, Emmanuel, God and man: the orient is his name——

SABININ [to VOLGIN]. Is that the end?

VOLGIN. Not yet.

BISHOP'S CHOIR. —whom magnifying, we call the virgin blessed.

[FATHER IVAN walks around the lectern for the second time.]

CATHEDRAL CHOIR [sings]. O holy martyrs, who valiantly contended, and are crowned; pray ye the Lord for mercy on our souls——

FATHER IVAN [*goes round for the third time and sings*]. —on our souls.

SABININ. My God, will this never end?

BISHOP'S CHOIR [*sings*]. Glory to thee, Christ God, apostles' boast and martyrs' joy, whose preaching was the consubstantial Trinity.

OFFICER IN THE CONGREGATION [*to* KOTELNIKOV]. Warn Sabinin that the students and grammar school boys are going to hiss him in the street.

KOTELNIKOV. Thank you. [*To the* ASSISTANT PROSECUTOR.] But how long this business drags out! Will the service never be done? [*Wipes his face on his handkerchief.*]

ASSISTANT PROSECUTOR. But your own hands are shaking—you're such a lot of sissies.

KOTELNIKOV. I can't get Tatyana out of my head. I keep imagining Sabinin singing and her crying.

FATHER IVAN [*taking the crown from* VOLGIN, *to* SABININ]. Be thou magnified, O bridegroom, as Abraham, and blessed as Isaac, and increased as Jacob, walking in peace, and performing in righteousness the commandments of God.

YOUNG ACTOR. What pearls to cast before swine like that!

MATVEYEV. It's the same God for us all.

FATHER IVAN [*taking the crown from the* ASSISTANT PROSECUTOR, *to* VERA]. And thou, O bride, be thou magnified as Sara, and rejoiced as Rebecca, and increased as Rachel, being glad in thy husband, and keeping the paths of the law, for so God is well pleased.

[*There is a great rush towards the exit.*]

VOICES. 'Be quiet, all of you. It's not over yet.' 'Shush! Don't push!'

DEACON. Let us pray to the Lord.

CHOIR. Lord, have mercy.

FATHER ALEXIS [*reads, after taking off his dark glasses*]. O God, our God, who wast present in Cana of Galilee, and didst bless the marriage there; do thou bless also these thy servants, who, by thy providence, are conjoined in the community of marriage. Bless their incomings and outgoings, replenish their life with good things, accept their crowns in thy kingdom unsullied and undefiled, and preserve them without offence to ages of ages.

CHOIR [*sings*]. Amen.

VERA [*to her brother*]. Ask them to fetch me a chair. I feel ill.

STUDENT. It will soon be over. [*To the* ASSISTANT PROSECUTOR.] Vera feels ill.

ASSISTANT PROSECUTOR. It'll be over in a moment, Vera. Just a moment. Hold on, my dear.

VERA [*to her brother*]. Peter doesn't hear me, he's like a man in a trance. My God, my God! [*To* SABININ.] Peter!

FATHER IVAN. Peace to all.

CHOIR. And on thy spirit.

DEACON. Bow your heads to the Lord.

FATHER IVAN [*to* SABININ *and* VERA]. The Father, the Son, and the Holy Ghost, the all-holy, and consubstantial and life-originating Trinity, one Godhead and sovereignty, bless you, and vouchsafe unto you long life, well-favoured children, progress in life and faith, and replenish you with all the good things of earth, and count you worthy of the obtaining of promised blessings, through the prayers of the holy God-bearing one, and of all the Saints. Amen! [*To* VERA, *with a smile*.] Kiss your husband.

VOLGIN [*to* SABININ]. Don't just stand around—kiss each other.

[*The bride and groom kiss.*]

FATHER IVAN. Congratulations. God grant——

MRS. KOKOSHKIN [*goes up to* VERA]. My dear, I'm so glad, darling. Congratulations!

KOTELNIKOV [*to* SABININ]. Congratulations on getting spliced. No need to look pale any more, the whole rigmarole's over.

DEACON. Wisdom!

[*Congratulations.*]

CHOIR [*sings*]. Thee more honourable than the Cherubim, and in-comparably more glorious than the Seraphim, thee who bearest without corruption God the word, O true Mother of God, thee we magnify! In the Lord's name, bless us, Father.

[*The crowd presses out of the church.* KUZMA *puts out the large candles.*]

FATHER IVAN. May Christ, our true God, that by his presence in Cana of Galilee declared marriage to be honourable, Christ our true God, through the prayers of his most pure Mother; of the holy, glorious, and all-praised apostles; of the holy god-crowned sovereigns and equals of the apostles, Constantine and Helen; of the holy great martyr Procopius, and of all the Saints, have mercy upon us and save us, as being good and the lover of mankind.

CHOIR [*singing*]. Amen. Lord, have mercy. Lord, have mercy. Lord, have me-e-rcy.

LADIES [*to* VERA]. Congratulations, dear. May you be very happy! [*Kisses.*]

SONNENSTEIN. Mrs. Sabinin, er, to put it in plain language, isn't it——

BISHOP'S CHOIR [*singing*]. Long life, long life, lo-o-ng life!

SABININ. So sorry, Vera. [*Grips* KOTELNIKOV's *arm and quickly takes him to one side; trembling and choking.*] Let's go to the cemetery immediately.

KOTELNIKOV. You must be out of your mind. It's night now. What are you going to do there?

SABININ. Come on, for God's sake—please.

KOTELNIKOV. Take your bride home, you lunatic.

SABININ. I don't give a damn, blast everything to hell! I—I'm going. Must hold a requiem service. But I must be mad—I almost died. Oh, Kotelnikov, Kotelnikov!

KOTELNIKOV. Come, come.

[*Leads him to his bride. A minute later a piercing whistle can be heard from the street. The congregation gradually leaves the church. Only the* ACOLYTE *and* KUZMA *remain behind.*]

KUZMA [*puts out the candelabras*]. What a huge crowd——

ACOLYTE. Well, yes. It's a smart wedding. [*Puts on a fur coat.*] These people know how to live.

KUZMA. It's all so pointless. No sense in it.

ACOLYTE. What?

KUZMA. Take this wedding. We marry them, christen them and bury them every day and there ain't no sense in it all.

ACOLYTE. Then what exactly would you like to do?

KUZMA. Nothing. Nothing at all. What's the point? They sing, burn incense, recite the liturgy—but God don't listen. Forty years I've worked here and never heard God's voice. Where God is, I just don't know. There's no point in anything.

ACOLYTE. Well, yes. [*Puts on his galoshes.*] 'It's talk like this that makes your head go round.' [*Moves off with squeaking galoshes.*] Cheerio! [*Goes out.*]

KUZMA [*on his own*]. We buried a local squire this afternoon, we've just had this wedding, and we've a christening tomorrow morning. Where will it all end? What use is it to anyone? None, it's just pointless.

[*A groan is heard.* FATHER IVAN *and* FATHER ALEXIS, *he of the flowing locks and dark glasses, come out from the chancel.*]

FATHER IVAN. I daresay he picked up a decent dowry too.

FATHER ALEXIS. Bound to have.

FATHER IVAN. Oh, what a life, when you come to look at it. Why, I courted a girl myself once, married her and received a dowry, but that's all buried in the sands of time now. [*Shouts.*] Kuzma, why did you put out all the candles? You'll have me falling over in the dark.

KUZMA. Oh, I thought you'd left.

FATHER IVAN. Well, Father Alexis? Shall we go and have tea over at my place?

FATHER ALEXIS. No, thank you, Father. I've no time, there's another report to write.

FATHER IVAN. As you wish.

WOMAN IN BLACK [*comes out from behind a column, staggering*] Who's there? Take me away, take me away.

FATHER IVAN. What's this? Who is it? [*Frightened.*] What do you want, my dear?

FATHER ALEXIS. Lord forgive us miserable sinners.

WOMAN IN BLACK. Take me out, please. [*Groans.*] I'm the sister of Ivanov, the army officer—his sister.

FATHER IVAN. What are you doing here?

WOMAN IN BLACK. I've taken poison—because I hate him. He insulted—. So why is he so happy? My God! [*Shouts.*] Save me, save me! [*Sinks to the floor.*] Everyone should take poison, everyone! There's no justice in this world!

FATHER ALEXIS [*in horror*]. What blasphemy! O God, what blasphemy!

WOMAN IN BLACK. Because I hate him. We should all poison ourselves. [*Groans and rolls on the floor.*] She's in her grave and he, he— the wrong done to a woman is a wrong done to God. A woman has been destroyed.

FATHER ALEXIS. What blasphemy against religion! [*Throws up his arms.*] What blasphemy against life!

WOMAN IN BLACK [*tears all her clothes and shouts*]. Save me! Save me! Save me!

CURTAIN

And all the rest I leave to A. S. Suvorin's imagination.

A TRAGIC ROLE

(*A holiday episode*)

[*Трагик по неволе (из дачной жизни)*]

A FARCE IN ONE ACT

(1889–1890)

IVAN TOLKACHOV, a family man
ALEXIS MURASHKIN, his friend

The action takes place in Murashkin's flat in St. Petersburg

MURASHKIN's *study. Easy chairs.* MURASHKIN *is sitting at his desk.* TOLKACHOV *comes in. He carries a glass lamp-globe, a child's bicycle, three hat-boxes, a large bundle of clothes, a shopping-bag full of beer and a lot of small parcels. He rolls his eyes in a dazed sort of way, and sinks exhausted on the sofa.*

MURASHKIN. Hallo, old man—nice to see you! Where are you sprung from?

TOLKACHOV [*breathing hard*]. Will you do me a favour, dear boy? Have a heart—lend me a revolver till tomorrow, there's a good chap.

MURASHKIN. A revolver? Whatever for?

TOLKACHOV. I need one. Oh Lord, give me water! Water, quick! I need one—got to drive through a dark wood tonight, so I, er—always be prepared. Lend me one, please.

MURASHKIN. Oh, rubbish, old man! 'Dark wood'—what the devil do you mean? Up to something, aren't you? And up to no good too, from the look of you. Now, what's the matter? Are you ill?

TOLKACHOV. Stop, let me get my breath. Whew, I'm all in! My whole body, the old brain-box—I feel as if they'd been chopped up and stuck on a skewer. Like a dog's dinner I feel, I'm at the end of my tether. Don't ask questions or go into details, there's a good fellow—just give me the revolver, I implore you.

MURASHKIN. Come, come, old boy, don't say you've got the wind up! And you a family man, high up in the civil service and all that! You should be ashamed!

TOLKACHOV. A family man? A martyr, more like—a complete drudge, a slave, a chattel, the lowest thing that crawls. Why don't I end it all—what am I waiting for, like some benighted idiot? I'm a regular doormat. What have I to live for? Eh? [*Jumps up.*] Come on, tell me what I have to live for, why the unbroken chain of moral and physical tortures? Certainly I can understand a man who sacrifices himself for an ideal, but to martyr yourself to women's petticoats, lampshades and that sort of damn tomfoolery—no, thank you very much. No, no, no! I've had enough! Enough, I tell you!

MURASHKIN. Don't talk so loud, the neighbours will hear.

TOLKACHOV. Then let the neighbours hear, I don't care. If you won't lend me a revolver, someone else will—I'm not long for this world anyway, that's settled.

MURASHKIN. Hey, you've pulled off one of my buttons. Cool off, can't you? What's wrong with your life? That's what I still don't see.

TOLKACHOV. Oh, don't you! What's wrong, he asks! All right then, I'll tell you. By all means! I'll get it off my chest and perhaps I'll feel better. Let's sit down. Now, you listen—. Lord, I'm out of breath. Take today, for instance. Yes, take it by all means! From ten till four I have my nose to the old office grindstone, as well you know. There's this ghastly heat-wave, the flies—sheer chaos, old boy, all hell let loose. My secretary's on leave, my assistant's gone off to get married, the office rank and file are all mad on week-ends in the country, love affairs and play-acting. The whole bunch are so drowsy, jaded and haggard, you can get no sense out of them. The secretary's job's being done by a creature who's deaf in his left ear and in love. Our clients are crazy, all in a tearing hurry, all losing their tempers and threatening us—there's such a god-almighty hullabaloo, it's enough to make you scream. It's a real mix-up—sheer hell on earth. And the work itself is so damn awful, the same thing over and over again, answering endless inquiries, writing endless minutes—just one damn boring thing after another. It's enough to send you pop-eyed, see? Give me water—. You come out of the office dead beat, absolutely whacked. All you're fit for is a meal and flopping into bed, but not a bit of it! Don't forget your family's staying out at the holiday cottage—in other words you're a complete dogsbody, a worm, a nonentity, an errand-boy expected to rush round like a scalded cat at everyone's beck and call. There's a charming custom where we're staying: if a husband travels in to the office every day, then not only his wife, but any little squirt in the place is fully entitled to load him with masses of errands. The wife tells me to go to her dressmaker and kick up a row because she made a bodice too full, but too narrow in the shoulders. Sonya needs a pair of shoes changed, my sister-in-law wants twenty copecks' worth of crimson silk to match a pattern, and seven foot of ribbon. Just a moment—here, I'll read it to you. [Takes a list out of his pocket and reads.] One globe for lamp; one pound ham-sausage; five copecks' worth of cloves and cinnamon; castor oil for Misha; ten pounds granulated sugar; fetch copper bowl and mortar for pounding sugar from home; carbolic acid; insect powder; ten copecks' worth face powder; twenty bottles beer; vinegar and a size eighty-two corset for Mlle Chanceau—ugh! And fetch Misha's overcoat and galoshes from home. So much for the domestic order. Now for my charming friends and neighbours, blast 'em—now for *their* commissions. It's young Vlasin's birthday tomorrow, so I have to buy him a bicycle. Colonel Vikhrin's missus is in the family way, so it's call on the midwife every day and ask her to come along. And so on and so forth. I've five lists in my pocket and my handkerchief's all knots. And so, old man, between leaving the office and catching your train you dash round town like a mad dog with your tongue hanging out, rushing here there and everywhere and cursing your fate. You traipse around from draper's to chemist's, from chemist's to dressmaker's, from dressmaker's to sausage-shop, then back to the chemist's again. You trip over yourself, you lose your money, you forget to pay, so they run after you and kick up a fuss, and somewhere else you tread on a woman's skirt—ugh! This mad rush puts you in a frenzy, makes you ache something chronic all night through, and you dream of crocodiles. All right, your errands are done, everything's bought—but how exactly are you going to parcel up all this junk? Are you going to lump the lampshade along with your heavy copper mortar and pestle, for instance? Or mix carbolic acid and tea? How do you fit the beer bottles in with this bicycle? It's a regular labour of Hercules, it is—a proper Chinese puzzle. Rack your brains, flog your wits as you like, you always end up breaking and spilling something, then on the station and in the train you find yourself standing with your arms stuck out and your legs straddled, a package under your chin, and with shopping-bags, cardboard boxes and the rest of the tripe strung all over you. Then the train starts and the passengers chuck your stuff all over the place because you've put it on people's seats. They shout, call the ticket-collector, say they'll have you put off. And all you can do is stand there cringing like a whipped cur. And then what? You reach the cottage keyed up for a real drink after all these good works—now for a meal and a bit of a snooze, eh? Some hope! The wife's had her eye on you all along, and you've scarce downed a mouthful of soup, poor devil, before she shoves her dirty great oar in: 'You'd like to see the amateur theatricals, wouldn't you, dear? Or go to the dancing club?' Just you try and get out of it! You're a husband. And in holiday parlance the word 'husband' means a dumb beast to be driven and loaded with all the baggage in sight—no

Society for the Prevention of Cruelty to Animals to bother about! You go and goggle at *A Scandal in a Respectable Family* or some other damn silly play, you clap when the wife tells you, you feel your strength ebbing away, and expect to have an apoplectic fit any minute. And at the club you've got to watch the dances and find partners for the wife, and if there aren't enough gentlemen to go round you have to dance the quadrille yourself. You get home from that theatre or dance after midnight more dead than alive, and fit for nothing. But you've made it at last, and it's off with your various trappings and climb into bed! Wonderful! Just shut your eyes and sleep. Nice and snug, isn't it—like a dream come true? The children aren't screaming in the next room, the wife isn't there, and you've nothing on your conscience—what could be better? You drop off. Then, all of a sudden—bzzzzzz! Gnats! [*Jumps up.*] Gnats! Damn and blast those bleeding gnats! [*Shakes his fist.*] Gnats! The Plagues of Egypt aren't in it—*or* the Spanish Inquisition! Buzz, buzz, buzz! There's this pathetic, mournful buzzing as if it was saying how sorry it was, but you wait till the little nipper gets his fangs in—it means an hour's hard scratching. You smoke, you lash out, you shove your head under the blankets—but you're trapped. You end by giving yourself up like a lamb to the slaughter—let the bastards have their meal and get stuffed! But before you've got used to the gnats, horror strikes again! Your wife starts practising songs in the drawing-room with some friends. Tenors! They sleep all day and spend their nights getting up amateur concerts. Ye gods! For sheer undiluted hell give me your average tenor! Gnats aren't in the same street! [*Sings.*] 'Oh, tell me not your young life's ruined.' 'Once more I stand entranced before thee.' It's the death by a thousand cuts, blast 'em! To deaden their voices a bit, I have this dodge of tapping my head near the ear. So there I am tapping away till they leave at about four o'clock. Whew! More water, old boy, I'm about played out. Well, anyway, at six o'clock you get up after a sleepless night and set off to the station to catch your train. You dash along afraid of missing it. The mud! The mist! And the cold—brrr! And when you get to town the whole ruddy rigmarole starts all over again. That's the way of it, old boy. It's a rotten life, I can tell you—I wouldn't wish it on my worst enemy. It's made me ill, you know—I've asthma, I've heartburn, I'm always on edge, I've indigestion and these dizzy spells. I've become quite a psychopath, you know! [*Looks about him.*] Keep this under your hat, but I feel like calling in one of our leading head-shrinkers. I get this funny mood, old man. You see, when you're really bitched, bothered and bewildered, when gnats do bite or tenors do sing, suddenly everything goes blank and you jump up and run round the house as if you were berserk, shouting: 'I must have blood! Blood!' At such times you really do feel like sticking a knife in someone's gizzard or bashing his head in with a chair. That's what this holiday commuting does for you! And you get no sympathy or pity, either, everyone takes it so much for granted. You even get laughed at. But I'm alive, aren't I? So I want a bit of life! This isn't funny, it's downright tragic. Look here, if you won't lend me a revolver, at least show a spot of fellow-feeling.

MURASHKIN. But I do feel for you.

TOLKACHOV. Yes, I can see how much you do. Well, good-bye. I'll get some sprats and salami, er, and I want some toothpaste too—and then to the station.

MURASHKIN. Whereabouts are you taking your holiday?

TOLKACHOV. At Corpse Creek.

MURASHKIN [joyfully]. Really? I say, you don't happen to know someone staying there called Olga Finberg?

TOLKACHOV. Yes. In fact she's a friend of ours.

MURASHKIN. You don't say! Well, I never! What a stroke of luck and how nice if you——

TOLKACHOV. Why, what is it?

MURASHKIN. My dear old boy, could you possibly do me a small favour, there's a good chap? Now, promise me you will.

TOLKACHOV. What is it?

MURASHKIN. Be a friend in need, old man—have a heart! Now, first give my regards to Olga and say I'm alive and well, and that I kiss her hand. And secondly, there's a little thing I want you to take her. She asked me to buy her a sewing-machine and there's no one to deliver it. You take it, old man. And you may as well take this cage with the canary while you're about it—only be careful or the door will break. What are you staring at?

TOLKACHOV. Sewing-machine—. Cage—. Canary—. Why not a whole bloody aviary?

MURASHKIN. What's up, man? Why so red in the face?

TOLKACHOV [*standing*]. Give me that sewing-machine! Where's the bird-cage? Now you get on my back too! Gobble me up! Rend me limb from limb! Do me in! [*Clenching his fists.*] I must have blood! Blood!

MURASHKIN. Have you gone mad?

TOLKACHOV [*bearing down on him*]. I must have blood! Blood! Blood!

MURASHKIN [*in horror*]. He's gone mad! [*Shouts.*] Peter! Mary! Where are the servants? Help!

TOLKACHOV [*chasing him round the room*]. I must have blood! Blood, blood, blood!

CURTAIN

THE WEDDING

[*Свадьба*]

A PLAY IN ONE ACT

(1889–1890)

CHARACTERS

YEVDOKIM ZHIGALOV, a minor civil servant, retired

NASTASYA, his wife

DASHA, their daughter

EPAMINONDAS APLOMBOV, her fiancé

COMMANDER THEODORE REVUNOV-KARAULOV,
  Imperial Russian Navy, retired

ANDREW NYUNIN, insurance agent

MRS. ANNA ZMEYUKIN, midwife; wears a bright
  crimson dress; aged 30

IVAN YAT, telegraph clerk

KHARLAMPY DYMBA, a Greek confectioner

DMITRY MOZGOVOY, sailor in the Volunteer Fleet

The best man, other young men, servants etc.

*The action takes place in a reception room at a second-class
restaurant*

A large, brilliantly lit room. A big table laid for supper with tail-coated waiters fussing round it. A band plays the last figure of a quadrille off-stage.

MRS. ZMEYUKIN, YAT *and the* BEST MAN *cross the stage.*

MRS. ZMEYUKIN. No, no, no!

YAT [*following her*]. Oh come on, have a heart.

MRS. ZMEYUKIN. No, no, no!

BEST MAN [*hurrying after them*]. This won't do, you two. Where do you think you're off to? What about the dancing? *Grand-rond, seel voo play!*

[*They go out.* MRS. ZHIGALOV *and* APLOMBOV *come in.*]

MRS. ZHIGALOV. Don't bother me with this stuff—you go and dance instead.

APLOMBOV. I'm not spinning round like a top, thank you. Me spin? No sir, I'm no Spinoza! I'm a solid citizen, a pillar of society, and I am not amused by such idle pursuits. But the dancing's neither here nor there. I'm sorry, Mother, but some things you do have me baffled. Take the dowry, for instance. Besides certain household utilities, you also promised me two lottery tickets. Well, where are they?

MRS. ZHIGALOV. I've got a bit of a headache. It must be the weather, there's a thaw in the offing.

APLOMBOV. Don't you try and fob me off! I've just found out that you've pawned those tickets. I'm sorry, Mother, but that's a pretty mean trick. I don't say so from selfishness—I don't want your lottery tickets, it's the principle of the thing. No one makes a monkey out of me. I've brought your daughter happiness, but if I don't get those tickets today I'll make her wish she'd never been born—as I'm a man of honour!

MRS. ZHIGALOV [*looking at the table and counting the number of places laid*]. One, two, three, four, five——

A WAITER. The chef asks how you want the ice-cream served—with rum or madeira or on its own?

APLOMBOV. Rum. And you can tell your boss there's not enough wine, Get him to bring on more Sauterne. [*To* MRS. ZHIGALOV.] You also promised to invite a General to this evening's celebration—that was clearly understood. Well, where is he, I should like to know?

MRS. ZHIGALOV. It's not my fault, dear.

APLOMBOV. Whose is it then?

MRS. ZHIGALOV. Andrew Nyunin's. He was here yesterday and promised to bring along a General—the genuine, guaranteed article. [Sighs.] He can't have run across any, or he'd certainly have brought one. It's not that we're mean—nothing's too much for our darling daughter. If you want a General, a General you shall have.

APLOMBOV. And another thing, Mother. Everyone, you included, knows that this telegraph-clerk Yat was going round with Dasha before I asked her to marry me. Why did you have to invite him? Surely you knew I'd find it awkward?

MRS. ZHIGALOV. Oh—what's your name?—Epaminondas, you haven't been married twenty-four hours and you've nearly been the death of me and Dasha already with your talk, talk, talk. What will it be like after a year of it? You do nag so, you really do.

APLOMBOV. So you don't like hearing a few home truths, eh? Just as I thought. Then behave yourself. That's all I ask, behave properly.

[Couples dance the grand-rond, crossing the room from one door to the other. The first couple are DASHA and the BEST MAN, the last consists of YAT and MRS. ZMEYUKIN. These last two drop behind and stay in the ballroom. ZHIGALOV and DYMBA come in and go up to the table.]

BEST MAN [shouts]. Promenade! Mess-sewers, promenade! [Off-stage.] Promenade!

[The couples go out.]

YAT [to MRS. ZMEYUKIN]. Have a heart—take pity on us, enchanting Anna Zmeyukin.

MRS. ZMEYUKIN. Oh, you are a one, really! I'm not in voice tonight, I've told you that already.

YAT. Sing something, I beg you, if only one note! For pity's sake! A single note!

MRS. ZMEYUKIN. Don't be such a bore. [Sits down and waves her fan.]

YAT. Oh, you're quite heartless! That a being so cruel, pardon the expression, should have such a simply divine voice! You shouldn't be a midwife with a voice like that, if you'll pardon my saying so—you should sing in the concert hall. For instance, there's the heavenly way you take that twiddly bit—how does it go? [*Sings softly.*] 'I loved you, but my love in vain—.' Superb!

MRS. ZMEYUKIN [*sings softly*]. 'I loved you once and love perhaps might still—.' Is that it?

YAT. That's the one. Super!

MRS. ZMEYUKIN. No, I'm not in voice today. Here—you fan me, it's hot! [*To* APLOMBOV.] Why so downhearted, Mr. Aplombov? And on your wedding day too! You should be ashamed of yourself, you naughty man. Well, why so pensive?

APLOMBOV. Marriage is a serious step. You have to weigh the whole thing up from every angle.

MRS. ZMEYUKIN. What revolting cynics you all are. This atmosphere makes me choke. Give me air, do you hear? Atmosphere! [*Sings softly.*]

YAT. Too, too divine!

MRS. ZMEYUKIN. Fan me, fan me! Or I think I'll burst. Tell me, please, why do I have this choking feeling?

YAT. Because you're sweating.

MRS. ZMEYUKIN. Oh, don't you be so common! How dare you speak to me like that?

YAT. Pardon, I'm sure. Of course, you're used to high society, if you don't mind my saying so, and——

MRS. ZMEYUKIN. Oh, let me alone. Give me romance, excitement! Fan me, fan me!

ZHIGALOV [*to* DYMBA]. Have another? [*Pours.*] A drink always comes in handy. The great thing is—don't neglect your business, my dear Dymba. Drink, but keep your wits about you. And if you want a little drink, why not have a little drink? A little drink does no harm. Your health! [*They drink.*] Tell me, are there tigers in Greece?

DYMBA. Yes, is tigers.

ZHIGALOV. And lions?

DYMBA. Is lions too. In Russia is nothing, in Greece is everything! In Greece is my father, my uncle, my brothers. Here is nothing, isn't it?

ZHIGALOV. I see. And are there whales in Greece?

DYMBA. In Greece is every damn thing.

MRS. ZHIGALOV [*to her husband*]. Why are you all eating and drinking any old how? It's time everyone sat down to table. Don't stick your fork in the lobsters, they're meant for the General. Perhaps he'll still come——

ZHIGALOV. Have you got lobsters in Greece?

DYMBA. We have. In Greece is damn all, I tell you!

ZHIGALOV. I see. Have you established civil servants too?

MRS. ZMEYUKIN. I can imagine what a terrific atmosphere there is in Greece!

ZHIGALOV. And a terrific lot of funny business goes on too, I'll bet. The Greeks are just like the Armenians or gipsies, aren't they? Can't sell you a sponge or a goldfish without trying to do you down. How about another?

MRS. ZHIGALOV. Why keep knocking it back? It's time everyone sat down, it's nearly midnight.

ZHIGALOV. If we're to sit, then sit we will. Ladies and gentlemen, I humbly beg you—this way, please. [*Shouts.*] Supper's ready! Come on, young people.

MRS. ZHIGALOV. Come and have supper, please, all of you. Take your places.

MRS. ZMEYUKIN [*sitting down at table*]. Give me a bit of poetry!

   'Restless, he seeks the raging storm,
    As if the storm could give him rest.'

YAT [*aside*]. Superb creature! Oh for a storm! I'm in love, head over heels!

 [*Enter* DASHA, MOZGOVOY, BEST MAN, *young men, girls and so on. All sit down noisily at table. There is a minute's pause. The band plays a march.*]

MOZGOVOY [*standing up*]. Ladies and gentlemen, I've something to say. There are lots of toasts and speeches to come, so let's not mess about, but plunge straight in. Ladies and gentlemen, I propose: the bride and bridegroom!

 [*The band plays a flourish. Cheers. Clinking of glasses.*]

MOZGOVOY. The bride and bridegroom!

ALL. The bride and bridegroom!

[APLOMBOV *and* DASHA *kiss.*]

YAT. Superb, divine! I must say, ladies and gentlemen—always give credit where credit is due—this room and whole establishment are magnificent! They're terrific, charming! But you know, we do need one thing to set things off to perfection—electric light, if you'll pardon the expression. Electric light's come in all over the world—only Russia lags behind.

ZHIGALOV [*with an air of profundity*]. Electric light. I see. If you ask me, there's a lot of funny business about electric light. They shove in a little bit of coal and think no one will notice. No, dear boy, if we're to have light, don't give us your coal, but something with a bit of body to it, something solid that a man can get his teeth in. Give us real light, see? Natural light, not something imaginary.

YAT. If you'd seen what an electric battery's made of, you'd tell a different tale.

ZHIGALOV. I don't want to see. It's all a lot of funny business, to cheat the common man—squeeze him dry, they do, we know their sort! As for you, young feller-me-lad, don't you stick up for swindlers. Have a drink instead and fill up the glasses, that's my message to you!

APLOMBOV. I quite agree, Dad old man. Why trot out all the long words? Not that I mind discussing modern inventions, like, in a scientific manner of speaking. But there's a time and place for everything. [*To* DASHA.] What do you think, dear?

DASHA. The gentleman's only trying to show how brainy he is, talking about things no one understands.

MRS. ZHIGALOV. We've lived our lives without book-learning, praise the Lord, and it didn't stop us finding good husbands for three daughters. If you think us so ignorant, why come here? Go and visit your smart friends.

YAT. I've always thought highly of your family, Mrs. Zhigalov, and if I did mention electric light, it doesn't mean I was trying to show off. I'm quite prepared to have a drink. I've always wished Dasha a good husband with all my heart. They don't grow on trees these days, Mrs. Zhigalov, good husbands don't. Nowadays everyone's out for what he can get, they all want to marry for money.

APLOMBOV. That's an insinuation!

YAT [*taking fright*]. No harm intended, I'm sure. I wasn't speaking of present company, it was just, er, a general remark. Oh, for heaven's sake—everyone knows you're marrying for love. It's not as if the dowry was up to much!

MRS. ZHIGALOV. Oh, isn't it? You mind your Ps and Qs, young man. Besides a thousand roubles in cash, we're giving three lady's coats, a bed and all the furniture. You'll not find many dowries to match that!

YAT. I meant no harm. Certainly the furniture's nice, and, er, so are the coats, of course. I was merely concerned with this gent being offended on account of my insinuations.

MRS. ZHIGALOV. Then don't *make* any. We ask you to the wedding out of regard for your mother and father, and now we get all these remarks! If you knew Mr. Aplombov was marrying for money, why not say so before? [*Tearfully.*] I've reared her, nurtured her, looked after her. She was the apple of her mother's eye, my darling little girl——

APLOMBOV. You mean you actually believe him! Thank you very much! Most grateful, I'm sure! [*To* YAT.] Mr. Yat, though you're a friend of mine, I won't have you behaving so outrageously in other people's houses. Be so good as to make yourself scarce!

YAT. I *beg* your pardon!

APLOMBOV. I wish you were as much of a gentleman as what I am. In a word, kindly buzz off!

[*The band plays a flourish.*]

YOUNG MEN [*to* APLOMBOV]. Oh, leave him alone, can't you? Stop it. What's the good? Sit down. Leave him alone.

YAT. I never said a thing, I was only—. I must say, I can't see why—. All right, I'll go then. But first you pay back the five roubles you borrowed last year to buy yourself a fancy, pardon the expression, waistcoat. I'll have another drink and, er, go. But you pay up first.

YOUNG MEN. Oh, stop it, stop it! That'll do. A lot of fuss about nothing.

BEST MAN [*shouts*]. To the health of the bride's mother and father! Mr. and Mrs. Zhigalov!

[*The band plays a flourish. Cheers.*]

ZHIGALOV [*bows in all directions, deeply moved*]. Thank you very much. My dear guests, I'm most grateful to you for remembering us and coming along and not turning up your noses. Now, don't go thinking this is all a put-up job or a lot of funny business. I'm just saying what I feel, speaking from the bottom of my heart. Nothing's too good for decent folk. My humble thanks. [*Exchanges kisses.*]

DASHA [*to her mother*]. Why are you crying, Mum? I'm so happy.

APLOMBOV. Your mother's upset at the thought of being separated from you. My advice to her is—remember what I told her just now.

YAT. Don't cry, Mrs. Zhigalov. Think what human tears are—a weakness in the psychology department, that's all.

ZHIGALOV. Are there mushrooms in Greece?

DYMBA. Is plenty. Is everything.

ZHIGALOV. Well, I bet there aren't any white and yellow ones like ours.

DYMBA. Is white. Is yellow. Is everything.

MOZGOVOY. Mr. Dymba, it's your turn to make a speech. Let him speak, ladies and gentlemen.

ALL [*to* DYMBA]. Speech! Speech! Your turn!

DYMBA. Pliss? Do not understand—. What is which?

MRS. ZMEYUKIN. Oh, no you don't—don't you dare try and wriggle out of it! It's your turn. Up you get!

DYMBA [*stands up in embarrassment*]. I speak, isn't it? Is Russia. Is Greece. Russian peoples is in Russia. Greek peoples is in Greece, isn't it? In sea is sailing-boats that Russians call sheep. Is railways on land. I am understanding very well, isn't it? We are Greeks, you are Russians and I am not needing anything, isn't it? I am also saying—. Is Russia. Is Greece——.

[NYUNIN *comes in.*]

NYUNIN. Just a moment, all of you—don't start eating just yet. One moment, Mrs. Zhigalov, please come here. [*Takes* MRS. ZHIGALOV *on one side, panting.*] Listen. The General's on his way, I've got hold of one at last. Had a terrible time. It's a real General, very dignified, very old. He must be about eighty—ninety, even.

MRS. ZHIGALOV. But when will he get here?

NYUNIN. Any moment now. You'll be grateful to me all your life. He's a General and a half, a regular conquering hero! Not some wretched footslogging old square-basher, this—he's a General of the Fleet. His rank's Commander, and in naval lingo that's equal to a Major-General, or an Under-Secretary in the civil service, there's nothing in it. It's higher, in fact.

MRS. ZHIGALOV. You're not pulling my leg are you, Andrew?

NYUNIN. What—think I'd swindle you, eh? Set your mind at rest.

MRS. ZHIGALOV [sighing]. I don't want us to waste our money, Andrew.

NYUNIN. Don't worry. He's a cracking good General! [Raising his voice.] I said to him: 'You've quite forgotten us, sir,' says I. 'You shouldn't forget old friends, sir. Mrs. Zhigalov's very annoyed with you,' I say. [Goes to the table and sits down.] 'But look here, young man,' says he, 'how can I go when I don't know the groom?' 'Oh really, sir, don't stand on ceremony.' 'The groom's a grand chap,' I tell him. 'Good mixer and all that. Works for a pawnbroker, writes out the price-tickets,' says I. 'But don't think he's some awful little tick, sir, or a frightful bounder. Respectable ladies serve in pawn-shops nowadays.' He slaps me on the shoulder, we each smoke a Havana, and now he's on his way. Wait, all of you, don't start eating.

APLOMBOV. But when will he get here?

NYUNIN. Any moment. He was putting on his galoshes when I left. Wait a bit, everyone, don't start.

APLOMBOV. Then you'd better tell them to play a march.

NYUNIN [shouts]. Hey, you in the band! A march!

[The band plays a march for a minute.]

WAITER [announces]. Mr. Revunov-Karaulov!

[ZHIGALOV, MRS. ZHIGALOV and NYUNIN run to meet him. Enter REVUNOV-KARAULOV.]

MRS. ZHIGALOV [bowing]. Make yourself at home, sir. Pleased to meet you, I'm sure.

REVUNOV. Delighted!

ZHIGALOV. We're plain, ordinary, humble folk, sir, but don't imagine we'd go in for any funny business. We set great store by nice people here, nothing's too good for them. So make yourself at home.

REVUNOV. Delighted indeed!

NYUNIN. May I introduce, General? This is the bridegroom, Mr. Epaminondas Aplombov and his newly-born—that is, his newly-wedded wife. Mr. Ivan Yat, who works in the telegraph office. Mr. Kharlampy Dymba, a foreigner of Greek extraction who's in the confectionery line. Mr. Osip Babelmandebsky. And so on and so forth. The rest are pretty small beer. Sit down, sir.

REVUNOV. Delighted! Excuse me, ladies and gentlemen, I must have a word with young Andrew. [*Takes* NYUNIN *aside.*] I feel a bit awkward, my boy. Why all this 'General' stuff? It's not as if I was one—I'm a naval Commander, and that's even lower than a Colonel.

NYUNIN [*speaks into his ear as if he was deaf*]. I know, but please let us call you General, Commander. This is an old-fashioned family, see. They look up to their betters, they like to show due respect.

REVUNOV. Oh, in that case of course. [*Going to the table.*] Delighted!

MRS. ZHIGALOV. Do sit down, General. Be so kind! And have something to eat and drink, sir. But you must excuse us, you being used to fancy things, like—we're plain folk, we are.

REVUNOV [*not hearing*]. What's that? I see. Very well. [*Pause.*] Very well. In the old days people all lived the simple life and were content. I live simply too, for all my officer's rank. Young Andrew comes to see me today and asks me to this wedding. 'How can I go,' I ask, 'when I don't know 'em? It's rather awkward.' 'Well,' says he, 'they're old-fashioned folk with no frills, always glad to have someone drop in.' Well, of course, if that's the way of it—why not? Delighted! It's boring being on your own at home, and if having me at a wedding can please anyone, they're only too welcome, say I.

ZHIGALOV. So it was out of the kindness of your heart, General? I hand it to you. I'm a plain man too, I don't hold with any sort of funny business, and I respect people like myself. Help yourself, sir.

APLOMBOV. Have you been retired long, sir?

REVUNOV. Eh? Yes, yes, I have. Quite true. Yes. I say, look here, what's all this? The herring tastes sour, and so does the blasted bread.

ALL. Blasted bread? Bless the bride! To the bride and groom!

[APLOMBOV *and* DASHA *kiss.*]

REVUNOV. Tee hee hee! Good health! [*Pause.*] Yes, in the old days things were straightforward and everyone was content. I like things shipshape. I'm an old man, after all—retired back in 'sixty-five! I'm seventy-two. Yes. There were times in the old days when they liked to cut a bit of a dash, of course. [*Seeing* MOZGOVOY.] You, er—a sailor, are you?

MOZGOVOY. Yessir.

REVUNOV. Aha! I see. Yes, the navy's always been a pretty rugged service—makes a man think and cudgel the old brain. Every little word has its special kind of meaning. For instance: 'Topmen aloft! To the foresail and mainsail yards!' What does that mean? You can bet your sailor knows! Tee hee hee! It's as tricky as geometry!

NYUNIN. To the health of General Theodore Revunov-Karaulov!

[*The band plays a flourish. Cheers.*]

YAT. Now, sir, you've just been telling us about the difficulties of naval service. But telegraphing's no easier, you know. Nowadays, sir, no one can get a job on the telegraph unless he can read and write French and German. But the hardest thing we do is sending morse. It's a very tough job! Listen to me, sir. [*Bangs his fork on the table in imitation of someone sending morse.*]

REVUNOV. What does that mean?

YAT. It means: 'I much respect you, sir, for your distinguished qualities.' Think it's easy, eh? Here's some more. [*Taps.*]

REVUNOV. Make it a bit louder, I can't hear.

YAT. That means: 'Madam, how happy I am to hold you in my arms.'

REVUNOV. Who's this 'madam'? Yes—. [*To* MOZGOVOY.] Now, if you're running before a good breeze and want to, er, set your topgallants and royals, you must order: 'Hands aloft to the topgallants and royals!' And while they cast loose the sails on the yards, down on deck they're manning the topgallant and royal sheets, halyards and braces.

BEST MAN [*getting up*]. Ladies and gent——

REVUNOV [*interrupting*]. Yes indeed. We've plenty of words of command, we have that. 'In on the topgallant and royal sheets! Haul taut the halyards!' Not bad, eh? But what does it all mean, what's the sense of it? It's all very simple. They haul the topgallant and royal sheets, see? And lift the halyards all at once, squaring off the royal sheets and royal halyards as they hoist, at the same time easing the braces from the sails by the required amount. So when the sheets are taut and the halyards all run right up, the topgallants and royals are drawing and the yards are braced according to the wind direction——

NYUNIN [to REVUNOV]. Our hostess asks, would you mind talking about something else, sir? The guests can't make this out, and they're bored.

REVUNOV. What! Who's bored? [To MOZGOVOY.] Young man! Now, if she's close-hauled under full sail on the starboard tack and you have to wear ship—what command must you give? Why, pipe all hands on deck! Wear ship! Tee hee hee!

NYUNIN. That's quite enough, Commander. Have something to eat.

REVUNOV. As soon as they all run up, the command's given at once: 'Stand by to wear ship!' What a jolly life! As you give the commands you watch the sailors run to their stations like greased lightning and unfurl the topgallants. You can't help shouting: 'Well done, lads!' [Chokes and coughs.]

BEST MAN [hastens to take advantage of the ensuing pause]. This evening, as we are, so to speak, gathered together to honour our dear——

REVUNOV [interrupting]. Yes, there's all that to remember, you know! For instance—let fly the foresheet, let fly the main!

BEST MAN [offended]. Why does he keep interrupting? We shan't get through a single speech at this rate.

MRS. ZHIGALOV. We're poor benighted folk, sir, we can't make sense of all that. Why not tell us something about——

REVUNOV [not hearing]. I've already eaten, thanks. Goose, you say? No, thank you. Yes, it all comes back to me—what jolly times those were, boy! You sail the seas without a care in the world, and [in a trembling voice]—remember the excitement of tacking? What sailor isn't fired by the thought of that manœuvre? Why, as soon as the command rings out, 'Pipe all hands on deck! Ready about!'—it's as if an electric spark ran through them all. Everyone, from the captain to the last sailor, is galvanized!

MRS. ZMEYUKIN. Oh, what a bore!

[*A general murmur of complaint.*]

REVUNOV [*not hearing*]. Thanks, I've already eaten. [*Carried away.*] Everyone stands by, and all eyes are glued on Number One. 'Haul taut the fore and main starboard braces and the port mizzen top braces and counterbraces on the port side!' shouts Number One. It's all done in a flash. 'Let fly the fore-sheet, let fly the jib-sheet! Hard a' starboard!' [*Stands up.*] She comes up into the wind and at last the sails start flapping. 'The braces! Look alive on those braces!' yells Number One. His eyes are glued to the main topsail, then at last that starts flapping too—so she's started to come about, and the command is given like a crack of thunder: 'Let go the main top bowline! Pay out the braces!' Then everything flies and cracks, a regular pandemonium, and it's all been done to perfection. We've brought her about!

MRS. ZHIGALOV [*flaring up*]. And you a General! A hooligan, more like! You should be ashamed, at your time of life!

REVUNOV [*mishearing*]. A slice of tripe? Thanks, I don't mind if I do.

MRS. ZHIGALOV [*loudly*]. I say you should be ashamed at your age! Call yourself a General, behaving like that!

NYUNIN [*embarrassed*]. Oh, look, everyone—why all the fuss? Really——

REVUNOV. Firstly, I'm not a General—I'm a naval Commander, which is equal to Lieutenant-Colonel in the army.

MRS. ZHIGALOV. If you aren't a General, why take the money? We didn't pay good money for you to break up the happy home!

REVUNOV [*bewildered*]. Pay what money?

MRS. ZHIGALOV. You know very well what money. You got your twenty-five roubles from Mr. Nyunin right enough. [*To* NYUNIN.] You should be ashamed of yourself, Andrew. I didn't ask you to hire something like this!

NYUNIN. Oh, I say, cut it out. Why make a fuss?

REVUNOV. Hired? Paid? What do you mean?

APLOMBOV. I say, just one moment—you did receive twenty-five roubles from Andrew Nyunin, I take it?

REVUNOV. Twenty-five roubles? [*The truth dawns.*] So that's it! I see! What a rotten, dirty trick!

APLOMBOV. Well, you took the money, I gather?

REVUNOV. I took no money. Get away from me! [*Stands up from the table.*] What a filthy, rotten trick! To insult an old sailor, an officer who's seen honourable service. If this was a respectable house I could challenge someone to a duel, but what can I do here? [*In despair.*] Where's the door? Which is the way out? Waiter, take me out! Waiter! [*Moves off.*] What a filthy, rotten trick! [*Goes out.*]

MRS. ZHIGALOV. But where are the twenty-five roubles, Andrew?

NYUNIN. Oh, what a lot of fuss about nothing! A fat lot that matters, with everyone enjoying themselves, damn it—I don't know what you're talking about. [*Shouts.*] To the health of bride and groom! You in the band! Play a march! Band! [*The band plays a march.*] To the bride and groom!

MRS. ZMEYUKIN. I'm choking. Let me have air! I choke when I'm near you.

YAT [*ecstatically*]. Superb creature!

[*A lot of noise.*]

BEST MAN [*trying to shout them down*]. Ladies and gentlemen! On this, er, so to speak, day——

CURTAIN

THE ANNIVERSARY

[Юбилей]

A FARCE IN ONE ACT

(1891)

CHARACTERS

ANDREW SHIPUCHIN, chairman of the board of a mutual credit bank, a man in his forties who wears a monocle

TATYANA, his wife, aged 25

KUZMA KHIRIN, an elderly bank clerk

MRS. NASTASYA MERCHUTKIN, an old woman who wears an old-fashioned overcoat

Shareholders and bank clerks

The action takes place at the offices of the N. Mutual Credit Bank

The Chairman's office. A door, left, leading into the main office.
Two desks. The furnishings have pretensions to extreme luxury:
velvet-upholstered furniture, flowers, statues, carpets and a tele-
phone.

Noon.

KHIRIN *is alone. He wears felt boots.*

KHIRIN [*shouts through the door*]. Send someone to get fifteen copecks'
worth of valerian drops from the chemist's and have some fresh
water brought into the Chairman's office. Must I tell you a hundred
times? [*Goes towards the desk.*] I'm all in. I've been writing for over
seventy-two hours on end without a wink of sleep. I write here all
day, I write at home all night. [*Coughs.*] I ache all over, what's more.
I've a feverish chill and a cough, my legs ache and I keep seeing stars
or exclamation marks or something. [*Sits down.*] And today that
swine, that simpering buffoon—our Chairman, I mean—is to speak
at the General Meeting on 'Our Bank: its Present and its Future'.
He doesn't half fancy himself, I must say! [*Writes.*] Two . . . one . . .
one . . . six . . . oh . . . seven. Then—six . . . oh . . . one . . . six. He
only wants to put over a lot of eyewash, and I'm to sit here working
my fingers to the bone, if you please! Fills his speech with high-
falutin' poppycock and expects me to tot up figures day in day out,
God damn and blast him! [*Clicks his counting frame.*] I can't stand it.
[*Writes.*] Ah well—one . . . three . . . seven . . . two . . . one . . . oh.
He's promised to see I don't lose by it. If all goes well this afternoon
and he manages to bamboozle his audience, he's promised me a gold
medal and a three-hundred-rouble bonus. We shall see. [*Writes.*]
But if I get nothing for my pains, my lad, then you can watch out—
I'm apt to fly off the handle! You put my back up, chum, and you'll
find yourself in Queer Street, believe you me!

[*Noise and applause off-stage.* SHIPUCHIN'S *voice:* 'Thank you,
thank you. Most touched.' SHIPUCHIN *comes in. He wears evening
dress with a white tie and carries an album which has just been presented
to him.*]

SHIPUCHIN [*standing in the doorway and turning to the main office*].
Dear colleagues, I shall treasure this gift of yours till my dying day
as a memento of the happiest years of my life. Yes, gentlemen. Thank

you again. [*Blows a kiss and goes towards* KHIRIN.] My dear, good
Khirin.

[*While he is on stage, clerks come and go from time to time with papers
for him to sign.*]

KHIRIN [*getting up*]. Mr. Shipuchin, may I felicitate you on the Bank's
fifteenth anniversary and wish——

SHIPUCHIN [*shakes his hand vigorously*]. Thank you very much, my
dear fellow. Thank you. On this auspicious occasion we may, I
think, embrace. [*They kiss.*] So glad, so glad. Thank you for your
services, thank you for everything, everything. If I've ever done
anything useful since I had the honour to be Chairman of the Bank,
I owe it mainly to my colleagues. [*Sighs.*] Yes, my dear fellow, fifteen
years! Fifteen years, or my name's not Shipuchin! [*Briskly.*] Well,
how's my speech? Is it coming along?

KHIRIN. Yes, I've only about five pages to do.

SHIPUCHIN. Fine. So it will be ready by three o'clock, will it?

KHIRIN. It will if I'm not interrupted, there's only a bit to do.

SHIPUCHIN. Marvellous. Marvellous, or my name's not Shipuchin.
The General Meeting's at four. Tell you what, old man—let me have
the first part to look through. Come on, hurry up. [*Takes the
speech.*] I'm hoping for a lot from this speech. It's a statement of
faith—a firework display, rather. There's some pretty hot stuff in
this, or my name's not Shipuchin. [*Sits down and reads the speech to
himself.*] I'm dead beat, my word I am. I had a spot of gout last night,
I've been rushed off my feet doing errands all morning, and now
there's all this excitement, applause and fuss. I'm worn out.

KHIRIN [*writes*]. Two . . . oh . . . oh . . . three . . . nine . . . two . . . oh.
These figures make me dizzy. Three . . . one . . . six . . . four . . .
one . . . five. [*Clicks his counting-frame.*]

SHIPUCHIN. There was some more unpleasantness too. Your wife
was here this morning, complaining about you again—said you ran
after her with a knife last night, and your sister-in-law too. Whatever next, Khirin! This won't do.

KHIRIN [*sternly*]. Mr. Shipuchin, may I venture to ask you a favour
on this anniversary occasion, if only out of consideration for the
drudgery I do here? Be so good as to leave my family life alone,
would you mind?

SHIPUCHIN [*sighs*]. You're quite impossible, Khirin. You're a very decent, respectable fellow, but with women you're a regular Jack the Ripper. You are, you know. I can't see why you hate them so.

KHIRIN. Well, I can't see why you like them so. [*Pause.*]

SHIPUCHIN. The clerks have just given me an album, and I hear the shareholders want to present me with an address and a silver tankard. [*Playing with his monocle.*] Very nice, or my name's not Shipuchin— no harm in it at all. A little ceremony's needed for the sake of the Bank's reputation, damn it. You're one of us, so you're in the know, of course. I wrote the address myself—and as for the tankard, well, I bought that too. Yes, and it set me back forty-five roubles to have the address bound, but there was nothing else for it. *They'd* never have thought of it. [*Looks round.*] What furniture and fittings! Not bad, eh? They call me fussy—say I only care about having my door-handles polished, my clerks turned out in smart neck-ties and a fat commissionaire standing at my front door. Not a bit of it, sirs. Those door-handles and that commissionaire aren't trifles. At home I can behave like some little suburban tyke—sleep and eat like a hog, drink like a fish——

KHIRIN. I'll thank you not to make these insinuations.

SHIPUCHIN. Oh, no one's insinuating anything, you really are impossible! Now, as I was saying, at home I can be a jumped-up little squirt with my own nasty little habits. But *here* everything must be on the grand scale. This is a bank, sir! Here every detail must impress and wear an air of solemnity, as you might say. [*Picks up a piece of paper from the floor and throws it on the fire.*] My great merit is simply that I've raised the Bank's prestige. Tone's a great thing. A great thing is tone, or my name's not Shipuchin. [*Looking* KHIRIN *over.*] My dear fellow, a shareholders' deputation may come in any moment, and here are you in those felt boots and that scarf and, er, that jacket thing—what a ghastly colour! You might have worn tails or at least a black frock-coat——

KHIRIN. My health matters more to me than your shareholders. I feel sore all over.

SHIPUCHIN [*excitedly*]. Well, you must admit you look an awful mess. You're spoiling the whole effect.

KHIRIN. If the deputation comes, I can make myself scarce. What a fuss about nothing. [*Writes.*] Seven . . . one . . . seven . . . two . . .

one . . . five . . . oh. I can't stand messes either. Seven . . . two . . . nine. [*Clicks his counting-frame.*] I don't like messes and muddles, which is why I wish you hadn't invited women to tonight's celebration dinner.

SHIPUCHIN. Oh, don't talk rot.

KHIRIN. I know you'll fill the place with women tonight just for the look of the thing, but you watch out—they'll muck everything up for you. Mischief and trouble—it all comes from women.

SHIPUCHIN. Not at all. Ladies' company is elevating.

KHIRIN. It is, is it? Your wife's an educated woman, I think, but last Monday she blurted out something—well, it took me two days to get over it. She suddenly asks in front of some strangers: 'Is it true my husband bought some shares in the Dryazhsky-Pryazhsky business for our bank, and then the price came down on the stock exchange? Oh, my husband's so worried!' she says. Before total outsiders! Why do you confide in them? That's what I don't see. Want them to land you in clink?

SHIPUCHIN. Oh, do cut it out, this is all much too gloomy for a celebration. By the way, you just reminded me. [*Looks at his watch.*] My dear wife's due here any moment. I really should have popped over to the station to meet the poor thing, but I'm too busy and—and too tired. And the fact is, I'm not all that keen on her coming. Actually, I am quite keen, but I'd rather she stayed on at her mother's for a day or two. She'll insist I spend the whole evening with her, when we were planning a little trip after dinner. [*Gives a start.*] I say, I'm getting as nervous as a kitten—I'm so on edge, I feel I'll burst into tears at the slightest provocation. Yes, one must be firm, or my name's not Shipuchin.

[TATYANA *comes in, wearing a mackintosh, with a travelling hand-bag slung over her shoulder.*]

SHIPUCHIN. I say! Talk of the devil!

TATYANA. Darling! [*Runs to her husband; a prolonged kiss.*]

SHIPUCHIN. Why, we were just talking about you. [*Looks at his watch.*]

TATYANA [*out of breath*]. Have you missed me? How are you? I haven't been home yet, I came straight here from the station. I've such a lot to tell you, I can hardly wait. I won't take my coat off, I'm just going. [*To* KHIRIN.] Good afternoon, Mr. Khirin. [*To her husband.*] Is all well at home?

SHIPUCHIN. Yes. And you've grown plumper and prettier during the week. Now, how was the trip?

TATYANA. Fine. Mother and Katya send their love. Vasily told me to give you a kiss. [*Kisses him.*] Aunty's sent a pot of jam and everyone's angry with you for not writing. Zina sends a kiss too. [*Kisses him.*] Oh, if you only knew what's been going on, if you had any idea! I'm scared to talk about it, really. What a business! But you don't look very pleased to see me.

SHIPUCHIN. On the contrary—. Darling——

[*Kisses her.* KHIRIN *gives an angry cough.*]

TATYANA [*sighs*]. My poor, poor Katya! I'm so, so sorry for her!

SHIPUCHIN. My dear, we're celebrating our anniversary today, and a shareholders' deputation may turn up any moment. And you're not properly dressed.

TATYANA. But of course! The anniversary! Congratulations, gentlemen. I wish you—. So it's the day of the meeting and the dinner. I adore all that. Remember that lovely shareholders' address? It took you such a long time to write. Are they going to present it today?

[KHIRIN *coughs angrily.*]

SHIPUCHIN [*embarrassed*]. Darling, one doesn't talk about such things. Now, look—why don't you go home?

TATYANA. Yes, yes, of course. It won't take a moment to tell you, and then I'll go. I'll tell you it all from the beginning. Now then, after you'd seen me off, I sat next to that stout lady, remember? And I started reading. I don't like talking in trains, so I went on reading for three stops, and not a word did I utter to a soul. Then evening came on and I began to feel depressed, see? There was this dark-haired young fellow sitting opposite me—not bad-looking, quite attractive, actually. Well, we got talking. A sailor came along and some student or other. [*Laughs.*] I told them I wasn't married. Oh, they were all over me! We chattered away till midnight—the dark young man told some screamingly funny stories and the sailor kept singing! I laughed till my sides ached. And when the sailor—

oh, those sailors!—when it came out that I was called Tatyana, do
you know what he sang? [*Sings in a bass voice.*]

> 'Onegin, how can I deny
> I'll love Tatyana till I die?'

[*Roars with laughter.* KHIRIN *coughs angrily.*]

SHIPUCHIN. I say, Tatyana, we're annoying Mr. Khirin. You go
home, darling. Tell me about it later.

TATYANA. Never mind, never mind, let him listen too, he'll find it
very interesting. I'll be through in a moment. Sergey met me at the
station. And then another young man turned up, a tax inspector,
I think—quite nice-looking, charming in fact, especially his eyes.
Sergey introduced us and the three of us went off together. The
weather was glorious.

[*Voices off-stage*: 'You mustn't go in there. What do you want?'
MRS. MERCHUTKIN *comes in.*]

MRS. MERCHUTKIN [*in the doorway, waving people off*]. You take your
hands off of me, I never heard of such a thing! I want to see His Nibs.
[*Coming in, to* SHIPUCHIN.] May I introduce myself, sir? Nastasya
Merchutkin's the name, and my husband's in the civil service, like.

SHIPUCHIN. And what can I do for you?

MRS. MERCHUTKIN. Well, it's this way, sir. My husband, him that's
in the service, has been real poorly these five months, and while he
was laid up at home under the doctor he was given the sack for no
reason, sir, and when I went to get his pay, do you know what they'd
done? Gone and docked him twenty-four roubles thirty-six copecks,
they had. What for? That's what I'd like to know. 'He borrowed it
from the kitty,' they tell me, 'and other people guaranteed the loan.'
What an idea—as if he'd borrow money without asking me first!
They can't do this to me, sir. I'm a poor woman, I only manage by
taking lodgers. I'm a weak, defenceless woman. Everyone insults me,
no one says a kind word to me.

SHIPUCHIN. Very well then. [*Takes her application and reads it standing up.*]

TATYANA [*to* KHIRIN]. Well, I must begin at the beginning. Last week
I suddenly get a letter from Mother. She writes that my sister
Katya's had a proposal from a certain Grendilevsky—a very nice,
modest young man, but with no means or position at all. Now, by

rotten bad luck Katya was rather gone on him, believe it or not. So what's to be done? Mother writes and tells me to come at once and influence Katya.

KHIRIN [*sternly*]. Look here, you're putting me off. While you go on about Mother and Katya, I've lost my place and I'm all mixed up.

TATYANA. Well, it's not the end of the world! And you listen when a lady talks to you! Why so peeved today? Are you in love? [*Laughs.*]

SHIPUCHIN [*to* MRS. MERCHUTKIN]. I say, look here, what's all this about? I can't make sense of it.

TATYANA. In love, eh? Aha—blushing, are we?

SHIPUCHIN [*to his wife*]. Tatyana, go into the office for a moment, dear. I won't be long.

TATYANA. All right. [*Goes out.*]

SHIPUCHIN. It makes no sense to me. You've obviously come to the wrong address, madam—your business is really no concern of ours. You should apply to the institution where your husband was employed.

MRS. MERCHUTKIN. I've been in half a dozen different places already, mister, and they wouldn't even listen. I was at my wits' end when Boris, that's my son-in-law, has the bright idea of sending me to you. 'You go to Mr. Shipuchin, Mum,' says he. 'The gentleman carries a lot of weight, and he can do anything.' Please help me, sir!

SHIPUCHIN. Mrs. Merchutkin, there's nothing we can do for you. Look here—as far as I can see, your husband worked for the War Office medical department, but this establishment is a completely private business. This is a bank, can't you see?

MRS. MERCHUTKIN. Now, about my husband's illness, sir, I have a doctor's certificate. Here it is, if you'll kindly have a look——

SHIPUCHIN [*irritatedly*]. All right, I believe you. But I repeat, it's no concern of ours.

[TATYANA's *laughter is heard off-stage, followed by a man's laughter.*]

SHIPUCHIN [*glancing at the door*]. She's stopping them working out there. [*To* MRS. MERCHUTKIN.] This is odd—a bit funny, really. Surely your husband knows where to apply?

MRS. MERCHUTKIN. The poor man knows nothing, sir. 'It's none of your business,' he keeps saying. 'So hop it!' I can't get another word out of him.

SHIPUCHIN. I repeat, madam. Your husband was employed by the War Office medical department, but this is a bank, a private business.

MRS. MERCHUTKIN. Quite so, quite so. I understand, mister. Then tell them to give me fifteen roubles, say. I don't mind waiting for the rest, sir.

SHIPUCHIN [sighs]. Phew!

KHIRIN. Mr. Shipuchin, I'll never finish the speech at this rate.

SHIPUCHIN. Just a moment. [To MRS. MERCHUTKIN.] You won't listen to reason. But you must see—it's as absurd for you to come to us with an application like this as it would be for someone to try and get a divorce at—let's say at a chemist's shop or the Assay Office.

[A knock on the door.]

TATYANA [off-stage]. Can I come in, Andrew?

SHIPUCHIN [shouts]. Just a moment, darling. [To MRS. MERCHUTKIN.] They underpaid you, but what business is that of ours? Besides, this is our anniversary celebration, madam, we're busy—and someone may come in any moment. Please excuse me.

MRS. MERCHUTKIN. Pity a helpless orphan, sir. I'm a weak, defenceless woman. Fair worried to death I am, what with lodgers to have the law on, my husband's affairs to handle, a house to run—and my son-in-law out of work as well.

SHIPUCHIN. Mrs. Merchutkin, I—. No, I'm sorry, I can't talk to you. My head's going round and round. You're annoying us, besides wasting your own time. [Sighs, aside.] The woman's daft, or my name's not Shipuchin. [To KHIRIN.] Mr. Khirin, would you mind explaining to Mrs. Merchutkin? [Makes a gesture of despair and goes off into the board-room.]

KHIRIN [goes up to MRS. MERCHUTKIN, sternly]. What do you want?

MRS. MERCHUTKIN. I'm a weak, defenceless woman. I may look strong, but if you took me to pieces you wouldn't find one healthy vein in my body. I can hardly stand, and my appetite's gone. I drank some coffee this morning, but it didn't go down well at all, it didn't.

KHIRIN. I asked you a question: what is it you want?

MRS. MERCHUTKIN. Just tell them to pay me fifteen roubles, mister, and the rest in a month, say.

KHIRIN. But I thought you'd already been told in words of one syllable. This is a bank!

MRS. MERCHUTKIN. Yes, yes, of course. And I can show you the doctor's certificate if you want.

KHIRIN. Have you taken leave of your senses, or what?

MRS. MERCHUTKIN. I'm only asking for my rights, kind sir. I don't want what isn't mine.

KHIRIN. I'm asking you if you've taken leave of your senses, madam. Oh, damn and blast me, I've no time to bandy words with you, I'm busy. [*Points to the door.*] Would you mind?

MRS. MERCHUTKIN [*astonished*]. But what about my money?

KHIRIN. The fact is, you've no senses to take leave of. This is your trouble. [*Taps his finger on the table and then on his forehead.*]

MRS. MERCHUTKIN [*taking offence*]. What! Who do you think you are! You do that to your own wife. My husband's in the executive branch, so don't you try your tricks on me.

KHIRIN [*losing his temper, in a low voice*]. Get out of here!

MRS. MERCHUTKIN. Cor, hark at him! You mind what you're saying!

KHIRIN [*in a low voice*]. If you don't leave this instant I'll send for the porter. Get out. [*Stamps.*]

MRS. MERCHUTKIN. Who do you think you're talking to? You don't scare me, I know your sort! You're crackers.

KHIRIN. I don't think I've ever seen anything nastier in my life. Ugh, what a pain in the neck! [*Breathes heavily.*] I repeat, do you hear? If you won't clear out, I'll pulverize you, you old horror. I'm quite capable of crippling you for life, that's the sort of man I am. I'll stop at nothing.

MRS. MERCHUTKIN. You're all bark and no bite. You don't scare me, I know your sort.

KHIRIN [*in despair*]. I can't stand the sight of her. Sickening! This is too much! [*Goes to the table and sits down.*] They unleash a horde of women in the bank and I can't get on with the speech. It's too much.

MRS. MERCHUTKIN. I'm not asking for what isn't mine. I want my rights, I do. Cor, look at him! Sits around in the office with his felt boots on! Cheek! Where was you brought up?

[SHIPUCHIN *and* TATYANA *come in.*]

TATYANA [*coming in after her husband*]. We went to a party at the Berezhnitskys'. Katya was wearing a dear little blue silk frock with an open neck, and trimmed with fine lace. She does look nice with her hair up, and I arranged it myself. Her dress and hair were quite devastating!

SHIPUCHIN [*who now has migraine*]. Yes, yes, I'm sure. Someone may come in here any moment.

MRS. MERCHUTKIN. Sir!

SHIPUCHIN [*despondently*]. What now? What do you want?

MRS. MERCHUTKIN. Sir! [*Points to* KHIRIN.] This man here, this creature—he taps his forehead at me and then on the table. You tell him to look into my case, but he sneers at me and makes nasty remarks. I'm a weak, defenceless woman, I am.

SHIPUCHIN. Very well, madam, I'll see about it. I'll take steps. Now do go, I'll deal with it later. [*Aside.*] My gout's coming on.

KHIRIN [*goes up to* SHIPUCHIN, *quietly*]. Mr. Shipuchin, let me send for the hall-porter and have her slung out on her ear. This beats everything.

SHIPUCHIN [*terrified*]. No, no! She'll only raise Cain and there are a lot of private apartments in this block.

MRS. MERCHUTKIN. Sir!

KHIRIN [*in a tearful voice*]. But I have a speech to write. I shan't get it done in time. [*Goes back to the desk.*] I can't stand this.

MRS. MERCHUTKIN. Please sir, when do I get my money? I need it at once.

SHIPUCHIN [*aside, indignantly*]. What a perfectly horrible old bitch! [*To her, gently.*] As I've said already, madam, this is a bank—a private business establishment.

MRS. MERCHUTKIN. Have mercy, kind sir. Think of yourself as my father. If the doctor's certificate isn't enough, I can bring a paper from the police too. Tell them to pay me the money.

SHIPUCHIN [*sighs heavily*]. Phew!

TATYANA [*to* MRS. MERCHUTKIN]. I say, old girl, you're in the way, do you hear? This won't do, you know.

MRS. MERCHUTKIN. Pretty lady, I've no one to stick up for me. Food and drink don't mean a thing, dearie, and I had some coffee this morning, but it didn't go down well at all, it didn't.

SHIPUCHIN [*exhausted, to* MRS. MERCHUTKIN]. How much do you want?

MRS. MERCHUTKIN. Twenty-four roubles, thirty-six copecks.

SHIPUCHIN. Very well then. [*Gets twenty-five roubles out of his wallet and gives it to her.*] Here's your twenty-five roubles. Take it and be off with you.

[KHIRIN *coughs angrily.*]

MRS. MERCHUTKIN. Thanking you kindly, sir. [*Puts the money away.*]

TATYANA [*sitting down near her husband*]. I must be off home, though. [*Glances at her watch.*] But I haven't finished yet. I'll only be a minute, and then I'll go. What a business, though, what a to-do! Well, off we go to the Berezhnitskys' party. It was all right, quite amusing, if nothing special. Katya's young man Grendilevsky was there too, of course. Well, I have a word with Katya, I shed a few tears, and I use my influence on her, so she has it out with Grendilevsky then and there at the party and turns him down. Well, thinks I, this has all gone like clockwork—I've set Mother's mind at rest, I've saved Katya, and now I can relax. But what do you think? Katya and I are walking in the garden just before supper, when suddenly—. [*Excitedly.*] When suddenly we hear a shot! No, I can't talk about it calmly. [*Fans herself with her handkerchief.*] It's too much for me!

[SHIPUCHIN *sighs.*]

TATYANA [*weeps*]. We rush to the summer-house, and there—there lies poor Grendilevsky with a pistol in his hand.

SHIPUCHIN. Oh, I can't stand this—can't stand it, I tell you! [*To* MRS. MERCHUTKIN.] What more do you want?

MRS. MERCHUTKIN. Please sir, can my husband have his job back?

TATYANA [*weeping*]. He shot himself straight through the heart, just here. Katya fainted, poor dear. And he got the fright of his life. He just lies there and asks us to send for the doctor. The doctor turns up quite soon and—and saves the poor boy.

MRS. MERCHUTKIN. Please sir, can my husband have his job back?

SHIPUCHIN. Oh, this is *too* much! [*Weeps.*] I can't cope! [*Stretches out both hands to* KHIRIN, *in despair.*] Get rid of her, chuck her out, for God's sake!

KHIRIN [*going up to* TATYANA]. You clear out!

SHIPUCHIN. No, not her, this one—this monster. [*Points to* MRS. MERCHUTKIN.] This one!

KHIRIN [*not understanding him, to* TATYANA]. Buzz off! [*Stamps.*] Beat it!

TATYANA. What! *What* did you say? Are you stark, staring mad?

SHIPUCHIN. This is ghastly! Oh, I'm so unhappy! Get her out of here, I tell you.

KHIRIN [*to* TATYANA]. You get out of here, or I'll cripple you for life! Mutilate you, I will. I'll stick at nothing!

TATYANA [*runs away from him, as he chases her*]. How dare you! I like your cheek! [*Shouts.*] Andrew, save me! Andrew! [*Shrieks.*]

SHIPUCHIN [*runs after them*]. Stop that, please. Be quiet. Have a heart!

KHIRIN [*chases* MRS. MERCHUTKIN]. Get out of here! Get hold of her, beat her, slit her throat!

SHIPUCHIN [*shouts*]. Stop that, please, I beg you!

MRS. MERCHUTKIN. Oh, goodness me! [*Shrieks.*] Heavens!

TATYANA [*shouts*]. Save me, save me! Oh, oh, I feel faint! Faint, I tell you! [*Jumps on a chair, then falls on the sofa and groans as if in a faint.*]

KHIRIN [*chases* MRS. MERCHUTKIN]. Get hold of her, thrash her, slit her throat!

MRS. MERCHUTKIN. Oh dearie me, I've come over all queer. Oh! [*Faints in* SHIPUCHIN'*s arms. There is a knock on the door, and a voice off-stage:* 'The deputation!']

SHIPUCHIN. Deputation, reputation, occupation——

KHIRIN [*stamps*]. Get out of here, God damn me! [*Rolls up his sleeves.*] Let me get at her! I may commit an atrocity!

[*Enter a deputation of five men, all in evening dress. One carries the address bound in velvet, another the tankard. Bank employees look through the office door.* TATYANA *is on the sofa,* MRS. MERCHUTKIN *is in* SHIPUCHIN's *arms, and both are quietly groaning.*]

A SHAREHOLDER [*reads in a loud voice*]. Mr. Shipuchin, our dear and most respected friend. As we turn a retrospective glance on the history of this financial establishment, running the mind's eye over the story of its gradual evolution, the impression we receive is highly gratifying. In the early stages of the Bank's existence the limited extent of our basic capital and the absence of any serious operations, as also the vagueness of our aims, did, it is true, confront us with Hamlet's question: 'To be or not to be?' At one time voices were even heard in favour of closing the Bank. But then *you* became head of the establishment. Your knowledge, energy and natural tact have accounted for our tremendous success and exceptional prosperity. The reputation of the Bank [*coughs*], the Bank's reputation——

MRS. MERCHUTKIN [*groans*]. Oh, oh!

TATYANA [*groans*]. Water, water!

SHAREHOLDER [*continues*]. The reputation——. [*Coughs.*] The Bank's reputation has been raised by you to such heights that our establishment can now compete with the best foreign establishments——

SHIPUCHIN. Deputation, reputation, occupation——.

> 'Two friends one night went for a walk,
> And on that walk they had a talk.'

> 'Oh, tell me not your young life's ruined
> And poisoned by my jealousy.'

SHAREHOLDER [*continues in embarrassment*]. And now, dear respected friend, casting the eye of objectivity at the present, we, er——. [*Lowering his voice.*] Under the circumstances we'd better come back later. Later.

[*They go out in embarrassment.*]

CURTAIN

SMOKING IS BAD FOR YOU

[О вреде табака]

A MONOLOGUE IN ONE ACT

(1903)

CHARACTER

IVAN NYUKHIN, a hen-pecked husband whose wife
keeps a music school and a girls' boarding-school

The stage represents the platform in the hall of a provincial club

NYUKHIN *struts in majestically. He has long side-whiskers, his upper lip is clean-shaven, and he wears an old, worn, tail-coat. He bows and adjusts his waistcoat.*

NYUKHIN. Ladies and er, in a manner of speaking, gentlemen. [*Strokes his side-whiskers.*]

It's been suggested to the wife that I should lecture here in aid of charity on some topic of general interest. I don't see why not. If I'm to lecture, I'll lecture—I just couldn't care less.

I'm not a professor, of course, and university degrees have passed me by. Still, for the last thirty years I've been working—non-stop, you might even say, ruining my health and all that—on problems of a strictly academic nature. I've done a lot of thinking, and even written some learned scientific articles, believe it or not—well, not exactly learned, but in the scientific line, as you might say. By the way, I wrote a great screed the other day on 'The Ill Effects Caused by Certain Insects'. My daughters really took to it, especially the bit about bed-bugs, but I read it through and tore it up. After all said and done and whatever you write, it comes down to good old Keating's Powder in the end, doesn't it? We've even got bugs in our piano. As the subject for my lecture today, I've chosen, as it were, the harmful effects of smoking on the human race. I'm a smoker myself, actually. But the wife told me to give today's lecture on why tobacco's bad for you, so what's the use of arguing? About tobacco as such, I just couldn't care less. But I suggest, ladies and gentlemen, that you attend to my present lecture with all due seriousness, or something worse may happen. If anyone's scared or put off by the idea of a dry, scientific lecture, he can stop listening and go. [*Adjusts his waistcoat.*]

I should like to ask the doctors in my audience to pay particular attention. My lecture is a mine of useful information for them, since nicotine not only has harmful effects, but is also used in medicine. For instance, if you put a fly in a snuff-box it will die—from a nervous breakdown, probably. Tobacco is, essentially, a plant. When I lecture my right eye usually twitches, but you can ignore that—it's pure nervousness. I'm a nervous wreck by and large, and this eye-twitching business started back in September 1889, on the thirteenth of the month—the very day when my wife gave birth, in a manner of speaking, to our fourth daughter Barbara. My daughters were all born on the 13th. Actually [*with a look at his watch*], time being short, let's not wander from the subject in hand.

My wife runs a school of music, I might add, and a private boarding-school—well, not a boarding-school exactly, but something in that line. Between you and me, my wife likes to complain of being hard up, but she's got a tidy bit salted away—a cool forty or fifty thousand—while I haven't a penny to my name, not a bean. But what's the use of talking? I'm the school matron. I buy food, keep an eye on the servants, do the accounts, make up exercise-books, exterminate bed-bugs, take the wife's dog for walks and catch mice. Last night I had the job of issuing flour and butter to Cook because we were going to have pancakes today. Well, this morning—to cut a long story short—when the pancakes are already cooked, in comes the wife to the kitchen to say three girls won't get any because they have swollen glands. It thus transpires that we have a pancake or two in hand. What are we to do with them? First my wife wants 'em put in the larder, then she changes her mind. 'You eat 'em, imbecile,' says she. That's what she calls me when she's in a bad mood—you imbecile, you snake, you hell-hound. Now how could anyone take me for a hell-hound? She's always in a bad mood, actually. Well, I didn't eat the pancakes properly, I just gulped them down because I'm always so hungry. Yesterday, for instance, she gave me no dinner. 'Why feed you, imbecile?' she asks.

However [*looks at his watch*], we've somewhat erred and strayed from our subject. So let's go on, though I've no doubt you'd rather hear a song, a symphony or an aria or something. [*Sings.*] 'We'll not be daunted in the heat of battle.' I don't remember where that comes from. By the way, I forgot to say that besides being matron in the wife's school of music, I also have the job of teaching mathematics, physics, chemistry, geography, history, singing scales, literature and all that. The wife charges extra for dancing, singing and drawing, though I'm also the singing and dancing master. Our school of music is at Number Thirteen, Five Dogs Lane. That's probably why I've always had such bad luck—living at Number Thirteen. My daughters were born on the thirteenth of the month too, and the house has thirteen windows. But what's the use of talking? The wife's available at home to interview parents at any time, and if you want a prospectus, they're on sale in the porter's lodge at thirty copecks each. [*Takes several prospectuses from his pocket.*] Or I can let you have some of these if you like. Thirty copecks a whack. Any takers? [*Pause.*] None? All right then, I'll make it twenty. [*Pause.*] How annoying. That's it, house Number Thirteen.

I'm a complete failure, I've grown old and stupid. Here am I lecturing and looking pretty pleased with myself, when I really feel like screaming or taking off for the ends of the earth. There's no one to complain to, it's enough to bring tears to your eyes. You'll say I have my daughters. What of my daughters? They only laugh when I talk to them. My wife has seven daughters. No, sorry—six, I think. [*Eagerly.*] It's seven! Anna, the eldest, is twenty-seven, and the youngest is seventeen. Gentlemen! [*Looks around him.*] Down on my luck I may be, pathetic and foolish I may have become, but in fact you see before you the happiest of fathers—I've no choice in the matter actually, I don't dare say anything else. But if only you knew! Thirty-three years I've lived with my wife—the best years of my life, I might say. Or then again I might not. But in fact they've flashed past like a single moment of ecstasy actually, God damn and blast them! [*Looks round.*]

Anyway, I don't think she's turned up yet—she isn't here, so I can say what I like. I really get the willies when she looks at me. Anyway, as I was saying—the reason why my daughters have been so long finding husbands is probably that they're shy and never meet any men. The wife won't give parties and never has anyone in to a meal. She's a very stingy, bad-tempered bitchy kind of a lady, so no one ever comes to see us, but, er, I can tell you in confidence—. [*Approaches the footlights.*] My wife's daughters are on view on high days and holidays at their Aunt Natalya's—that's the one who has rheumatism and goes round in a yellow dress with black spots on, looking as if she had black-beetles all over her. Snacks are served too, and when my wife's away you can get a bit of you know what. [*Makes a suitable gesture to indicate drinking.*]

One glass is enough to make me drunk, I might add. It feels good, but indescribably sad at the same time. Somehow the days of my youth come back to me, I somehow long—more than you can possibly imagine—to escape. [*Carried away.*] To run away, leave everything behind and run away without a backward glance. Where to? Who cares? If only I could escape from this rotten, vulgar, tawdry existence that's turned me into a pathetic old clown and imbecile! Escape from this stupid, petty, vicious, nasty, spiteful, mean old cow of a wife who's made my life a misery for thirty-three years! Escape from the music, the kitchen, my wife's money and all these vulgar trivialities! Oh, to stop somewhere in the depths of the country and just stand there like a tree or a post or a scarecrow on some vegetable plot under the broad sky, and watch the quiet, bright moon above you all night long and forget, forget! How I'd love to lose my memory! How I'd love to tear off this rotten old tail-coat that I got married in thirty years ago [*tears off his tail-coat*], the one I always wear when I lecture for charity. So much for you! [*Stamps on the coat.*] Take that! I'm a poor, pathetic old man like this waistcoat with its shabby, moth-eaten back. [*Shows the back.*] I don't need anything. I'm above all these low, dirty things. Once I was young and clever and went to college. I had dreams and I felt like a human being. Now I want nothing—nothing but a bit of peace and quiet. [*Glancing to one side, quickly puts on his tail-coat.*]

I say, my wife's out there in the wings. She's turned up and she's waiting for me there. [*Looks at his watch.*] Time's up. If she asks, please, please tell her the lecture was, er—that the imbecile, meaning me, behaved with dignity. [*Looks to one side and coughs.*] She's looking this way.

[*Raising his voice.*] On the supposition that tobacco contains the terrible poison to which I have just alluded, smoking should on no account be indulged in. I shall therefore venture to hope, in a manner of speaking, that some benefit may accrue from this lecture on 'Smoking is Bad for you'.

That's the end. *Dixi et animam levavi!*

[*Bows and struts out majestically.*]

THE NIGHT BEFORE THE TRIAL

[*Ночь перед судом*]

(the 1890s)

CHARACTERS

FRED GUSEV, a gentleman of advanced years
ZINA, his young wife
ALEXIS ZAYTSEV, a traveller
The keeper of a coaching inn

The action takes place inside a coaching inn on a winter's night. A gloomy room with soot-blackened walls. Large sofas upholstered in oilcloth. A cast-iron stove with a chimney stretching across the whole room.

ZAYTSEV, *with a suitcase; the* INNKEEPER, *with a candle.*

ZAYTSEV. I say, what an awful stink, my good man! You can't breathe in here—there's a sort of sour smell mixed up with sealing-wax and bed-bugs. Ugh!

INNKEEPER. You can't help smells.

ZAYTSEV. Give me a call at six tomorrow, will you? And I want my carriage ready then, I'm due in town by nine.

INNKEEPER. All right.

ZAYTSEV. What time is it now?

INNKEEPER. Half past one. [*Goes out.*]

ZAYTSEV [*taking off his fur coat and felt boots*]. It's freezing! My brains have congealed, I'm so cold. I feel as if I'd been plastered with snow and drenched with water—and then flogged within an inch of my life! What with these snow-drifts and this hellish blizzard, another five minutes out there would have done for me, I reckon. I'm dead beat. And what's it all in aid of? I wouldn't mind if I was on my way to meet a girl or pick up some money I'd inherited—but in fact, you know, I'm on the road to ruin. What a frightful thought! The assizes meet in town tomorrow, and I'm headed for the dock on charges of attempted bigamy, forging my grandmother's will to the tune of not more than three hundred roubles, and the attempted murder of a billiards-marker. The jury will see I'm sent down, no doubt about it. It's here today, in jug tomorrow—and Siberia's frozen wastes in six months' time. Brrr! [*Pause.*] There is a way out of this mess, though, oh yes there is! If the jury finds against me, I'll appeal to an old and trusty friend. Dear, loyal old pal! [*Gets a large pistol out of his suitcase.*] This is him! What a boy! I swapped him with Cheprakov for a couple of hounds. Isn't he lovely! Why, just shooting yourself with this would be a kind of enjoyment. [*Tenderly.*] Are you loaded, boy? [*In a reedy voice, as if answering for the pistol.*] I am that. [*In his own voice.*] I bet you'll go off with a bang—one hell of a ruddy great bang! [*In a reedy voice.*] One hell of a ruddy great bang! [*In his own voice.*] Ah, you dear, silly old thing. Well, lie down and go to sleep. [*Kisses the pistol and puts it in his suit-case.*] The moment they bring in that 'guilty' verdict, I'll put a bullet in my brains and that will be that. I say, I'm frozen stiff. Brrr! Must warm up. [*Does some jerks with his arms and jumps about near the stove.*] Brrr!

[ZINA *looks through the door and immediately disappears from view.*]

ZAYTSEV. What's that? Didn't someone look through the door just then? Well, now! Yes, so they did. So I have neighbours, eh? [*Listens by the door.*] Can't hear a thing, not a sound. Must be some other travellers. How about waking them and making up a four at bridge if they're reasonable people? Grand slam in no trumps! It might help to pass the time, so help me! Even better if it's a woman! Frankly, there's nothing I like more than a wayside romance. Travelling around, you sometimes run into an affair better than any in Turgenev's novels. I remember a situation like this when I was on my travels down Samara way. I put up at a post-house. It's night, see, with the cricket chirping away in the old stove and not another sound. I'm sitting at the table drinking tea, when suddenly there's this mysterious rustle. The door opens and——

ZINA [*from the other side of the door*]. This is maddening, it's grotesque! Call this a post-station! It's an absolute disgrace! [*Looking through the door, shouts.*] Landlord! Where's the landlord? Where are you?

ZAYTSEV [*aside*]. Lovely creature! [*To her.*] The landlord's not here, madam. The lout's asleep. What do you want? Can I be of service to you?

ZINA. It's horrible, ghastly! I think the bed-bugs must want to eat me alive.

ZAYTSEV. Really? Bed-bugs? I say, what awful cheek!

ZINA [*through tears*]. It's quite horrible, in fact. I'm leaving at once. Tell that scoundrel of an innkeeper to harness the horses. Those bugs have really done for me.

ZAYTSEV. You poor girl. To be so lovely and suddenly——. No, this is quite monstrous.

ZINA [*shouts*]. Landlord!

ZAYTSEV. Young lady, er, miss——

ZINA. Not miss—Mrs.

ZAYTSEV. So much the better. [*Aside.*] What a honey! [*To her.*] Madam, what I'm trying to say is this: not being privileged to know your name, and being for my part a gentleman and man of honour, I venture to offer my services. Let me aid you in distress.

ZINA. But how?

ZAYTSEV. I have an excellent habit—always carry insect-powder on my travels. May I offer you some sincerely, from the bottom of my heart?

ZINA. Oh, thank you very much.

ZAYTSEV. Then I'll give it you at once, this very instant—I'll get it out of my suitcase. [*Runs to his suitcase and rummages.*] Those eyes, that nose! This means an affair, I feel it in my bones! [*Rubbing his hands.*] I have all the luck—I've only to fetch up in some wayside inn to have a little romance. She's so lovely, she's even got *my* eyes flashing sparks! Here we are! [*Goes back to the door.*] Here he is, your friend in need!

[ZINA *stretches her arm out from behind the door.*]

ZAYTSEV. No, please—let me come to your room and put it down myself.

ZINA. Certainly not—ask you into my room! Whatever next!

ZAYTSEV. Now why not? There's nothing wrong in it, especially— especially as I'm a doctor. From their doctors and hairdressers ladies have no secrets.

ZINA. You really mean you're a doctor, you're not making it up

ZAYTSEV. On my word of honour.

ZINA. Oh well, in that case carry on. But why should you put your- self out? I can send my husband to you. Fred! Fred, wake up, you great lump!

GUSEV [*off-stage*]. Eh?

ZINA. Come here. The doctor's very kindly offered us some insect- powder. [*Disappears.*]

ZAYTSEV. Fred! Now that *is* a surprise! Most grateful, I'm sure. I need this Fred like a hole in the head, damn and blast him! Barely have I picked the girl up and had the bright idea of pretending to be a doctor, when up pops friend Fred! Talk about pouring cold water on things! I've a good mind not to give her any insect-powder. She's nothing to write home about, either, with that nondescript little face—two a penny, her sort are. Can't stand that kind of woman!

GUSEV [*in a dressing-gown and nightcap*]. How do you do, Doctor? My wife tells me you have some insect-powder.

ZAYTSEV [*rudely*]. That is so.

GUSEV. Please lend us a bit, we're eyebrow-deep in bugs.

ZAYTSEV. Take it.

GUSEV. Thank you very much indeed, most grateful to you. Did you get caught in the blizzard too?

ZAYTSEV. Yes.

GUSEV. Quite so. What awful weather! And where might you be making for?

ZAYTSEV. Town.

GUSEV. That's where we're going too. I've some hard work ahead of me in town tomorrow and I need my sleep, but there's this bed-bug business and I just can't cope. What with bugs, black-beetles and other creepy-crawlies, our coaching stations are revolting places. I know what I'd do if I had my way with these bug-ridden inn-keepers—run 'em in under Article 112 of the Local Magistrates' Penal Code for 'not keeping domestic beasts under proper control'. Most grateful to you, Doctor. Do you specialize in any particular field?

ZAYTSEV. Chest and, er, head complaints.

GUSEV. Quite so. Very pleased to have met you. [*Goes out.*]

ZAYTSEV [*alone*]. What a ghastly old frump! I'd bury him alive in insect-powder if I had my way. I'd like to beat the swine at cards and clean him out good and proper a dozen times over. Better still, I'd play him at billiards and accidentally fetch him one with a cue that would make him remember me for a whole week. With that blob of a nose, those blue veins all over his face and that wart on his forehead, he—he has the nerve to be married to a woman like that! What right has he? It's disgusting! Yes, it's a dirty trick, I must say. And then people ask why I take such a jaundiced view of things. But how can you help being pessimistic under these conditions?

GUSEV [*in the doorway*]. Don't be shy, Zina. He is a doctor, you know. Don't stand on ceremony, ask him. There's nothing to be scared of. If Shervetsov didn't help you, perhaps he will. [*To* ZAYTSEV.] Sorry to trouble you, Doctor, but could you please tell me why my wife has this constricted feeling in her chest? She has a cough, you know, and it feels tight as if she had some sort of congestion. What's the reason?

ZAYTSEV. That would take time. I can't do a diagnosis just like that.

GUSEV. Oh, never mind that—there's time enough. We can't sleep anyway. Look her over, my dear fellow.

ZAYTSEV [*aside*]. Talk about asking for trouble!

GUSEV [*shouts*]. Zina! Oh really, you are silly. [*To him.*] She's shy— quite the blushing violet, same as me. Modesty's all very well in its way, but why overdo things? What—stand on ceremony with your doctor when you're ill? That really is the limit.

ZINA [*comes in*]. Really, I'm hot and cold all over!

GUSEV. Now, that's quite enough of that. [*To him.*] She's been seeing Dr. Shervetsov, I might add. He's a good fellow, very nice chap, always the life and soul of the party, and he knows his stuff too. But—I don't know, I don't trust him! Somehow I don't like the cut of his jib. Now I can see you're not in the mood, Doctor, but do oblige us, please.

ZAYTSEV. I—I, it's all right. I don't mind. [*Aside.*] This beats everything!

GUSEV. You examine her while I go and tell mine host to put the good old samovar on. [*Goes out.*]

ZAYTSEV. Sit down, please. [*They sit.*] How old are you?

ZINA. Twenty-two.

ZAYTSEV. I see. A dangerous age. May I take your pulse? [*Takes it.*] I see. Quite so. [*Pause.*] What are you laughing at?

ZINA. You really are a doctor, I suppose?

ZAYTSEV. I say, whatever next! Who do you take me for? H'm—. Your pulse is all right. Very much so. A nice, plump little pulse—. I adore travelling adventures, damn it. You go on and on and on— then you suddenly meet a little, er, pulse like this. Do you love medicine?

ZINA. Yes.

ZAYTSEV. Now, isn't that nice! Terribly nice, it is! Let me take your pulse.

ZINA. But, but, but—. Don't go too far!

ZAYTSEV. That lovely little voice, those delightful rolling little eyes! One smile's enough to drive a man crazy. Is your husband jealous? Very jealous? Give me your hand. Only let me take your pulse and I'll die of happiness.

ZINA. Now look here, sir, I can see what's in your mind, but I'm not that kind of girl, sir. I'm a married woman and my husband has a position to keep up.

ZAYTSEV. Yes, yes, I know—but can I help it if you're so lovely?

ZINA. I won't permit liberties, sir—. Kindly leave me alone, or I shall have to take steps. I love and respect my husband too much to let some travelling cad make cheap remarks to me. You're quite wrong if you think I—. My husband's coming now, I think. Yes, yes, he's coming. Why don't you speak? What are you waiting for? Come on, then—kiss me, can't you?

ZAYTSEV. Darling! [*Kisses her.*] You pretty little poppet! [*Kisses her.*]

ZINA. Well, well, well——

ZAYTSEV. My little kitten! [*Kisses her.*] You dear little bit of fluff! [*Seeing* GUSEV *coming in.*] One more question—when do you cough more, on Tuesdays or on Thursdays?

ZINA. On Saturdays.

ZAYTSEV. I see. Let me take your pulse.

GUSEV [*aside*]. It looks as if there's been kissing—it's the Shervetsov business all over again. I can't make any sense of medicine. [*To his wife.*] Do be serious, Zina—you can't go on like this, you can't neglect your health. You must listen carefully to what the doctor tells you. Medicine's making great strides these days, great strides.

ZAYTSEV. Quite so. Now, what I have to say is this. Your wife's in no danger as yet, but if she doesn't have proper treatment she may end up badly with a heart attack and inflammation of the brain.

GUSEV. You see, Zina, you see! The trouble you cause me, oh, I'm so upset.

ZAYTSEV. I'll write a prescription at once. [*Tears a sheet of paper out of the register, sits down and writes.*] *Sic transit* . . . two drams. *Gloria mundi* . . . one ounce. *Aquae dest*— . . . two grains. Now, you take these powders, three a day.

GUSEV. In water or wine?

ZAYTSEV. Water.

GUSEV. Boiled?

ZAYTSEV. Boiled.

GUSEV. I'm really most grateful to you, Doctor——

[UNFINISHED]

THE WOOD-DEMON

[*Леший*]

A COMEDY IN FOUR ACTS

(1889–1890)

CHARACTERS

ALEXANDER SEREBRYAKOV, a retired professor

HELEN, his wife, aged 27

SONYA, his daughter by his first wife, aged 20

MRS. VOYNITSKY, widow of a high official and mother of the professor's first wife

GEORGE VOYNITSKY, her son

LEONID ZHELTUKHIN, a very wealthy man, once a student of technology

JULIA, his sister, aged 18

IVAN ORLOVSKY, a landowner

THEODORE, his son

MICHAEL KHRUSHCHOV, a landowner with a medical degree

ILYA DYADIN

VASILY, Zheltukhin's manservant

SIMON, a labourer employed at Dyadin's flour-mill

ACT ONE

The garden on ZHELTUKHIN'S *estate. The house and terrace. In the open space in front of the house are two tables, a large one laid for lunch, and a smaller one with hors d'œuvres. It is between two and three o'clock in the afternoon.*

SCENE I

[ZHELTUKHIN *and* JULIA *come out of the house.*]

JULIA. I wish you'd wear your nice grey suit. That one looks all wrong.

ZHELTUKHIN. Oh, who cares? I don't.

JULIA. Don't be such a bore, Leo. And on your birthday too. You *are* a naughty boy. [*Lays her head on his chest.*]

ZHELTUKHIN. Go easy on the love and kisses, will you?

JULIA [*through tears*]. Leo!

ZHELTUKHIN. Instead of all these boring kisses and loving looks of one kind or another, not to mention gadgets for standing my watch on that are no damn use to me, why don't you try doing what I ask you? Why didn't you write to the Serebryakovs?

JULIA. But I did, Leo.

ZHELTUKHIN. Which of them did you write to?

JULIA. Sonya. I told her to be sure to be here by one o'clock today. I did write. Honestly.

ZHELTUKHIN. But here it is past two and still no sign of them. Anyway, let them please themselves, I don't care. I must drop all that business. There's no future in it. It only means being humiliated and feeling one's behaved badly. That's all there is to it. She doesn't even notice me. I'm ugly, unattractive and not a bit romantic, and if she does marry me it'll only be because she has an eye on the main chance and is after my money.

JULIA. Unattractive! How can you tell what you're really like?

ZHELTUKHIN. Oh come, I do have eyes in my head. Look how my beard grows out of my neck here unlike any self-respecting beard. Then there's my moustache, damn it, and my nose.

JULIA. What are you holding your cheek for?

ZHELTUKHIN. I have that pain below my eye again.

JULIA. Yes, there is a bit of a swelling. Let me kiss it and make it better.

ZHELTUKHIN. Don't be so silly.

[IVAN ORLOVSKY *and* VOYNITSKY *come in*.]

SCENE II

[The above, ORLOVSKY *and* VOYNITSKY.]

ORLOVSKY. When do we get lunch, dear? It's after two.

JULIA. I know, but the Serebryakovs haven't turned up yet.

ORLOVSKY. Well, how much longer do we have to wait? I'm hungry, my dear, and so is George here.

ZHELTUKHIN [*to* VOYNITSKY]. Is your family really coming?

VOYNITSKY. Helen was dressing as I left the house.

ZHELTUKHIN. Does that mean we can count on them?

VOYNITSKY. I wouldn't say we could count on anything. The great man might have gout or one of his moods, in which case they'll stay put.

ZHELTUKHIN. Let's eat then. Why wait? [*Shouts*.] Come on, Dyadin. You too, Sergey Nikodimovich.

[DYADIN *and two or three other guests come in*.]

SCENE III

[The above, DYADIN *and guests.*]

ZHELTUKHIN. Come and start then. Please help yourselves. [*Attends to the table with the hors d'œuvres*.] The Serebryakovs haven't turned up, Theodore Orlovsky isn't here and the Wood-Demon hasn't come either. They've forgotten us.

JULIA. Some vodka for you, Godfather?

ORLOVSKY. Just a drop. That's right, thank you.

DYADIN [*tying his napkin round his neck*]. You do have things running splendidly here, Julia. When I go for a drive in your fields, or stroll in the shade of your garden or just gaze at this table here, everywhere I see the mighty power of your enchanting little hand. Your very good health!

JULIA. It's an awful lot of trouble, you know. For instance, last night Nazarka forgot to put the young turkeys in the shed, they were out in the garden all night and this morning five of them died.

DYADIN. He shouldn't have done that. Your turkey is a sensitive bird.

VOYNITSKY [*to* DYADIN]. Cut me a slice of ham, will you, Waffles?

DYADIN. With the greatest pleasure. What a splendid ham! Fabulous, like something out of the *Arabian Nights*. [*Cuts some.*] I'll slice it according to the book of rules, Georgie. Beethoven and Shakespeare couldn't have put more art into it. This knife's a bit blunt, though. [*Sharpens the knife on another knife.*]

ZHELTUKHIN [*shuddering*]. Brr! Steady on, Waffles, I can't stand that.

ORLOVSKY. Come on, George, tell us what's going on at your place.

VOYNITSKY. Nothing's going on.

ORLOVSKY. What's new?

VOYNITSKY. Nothing. It's the same old story, no different this year from last. I talk a lot as usual and don't get much done. And my dear mother, the old chatterbox, still keeps burbling on about the emancipation of women. She has one foot in the grave, but she still reads all those solemn pamphlets and thinks they'll lead her to a new life.

ORLOVSKY. What about Alexander?

VOYNITSKY. The professor? The moths haven't got him yet, I'm sorry to say. He still sits in his study writing from morning till last thing at night.

> 'With harassed brain and furrowed brow
> We pen heroic lays.
> But neither we nor they till now
> Have had one word of praise.'

I pity the paper he writes on. Sonya's just the same too, still reads serious books and keeps a most formidable diary.

ORLOVSKY. Ah, my darling Sonya.

VOYNITSKY. With my powers of observation I ought to write a novel. What a subject. It's just asking to be written up. A retired professor, an old fossil, a sort of academic stuffed trout. He suffers from gout, rheumatism, migraine, liver trouble and all the rest of it. He's as jealous as Othello. He lives on his first wife's estate, not that he wants to live there, but he can't afford to live in town. He's forever moaning about his misfortunes, though he's actually been pretty lucky.

ORLOVSKY. Oh, come.

VOYNITSKY. Of course he has. Just think what luck he's had. We won't say anything about him being the son of an ordinary parish clerk, who was educated at a church school, collected academic degrees and a university chair, became a person of consequence, married a senator's daughter and so on and so forth. None of that matters. But you note my next point. For precisely twenty-five years the man's been lecturing and writing about art. And what does he understand about art? Nothing. For precisely twenty-five years he's been chewing over other people's ideas on realism, tendentiousness and every other kind of tomfoolery. For twenty-five years he's been lecturing and writing about things which every intelligent person has known all along, and which don't interest fools anyway. In other words he's spent precisely twenty-five years chasing his own shadow. And all the time what fantastic success! What colossal fame! Why? What's it in aid of? What right has he to it?

ORLOVSKY [*guffaws*]. You're jealous, you're jealous.

VOYNITSKY. All right then, I'm jealous. And what success with women! Casanova himself couldn't have done better. His first wife, my own sister—a beautiful, gentle creature as pure as the blue sky above us, a fine, generous girl who had more admirers than he had pupils—she loved him as only angels in heaven can love beings as pure and lovely as themselves. My own mother, his mother-in-law, still idolizes him, still goes in awe of him. His second wife—you've seen her—is a beautiful, intelligent woman, and she married him when he was already an old man and gave him her youth, her beauty, her freedom, her radiance. Whatever for? Why? And she's so gifted, you know, a real artist. She plays the piano superbly.

ORLOVSKY. It's a very gifted family. There aren't many like it.

ZHELTUKHIN. I agree. Sonya, for instance, has quite a voice, a magnificent soprano. I've never heard anything to match it even in St. Petersburg. But you know, she is inclined to force her top notes. It's a great pity. Let me have those top notes. I must have them. Oh, if she only had the top notes, I bet you anything you like she'd really hit the heights, if you see what I mean. Sorry, all of you, I must have a word with Julia. [*Takes* JULIA *on one side.*] Send someone over there with a message. Tell them if they can't come now they must come to dinner. [*In a lower voice.*] And don't do anything silly or let me down by making spelling mistakes. Dinner is spelt with two ens. [*In a loud voice, affectionately.*] Please, darling.

JULIA. All right. [*Goes out.*]

DYADIN. I hear that Mrs. Helen Serebryakov, the professor's good lady, whom I have not had the honour of meeting, is distinguished not merely by spiritual beauty, but by the beauty of her physical attributes as well.

ORLOVSKY. Yes, she's a wonderful woman.

ZHELTUKHIN. Is she faithful to her professor?

VOYNITSKY. Yes, I'm sorry to say.

ZHELTUKHIN. Why sorry?

VOYNITSKY. Because she's faithful in a way that's so thoroughly bogus. Oh, it sounds impressive enough, but it just doesn't make sense. To be unfaithful to an elderly husband you can't stand, that's immoral. But if you make these pathetic efforts to stifle your own youth and the spark of life inside you, that isn't immoral at all. Where's the sense of that, damn it?

DYADIN [*in a tearful voice*]. Georgie, I hate it when you talk like that. Well, really. I'm actually trembling. I do not possess the gift of flowery expression, gentlemen, but allow me to give you my honest opinion without oratorical flourishes. Gentlemen, anyone who betrays a wife or husband could easily be unreliable enough to betray his country as well.

VOYNITSKY. Oh, turn the tap off.

DYADIN. No, let me go on, Georgie. Orlovsky, Leonid, my dear friends, you must remember the vicissitudes of my fate. There's no secret about it, nothing obscure or mysterious—the day after we were married my wife ran away with another man because of my unprepossessing appearance.

VOYNITSKY. Well, can you blame her?

DYADIN. Let me go on, please. Since that episode I've always done my duty. I still love her, I'm still faithful to her, I help her as much as I can and I've made a will leaving everything I possess to her children by this other man. I've done my duty and I'm proud of it. Proud of it, I tell you. I've lost my happiness, but I've kept my pride. What about her, though? She's no longer young, she's lost her looks—as was bound to happen sooner or later—and her lover is dead, poor chap. So what has she got left? [*Sits down.*] I'm perfectly serious and you laugh at me.

ORLOVSKY. You're a good chap, a splendid fellow in fact, but you do go on and on so, and wave your arms about.

[THEODORE *comes out of the house wearing a sleeveless coat of fine cloth and high boots. On his chest there are medals, decorations, and a massive gold chain with trinkets hanging from it. He wears expensive rings on his fingers.*]

SCENE IV

[*The above and* THEODORE.]

THEODORE. Hallo there, one and all.

ORLOVSKY [*delightedly*]. Theo, my dear boy!

THEODORE [*to* ZHELTUKHIN]. Happy birthday. You'll be a big man one day. [*Greets everyone.*] My revered parent! Waffles, hallo there! And may you all enjoy your meal. Let's hope it does you good.

ZHELTUKHIN. Where did you get to? You shouldn't be so late.

THEODORE. It's hot, I could do with a spot of vodka.

ORLOVSKY [*giving him an admiring look*]. You and your beard, dear boy, you look magnificent. I say, isn't he handsome? Look at him, the handsome devil.

THEODORE. Happy birthday. [*Drinks.*] Aren't the Serebryakovs here?

ZHELTUKHIN. They haven't turned up.

THEODORE. H'm! Where's Julia then?

ZHELTUKHIN. I don't know what's keeping her. It's time to serve the pie, I'll just go and call her. [*Goes out.*]

ORLOVSKY. What's up with friend Leo? It's baby's birthday, but he seems to have got out of bed on the wrong side. A bit down in the mouth——

VOYNITSKY. The man's a swine.

ORLOVSKY. His nerves have gone to pieces, he can't help it.

VOYNITSKY. He thinks too much of himself, hence the nerves. If you told him this herring tasted good he'd be up in arms at once because you praised the herring instead of him. Ghastly little squirt! Here he comes.

[JULIA *and* ZHELTUKHIN *come in.*]

SCENE V

[*The above,* ZHELTUKHIN *and* JULIA.]

JULIA. Good afternoon, Theo. [*They kiss.*] Help yourself, dear. [*To* ORLOVSKY.] Look what I'm giving Leo for his birthday. [*Shows him the watch-stand.*]

ORLOVSKY. My darling child! A watch-stand. Isn't that lovely!

JULIA. The gold thread alone came to eight-and-a-half roubles. And look at the edges, rows and rows and rows of tiny little pearls. And here's his name, 'Leonid Zheltukhin'. And look at this silk embroidery: 'To him I love.'

DYADIN. I say, let me have a look. Charming!

THEODORE. Oh, do pack it in, that's quite enough of that. Julia, tell them to bring in the champagne.

JULIA. But that's for this evening, Theo.

THEODORE. This evening, she tells me. You get going on it right now, or else I'm leaving. I really mean it, I shall go away. Where do you keep it? I'll go and get it myself.

JULIA. You're always turning the house upside down, Theo. [*To* VASILY.] Vasily, here's the key. The champagne's in the larder. You know, in a basket near the bag of raisins in the corner. And mind you don't break anything.

THEODORE. Bring three bottles, Vasily.

JULIA. You'd never learn to run a house, Theo. [*Serves everyone with pie.*] Mind you have plenty to eat, everybody. You won't get dinner for some time, not till about half past five. You'll never add up to anything in this world, Theo, you're hopeless.

THEODORE. Dear me, we are putting people in their places, aren't we?

VOYNITSKY. I think someone's just arrived. Can you hear anything?

ZHELTUKHIN. Yes, it's the Serebryakovs. Here at last.

VASILY. Mr. and Mrs. Serebryakov are here together with Miss Sonya.

JULIA [*shrieks*]. Sonya! [*Runs out.*]

VOYNITSKY [*sings*]. Come and meet them, come and meet them. [*Goes out.*]

THEODORE. Quite overjoyed, aren't they?

ZHELTUKHIN. Some people are tactless, I must say. He's carrying on with the professor's wife and can't even keep it to himself.

THEODORE. Who is?

ZHELTUKHIN. Why, George of course. The way he was singing her praises just before you came, it was downright improper.

THEODORE. How do you know he's carrying on with her?

ZHELTUKHIN. I'm not exactly blind. Anyway it's the talk of the whole neighbourhood.

THEODORE. Stuff and nonsense. No one's carrying on with her—yet. But I soon shall be. Do you hear me? *I* shall!

SCENE VI

[*The above, together with the following, who now come in:* SERE-BRYAKOV, MRS. VOYNITSKY, VOYNITSKY *with* HELEN *on his arm*, SONYA *and* JULIA.]

JULIA [*kissing* SONYA]. Darling, darling!

ORLOVSKY [*going to meet them*]. Hallo, Alexander, hallo, old boy. [*They kiss each other.*] Are you fit? Splendid!

SEREBRYAKOV. What about you, old man? You look terrific. Delighted to see you. Have you been back long?

ORLOVSKY. Since Friday. [*To* MRS. VOYNITSKY.] Mrs. Voynitsky! How are you keeping, madam? [*Kisses her hand.*]

MRS. VOYNITSKY. My dear—. [*Kisses him on the head.*]

SONYA. Godfather!

ORLOVSKY. Sonya, my dear. [*Kisses her.*] My darling little canary.

SONYA. You look just the same as ever, you nice sentimental old thing.

ORLOVSKY. Aren't you a big girl now! And you're as pretty as a picture, my pet.

SONYA. How are you getting on? Are you well?

ORLOVSKY. Fit as a fiddle.

SONYA. Good for you. [*To* THEODORE.] Oh, I didn't notice his lordship. [*They kiss.*] All sunburnt and covered with hair like a great spider.

JULIA. Darling!

ORLOVSKY [*to* SEREBRYAKOV]. How's life, old man?

SEREBRYAKOV. Oh, so so. How are you?

ORLOVSKY. How am I doing? I'm having quite a time. I've made over my estate to my son, found decent husbands for all my daughters and now I'm the freest man in the world. I'm having a whale of a time.

DYADIN [*to* SEREBRYAKOV]. I'm afraid you're a little on the late side, sir. The temperature of the pie has diminished considerably. May I introduce myself? Ilya Dyadin or, as certain persons have wittily nicknamed me on account of my pock-marked face, Waffles.

SEREBRYAKOV. How do you do?

DYADIN. *Madame! Mademoiselle!* [*Bows to* HELEN *and* SONYA.] These people are all friends of mine, Professor. I was pretty well off at one time. But domestic circumstances or, as people in intellectual circles put it, considerations for which the editor accepts no responsibility, compelled me to make over my share to my brother, who once had the bad luck to find himself short of seventy thousand roubles of government money. My profession is exploiting the stormy elements. I compel the tempestuous waves to turn the wheels of a flour-mill which I rent from my friend the Wood-Demon.

VOYNITSKY. Turn the tap off, Waffles.

DYADIN. I always bow down with reverence [*bows*] to the learned luminaries who shed lustre on our country's horizons. Forgive my audacity, sir, in hoping to pay you a visit and enjoy the spiritual pleasures of conversing about the latest findings of scholarship.

SEREBRYAKOV. Please do. Delighted.

SONYA. Come on, tell us what you've been up to, Godfather. Where did you spend the winter? Where did you get to?

ORLOVSKY. I've been in Gmunden, I've been in Paris, Nice, London. My dear I've been——

SONYA. Marvellous! You lucky man.

ORLOVSKY. Why don't you come with me this autumn? What do you say?

SONYA [*sings*]. 'Lead me not into temptation——'

THEODORE. Don't you sing at table, or your husband will find he has a silly wife.

DYADIN. It would be interesting to have a bird's eye view of this table. Such a charming floral arrangement, a combination of grace, beauty, profound erudition, distinc——

THEODORE. What a charming way to talk, dammit. You speak as if someone was running a carpenter's plane along your back. [*Laughter.*]

ORLOVSKY [*to* SONYA]. So you aren't married yet, dear?

VOYNITSKY. Have a heart! Who is she to marry? Humboldt's dead, Edison's in America, Lassalle's dead too. The other day I found her diary on the table, a thing this size. I opened it and read, 'No, I shall never fall in love. Love is an egoistic attraction of my person towards an object of the opposite sex.' She has a bit of everything there, dammit. 'Transcendental, culminating point of the integrating principle.' I ask you! Where did you get hold of that stuff?

SONYA. Spare us the irony, Uncle George, it's hardly your strong point.

VOYNITSKY. Why so annoyed?

SONYA. If you say another word one of us will have to go home. Either you or me.

ORLOVSKY [*gives a loud laugh*]. I say, what a girl!

VOYNITSKY. Yes, she's quite a handful, and no mistake. [*To* SONYA.] Give me your hand. Come on. [*Kisses her hand.*] Let peace and harmony reign, I'll behave myself in future.

SCENE VII

[*The above and* KHRUSHCHOV.]

KHRUSHCHOV [*coming out of the house*]. A pity I don't paint, you make such a marvellous group.

ORLOVSKY [*delighted*]. Michael! My dear godson.

KHRUSHCHOV. Many happy returns to Leo. Hallo there, Julia, you do look pretty today. Godfather. [ORLOVSKY *and he embrace.*] Sonya. [*Greets everybody.*]

ZHELTUKHIN. But why so late? Where have you been?

KHRUSHCHOV. Attending a patient.

JULIA. The pie's quite cold.

KHRUSHCHOV. Never mind, Julia, I'll eat it cold. Where do you want me to sit?

SONYA. Come and sit here. [*Points to the place next to her.*]

KHRUSHCHOV. What wonderful weather, and I'm absolutely ravenous. Just a moment, I'll have some vodka. [*Drinks.*] Happy birthday. Now for a spot of pie. Julia, give it a little kiss to make it taste better. [*She kisses it.*] Thank you. [*To* ORLOVSKY.] Well how are things with you? Haven't seen you for ages.

ORLOVSKY. Yes, it's been quite a while, hasn't it? I've been abroad, you know.

KHRUSHCHOV. So I heard, so I heard. Felt quite envious too. And how are you, Theodore?

THEODORE. Not so bad, thanks to your prayers, our ever-present help in trouble.

KHRUSHCHOV. And how's business?

THEODORE. I can't complain, I'm getting along very nicely. Only there's so much travelling, old boy, I'm quite worn out. From here to the Caucasus, back here again, then off back to the Caucasus. There's no end of this mad dashing about. I have two estates down there, you know.

KHRUSHCHOV. I do indeed.

THEODORE. I run my little colony and catch tarantulas and scorpions. On the whole things are really moving, but when we come to 'be still, ye raging passions' and all that, there's no change to report.

KHRUSHCHOV. You're in love, I take it.

THEODORE. We must have a drink on that, Mr. Wood-Demon. [*Drinks.*] Never fall in love with married women, gentlemen. Better have a bullet clean through the shoulder and another through the leg like your humble servant than be in love with a married woman, believe you me. It's more trouble than it's——

SONYA. Have you no hope?

THEODORE. Good grief, listen to her! 'No hope.' There's nothing hopeless in this world. Hopelessness, unhappy love affairs, moaning and groaning—that stuff's sheer self-indulgence. It's only a question of will-power. I don't want my shotgun to misfire and it doesn't. I do want a certain married woman to love me. And love me she will. That's the way it goes, Sonya old sport. Once I have my eye on a woman she has about as much chance of getting away as of taking a trip to the moon.

SONYA. Oh, you are a horrible man, I must say!

THEODORE. They don't escape my clutches in a hurry, oh dear me no. I haven't said more than a few words to her and she's already in my power. Yes indeed. I just told her, 'Madam, whenever you see a window anywhere, remember me. That's the way I want it.' So she thinks of me a thousand times a day. Besides, I bombard her with letters every day.

HELEN. That's pretty poor technique. She may not read the letters when she gets them.

THEODORE. You think so, do you? H'm! I've been on this earth for thirty-five years and somehow or other I've never run across any of these phenomenal women with the strength of mind not to open a letter.

ORLOVSKY [*looking at him admiringly*]. Isn't he terrific? You're a real chip off the old block, you handsome devil, you. I was just like him, you know, I was his living image. The only difference is, I was never in the war, but I did drink vodka and throw my money around like nobody's business.

THEODORE. You know, Michael, I love her damn seriously. Let her say the word and I'd give her everything I have. I'd take her off to my place in the Caucasus, in the mountains, and we'd be on top of the world. You know, Helen, I'd watch over her like a faithful hound and I'd treat her like the song one of our local big-wigs sings:

> 'Thou shalt of all the universe
> Be queen, o faithful mistress mine.'

She doesn't know her luck, believe me.

KHRUSHCHOV. And who is the lucky girl?

THEODORE. Curiosity killed the cat. But that's enough of that. Let's change the subject, shall we? I remember ten years ago when Leo was still at school and we were at his birthday party, just as we are now. I rode home with Sonya on my right arm and Julia on my left, both of them holding on to my beard. Come on, everyone, let's drink to the friends of my youth, Sonya and Julia.

DYADIN [*with a loud laugh*]. Charming, charming!

THEODORE. After the war I once got drunk with a Turkish pasha in Trebizond and he asked me whether——

DYADIN [*interrupting him*]. I say, let's drink a toast to friendliness. Long live friendship and the best of jolly good luck!

THEODORE. Stop, stop, stop! Your attention please, Sonya. I'll have a bet with you, damn it all. I'll stake three hundred roubles. Let's go and play croquet after lunch and I bet you I'll get through all the hoops and back in one go.

SONYA. I'd take you on, only I haven't got three hundred roubles.

THEODORE. Well, if you lose you must sing to me forty times.

SONYA. All right.

DYADIN. Charming, charming!

HELEN [*looking at the sky*]. What sort of bird is that?

ZHELTUKHIN. A hawk.

THEODORE. Its health, everyone! The hawk!

[SONYA *laughs loudly.*]

ORLOVSKY. I say, she *has* got a fit of the giggles. What's up?

[KHRUSHCHOV *laughs loudly.*]

ORLOVSKY. And what's got into you?

MRS. VOYNITSKY. Sonya, this is most unseemly.

KHRUSHCHOV. Oh dear, I'm sorry, everybody. I'll stop in a minute, I really will.

ORLOVSKY. This is what the Bible calls the laughter of fools.

VOYNITSKY. You only have to hold up a finger to either of those two and they burst out laughing. Sonya! [*Holds up a finger.*] See what I mean?

KHRUSHCHOV. All right, that will do. [*Looks at his watch and addresses himself.*] Well, Father Michael, your Reverence, you've had some food and drink and it's time to call it a day. Must be off.

SONYA. Where to?

KHRUSHCHOV. To see a patient. I'm sick and tired of my practice, it's like an unloved wife or a long winter.

SEREBRYAKOV. But look here, medicine is your profession after all —your business, so to speak.

VOYNITSKY [*ironically*]. He does have another profession. He digs peat on his land.

SEREBRYAKOV. What?

VOYNITSKY. Peat. Some engineer has it all worked out. There's seven hundred and twenty thousand roubles' worth of peat on his land. That's no joke.

KHRUSHCHOV. I don't dig peat to make money.

VOYNITSKY. Then what do you dig it for?

KHRUSHCHOV. To stop you cutting down the forests.

VOYNITSKY. And why shouldn't we cut them down? From the way you talk, anyone would think our forests only exist so that young lovers can bill and coo in them.

KHRUSHCHOV. I never said that.

VOYNITSKY. Whenever I've been favoured with your speeches on behalf of the forests every word has been stale, frivolous and biased. I'm sorry, but I know what I'm talking about, I know your speeches for the defence almost by heart. For instance. [*Raising his voice and making gestures as if in imitation of* KHRUSHCHOV.] O men and women, you destroy our forests, but they are the glory of our earth, they teach man to appreciate beauty and give him a sense of grandeur. Forests alleviate a harsh climate. In a mild climate less effort is spent on the struggle for existence, so that men and women are gentler and more affectionate. In countries with a mild climate, people are handsome, adaptable and sensitive, their speech is elegant and their movements are graceful. Art and learning flourish among them, their philosophy is cheerful and they treat their womenfolk with great delicacy and chivalry. And so on and so forth. That's all very charming, but so unconvincing that you must allow me to carry on burning logs in my stoves and building my barns of wood.

KHRUSHCHOV. By all means cut timber if you really need it, but it's time we stopped ruining the forests. All the forests of Russia are crashing down before the axe, millions upon millions of trees perish, the homes of birds and beasts are devastated, rivers grow shallow and dry up, wonderful scenery disappears without trace, and all because man's so lazy and hasn't the sense to bend down and take his fuel from the ground. Only an unreasoning brute could burn beauty like this [*points to the trees*] in his stove, destroying what we cannot create. Man has been granted reason and the power to create, so that he can add to what he's been given. But up to now he hasn't been a creator, only a destroyer. Forests keep disappearing, rivers dry up, wild life's become extinct, the climate's ruined and the land grows poorer and uglier every day. You look at me ironically and you find everything I say stale and frivolous, but when I walk past our village woodlands which I've saved from the axe or hear the rustle of my own saplings, planted with these hands, I feel that I too have some slight control over the climate and that if man is happy a thousand years from now I'll have done a bit towards it myself. When I plant a young birch and later see it covered with green and swaying in the breeze, my heart fills with pride at the thought that I'm helping God to create a living organism.

THEODORE [*interrupting*]. Your health, Mr. Wood-Demon.

VOYNITSKY. This is all very well, but if you looked at the thing less from a sensational and more from a scientific point of view, then——

SONYA. Uncle George, this leaves a nasty taste in the mouth. Please be quiet.

KHRUSHCHOV. Yes really, Voynitsky, let's not talk about it. Please.

VOYNITSKY. Have it your own way.

MRS. VOYNITSKY. Oh!

SONYA. What's the matter, Grandmother?

MRS. VOYNITSKY [*to* SEREBRYAKOV]. I forgot to tell you, Alexander, it slipped my mind. I had a letter today from Kharkov, from Paul Alekseyevich. He sends you his regards.

SEREBRYAKOV. Thank you, I'm delighted.

MRS. VOYNITSKY. He sent his new pamphlet and asked me to show you it.

SEREBRYAKOV. Is it interesting?

MRS. VOYNITSKY. Interesting, but rather odd. He attacks the very position he was defending seven years ago. Now isn't that so typical of our age? People have never been so ready to betray their own convictions as they are nowadays. It's dreadful.

VOYNITSKY. There's nothing dreadful about it. Have some fish, Mother.

MRS. VOYNITSKY. But I want to talk.

VOYNITSKY. For fifty years we've been talking about trends and schools of thought, and it's about time we stopped.

MRS. VOYNITSKY. For some reason you dislike the sound of my voice. I'm sorry, George, but this last year you've changed out of all recognition. You used to be a man of such firm principles, a shining example——

VOYNITSKY. Oh yes, I've been an example of something all right, but I haven't exactly shone. Do you mind if I get up? A shining example. That's a pretty poisonous sort of joke. I'm forty-seven. Until last year I was like you, I deliberately tried to befuddle myself with all sorts of abstract, pedantic humbug so as not to see life as it really is. I thought I was doing the right thing, but now—if you only knew what an ass I feel about the stupid way I've wasted time when I might have had everything I can't have now because I'm too old.

SEREBRYAKOV. Just a moment, George, you seem to be blaming your former principles for something——

SONYA. That's quite enough of that, Father. Don't be a bore.

SEREBRYAKOV. Just a moment. You seem to be blaming your former principles for something, but they're not to blame. You are. You're forgetting that principles are no good without deeds. You should have *done* something.

VOYNITSKY. 'Done something'? We can't all be non-stop writing machines.

SEREBRYAKOV. What exactly do you mean by that?

VOYNITSKY. Nothing. Let's stop talking like this. We're not at home now.

MRS. VOYNITSKY. Oh, it completely slipped my memory. Alexander, I forgot to remind you to take your medicine before lunch. I brought it with me, but I forgot to remind you.

SEREBRYAKOV. I don't want it.

MRS. VOYNITSKY. But you're not well, you know. In fact you're very ill.

SEREBRYAKOV. Well, there's no need to shout it from the roof-tops. I'm old and ill, I'm old and ill. That's all I ever hear. [*To* ZHEL-TUKHIN.] Do you mind if I get up and go indoors, Zheltukhin? It's a bit hot out here and I'm being bitten by mosquitoes.

ZHELTUKHIN. Please do, we've finished lunch anyway.

SEREBRYAKOV. I thank you. [*Goes off into the house followed by* MRS. VOYNITSKY.]

JULIA [*to her brother*]. You must go with the professor. This is most awkward.

ZHELTUKHIN [*to her*]. Oh, blast the man! [*Goes out.*]

DYADIN. Permit me to thank you from the bottom of my heart. [*Kisses her hand.*]

JULIA. Not at all. You ate so little. [*Everyone thanks her.*] Not at all, don't mention it. You've all eaten so little.

THEODORE. Well, what shall we do now, everybody? Let's go out on the croquet lawn and settle our wager. And then what?

JULIA. Then we'll have dinner.

THEODORE. And after that?

KHRUSHCHOV. You can all come over to my place. We'll go fishing on the lake this evening.

THEODORE. Splendid.

DYADIN. Charming.

SONYA. All right, come on then, everyone. We'll go and settle our bet on the croquet lawn. Then we'll have an early dinner here at Julia's, and at sevenish we'll drive over to the Wood—I mean to Mr. Khrushchov's place. Marvellous. Come on then, Julia, let's get the croquet balls. [*Goes into the house with* JULIA.]

THEODORE. Vasily, bring some wine out on to the croquet lawn. We'll drink the winners' health. Well, revered parent, shall we take part in this noble sport?

ORLOVSKY. In a moment, dear boy. I must spend five minutes or so with the professor or it would look bad. One must keep up appearances. You take my place for a bit, I'll be with you in a moment. [*Goes into the house.*]

DYADIN. I must go and sit at the feet of the learned Professor Serebryakov. Anticipating the exalted pleasure which——

VOYNITSKY. Waffles, you're a bore. Go.

DYADIN. I am going. [*Goes into the house.*]

THEODORE [*walks into the garden, singing*].

> 'Thou shalt of all the universe
> Be queen, o faithful mistress mine.' [*Goes out.*]

KHRUSHCHOV. I'm going to slip quietly away. [*To* VOYNITSKY.] Will you do me a great favour, Voynitsky? Let's never talk about forestry or medicine again. I don't know why, but when you get on to these things it leaves me with a nasty taste in my mouth for the rest of the day. I wish you a very good afternoon. [*Goes out.*]

SCENE VIII

[HELEN *and* VOYNITSKY.]

VOYNITSKY. What a narrow-minded fellow. I don't care how much nonsense people talk, but I don't like it when they put so much feeling into it.

HELEN. Once again you've behaved abominably, George. Did you have to quarrel with your mother and Alexander and bring in that stuff about non-stop writing machines? That's a pretty poor way to behave.

VOYNITSKY. But what if I hate him?

HELEN. There's no reason to hate Alexander, he's just the same as anyone else.

[SONYA *and* JULIA *cross into the garden with croquet balls and mallets.*]

VOYNITSKY. If you could only see your face and the way you move. It's as if life was too much for you, altogether too much.

HELEN. Dear me, it is, and I'm so bored too. [*Pause.*] Everyone runs down my husband to my face, just as if I wasn't there at all. Everyone looks at me as if they're sorry for me. 'Poor girl, she's married to an old man.' All of them, even the nicest ones, would like me to leave Alexander. This sympathy for me, all these pitying glances and compassionate sighs, add up to one thing. It's just what the Wood-Demon was saying just now, you all wantonly destroy the forests, and soon there won't be anything left on earth. You destroy men and women too, every bit as wantonly, and soon, thanks to your good offices, there will be no loyalty, integrity or unselfishness left on this earth. Why does it upset you so much to see a faithful wife who doesn't belong to you? Because—and the Wood-Demon's right—there's a demon of destruction in every one of you. You don't spare anything, whether it's the trees, the birds—or women or one another.

VOYNITSKY. I can't stand this sort of pretentious talk.

HELEN. And you can tell friend Theodore I'm sick and tired of his impertinence. It's thoroughly disgusting. To look me straight in the eyes and shout aloud to all and sundry about his love for some married woman, that is a bright way to behave, I must say.

[*Voices in the garden*: Hurray! Well done!]

HELEN. But isn't the Wood-Demon nice? He often comes to see us, but I'm rather shy, so we've never had a proper talk, and I've never been really friendly to him. He'll think I'm bad-tempered or proud. Do you know why you and I are such good friends, George? It must be because we're both such tiresome bores. Yes, bores! Don't look at me in that way, I don't like it.

VOYNITSKY. How else can I look at you when I love you? You are my happiness, my life, my youth. I know there's no chance of your loving me, but I don't want anything from you. Only let me look at you, listen to your voice——

SCENE IX

[*The above and* SEREBRYAKOV.]

SEREBRYAKOV [*at a window*]. Where are you, Helen?

HELEN. Here.

SEREBRYAKOV. Come and sit with us for a bit, dear. [*Disappears.*]

[HELEN *moves towards the house.*]

VOYNITSKY [*following her*]. Let me speak of my love. So long as you don't drive me away, that's all I need to be the happiest man on earth.

CURTAIN

ACT TWO

The dining-room of SEREBRYAKOV'*s house. There is a sideboard and—in the centre of the room—a dining table. It is between one and two o'clock in the morning. The watchman can be heard tapping his stick in the garden.*

SCENE I

[SEREBRYAKOV *sits dozing in an armchair by an open window while* HELEN, *also dozing, sits by his side.*]

SEREBRYAKOV [*opening his eyes*]. Who's there? Sonya, is it you?

HELEN. It's me.

SEREBRYAKOV. Oh, it's you, Helen. I'm in agony.

HELEN. Your rug's fallen on the floor. [*Wraps it round his legs.*] I'd better shut the window.

SEREBRYAKOV. No, it's too stuffy. Just now I dozed off and dreamed that my left leg didn't belong to me. I woke up with an excruciating pain. It can't be gout, it's more like rheumatism. What time is it?

HELEN. Twenty past one. [*Pause.*]

SEREBRYAKOV. You might look out Batyushkov's poems for me in the library tomorrow. I think we have them.

HELEN. What's that?

SEREBRYAKOV. Find me a Batyushkov in the morning. I seem to remember we had one. But why do I find it so hard to breathe?

HELEN. You're tired. This is the second night you've had no sleep.

SEREBRYAKOV. That's how Turgenev is supposed to have got angina, from having gout. I'm afraid it might happen to me. Old age, what a damnable, repulsive thing it is, confound it. Since I've aged so much I've even begun to disgust myself. And obviously none of you can stand the sight of me.

HELEN. The way you go on about your age, anyone would think it was all our fault.

SEREBRYAKOV. You're the one who really can't stand me.

HELEN. Don't be such a bore. [*Gets up and sits down further away.*]

SEREBRYAKOV. You're right of course. I'm not such a fool I can't see it. You're a good-looking, healthy young woman and you want a bit of life, while I'm an old man more dead than alive. Well? Do you really think I don't understand? Stupid of me of course to go on living at all. But just wait a bit, I'll soon set you all free. I shan't last much longer.

HELEN. I feel quite faint. If these sleepless nights have earned me any reward, all I ask is that you stop talking. For God's sake, stop it. That's all I ask.

SEREBRYAKOV. What it comes to is that you're all faint and weary and you're all wasting the best years of your lives on my account. While I'm the only person who's happy and enjoys life. Obvious, isn't it?

HELEN. Do stop it. You've completely worn me out.

SEREBRYAKOV. But then I've worn everybody out, haven't I? Obviously.

HELEN [*crying*]. I can't stand any more! Look here—what do you want from me?

SEREBRYAKOV. Nothing.

HELEN. Well, in that case stop talking. Please.

SEREBRYAKOV. It's a curious thing, but if George or that imbecile old mother of his ever say anything, that's perfectly in order and everyone listens. But I've only to open my mouth and everyone starts feeling miserable. Even my voice disgusts you. All right, I'm disgusting, I'm selfish, I'm a tyrant. But haven't I the right to a little selfishness in my old age? Haven't I earned it? My life hasn't been all that easy. Orlovsky and I were students together at one time. You ask him. He led a gay life, used to go off with gipsy girls and was a kind of benefactor to me, while I lived in cheap, dirty lodgings, slaving away day and night, going short of food and worrying because I was living at someone else's expense. Then I went to Heidelberg, though I saw nothing of Heidelberg while I was there. I went to Paris and saw nothing of Paris either. I was cooped up indoors the whole time working. And since I got my university chair I've spent my whole life serving faithfully, so to speak, in the ranks of scholarship, and I'm still soldiering on. I'm asking you, hasn't all

this earned me the right to a peaceful old age and a little consideration from others?

HELEN. No one's disputing that right. [*The window bangs in the wind.*]
There's a wind getting up, I'd better shut that window. [*Shuts it.*]
It's going to rain. Nobody's disputing your rights.

> [*Pause. The watchman in the garden is heard tapping his stick and
> singing a song.*]

SEREBRYAKOV. You give your whole life to scholarship, you grow used
to your study, your lecture-room and your distinguished colleagues.
Then, God knows why, you turn up in this dead-and-alive hole
where you can't get away from second-rate people and their inane
chatter. I want some life, I like success, I like to be well known and
make a bit of a stir, but here—I might as well be exiled to the depths
of Siberia. To spend every moment regretting one's past, watching
others succeed and going in fear of death—I can't stand it. It's too
much! And now they won't even forgive me for growing old.

HELEN. Just wait and be patient. In five or six years I'll be old too.

[SONYA *comes in.*]

SCENE II

[*The above and* SONYA.]

SONYA. I can't think why there's no doctor here yet. I told Stephen to
go and fetch the Wood-Demon if the local man's out.

SEREBRYAKOV. What do I want with this Wood-Demon of yours?
He knows as much about medicine as I do about astronomy.

SONYA. We can hardly bring an entire medical faculty out here to
attend to your gout.

SEREBRYAKOV. I won't even talk to him, he's a complete crack-pot.

SONYA. Have it your own way. [*Sits down.*] I don't care.

SEREBRYAKOV. What time is it?

HELEN. Past one o'clock.

SEREBRYAKOV. It's stuffy in here. Sonya, will you get me that medicine from the table?

SONYA. Here you are. [*Hands him the medicine.*]

SEREBRYAKOV [*irritably*]. Oh, really, not that one! It's no use asking for anything.

SONYA. Please stop behaving like a child. It may appeal to some people, but don't treat me that way, thank you very much. I dislike that sort of thing.

SEREBRYAKOV. The girl's quite impossible. Why are you so angry?

SONYA. And why do you sound so dismal? Anyone might think you were really unhappy, when actually you're one of the happiest people on earth.

SEREBRYAKOV. Oh yes, of course, I couldn't be happier.

SONYA. Of course you're happy. And even if you do have gout you know perfectly well it will be gone by morning. So why all the groans? What a lot of fuss about nothing!

[*Enter* VOYNITSKY *wearing a dressing-gown and carrying a candle.*]

SCENE III

[*The above and* VOYNITSKY.]

VOYNITSKY. There's going to be a storm. [*A flash of lightning.*] Did you see that! Helen and Sonya, you go to bed. I've come to relieve you.

SEREBRYAKOV [*terrified*]. No, no! Don't leave me alone with him. No! He'll talk my head off.

VOYNITSKY. But you must let them have some rest, they were up all last night.

SEREBRYAKOV. Let them go to bed, but you go away too, thank you very much. I implore you in the name of our past friendship, don't argue. We'll talk some other time.

VOYNITSKY. Our past friendship? That's news to me, I must say.

HELEN. Please be quiet, George.

SEREBRYAKOV. My dear, don't leave me alone with him. He'll talk my head off.

VOYNITSKY. This is becoming quite ridiculous.

KHRUSHCHOV [*off stage*]. Are they in the dining-room? In here? Will you have someone look after my horse, please?

VOYNITSKY. Look, the doctor's come.

[*Enter* KHRUSHCHOV.]

SCENE IV

[*The above and* KHRUSHCHOV.]

KHRUSHCHOV. I say, what do you think of the weather? There was a shower coming up behind me, I only just dodged it. How are you? [*Shakes hands.*]

SEREBRYAKOV. I'm sorry you've been bothered. It wasn't my idea.

KHRUSHCHOV. Oh come, come, that's all right. But what do you mean by falling ill like this, Professor? Whatever next! This won't do, oh dear me no. What's the matter?

SEREBRYAKOV. Why do doctors always have to talk to their patients in this patronizing way?

KHRUSHCHOV [*laughs*]. You shouldn't be so observant. [*Affectionately.*] Come, we'd better go to bed. We're not comfortable here. It'll be warmer and more restful in bed. Come on. Then I'll listen to your chest and everything will be fine.

HELEN. Go on, Alexander, do what he says.

KHRUSHCHOV. If it hurts you to walk we'll carry you in your chair.

SEREBRYAKOV. It's all right, I can manage. I'll walk. [*Gets up.*] Only they shouldn't have troubled you. [KHRUSHCHOV *and* SONYA *lead him by the arms.*] Besides I haven't all that much faith in—in medicaments. Why are you helping me? I can manage on my own. [*Goes off with* KHRUSHCHOV *and* SONYA.]

SCENE V

[HELEN *and* VOYNITSKY.]

HELEN. He's completely worn me out, I can hardly stand.

VOYNITSKY. He wears you out and I wear myself out. This is the third night I've had no sleep.

HELEN. We are in a bad way in this house. Your mother hates everything except her pamphlets and the professor. The professor's overwrought, he doesn't trust me and he's afraid of you. Sonya's annoyed with her father and not on speaking terms with me. You loathe my husband and openly sneer at your mother. I'm a complete wet blanket and I'm so much on edge, I've been on the verge of tears a dozen times today. In fact we're all fighting each other, but what

I want to know is—what's the point of this free-for-all? What's it all in aid of?

VOYNITSKY. We can do without the moralizing, thank you.

HELEN. Yes, we are in a bad way here. You're an intelligent and civilized man, George. I should have thought you must see why the world's heading for disaster. It's not bandits and thieves, so much as all this concealed hatred, this hostility between nice people, all these sordid little squabbles. There are people who call our house a cultural haven, but they never notice these things. Do help me to make peace here. I can't do it on my own.

VOYNITSKY. First help me make peace with myself. My darling——.

[*Bends down and kisses her hand.*]

HELEN. Leave me alone. [*Removes her hand.*] Go away.

VOYNITSKY. Soon the rain will be over. All living things will revive and breathe more freely. Except me. The storm won't revive me. Day and night my thoughts choke me, haunt me with the spectre of a life hopelessly wasted. I've never lived. My past life has been thrown away on stupid trivialities and the present is so futile, it appals me. My life and my love—well, there you have it. What can I do with them? What can I make of them? My feelings are wasted like a ray of sunlight falling in a well, and I'm running to waste too.

HELEN. When you talk about love I somehow can't think or feel—words fail me. I'm sorry, but I've nothing to say to you. [*Makes to leave.*] Good night.

VOYNITSKY [*barring her way*]. And if you only knew how it hurts me to think that in this very house another life is wasting away besides my own. I mean yours. What are you waiting for? What's stopping you, dammit? Some wretched theory or other? You may suppress your youthful high spirits or even try to bury them alive. But that's not what being moral means in the best sense of the word, so get that into your head.

HELEN [*stares at him*]. George, you're drunk.

VOYNITSKY. Possibly, very possibly.

HELEN. Is Theodore with you?

VOYNITSKY. He's sleeping in my room tonight. Possibly, very possibly. Anything's possible.

HELEN. So you've been celebrating again today, have you? What do you do it for?

VOYNITSKY. It at least gives one the illusion of being alive. Don't try and stop me, Helen.

HELEN. You never used to drink. And you never used to talk so much as you do now. Go to bed. You bore me. And tell your friend Theodore Orlovsky that if he doesn't stop annoying me I intend to do something about it. Now go.

VOYNITSKY [*bending down to kiss her hand*]. My darling. Wonderful woman!

[KHRUSHCHOV *comes in.*]

SCENE VI

[*The above and* KRUSHCHOV.]

KHRUSHCHOV. Your husband's asking for you.

HELEN [*snatching her hand away from* VOYNITSKY]. Right, I'm coming. [*Goes out.*]

KHRUSHCHOV [*to* VOYNITSKY]. Is nothing sacred to you? You might remember, you and that dear lady who's just gone out, that her husband was once married to your sister. And that you have a young girl living under the same roof. Your affair's already the talk of the whole county. You should be thoroughly ashamed of yourselves. [*Goes off to his patient.*]

VOYNITSKY [*alone*]. She's gone. [*Pause.*] Ten years ago I used to meet her at my sister's. She was seventeen then and I was thirty-seven. Why didn't I fall in love then and ask her to marry me? It would have been the most natural thing in the world. And she'd be my wife now. Yes. And tonight the storm would have woken us both. She'd be scared of the thunder and I'd hold her in my arms and whisper, 'Don't be afraid. I'm here.' Oh, what wonderful thoughts, I could laugh for sheer joy. But oh God, my head's in such a whirl. Why am I so old? Why can't she understand me? The affected way she talks, her languid moralizing, those trivial, tired ideas about the world heading for disaster—how utterly I loathe it all. [*Pause.*] Why am I such an awful character? How I envy that gay spark Theodore or that stupid Wood-Demon! They're natural, sincere and stupid —and free from this damned irony that poisons everything.

[*Enter* THEODORE ORLOVSKY *wrapped in a blanket.*]

SCENE VII

[VOYNITSKY *and* THEODORE ORLOVSKY.]

THEODORE [*speaking through the door*]. Here on your own? None of the ladies about? [*Comes in.*] The storm woke me up. Quite a shower. What time is it?

VOYNITSKY. How the hell should I know?

THEODORE. I thought I heard Helen speaking.

VOYNITSKY. She was in here a moment ago.

THEODORE. Gorgeous creature. [*Looks at the medicine bottles on the table.*] What are those? Peppermints? [*Eats some.*] Yes indeed, a gorgeous creature. Is the professor ill then?

VOYNITSKY. Yes, he is.

THEODORE. That kind of existence makes no sense to me. It's said the ancient Greeks used to throw weak and sickly babies over a precipice on Mont Blanc. That's the way to treat his sort.

VOYNITSKY [*irritably*]. It wasn't Mont Blanc, it was the Tarpeian Rock. What gross ignorance!

THEODORE. All right, make it a rock then. What the hell does it matter? And why so mournful tonight? Feeling sorry for the professor or something?

VOYNITSKY. Leave me alone. [*Pause.*]

THEODORE. Or could it be that you're in love with Mrs. Professor? Eh? Oh well, there's nothing wrong with that. Languish away. But just get this straight. If I find there's one grain of truth in the gossip that's going round the place you can expect no mercy. I'll chuck you off the Tarpeian Rock.

VOYNITSKY. She's a friend of mine.

THEODORE. Already?

VOYNITSKY. What do you mean, 'already'?

THEODORE. A woman can become a man's friend only under the following conditions—first an acquaintance, next a mistress, and only then a friend.

VOYNITSKY. That's a pretty cheap line of talk.

THEODORE. Then let's have a drink on it. Come on, I think I still have a bit of Chartreuse. Let's have a drink. And as soon as it gets light we'll drive over to my place. Wodger say? I have a manager on one of my estates called Luke, who can't say 'what do you', always says 'wodger'. A frightful rogue. So wodger say? [*Seeing* SONYA, *who is coming in.*] Heavens alive, excuse me, I haven't got a tie on. [*Runs out.*]

SCENE VIII

[VOYNITSKY *and* SONYA.]

SONYA. So you've been drinking champagne with Theo again, have you, Uncle George? And driving about in a troika? The boys *have* been getting together, haven't they? All right then, he's quite hopeless, he's been a rake since the day he was born, but what's got into you? It doesn't suit you at your time of life.

VOYNITSKY. My time of life is neither here nor there. When people aren't really alive they live on illusions. It's better than nothing anyway.

SONYA. We haven't got the hay in yet. Gerasim told me today it would all rot in the rain, and you spend your time on illusions. [*Alarmed.*] Uncle, you have tears in your eyes!

VOYNITSKY. What do you mean, tears? Nothing of the sort. Rubbish. The way you looked at me just now, your poor dear mother used to look like that. My darling—. [*Eagerly kisses her hands and face.*] My sister, my darling sister—. Where is she now? If she only knew! Oh, if she only knew!

SONYA. Knew what? What do you mean, Uncle?

VOYNITSKY. It's so painful, such a wretched business. Never mind. [KHRUSHCHOV *comes in.*] I'll tell you later. It doesn't matter—I'll go. [*Goes.*]

SCENE IX

[SONYA *and* KHRUSHCHOV.]

KHRUSHCHOV. Your father won't listen to me at all. I tell him it's gout, he says it's rheumatism, and if I ask him to lie down he sits up. [*Picks up his peaked cap.*] It's all nerves.

SONYA. He's spoilt. Put your hat down and wait till the rain stops. Do you want something to eat?

KHRUSHCHOV. Well, yes perhaps.

SONYA. I like eating in the middle of the night. We have some food in the sideboard, I think. [*Rummages in the sideboard.*] What does he want with a doctor? What he wants is a dozen women sitting round him, gazing into his eyes and groaning, 'Professor!' Here, have some cheese.

KHRUSHCHOV. That's not the way to talk about your father. I agree, he is difficult, but compared with other people—why, all these Uncle Georges and Ivan Orlovskys aren't worth his little finger.

SONYA. Here's a bottle of something. I wasn't speaking of him as a father, but as a great man. I love my father, but I'm bored stiff with great men and all the oriental ceremonial that goes with them. [*They sit down.*] What a downpour! [*Lightning.*] I say!

KHRUSHCHOV. The storm's passing over, we shall pretty well miss it.

SONYA [*pouring out*]. Have something to drink.

KHRUSHCHOV. Your very good health. [*Drinks.*]

SONYA. Are you angry with us for bringing you out in the middle of the night?

KHRUSHCHOV. Not a bit. If you hadn't sent for me I'd be asleep now, and it's so much nicer to see you in the flesh than in my dreams.

SONYA. Then why do you look angry?

KHRUSHCHOV. Because I happen to be angry. There's no one about, so I can speak frankly. Oh, Sonya, how I'd love to take you away from here this very instant. I simply can't breathe the air in this house and I think it's poisoning you. Your father, so obsessed with his gout and his books and refusing to notice anything else, your Uncle George, and then your step-mother——

SONYA. What about my step-mother?

KHRUSHCHOV. There are some things one doesn't talk about, one can't. My dear, wonderful girl, there's so much I don't understand about people. People should be beautiful in every way—in their faces, in the way they dress, in their thoughts and in their innermost selves. Oh, I've seen plenty of pretty faces and dresses, been quite swept off my feet at times. But the mind and spirit that go with them, well, the less said about those the better. A pretty face can conceal a nature so black that no amount of make-up could hide it. I'm sorry, I'm rather worked up. You're very precious to me, you know,

SONYA [*drops a knife*]. Oh dear, I've dropped it.

KHRUSHCHOV [*picks it up*]. Never mind. [*Pause.*] When you walk in a wood on a dark night there's sometimes a glimmer of light shining in the distance, isn't there? Then you somehow feel so wonderful that you don't notice how tired you are or how dark it is or how the thorns and twigs hit you in the face. I work from morning till night with never a moment's peace, winter or summer, battling away against people who don't understand me, and things sometimes get too much for me. But now at last I've found my light shining in the distance. I'm not going to make out I love you more than anything in the world. Love isn't the whole of my life, it's my reward. But my darling, there's no higher reward for anyone who works, struggles and suffers.

SONYA [*most upset*]. I'm sorry. Can I ask you something, Michael?

KHRUSHCHOV. What is it? Tell me quickly.

SONYA. Well, look, you come here pretty often, and I sometimes go over to your place with my family. And you feel terribly guilty about it all, don't you?

KHRUSHCHOV. What do you mean?

SONYA. I mean this—your democratic feelings are offended by your friendship for us. I went to an exclusive school, Helen comes from a titled family and we dress fashionably, while you hold these democratic views——

KHRUSHCHOV. Well, really! Don't let's talk about that. This isn't the time.

SONYA. The point is, you go round digging up peat and planting trees. Well, it is a bit odd. In fact you're a kind of socialist.

KHRUSHCHOV. 'Democratic, socialist.' Sonya, don't tell me you can use such words seriously. Why, you even sound quite worked up about it.

SONYA. Well, I am serious. Very much so.

KHRUSHCHOV. Oh really, you can't be.

SONYA. I'll tell you something else and I'll bet you anything you like it's true. Suppose I had a sister and suppose you fell in love with her and asked her to marry you, you'd never forgive yourself. You'd be ashamed to show yourself to your doctor friends, including those women, in the council health department—ashamed of loving someone who went to a fashionable girls' school, a namby-pamby young lady who never learned anything useful and who dresses according to the latest fashion. I know you would, I can see it in your eyes. In fact, to put it in a nutshell, those woods of yours, your peat and your embroidered shirts, they're all an affectation, a pretentious piece of play-acting and nothing more.

KHRUSHCHOV. What have I done to deserve this? Why do you insult me, child? Anyway, I'm a fool, it serves me right for not knowing my place. Good-bye. [*Moves towards the door.*]

SONYA. Good-bye. I was rude, please forgive me.

KHRUSHCHOV [*returning*]. If you only knew what an oppressive, stuffy atmosphere you have here. You're surrounded by people who come crawling up to a man, look at him sideways on and try to discover in him a socialist, a psychopath or an idle chatterbox—anything you like except a human being. 'Oh, he's a psychopath,' they say. And they're delighted. Or, 'He talks a lot of hot air.' And they're as pleased as if they'd discovered America. And when they don't understand me and don't know what label to stick on me, they don't blame themselves. They blame me and say, 'He's an odd fellow, odd.' You're only twenty, but you're already as old and canny as your father and your Uncle George, and I wouldn't be the least surprised if you were to call me in to cure your gout. That's no way to live. Never mind who I am, you should look me straight in the eye—openly, without reservations or preconceived ideas—and above all try to see me as a human being, or else you'll never really get on with people. Good-bye. And just remember this. With calculating, suspicious eyes like yours you'll never fall in love.

SONYA. That's not true.

KHRUSHCHOV. Oh yes, it is.

SONYA. It's not true. Well, just to show you—I am in love, so there. I'm in love and I'm terribly, terribly unhappy. Now leave me alone. Go away, for heaven's sake. And stop coming here, don't you come here any more.

KHRUSHCHOV. I wish you a very good night. [*Goes off.*]

SONYA [*alone*]. Oh, I *have* made him angry. I hope to God I never have a temper like that. [*Pause.*] He speaks very well, but who can be sure it's not a lot of hot air? Then he has those woods on the brain, he can talk of nothing else, and he plants trees. That's all very well, but it could so easily turn out to be psychopathic. [*Covers her face with her hands.*] I can't make him out at all. [*Cries.*] He studied medicine, but his interests are right outside medicine. It's all very odd, it really is. Lord, help me to make some sense of it.

[HELEN *comes in.*]

SCENE X

[SONYA *and* HELEN.]

HELEN [*opens the windows*]. The storm's over. What wonderful air. [*Pause.*] Where's the Wood-Demon?

SONYA. Gone home. [*Pause.*]

HELEN. Sonya.

SONYA. What?

HELEN. When are you going to stop sulking? We've done each other no harm, so why should we be enemies? Can't we call it off?

SONYA. I've wanted to myself. [*Embraces her.*] Darling!

HELEN. That's splendid. [*Both are very moved.*]

SONYA. Has Father gone to bed?

HELEN. No, he's in the drawing-room. We don't speak to each other for a whole month and heaven knows why. It's high time we did call it off. [*Looks at the table.*] What's this?

SONYA. The Wood-Demon has been having some supper.

HELEN. There's wine too. Let's drink to our friendship.

SONYA. Yes, let's.

HELEN. From the same glass. [*Fills it.*] That's better. So we're friends now, Sonya?

SONYA. Friends, Helen. [*They drink and kiss each other.*] I've wanted to make it up for ages, but I felt too embarrassed somehow. [*Cries.*]

HELEN. But why are you crying?

SONYA. Never mind, it's nothing.

HELEN. There, there, that'll do. [*Cries.*] You silly girl, now you've made me cry. [*Pause.*] You're angry with me because you think I married your father for selfish reasons. I give you my word of honour, if that means anything to you, that I married him for love. He attracted me as a scholar and public figure. It wasn't real love, it was quite artificial, but it seemed real enough at the time. It wasn't my fault. But since the day we were married you've been tormenting me by looking at me with those calculating, suspicious eyes.

SONYA. Please, please, remember we're friends now. Let's forget all that. That's the second time today I've been told about my calculating, suspicious eyes.

HELEN. You shouldn't look so calculating then, it doesn't suit you. You must trust people or life becomes impossible.

SONYA. Once bitten, twice shy. I've been let down so often.

HELEN. Who by? Your father's a good, honest man and he works hard. You were on at him today about being happy. If he's really been happy then he hasn't noticed it himself because he's been working too hard. I've never tried to hurt either you or your father. Your Uncle George is a very kind, honest man, but he's unhappy and discontented. So who is it you can't trust? [*Pause.*]

SONYA. Tell me honestly as a friend. Are you happy?

HELEN. No.

SONYA. I knew it. Another question. Tell me frankly, do you wish you were married to somebody younger?

HELEN. What a child you are. Of course I do. [*Laughs.*] All right, ask me something else, go on.

SONYA. Do you like the Wood-Demon?

HELEN. Yes I do, very much.

SONYA [*laughs*]. I have a foolish expression on my face, haven't I? He's just left, but I can still hear his voice and footsteps. And if I look into a dark window I seem to see his face in it. Let me finish what I have to say. But I can't say it out loud like this, I feel too embarrassed. Let's go to my room and talk there. Do you think I'm silly? You do, don't you? Is he a good man?

HELEN. Yes, indeed he is.

SONYA. I'm puzzled by this forestry and peat business. I can't make sense of it.

HELEN. There's a bit more to it than forestry, you know. Don't you see, my dear? He's a brilliant man! You know what that means? It means he has courage, flair, tremendous vision. When he plants a tree or digs up half a hundredweight of peat he's already working out what the result will be in a thousand years' time, already dreaming of man's happiness. People like that are precious and should be cherished. God bless you both. You're decent, courageous, honest people. He's a bit unhinged, but you're clear-headed and sensible. You'll make a very good match. [*Stands up.*] As for me, I'm just a tiresome character and not a very important one. In my music, in my husband's house, in all your romantic affairs—in everything, that is— I've always played a minor role. Come to think of it, Sonya, I really must be very, very unhappy. [*Walks agitatedly up and down the stage.*] There's no happiness for me in this world. None at all. What are you laughing at?

SONYA [*laughing and hiding her face*]. I'm so happy. Oh, how happy I am!

HELEN [*wringing her hands*]. Oh, really, how unhappy I am!

SONYA. I'm happy—happy.

HELEN. I feel like playing the piano. I'd like to play something now.

SONYA. Yes, do. [*Embraces her.*] I can't sleep. Do play something.

HELEN. Just a minute, your father's still awake. Music annoys him when he's unwell. Go and ask him and I'll play something if he doesn't mind. Go on.

SONYA. All right. [*Goes out.*]

[*The watchman is heard tapping his stick in the garden.*]

HELEN. It's ages since I played anything. I'll play and cry, cry my eyes out like a silly girl. [*Through the window.*] Is that you knocking, Yefim?

WATCHMAN [*off stage*]. Hallo there!

HELEN. Stop it then. The master's unwell.

WATCHMAN [*off stage*]. I'm just going. [*Whistles under his breath.*] Hey there, good dogs. Come on, dogs! [*Pause.*]

SONYA [*returning*]. He says no.

CURTAIN

ACT THREE

The drawing-room of SEREBRYAKOV's *house. There are three doors—right, left and centre. Afternoon.* HELEN *can be heard playing the piano off stage. She is playing Lensky's aria which precedes the duel in* Eugene Onegin.

SCENE I

[ORLOVSKY, VOYNITSKY *and* THEODORE, *the latter in Circassian costume and carrying a fur cap.*]

VOYNITSKY [*listening to the music*]. Helen's playing my favourite aria. [*The music stops.*] Yes, it's a lovely thing. I don't think it's ever been quite so boring here before.

THEODORE. You don't know the meaning of the word boredom, old boy. When I was with the volunteers in Serbia we had the genuine article there all right, what with the stifling heat and the dirt and your head practically splitting in two because you had a hangover. I remember once sitting in some filthy little shed along with a Captain Kashkinazi. We'd long ago said all we had to say, there was nowhere to go and nothing to do, and we didn't want a drink. It was sickening, you know, enough to drive you round the bend. We sit there like a couple of snakes trying to hypnotize each other. He stares at me and I stare at him. I stare at him and he stares at me, and we go on staring like that without knowing why. Well, an hour passes, you see, and then another, and there we are still staring at each other. Then suddenly, God knows why, he jumps to his feet, whips out his sabre and goes for me. How do you like that! Well of course, I draw my own sabre pretty smartly—no point in being killed—and then the fun begins. Bim bam bim bam! They had a job separating us. I didn't get hurt, but Captain Kashkinazi's still going round with a scar on his cheek. It shows how crazy people can be.

ORLOVSKY. Yes, such things happen.

[*Enter* SONYA.]

SCENE II

[*The above and* SONYA.]

SONYA [*aside*]. I don't know what to do with myself. [*Laughs as she crosses the stage.*]

ORLOVSKY. Where are you off to, Kitten? Sit with us for a bit.

SONYA. Come here a moment, Theo. [*Takes* THEODORE *on one side.*] Come over here.

THEODORE. What do you want? What do you look so happy about?

SONYA. Promise you'll do what I ask.

THEODORE. Well, what is it?

SONYA. Drive over to the—Wood-Demon's.

THEODORE. What for?

SONYA. Oh, nothing. Just drive over and ask him why he hasn't been near us for so long. It's been a whole fortnight.

THEODORE. She's blushing. You should be ashamed of yourself. I say, everyone, Sonya's in love.

EVERYONE. Shocking. You should be ashamed of yourself.

[SONYA *covers her face with her hands and runs out.*]

THEODORE. She drifts around from one room to another as if she was half dead and doesn't know what to do with herself. She's in love with the Wood-Demon.

ORLOVSKY. She's a splendid child, I'm very fond of her. I did think you might marry her, Theo. You couldn't find a better wife. Ah well, things haven't worked out that way. But it would have given me such pleasure, I'd have been delighted. I'd have come to see you, and there you'd have been with your young wife in the bosom of your family with the good old samovar on the boil.

THEODORE. That's not my line of country. But if I ever was crazy enough to get married I'd marry Julia anyway. She is at least small, and one should always choose the lesser of two evils. And she does know how to run a house. [*Claps his forehead.*] I've had an idea.

ORLOVSKY. What's that?

THEODORE. Let's have some champagne.

VOYNITSKY. It's a bit early and it's too hot. Let's leave it a bit.

ORLOVSKY [*with an admiring look*]. My own boy, handsome devil! Wants champagne, the dear fellow.

[*Enter* HELEN.]

SCENE III

[*The above and* HELEN. HELEN *crosses the stage.*]

VOYNITSKY. Look at that. There she goes, nearly falling over from sheer laziness. A charming sight, I must say.

HELEN. Stop it, George. Things are quite boring enough without you going on all the time.

VOYNITSKY [*barring her way*]. Our brilliant pianist! But you don't look much like one. Lazy, indolent, sluggish and so virtuous that I can't bear to look at you.

HELEN. Then don't look at me, let me go.

VOYNITSKY. Why so downhearted? [*Vigorously.*] No really, my dear, splendid creature, do be sensible. There's mermaid's blood flowing in your veins. So go on, be a mermaid.

HELEN. Leave me alone.

VOYNITSKY. Let yourself go for once in your life and fall madly in love with a river god——

THEODORE. And dive head first into deep water with him and leave the learned professor and the rest of us gasping on the shore.

VOYNITSKY. A mermaid, eh? How about a little love affair before it's too late?

HELEN. Why are you telling me what to do? If I had my way, I wouldn't need you to show me how to live. I'd fly away, free as a bird, far away from you all, away from your sleepy faces and your dull, boring talk. I'd forget that you so much as exist, and then no one would dare to tell me what to do. But I have no will of my own. I'm such a coward, I'm so shy. I keep feeling that if I was unfaithful all other wives would do the same and leave their husbands. I feel that God would punish me and my conscience would torment me, otherwise I'd show you a thing or two about leading a free life. [*Goes out.*]

ORLOVSKY. My dear, my beautiful——

VOYNITSKY. I think I'll soon find myself despising that woman. She's as bashful as a young girl, but she lays down the law like some stuffy old parish clerk who's never done anything wrong in his life. What sickly, wishy-washy stuff!

ORLOVSKY. All right, that will do. Where's the professor now?

VOYNITSKY. In his study, writing.

ORLOVSKY. He wrote and asked me to come and talk over some business matter. You don't know what it's all about, I suppose?

VOYNITSKY. He has no business affairs. All he ever does is write nonsense, grumble and feel jealous.

[ZHELTUKHIN *and* JULIA *come in through the door, right.*]

SCENE IV

[*The above*, ZHELTUKHIN *and* JULIA.]

ZHELTUKHIN. Hallo, everybody. [*Greets everyone.*]

JULIA. Hallo, Godfather. [*They kiss.*] Hallo, Theo. [*They kiss.*] Hallo, Mr. Voynitsky. [*They kiss.*]

ZHELTUKHIN. Is Professor Serebryakov in?

ORLOVSKY. Yes, he's in his study.

ZHELTUKHIN. I must go and see him. He wrote and told me he wanted to talk business. [*Goes out.*]

JULIA. Mr. Voynitsky, that barley you ordered—did you get it yesterday?

VOYNITSKY. Yes, thank you. What do I owe you? We had something from you in the spring as well, I don't remember what. We must settle up. I can't bear having my accounts in a mess or neglecting them.

JULIA. In the spring you had sixty-four bushels of rye, two heifers and one calf. And the people from your farm sent for some butter.

VOYNITSKY. Then what do I owe you?

JULIA. I can't tell you. Not without my counting frame.

VOYNITSKY. Well, I'll go and get it for you if you need it.

[*Goes out and returns at once with the counting frame.*]

ORLOVSKY. How's big brother Leo, my dear?

JULIA. Fine, thanks. I say, where did you buy that lovely tie?

ORLOVSKY. In town. At Kirpichov's.

JULIA. It's jolly nice. I must get one like that for Leo.

VOYNITSKY. Here's your counting frame.

[JULIA *sits down and rattles the beads on the frame.*]

ORLOVSKY. Leo should thank his lucky stars he has Julia to run the place. A tiny little thing, so small you can hardly see her, but look at the way she works! Not bad, eh?

THEODORE. While all he does is walk round clutching his cheek, the lazy so-and-so.

ORLOVSKY. My dearest beggar maid. Do you know, she goes round wearing an old-fashioned cloak? While I drive round the market on a Friday she walks about among the carts wearing this cloak.

JULIA. Now you've put me off.

VOYNITSKY. Let's go somewhere else, everybody. How about the ballroom? I'm fed up with being in here. [*Yawns.*]

ORLOVSKY. Whatever you say. I don't mind.

[*They go out through the door, left.*]

JULIA [*alone, after a pause*]. Theo's wearing Caucasian dress. That's what happens when parents don't discipline their children properly. He's the best-looking man in the county, he's clever, he's rich, but he's just no good. He's a complete ass. [*Rattles the counting frame.*]

[*Enter* SONYA.]

SCENE V

[JULIA *and* SONYA.]

SONYA. You here, Julia? I didn't know.

JULIA [*they kiss each other*]. Darling!

SONYA. What are you up to? Doing some sums? You look so efficient, I feel quite envious. My dear, why don't you get married?

JULIA. Oh, I don't know. Approaches have been made, but I've turned them down. No real man would ever want to marry me. [*Sighs.*] That's impossible.

SONYA. But why not?

JULIA. I'm uneducated. I was taken away from school in the second form, you know.

SONYA. Whatever for?

JULIA. I just wasn't any good.

[SONYA *laughs.*]

JULIA. Why do you laugh?

SONYA. I have a funny sort of feeling. I'm so happy today, oh so happy, I'm almost bored with my own happiness. I don't know what to do with myself. Well, come on, let's talk about something, shall we? Have you ever been in love?

[JULIA *nods her head.*]

SONYA. Really? With someone attractive?

[JULIA *whispers in her ear.*]

SONYA. Who? Theodore?

JULIA [*nods her head*]. And what about you?

SONYA. Yes, me too. Only not with Theodore. [*Laughs.*] Go on then, tell me more.

JULIA. I've wanted to talk to you for ages, Sonya.

SONYA. Well, carry on then.

JULIA. I want to clear things up. You see, I've always liked you. I've plenty of girl friends, but you're the nicest of the lot. If you asked me to give you ten horses or two hundred sheep, say, I'd be delighted. I'd do anything for you.

SONYA. But why be so embarrassed about it?

JULIA. I feel ashamed. I—like you so much. You're the nicest friend I have, you're not the least bit proud. What a lovely dress you're wearing!

SONYA. Let's leave my dress till later. Go on.

JULIA [*agitatedly*]. I don't know how to put it in clever language. May I propose to you—that you should make me happy. I mean, er, I mean—you must marry Leo. [*Covers her face.*]

SONYA [*getting up*]. Let's not say any more about that, Julia. Don't let's talk about it, please.

[HELEN *comes in.*]

SCENE VI

[*The above and* HELEN.]

HELEN. There's absolutely nowhere to go in this house. George and the two Orlovskys are wandering round and wherever I go I find them. It really is depressing. What do they want here? Why don't they go off somewhere?

JULIA [*through tears*]. Hallo, Helen. [*Is about to kiss her.*]

HELEN. Hallo, Julia. I'm sorry, I don't like kissing all the time. What's your father doing, Sonya? [*Pause.*] Sonya, why don't you answer me? I asked you what your father's doing. [*Pause.*] Why don't you answer me? Sonya!

SONYA. So you want to know, do you? Come here then. [*Takes her slightly to one side.*] All right, I'll tell you. I feel so honest today, I just can't keep up the usual pretence while talking to you. Here, take this. [*Hands over a letter.*] I found it in the garden. Come on, Julia. [*Goes out with* JULIA *through door, left.*]

SCENE VII

[HELEN *and—later—*THEODORE.]

HELEN [*alone*]. What's all this? A letter from George to me. But what have I done wrong? Why, how rude and heartless of her! She feels so honest that she can't talk to me. My God, what an insult! My head's going round, I think I'm going to faint.

THEODORE [*comes through the door, left, and starts crossing the stage*]. Why do you always shudder when you see me? [*Pause.*] H'm! [*Takes the letter out of her hands and tears it to pieces.*] You must give all this up. You must only think of me. [*Pause.*]

HELEN. What do you mean?

THEODORE. I mean that if I have my eye on a girl she doesn't get out of my clutches in a hurry.

HELEN. No, what you really mean is that you're stupid and insolent.

THEODORE. You'll wait for me by the bridge on the other side of the garden at half past seven this evening. All right? That's all I have to say. Till half past seven then, my angel. [*Tries to take her hand.*]

[HELEN *slaps his face.*]

THEODORE. You put it rather forcibly.

HELEN. Get out of here.

THEODORE. Very well then. [*Moves off and then comes back.*] I'm most touched. Let's discuss the thing calmly. You see, I've experienced everything in this world. I've even eaten goldfish soup a couple of times. But I've still never been up in a balloon or run off with the wife of a learned professor.

HELEN. Please go away.

THEODORE. Certainly, at once. I've experienced everything, that's why I'm so full of impudence I don't know what to do with it. Anyway, the point is, if you ever need a friend or a faithful hound, apply to me. My feelings have been profoundly touched.

HELEN. I don't require any hounds. Please go away.

THEODORE. All right. [*Deeply moved.*] Still, I'm very touched all the same. Of course I am. Yes indeed. [*Goes out hesitantly.*]

HELEN [*alone*]. I have a headache. Every night I have nightmares and I feel as if something terrible was going to happen. What a loathsome business, though. These young people were born here and brought up together, they're close friends, they're always embracing, and they ought to be on the best of terms. But they look ready to eat one another alive. The Wood-Demon's saving our forests, but what about people? There's no one to save them.

[*Moves off towards the door, left, but seeing* ZHELTUKHIN *and* JULIA *advancing to meet her goes out through the centre door.*]

SCENE VIII

[ZHELTUKHIN *and* JULIA.]

JULIA. How unlucky we are, Leo. Dear me, we are unlucky.

ZHELTUKHIN. But who asked you to speak to her? Who do you think you are, a village match-maker? Now you've spoilt everything. She'll think I can't speak up for myself and—and oh, how vulgar and provincial! I've told you a thousand times we ought to drop the whole thing. It brings nothing but humiliation and these hints of one kind and another. It's a dirty, rotten business. The old man must have guessed I'm in love with her and he's already taking advantage of my feelings. He'd like me to buy this estate from him.

JULIA. How much does he want for it?

ZHELTUKHIN. Sh! Someone's coming.

[*Enter through the door, left,* SEREBRYAKOV, ORLOVSKY *and* MRS. VOYNITSKY, *the last reading a pamphlet as she comes in.*]

SCENE IX

[*The above,* SEREBRYAKOV, ORLOVSKY *and* MRS. VOYNITSKY.]

ORLOVSKY. I don't feel too grand myself, old boy. I've had this head-ache for two days and I ache all over.

SEREBRYAKOV. But where are the others? I hate this house. It's such a labyrinth, twenty-six enormous rooms with people wandering off in all directions so you can never find anyone. [*Rings.*] Ask George and my wife to come here.

ZHELTUKHIN. Julia, you're not doing anything. Go and find George and Helen.

[JULIA *goes out.*]

SEREBRYAKOV. One can put up with ill health. What does it matter anyway? But what I can't stand is my present state of mind. I feel as if I was already dead or had left the earth entirely and got stuck on some strange planet.

ORLOVSKY. It all depends on your point of view.

MRS. VOYNITSKY [*reading*]. Give me a pencil, someone. Here's an-other contradiction, I must mark it.

ORLOVSKY. Here you are, dear madam. [*Gives her a pencil and kisses her hand.*]

[VOYNITSKY *comes in.*]

SCENE X

[*The above,* VOYNITSKY *and—later—*HELEN.]

VOYNITSKY. Do you want me?

SEREBRYAKOV. Yes I do, George.

VOYNITSKY. What exactly do you require of me?

SEREBRYAKOV. 'Require of you'? But what are you so annoyed about? [*Pause.*] If I've offended you somehow, please forgive me.

VOYNITSKY. Oh, don't be so pompous, and let's get down to busi-ness. What do you want?

[HELEN *comes in.*]

SEREBRYAKOV. Ah, here is Helen. Sit down, ladies and gentlemen. [*Pause.*] Ladies and gentlemen, I have invited you here to announce that a government inspector is on his way. Actually, joking apart, I do have something serious to say. I have gathered you all here to ask for your help and advice. And, aware as I am of your unfailing kindness, I trust I shall receive the same. I'm an academic person, a man of books, and I've always been out of my depth in practical affairs. I cannot manage without the guidance of competent persons, so I appeal to you, Orlovsky, to you, Zheltukhin, and to you, George. The thing is that *manet omnes una nox*. In other words none of us is going to live for ever. I'm old and ill, so it seems to me high time to put my property and affairs in order in so far as they affect my family. My own life is over and I'm not thinking of myself, but I do have a young wife and an unmarried daughter. They simply cannot go on living in the country.

HELEN. It makes no difference to me.

SEREBRYAKOV. We are not cut out for country life. But we can't live in town either on the income from this estate. The day before yesterday I sold some woodland for four thousand roubles, but that's an abnormal measure which can't be repeated every year. We must find some procedure that guarantees us a constant, more or less stable income. Such a procedure has occurred to me and I have the honour to submit it for your consideration. I'll leave out the details and explain it in general terms. Our estate gives an average return of no more than two per cent on its capital value. I propose we sell it. If we invest the proceeds in securities we should get from four to five per cent on them. There may even be a few thousand roubles to spare, so that we can buy a cottage near St. Petersburg.

VOYNITSKY. Just a moment. My ears must be deceiving me. Say that again.

SEREBRYAKOV. Invest the money in securities and buy a cottage near St. Petersburg.

VOYNITSKY. No, it wasn't the bit about St. Petersburg. It was something else you said.

SEREBRYAKOV. I propose selling the estate.

VOYNITSKY. Ah, that was it. You're going to sell the estate. Wonderful. A very bright idea. And what do you suggest my old mother and I should do with ourselves?

SEREBRYAKOV. We'll discuss that all in good time. One can't do everything at once.

VOYNITSKY. Just a moment. It looks as if I've never had a scrap of ordinary common sense. Till now I've been stupid enough to think this estate belonged to Sonya. This estate was bought by my father as a dowry for my sister. So far I've been simple-minded enough to imagine that our laws weren't made in Turkey and I thought the estate had passed from my sister to Sonya.

SEREBRYAKOV. Yes, the estate does belong to Sonya. Nobody denies that. Without Sonya's consent I shouldn't venture to sell it. What's more, I'm acting in the girl's own best interests.

VOYNITSKY. But this is fantastic, utterly fantastic. Either I've gone stark, staring mad or—. Or else——

MRS. VOYNITSKY. Don't contradict the professor, George. He knows better than we do what's right and what's wrong.

VOYNITSKY. Oh, give me some water. [*Drinks water.*] Say what you like then, I give up.

SEREBRYAKOV. I don't know why you're so worked up, George. I'm not claiming my scheme is ideal. If you all decide it's no good I shan't insist on it.

[DYADIN *comes in wearing a tail-coat, white gloves and a broad-brimmed top hat.*]

SCENE XI

[*The above and* DYADIN.]

DYADIN. A very good day to you all. Excuse me venturing in here unannounced. I'm guilty, but I deserve to be let off lightly as there wasn't a single domestic in your hall.

SEREBRYAKOV [*embarrassed*]. Delighted. Do come in.

DYADIN [*bowing and scraping*]. Professor Serebryakov! Dear ladies! My intrusion on these premises has a double motive. I am here in the first place to visit you, sir, and pay my humble respects. Secondly, I've come to invite you all on an expedition to my part of the world to celebrate this excellent weather. I live at the water-mill which I rent from our mutual friend, the Wood-Demon. It's a secluded and romantic spot where you can hear water-nymphs splashing about at night, and in the daytime——

VOYNITSKY. One moment, Waffles, this is serious. Hold it, you can tell us later. [*To* SEREBRYAKOV.] Here, ask him. This estate was bought from his uncle.

SEREBRYAKOV. Oh really, and why should I ask him? Where would that lead us?

VOYNITSKY. This estate was bought for ninety-five thousand roubles as prices went in those days. My father paid only seventy thousand down and left twenty-five thousand on mortgage. Now listen to me. The estate would never have been bought at all if I hadn't given up my own share of the inheritance to my sister, of whom I was very fond. What's more, I slaved away for ten years and paid off the whole mortgage.

ORLOVSKY. What are you getting at, old boy?

VOYNITSKY. This estate is free from debt and in good order solely through my own personal efforts. And now I've grown old I'm to be pitched out of it neck and crop!

SEREBRYAKOV. I don't know what you're getting at.

VOYNITSKY. For twenty-five years I've run this estate. I've worked and sent the money to you. The best manager in the world couldn't have done more. And all this time you haven't thanked me once. All this time, when I was young and just the same today, I've been getting a salary of five hundred roubles a year from you—a miserable pittance! And not once has it occurred to you to give me a single extra rouble.

SEREBRYAKOV. But how was I to know, George? I'm an unpractical person, I don't understand these things. You could have helped yourself to as much as you liked, couldn't you?

VOYNITSKY. Why didn't I steal, you mean? Why don't you all despise me for not stealing? It would have been only fair if I had, and I shouldn't be a pauper now.

MRS. VOYNITSKY [*sternly*]. George!

DYADIN [*agitatedly*]. Do stop it, Georgie, for heaven's sake. I'm trembling all over. Why spoil good relations? [*Kisses him.*] Please don't.

VOYNITSKY. For twenty-five years I've been cooped up in this place with her—with this mother of mine. All our thoughts and feelings were for you alone. In the daytime we talked of you and your writings, we were proud of your reputation and spoke your name with reverence. And we wasted our nights reading books and journals that I utterly despise.

DYADIN. Oh Georgie, stop it, please. I can't stand this.

SEREBRYAKOV. What are you driving at? That's what I don't see.

VOYNITSKY. We thought of you as a superior being and we knew your articles by heart. But now my eyes have been opened. Everything's perfectly clear. You write about art, but you haven't the faintest idea what art is all about. Your entire works, which once meant so much to me, aren't worth a brass farthing.

SEREBRYAKOV. My friends, can't you stop him? Really! I'll go away.

HELEN. George, I insist you keep quiet. Do you hear me?

VOYNITSKY. I will not keep quiet. [*Barring* SEREBRYAKOV's *way.*] Wait, I haven't finished yet. You've ruined my life! I've not lived— not lived, I tell you. Thanks to you the best years of my life have been thrown down the drain. You are my worst enemy!

DYADIN. I can't stand this—I really can't. I'm going into another room. [*Goes out of the door, right, in terrible agitation.*]

SEREBRYAKOV. What do you want from me? And what right have you to talk to me like that? Nonentity! If the estate is yours, take it. I don't want it.

ZHELTUKHIN [*aside*]. I say, the sparks are flying! I'm off. [*Goes.*]

HELEN. If you won't keep quiet I shall get out of this madhouse this instant. [*Shouting.*] I've had about as much as I can take.

VOYNITSKY. My life's ruined! I'm gifted, intelligent and courageous. If I'd had a normal life I might have been a Schopenhauer or a Dostoyevsky. But I'm talking nonsense, I'm going mad. Mother dear, I'm desperate. Mother!

MRS. VOYNITSKY. Do as the professor says.

VOYNITSKY. Mother! What am I to do? Never mind, don't tell me. I know what to do all right. [*To* SEREBRYAKOV.] I'll give you something to remember me by! [*Goes out through centre door.*]

[MRS. VOYNITSKY *follows him.*]

SEREBRYAKOV. Really, everybody, what on earth is all this? Rid me of this maniac!

ORLOVSKY. It's quite all right, Alexander, just let him simmer down a bit. And don't you get so worked up.

SEREBRYAKOV. I cannot live under the same roof with him. His room is here [*points to the centre door*], almost next to mine. Let him move into the village, into a cottage in the grounds, or I'll move out myself, but I can't stay here with him.

HELEN [*to her husband*]. If anything like this happens again I'm leaving.

SEREBRYAKOV. Oh, don't try and frighten me, please.

HELEN. I'm not trying to frighten anyone, but you all seem to have conspired to make my life hell. I shall go away.

SEREBRYAKOV. Everyone knows perfectly well that you're young and I'm old and that you're doing me a great favour by living here at all.

HELEN. Go on, finish what you have to say.

ORLOVSKY. Oh come, come, my friends——

[KHRUSHCHOV *comes in hurriedly*.]

SCENE XII

[*The above and* KHRUSHCHOV.]

KHRUSHCHOV [*agitatedly*]. Oh, I am glad to find you in, Professor. Sorry if I've come at the wrong time or am being a nuisance, but that's not the point. How are you?

SEREBRYAKOV. What exactly do you want?

KHRUSHCHOV. I'm sorry, I'm rather distraught. Been riding so fast. Professor, I hear you sold your woods to Kuznetzov for timber the day before yesterday. If this is true and not just a rumour, then I say, please don't do it.

HELEN. My husband isn't in the mood to talk business just now. Let's go into the garden.

KHRUSHCHOV. But I must talk about it now.

HELEN. As you wish. I can't cope with this. [*Goes out.*]

KHRUSHCHOV. Let me go over and see Kuznetsov. Let me tell him you've changed your mind. How about it? You're going to fell a thousand trees. And what are you destroying them for? Just for two or three thousand roubles to buy a few miserable dresses for your wife and indulge yourself in a little luxury! Why destroy them? So that posterity may curse us as a lot of savages? If you, a scholar and a distinguished man, can be so cruel, what about those who haven't your advantages? This is quite appalling.

ORLOVSKY. We can talk about it later, Michael.

SEREBRYAKOV. Come on, Orlovsky, we'll never hear the end of this.

KHRUSHCHOV [*barring* SEREBRYAKOV'*s way*]. In that case I'll tell you what, Professor. Hold off a bit, and I'll get some money and buy it myself in three months' time.

ORLOVSKY. I'm sorry, Michael, but this is decidedly odd. All right, we all know you're a man of principle. We thank you humbly and respect you for it. [*Bows.*] But why all the fuss?

KHRUSHCHOV [*flaring up*]. Hark at the universal uncle! There are plenty of easy-going people in this world, and that's always struck me as suspicious. Because why are they all so easy-going? It's just that they don't care.

ORLOVSKY. You came here to pick a quarrel, old boy, and that's rather a poor show. Principles are all right in their way, but you need this little gadget as well, old sport. [*Points to his heart.*] Without this little contraption, old boy, all your woods and your peat aren't worth a damn. Don't take it the wrong way, but you've got a lot to learn, dear me, you have.

SEREBRYAKOV [*brusquely*]. And another time be kind enough not to come in unannounced. I must also ask you to spare me these psychopathic outbursts. You've all been trying to make me lose my temper and you've finally succeeded. Be so good as to leave me alone. In my opinion this stuff about woods and peat is all sheer raving lunacy. Come on, Orlovsky. [*Goes out.*]

ORLOVSKY [*following him*]. That was a bit steep, Alexander. No need to be quite so outspoken. [*Goes out.*]

KHRUSHCHOV [*alone, after a pause*]. 'Raving lunacy.' So I'm a madman according to this distinguished academic figure. I bow to your professorial authority and I'm going straight home to shave my head. I must say, it's the earth itself that's mad for still putting up with us.

[*Goes quickly towards the door, right. Enter* SONYA *through the door, left, where she has been eavesdropping throughout the whole of* SCENE XII.]

SCENE XIII

[KHRUSHCHOV *and* SONYA.]

SONYA [*runs after him*]. Just a moment. I heard all that. Hurry up and say something or else I'll break down and say a thing or two myself.

KHRUSHCHOV. I've already said my piece. I begged your father to spare those trees. I know I was right, but he insulted me and called me a madman. All right then, I'm mad.

SONYA. Oh, don't go on like that, please.

KHRUSHCHOV. But those who hide their cruel, stony hearts behind a façade of learning, those who try to pass off their own insensitivity as the height of wisdom—they aren't mad, oh dear no! Nor, I suppose, are those who marry old men with the sole purpose of blatantly deceiving them and of buying themselves fashionable, elegant dresses on the proceeds of destroying our trees.

SONYA. Do listen to me, please. [*Presses his hands.*] Do let me tell you——

KHRUSHCHOV. That's quite enough of that. We've nothing in common. I know what you think of me already, and there's no place for me here any more. So good-bye. Our friendship has meant a lot to me and I'm sorry I shall now only be left with the memory of your father's gout and your remarks about my democratic sentiments. But that's not my fault. It's not I who——

[SONYA *weeps, covers her face and quickly goes out of the door, left.*]

KHRUSHCHOV. I was rash enough to fall in love here and that will be a lesson to me. I must get out of this dump.

[*Goes towards the door, right. Enter* HELEN *through the door, left.*]

SCENE XIV

[KHRUSHCHOV *and* HELEN.]

HELEN. Are you still here? Wait a moment. Mr. Orlovsky has just told me that my husband was rather sharp with you. I'm sorry, he's in a bad temper today and he didn't understand you. As for me, I'm entirely on your side. I think most highly of you, believe me, I really mean it. I sympathize with you and I feel for you, so allow me to offer you my sincere friendship. [*Holds out both her hands.*]

KHRUSHCHOV [*with aversion*]. Get away from me. I despise your friendship! [*Goes out.*]

HELEN [*alone, groans*]. What was that for? Why?

[*A shot is heard off stage.*]

SCENE XV

[HELEN, MRS. VOYNITSKY *and—later—*SONYA, SEREBRYAKOV, ORLOVSKY *and* ZHELTUKHIN. MRS. VOYNITSKY *staggers through the door, centre, shrieks and falls down in a faint.* SONYA *comes in and runs out through the door, centre.*]

SEREBRYAKOV.
ORLOVSKY.   } What's the matter?
ZHELTUKHIN.

[SONYA *is heard to scream. She comes back and shouts,* 'Uncle George has shot himself!' SONYA, ORLOVSKY, SEREBRYAKOV *and* ZHELTUKHIN *run out of the next door.*]

HELEN [*groans*]. What for? What ever for?

[DYADIN *appears in the doorway, right.*]

SCENE XVI

[HELEN, MRS. VOYNITSKY *and* DYADIN.]

DYADIN [*in the doorway*]. What's the matter?

HELEN [*to him*]. Take me away from here. Throw me off a precipice or kill me if you like, but I can't stay here any longer. Quickly, quickly—please! [*Goes out with* DYADIN.]

CURTAIN

ACT FOUR

The forest and the house by the mill which DYADIN *rents from* KHRUSHCHOV.

SCENE I

[HELEN *and* DYADIN *are sitting on a bench beneath a window.*]

HELEN. I wonder if you'd mind driving over to the post office again tomorrow.

DYADIN. Not in the slightest.

HELEN. I'll wait another three days. If my brother hasn't answered my letter by then I'll borrow some money from you and go to Moscow myself. After all I can't spend the rest of my life at your mill, can I?

DYADIN. No, of course not. [*Pause.*] It's not for me to advise you, dear lady, but all these letters and telegrams and my daily trips to the post office—well, they're all a waste of time, I'm sorry. Whatever your brother tells you, you'll still go back to your husband in the end.

HELEN. Oh no I shan't. Let's be rational, shall we? I don't love my husband. I did like those young people, but they've been unfair to me all along. So why should I go back? You'll say it's my duty. I know that all right, but I repeat, we must be rational. [*Pause.*]

DYADIN. Yes indeed. The great Russian poet Lomonosov ran away from Archangel Province to seek his fortune in Moscow. A fine thing to do, of course. But you—why did you run away? Quite frankly, there's no happiness for you in this world. A canary should sit in its cage and watch others being happy. It should stay put, in fact.

HELEN. Perhaps I'm not a cage-bird. Perhaps I'm free to fly where I like.

DYADIN. Don't you believe it. With due respects, you must expect to be judged by results like anyone else. This last fortnight another woman in your position might have popped up in a dozen different towns and had everyone running round in small circles, but you've only got as far as this mill and even that's been too much for you. Oh, come down to earth, can't you? You'll stay on here a bit till you've calmed down and then back you'll go to your husband. [*Pricks up his ears.*] I hear a carriage coming. [*Gets up.*]

HELEN. I'll go away.

DYADIN. I won't venture to impose on you further. I'll go into my mill and have a little snooze. I was up with the lark today.

HELEN. Come back here when you wake up and we'll have tea. [*Goes into the house.*]

DYADIN [*alone*]. If I lived somewhere with a bit of cultural life, I can see a caricature of myself appearing in a magazine. It could have a most amusing satirical caption. Just think of someone as old and unattractive as me running off with the young wife of a distinguished professor. Charming! [*Goes out.*]

SCENE II

[SIMON, *carrying buckets, and* JULIA, *coming in.*]

JULIA. Good afternoon, Simon. Nice to see you. Is Mr. Dyadin in?

SIMON. Yes, he's down at the mill.

JULIA. Would you mind calling him?

SIMON. Not at all, miss. [*Goes out.*]

JULIA [*alone*]. He's probably having a nap. [*Sits down on the bench beneath the window and gives a deep sigh.*] Some of them sleep, others enjoy themselves, but I'm run off my feet all day long. Ah well, no peace for the wicked. [*Gives an even deeper sigh.*] Heavens, how can anyone be as stupid as old Waffles? I was driving past his barn just now and a little black pig came out of the door. If other people's pigs start getting at his corn sacks it will just serve him right. [DYADIN *comes in.*]

SCENE III

[JULIA *and* DYADIN.]

DYADIN [*putting on a frock-coat*]. Is that you, Julia? Excuse my *déshabillé*, I was going to rest awhile in the arms of Morpheus.

JULIA. How are you?

DYADIN. I'm sorry I can't ask you in, the house isn't tidy and all that. Would you care to come over to the mill?

JULIA. No, I'm all right here for a bit. Let me tell you why I came. Leo and the professor have decided on an outing and they'd like to picnic at your mill this afternoon.

DYADIN. Delighted.

JULIA. I've come on ahead. The others will be here soon. Could you have a table brought out—oh, and a samovar too of course? And would you mind telling Simon to get the picnic baskets out of my carriage?

DYADIN. Very well. [*Pause.*] Well, what news? How are things?

JULIA. Bad. I'm sick with worry, I can tell you. You know the professor and Sonya are staying with us now, don't you?

DYADIN. Yes.

JULIA. They can't bear their own house since George's suicide. They were scared. It wasn't too bad during the day, but at night they all used to sit huddled in one room till dawn, terrified of George's ghost appearing in the dark.

DYADIN. That's all superstition. Do they ever mention Helen?

JULIA. Of course they do. [*Pause.*] She's cleared out.

DYADIN. Yes, it's a subject worthy of the brush of Ayvazovsky. She just cleared out.

JULIA. And now no one knows where she is. Perhaps she's gone away or perhaps she was desperate enough to——

DYADIN. God is merciful, my dear. It'll be all right.

[KHRUSHCHOV *comes in carrying a portfolio and a drawing-case.*]

SCENE IV

[*The above and* KHRUSHCHOV.]

KHRUSHCHOV. Hey! Is anyone here? Simon!

DYADIN. Try looking this way.

KHRUSHCHOV. Ah! Good afternoon, Julia.

JULIA. Good afternoon.

KHRUSHCHOV. Well, I came out here to do some work again, Dyadin. I don't feel like staying at home. Would you ask them to put my table under this tree the way I had it yesterday, and tell them to have two lamps ready? It's getting dark.

DYADIN. At your service, sir. [*Goes out.*]

KHRUSHCHOV. How are you, Julia?

JULIA. Oh, all right. [*Pause.*]

KHRUSHCHOV. The Serebryakovs are staying with you, aren't they?

JULIA. Yes.

KHRUSHCHOV. H'm! And what's brother Leo up to?

JULIA. He stays at home, spends his time with Sonya.

KHRUSHCHOV. I'll bet he does. [*Pause.*] Why doesn't he marry the girl?

JULIA. Why indeed? [*Sighs.*] I only wish he would. He's educated, he's a gentleman, and she comes of a good family too. I've always wanted it.

KHRUSHCHOV. She's a fool.

JULIA. Don't say such things.

KHRUSHCHOV. And your Leo's a bright specimen, I must say. You and your friends are a pretty prize collection one way and another. Quite a glut of intellect there, and no mistake.

JULIA. You must have missed your lunch today.

KHRUSHCHOV. Oh? Why?

JULIA. You're in such a bad temper.

[DYADIN *and* SIMON *come in carrying a small table.*]

SCENE V

[*The above,* DYADIN *and* SIMON.]

DYADIN. You do know how to look after yourself, Michael. You've picked a splendid place to work. It's an oasis. Yes, I mean it. Can't you see yourself surrounded by palm trees? Julia's a gentle doe, you're a lion and I'm a tiger.

KHRUSHCHOV. You're a very nice fellow, Dyadin, but why carry on like this? These sugary words, all this foot-scraping and shoulder-twitching—anyone who didn't know you wouldn't take you for a human being at all. Devil knows what he'd think of you. Pity.

DYADIN. It must be the way I'm made. Such are the dictates of destiny.

KHRUSHCHOV. There you go again, 'dictates of destiny'. Can't you drop that stuff? [*Pins a chart on the table.*] I think I'll stay the night here.

DYADIN. Delighted. You're in a bad temper, but I feel inexpressibly cheerful as though there was a dear little bird inside me singing a song.

KHRUSHCHOV. Well, make the most of it. [*Pause.*] You may have a dear little bird inside you. I haven't. Quite the opposite in fact. It's been just one damn thing after another. Shimansky's sold his wood for timber for a start. And then Helen's run away from her husband and no one knows where she's got to. And thirdly, I feel I'm becoming stupider, cheaper and more second-rate every day. There was something I wanted to tell you yesterday, but couldn't—couldn't pluck up the courage. You may congratulate me. George's diary turned up after his death. Mr. Orlovsky got hold of it first and I went over there and read it a dozen times.

JULIA. Yes, we read it too.

KHRUSHCHOV. George's affair with Helen had the entire district buzzing like a hive, but it turns out the whole story was a filthy pack of lies. I believed it and joined in the general mud-slinging—the hatred, the contempt, the insults.

DYADIN. That was very wrong of course.

KHRUSHCHOV. I first heard it from your brother, Julia. A prize specimen I am! I don't think much of your brother, but I believed him rather than Helen, though I only had to open my eyes to see how unselfishly she was behaving. I'd rather believe evil than good and I can't see further than the end of my own nose, which means I'm just as second-rate as the rest of them.

DYADIN [*to* JULIA]. Let's go down to the mill, child, and leave our bad-tempered friend to his work while we amuse ourselves. Come on. And you do your work, Michael. [*Goes out with* JULIA.]

KHRUSHCHOV [*alone, mixes some paint in a saucer*]. One night I saw him press his face against her hand. There's a detailed description of that night in his diary, how I came in and what I said. He quotes my words, calls me a narrow-minded fool. [*Pause.*] This colour's too dark. Must get it lighter. Then he blames Sonya for loving me. She never loved me. Now I've made a blot. [*Scrapes the paper with a knife.*] Even supposing there was something in it, there's no point in thinking about that now. It began and ended in foolishness. [SIMON *and some workmen bring in a large table.*] What are you doing? What's that for?

SIMON. Mr. Dyadin's orders. The ladies and gentlemen from the Zheltukhin estate are going to have tea here.

KHRUSHCHOV. Oh, that's just wonderful. So there's no point in me bothering about my work any more. I'll pack up and go home.

[ZHELTUKHIN *comes in with* SONYA *on his arm.*]

SCENE VI

[KHRUSHCHOV, ZHELTUKHIN *and* SONYA.]

ZHELTUKHIN [*sings*]. 'Against my will to these sad shores
                 An unknown force has drawn me.'

KHRUSHCHOV. Who's there? Oh! [*Hurriedly puts his drawing materials away in their cases.*]

ZHELTUKHIN. One more question, Sonya. Do you remember lunching with us on my birthday? You thought I looked funny, didn't you? You laughed at me.

SONYA. Oh, please stop it. How can you? I wasn't laughing at anything in particular.

ZHELTUKHIN [*catching sight of* KHRUSHCHOV]. I say, who's this I see? You here as well? Hallo.

KHRUSHCHOV. Hallo.

ZHELTUKHIN. Working? Splendid. Where's Waffles?

KHRUSHCHOV. Over there.

ZHELTUKHIN. Where's over there?

KHRUSHCHOV. I should have thought I'd made myself clear. Over there at the mill.

ZHELTUKHIN. I must go and call him. [*Goes off singing.*] 'Against my will to these sad shores—' [*Goes out.*]

SONYA. Good afternoon.

KHRUSHCHOV. Good afternoon. [*Pause.*]

SONYA. What are you drawing?

KHRUSHCHOV. Oh, nothing of any interest.

SONYA. Is it a plan?

KHRUSHCHOV. No, it's a map of the forests in our district. I made it. [*Pause.*] The green colouring shows the forests of our grandfathers' time and before. Light green shows where they've been felled during the last twenty-five years—oh, and the blue shows where they're still standing. Yes. [*Pause.*] Well now, how are you? Happy?

SONYA. This is no time to think about happiness.

KHRUSHCHOV. Then what should we think about?

SONYA. That's what caused the tragedy, thinking too much about happiness.

KHRUSHCHOV. Just as you say. [*Pause.*]

SONYA. It's an ill wind that blows nobody any good. Misfortune has taught me to forget my own happiness and think only of others. Life should be an act of constant self-sacrifice.

KHRUSHCHOV. As you say. [*Pause.*] Mrs. Voynitsky's son shot himself. But she's still chasing contradictions in her wretched pamphlets. You've had a ghastly experience, and now you try to cripple your whole life, and call that self-sacrifice—which is just pandering to your own vanity. Everyone's heartless. You are. And so am I. All the wrong things are done and everything's going to rack and ruin. I'm just off, I don't want to be in the way of you ánd Zheltukhin. But why the tears? I wasn't trying to make you cry.

SONYA. Never mind, it doesn't matter. [*Wipes her eyes.*]

[*Enter* JULIA, DYADIN *and* ZHELTUKHIN.]

SCENE VII

[*The above,* JULIA, DYADIN *and* ZHELTUKHIN, *then—later—* SEREBRYAKOV *and* ORLOVSKY.]

SEREBRYAKOV [*off stage*]. Hallo there! Where are you all?

SONYA [*shouts*]. We're here, Father.

DYADIN. They're bringing the samovar. Charming. [*He and* JULIA *attend to the table.*]

[SEREBRYAKOV *and* ORLOVSKY *come in.*]

SONYA. This way, Father.

SEREBRYAKOV. All right, I can see you.

ZHELTUKHIN [*in a loud voice*]. Ladies and gentlemen, I declare the meeting open. Take out the cork, Waffles.

KHRUSHCHOV [*to* SEREBRYAKOV]. Let's forget what happened, shall we? [*Holds out his hand.*] Forgive me, please.

SEREBRYAKOV. Thank you, only too delighted. And you must forgive me. When I tried to think about that business next day and remembered what we said, I felt very bad about it. Let's be friends. [*Takes him by the arm and goes to the table.*]

ORLOVSKY. This was long overdue, old boy. A bad peace is better than a good war.

DYADIN. I am indeed happy, sir, that you have honoured my oasis with a visit. It gives me more pleasure than I can say.

SEREBRYAKOV. Thank you, my dear sir. It's really lovely out here, an oasis indeed.

ORLOVSKY. You're fond of nature, are you?

SEREBRYAKOV. Very much so. [*Pause.*] Well, come on, all of you, don't let the conversation flag. In our position it's best to keep talking. We've got to face up to our misfortunes. I'm putting a better face on things than all of you just because I'm the most unfortunate of us all.

JULIA. I say, I'm not giving you any sugar, you must all have jam with your tea.

DYADIN [*bustling about among his guests*]. I'm delighted, delighted.

SEREBRYAKOV. Recently, Michael, I've had so much to put up with and I've thought so many thoughts, I could probably write a whole treatise on the art of living for the benefit of posterity. One's never too old to learn. Misfortune is a great teacher.

DYADIN. Let bygones be bygones. With God's mercy it will turn out all right.

[SONYA *gives a start.*]

ZHELTUKHIN. What made you jump like that?

SONYA. I heard someone shout.

DYADIN. It's some of the locals catching crayfish in the river. [*Pause.*]

ZHELTUKHIN. Didn't we agree to spend the evening as if nothing had happened? Yet there's a feeling of tension somehow.

DYADIN. I revere scholarship, sir, and even have a kind of family feeling for it. My brother Gregory's wife's brother, a Mr. Konstantin Novosyolov—you may possibly know him—held a master's degree in foreign literature.

SEREBRYAKOV. I don't know him, but I know of him. [*Pause.*]

JULIA. It's exactly a fortnight since George died.

KHRUSHCHOV. Don't let's talk about it, please.

SEREBRYAKOV. Well come on, don't be downhearted.

ZHELTUKHIN. All the same, there is a feeling of tension somehow.

SEREBRYAKOV. Nature abhors a vacuum. She robbed me of two dear ones, but soon sent some new friends along to fill the gap. Your health, Zheltukhin.

ZHELTUKHIN. Thank you, Professor. Permit me in turn to drink to your fruitful academic work.

> 'Scatter the seed for a harvest of kindliness,
> Reason and goodness—and Russia will gratefully
> Offer her thanks.'

SEREBRYAKOV. I appreciate the compliment. I sincerely hope our friendship will ripen in the not too distant future.

[THEODORE *comes in.*]

SCENE VIII

[*The above and* THEODORE.]

THEODORE. So that's what's going on. A picnic.

ORLOVSKY. My dear boy—you handsome fellow, you.

THEODORE. Good evening, all. [*Kisses* SONYA *and* JULIA.]

ORLOVSKY. It's a whole fortnight since we met. What have you been up to, eh?

THEODORE. I've just been over to Leo's place and they told me you were here, so I drove out.

ORLOVSKY. Where did you get to all this time?

THEODORE. I haven't slept for three nights. I lost five thousand roubles at cards last night, Father. I've been drinking and gambling, and made half a dozen trips to town. I've gone completely off my rocker.

ORLOVSKY. Good for you! I daresay you're a bit drunk now, eh?

THEODORE. Not on your life. Julia! Tea, girl! But I'd like it on the tart side with a bit of lemon in it. What price old George, eh? Going and putting a bullet through his head like that. And what possessed him to use a French revolver? Wasn't a Smith and Wesson good enough?

KHRUSHCHOV. Hold your tongue, you swine.

THEODORE. I may be a swine, but I'm a pedigree animal. [*Strokes his beard.*] My beard alone is worth a fortune. Yes, I'm a swine, a fool, a scoundrel. But if I said the word, any young woman would marry me like a shot. Sonya, marry me. [*To* KHRUSHCHOV.] All right, I'm sorry. *Pardonnez-moi*, I'm sure.

KHRUSHCHOV. Oh, stop fooling around.

JULIA. You're hopeless, Theo. You're the worst drunkard and spend-thrift in the county. Just look at you. You're pathetic. You're the absolute limit, you wicked, wicked man.

THEODORE. Oh, don't be such a spoil-sport. Come and sit next to me. That's right. I'll come and stay with you for a fortnight. Must get some rest. [*Kisses her.*]

JULIA. You ought to be ashamed of yourself. You should comfort your father in his old age and you only disgrace him. It's a crazy way to carry on, that's all I can say.

THEODORE. I'm giving up drinking. I'm finished with that. [*Pours himself a drink.*] Is this plum wine or cherry?

JULIA. Don't drink it. Leave it alone.

THEODORE. I'm allowed one glass. [*Drinks.*] I'll give you a pair of horses and a gun, Mr. Wood-Demon. I'm going to stay at Julia's, going to spend a fortnight over there.

KHRUSHCHOV. A spot of corrective detention is more what you need.

JULIA. Come on, drink your tea, do.

DYADIN. Have some biscuits with it.

ORLOVSKY [*to* SEREBRYAKOV]. You know, old man, I lived just like young Theodore till I was forty. I once started counting how many women I'd made unhappy in my life and I got as far as seventy, old boy, and then stopped counting. Yes indeed. But something sud-denly came over me at the age of forty, old boy. I felt depressed and out of things. In fact I felt terribly mixed up inside, and that was that.

I tried everything—reading, work, travel—but it was no good. Anyway, old boy, I once went to see an old pal of mine who's not with us any longer, Prince Dmitry Pavlovich. We had dinner, hors d'œuvres and all that, and instead of a nap afterwards we laid on some target practice outside. There were masses of people there, friend Waffles among them.

DYADIN. Indeed I was, I haven't forgotten.

ORLOVSKY. You know, I felt absolutely miserable, my God I did! I couldn't stand it. I suddenly burst into tears, staggered and bellowed across the yard at the top of my voice, 'Good people, my friends, forgive me in the name of Christ!' And all at once I began to feel kind, pure and warm inside. And ever since then, old boy, I've been the happiest man in these parts. You ought to try it yourself.

SEREBRYAKOV. Try what?

[*A glow appears in the sky.*]

ORLOVSKY. Do the same as me. Surrender. Capitulate.

SEREBRYAKOV. A fine piece of homespun philosophy. You're telling me to apologize. Why should I? Let other people apologize to me.

SONYA. But it's *we* who're at fault, Father.

SEREBRYAKOV. Is it? At the moment you're all thinking of my attitude to my wife, I presume. Do you really think that's my fault? Why, that's absurd, you know. She's neglected her duty and left me just when I most needed her.

KHRUSHCHOV. Listen to me, Serebryakov. For twenty-five years you've been a professor and done academic work while I've planted trees and practised medicine. But what's the point of these things, and who gets anything out of them, if we're not kind to those we're working for? We say we're serving humanity, while all the time we're callously wrecking each other's lives. For instance, did you or I do anything to save George? Where's your wife, whom we've all insulted? Where's your peace of mind and your daughter's? Everything's gone to rack and ruin, it's all going to blazes. You people call me a wood-demon, but I'm not the only one, you know. You've all got a demon inside you, and you're all wandering in a dark wood and feeling your way. You're all just about bright enough, and have just about enough sense, to ruin your own and other people's lives.

[HELEN *comes out of the house and sits on the bench beneath the window.*]

SCENE IX

[*The above and* HELEN.]

KHRUSHCHOV. I thought I was a man of integrity and understanding, when I couldn't forgive anyone the slightest mistake, believed in gossip and joined in the general mud-slinging. And then when your wife sincerely offered me her friendship, I came down on her like a ton of hot bricks—told her to leave me alone, said I despised her friendship. That's what I'm like. There's a demon inside me, and I'm narrow-minded, blind, second-rate, but you're not all that wonderful yourself, Professor. Meanwhile everyone round here thinks I'm a hero and a man of the future. All the women certainly think so. And your name's a byword throughout Russia. Now if my sort are seriously taken for heroes and your sort are seriously regarded as celebrities—well, all I can say is we *are* in a bad way, and we haven't any real heroes or brilliant men or anyone else to lead us out of this dark wood and put right the damage we do. There are no really first-class people with a genuine right to fame and honour——

SEREBRYAKOV. I'm very sorry, I didn't come here to cross swords with you or defend my claims to distinction.

ZHELTUKHIN. We might change the subject anyway, Michael.

KHRUSHCHOV. I'll be through in a moment and then I'll go. All right, I'm not much good, but you're no great shakes yourself, Professor. And George, who couldn't find anything better to do than put a bullet through his brains, he wasn't up to much either. You're none of you very much good if it comes to that. And the women——

HELEN [*interrupting*]. And the women are no better. [*Approaches the table.*] There was a woman called Helen who left her husband, but will she make any use of her freedom? Don't worry, she'll be back. [*Sits down at the table.*] In fact here I am.

[*General consternation.*]

DYADIN [*with a loud laugh*]. Charming! Now, everybody, let me say a word before you all shout 'Off with his head!' Professor, it was I who ran off with your wife, as a certain Paris once carried off Helen of Troy. Yes, I did it. True, you don't get pock-marked Parises, but there are more things in heaven and earth, Horatio, than are dreamt of in your philosophy.

KHRUSHCHOV. I don't get this. Can it really be you, Helen?

HELEN. Yes, I've been staying here for the last fortnight. Well, why do you all stare at me like that? How are you all? I was sitting by the window and I could hear everything you said. [*Embraces* SONYA.] Let's be friends again. How are you, dear? Do let's be friends.

DYADIN [*rubbing his hands*]. Charming!

HELEN [*to* KHRUSHCHOV]. Michael! [*Holds out her hand.*] Can't we let bygones be bygones? How are you, Theodore? Julia——

ORLOVSKY. My dear old girl, dear wife of our dear professor, you glorious, beautiful creature. She's returned, she's come back to us.

HELEN. I've missed you all so much. Hallo, Alexander. [*Holds out her hand to her husband, who turns away.*] Alexander!

SEREBRYAKOV. You've neglected your duty.

HELEN. Alexander!

SEREBRYAKOV. I won't deny I'm glad to see you and I'm quite willing to talk to you—but at home, not here. [*Moves away from the table.*]

ORLOVSKY. Alexander! [*Pause.*]

HELEN. I see. So the solution to our problem is a very simple one. It hasn't got a solution. Oh, all right then. I admit I don't count for very much. My happiness is that of a cage-bird, the sort of happiness suitable for a woman. That means being cooped up at home for the rest of my life, eating, drinking, sleeping and listening every day to people going on about their gout, and about their merits and their rights. Why do you all look away? You're not embarrassed, are you? How about a glass of wine? Oh, come on!

DYADIN. It will turn out all right in the end. Everything's going to be fine.

THEODORE [*approaches* SEREBRYAKOV, *agitatedly*]. I feel very much moved. Do be kind to your wife, say something nice to her, and on my word of honour you can count on my loyalty and friendship for the rest of my life. I'll present you with my best troika.

SEREBRYAKOV. Thank you, but I'm afraid I don't quite understand.

THEODORE. So you don't understand, eh? One day on my way back from a shooting trip I saw a brown owl in a tree, so I loosed off at him with small shot. He stayed put, so I let him have a charge of buck-shot. And he didn't budge an inch, there was absolutely nothing doing. Just sat there blinking.

SEREBRYAKOV. What was all that directed at?

THEODORE. A brown owl. [*Goes back to the table.*]

ORLOVSKY [*pricks up his ears*]. Just a moment, everyone. Quiet, please. I think I hear bells, it must be a fire-alarm.

THEODORE [*spotting the glow in the sky*]. I say! Take a look at the sky. See that glow?

ORLOVSKY. Good heavens, while we're sitting here and missing it all!

DYADIN. Pretty good, eh?

THEODORE. Phew, I say! Quite a display! It's near Alekseyevskoye.

KHRUSHCHOV. No, Alekseyevskoye must be further to the right. It's more likely Novo-Petrovskoye.

JULIA. How awful! I'm scared of fires.

KHRUSHCHOV. Yes, of course it's Novo-Petrovskoye.

DYADIN [*shouts*]. Simon, run along to the weir and see if you can tell where the fire is. You might be able to see from there.

SIMON [*shouts*]. It's the Telibeyev Woods.

DYADIN. What?

SIMON. The Telibeyev Woods.

DYADIN. The woods——.

[*A lengthy pause.*]

KHRUSHCHOV. I must get along there to the fire. Good-bye. I'm sorry I was so rude, but I've never felt quite so depressed in my life. Things have really got me down. Anyway, what does that matter? A man should stand on his own feet, and I shan't shoot myself or throw myself under the mill-wheel. I may not be much of a hero, but I'll be one some day, I'll grow an eagle's wings and I shan't fear that glow in the sky or the devil himself. Let the woods burn. I'll plant new ones, and if the one I love won't have me I'll find myself another. [*Rushes out.*]

HELEN. Good for him!

ORLOVSKY. Yes, indeed. 'If the one I love won't have me I'll find myself another.' Now I wonder what he meant by that pronouncement.

SONYA. Take me away, I want to go home.

SEREBRYAKOV. Yes, it is time we went, it's impossibly damp out here. My rug and overcoat must be somewhere around.

ZHELTUKHIN. Your rug's in the carriage and your overcoat's here. [*Gives him the overcoat.*]

SONYA [*in great agitation*]. Take me away, for heaven's sake.

ZHELTUKHIN. At your service.

SONYA. No, I'll go with my godfather. Please take me with you, Godfather.

ORLOVSKY. Come on then, girl, come on. [*Helps her on with her coat.*]

ZHELTUKHIN [*aside*]. Damnation! This is all so sordid and degrading.

[THEODORE *and* JULIA *pack the crockery and napkins in a basket.*]

SEREBRYAKOV. I've got a pain in my left foot, it must be rheumatism. That means another sleepless night.

HELEN [*buttoning up her husband's overcoat*]. Mr. Dyadin, would you bring me my hat and cape from the house, please?

DYADIN. Certainly. [*Goes into the house and comes back with her hat and cape.*]

ORLOVSKY. So you're scared of the fire, are you, girl? Don't be afraid, it's not so bad as it was. It'll soon be out.

JULIA. We've left half a jar of cherry jam. Oh well, Mr. Dyadin can have it. [*To her brother.*] Take the basket please, Leo.

HELEN. I'm ready. [*To her husband.*] Come on then, carry me off like the statue of the Commendatore in *Don Giovanni* and let's go to hell together in your twenty-six gloomy rooms. That's all I'm good for.

SEREBRYAKOV. 'Statue of the Commendatore.' I might find the comparison more amusing were it not for the pain in my foot. [*To the whole company.*] Good-bye, everyone, and thank you for your hospitality and pleasant company. It's been a wonderful evening, the tea was excellent and everything in the garden's lovely. But there's one thing I can't accept, I'm sorry, and that's all this hedgerow philosophy and your general attitude. What we need, ladies and gentlemen, is action. We can't go on like this. We must *do* things, indeed we must. Good-bye. [*Goes out with his wife.*]

THEODORE [*to* JULIA]. Come on, my little beggar maid. [*To his father.*] Good-bye, Your Reverence. [*Goes out with* JULIA.]

ZHELTUKHIN [*following them, carrying the basket*]. This basket's heavy, damn it. How I hate picnics! [*Goes out and shouts off stage.*] Drive up there, Aleksey.

SCENE X

[ORLOVSKY, SONYA and DYADIN.]

ORLOVSKY [*to* SONYA]. Well, what are you waiting for? Come on, my pet. [*Moves off with* SONYA.]

DYADIN [*aside*]. And nobody said good-bye to me. Charming! [*Puts out the candles.*]

ORLOVSKY [*to* SONYA]. What's the matter?

SONYA. I just can't move. I feel too weak. I'm desperate, completely desperate. I'm so utterly miserable.

ORLOVSKY [*alarmed*]. What's all this? My pretty darling——

SONYA. Let's stay here a bit.

ORLOVSKY. First it's take me away, then it's stay here a bit. I can't make you out.

SONYA. I've lost all my happiness here today. Oh, I do feel awful. Why, oh why, am I still alive? [*Embraces him.*] Oh, if you only knew, if you did but know.

ORLOVSKY. You need a drink of water. Come and sit down. Come on.

DYADIN. What's the matter? Sonya, my dear, this is awful, I'm all of a dither. [*Tearfully.*] I can't bear to see you like this. My child——

SONYA [*to* DYADIN]. Please take me to the fire. Please!

ORLOVSKY. What do you want at the fire? What can you do there?

SONYA. For goodness' sake take me, or I'll go on my own. I'm desperate. I'm so unhappy, so unbearably unhappy. Take me to the fire.

[KHRUSHCHOV *rushes in.*]

SCENE XI

[*The above and* KHRUSHCHOV.]

KHRUSHCHOV [*shouts*]. I say, Dyadin!

DYADIN. I'm here. What do you want?

KHRUSHCHOV. I can't walk all that way. Can you let me have a horse?

SONYA [*noticing* KHRUSHCHOV, *gives a happy shout*]. Michael! [*Goes towards him.*] Michael! [*To* ORLOVSKY.] Go away please, I must talk to him. [*To* KHRUSHCHOV.] Michael, you said you'd find someone else. [*To* ORLOVSKY.] Do go away, please. [*To* KHRUSHCHOV.] Well, I *am* someone else now. I only want the truth—the truth and nothing but the truth. I love you, I love you. I love you.

ORLOVSKY. So that's the reason for all this coming and going. [*Gives a loud laugh.*]

DYADIN. Charming!

SONYA [*to* ORLOVSKY]. Please go away. [*To* KHRUSHCHOV.] Yes, yes, the truth and nothing but the truth. Speak to me, for heaven's sake, I've said all I have to say.

KHRUSHCHOV [*embracing her*]. My darling.

SONYA. Don't go away now, Godfather. Michael, when you tried to tell me you loved me I was so happy I could hardly breathe, but I had all those absurd prejudices. And what stopped me telling you how I really felt? Why, the same thing that stops Father from smiling at Helen now. Now I'm free——

ORLOVSKY [*laughs*]. Journeys end in lovers' meetings. So you're safe on shore at last. I have the honour to congratulate you. [*Bows low.*] Oh, you naughty, naughty children—the way you've dragged the thing out, chasing each other up hill and down dale.

DYADIN [*embracing* KHRUSHCHOV]. You've made me very happy, my dear fellow.

ORLOVSKY [*embracing and kissing* SONYA]. My little canary, darling Sonya. [SONYA *laughs.*] I say, she's off again.

KHRUSHCHOV. I'm in a complete daze, I'm sorry. Let me have another word with her. Please don't get in our way. Do go away, please.

[THEODORE *and* JULIA *come in.*]

SCENE XII

[*The above,* THEODORE *and* JULIA.]

JULIA. But you're always talking nonsense, Theo, you never do anything else.

ORLOVSKY. Sh! Be quiet, children. My son's coming, the young bandit. Hurry up, everybody, let's hide somewhere. Come on.

[ORLOVSKY, DYADIN, KHRUSHCHOV and SONYA *hide*.]

THEODORE. I left my whip somewhere round here, and a glove.

JULIA. But you're always talking nonsense.

THEODORE. Well, what if I am? I don't want to go over to your place just yet. Let's have a stroll and then drive over.

JULIA. Oh, you are a nuisance, you're the absolute limit. [*Claps her hands together.*] I say, isn't old Waffles an ass? He hasn't even cleared the table. Someone might have stolen the samovar. Oh, Waffles, Waffles, he seems quite old, but he's got no more sense than he was born with.

DYADIN [*aside*]. Thank you.

JULIA. I heard someone laughing as we were coming along.

THEODORE. It's some of the local women bathing. [*Picks up a glove.*] Somebody's glove. It's Sonya's. I don't know what's bitten Sonya today. She's in love with the Wood-Demon. She's quite crazy about him and the silly chump can't see it.

JULIA [*angrily*]. But where are you taking me?

THEODORE. To the weir. Let's go for a walk, it's the prettiest spot in the whole neighbourhood. Beautiful!

ORLOVSKY [*aside*]. That's my own boy, the handsome devil, with that whacking great beard of his——

JULIA. I heard someone speak just then.

THEODORE. 'Oh wondrous spot, wood-demons' haunt,
　　　　　Where water-nymphs sit in the trees.'
That's the way of it, old man. [*Claps her on the shoulder.*]

JULIA. I'm not an old man.

THEODORE. Let's talk things over calmly. Listen. I've been through hell and high water. I'm thirty-five and I've no position in life except that of lieutenant in the Serbian Army and sergeant of the Russian reserve. I'm neither one thing nor the other. I must turn over a new leaf, and, well, I've got the crazy idea, you see, that if I marry my whole life will be different. So will you marry me, eh? You're the girl for me.

JULIA [*embarrassed*]. H'm. Well, you see—. Hadn't you better mend your ways first?

THEODORE. Oh come on, don't beat about the bush! Say yes or no.

JULIA. I'm too embarrassed. [*Looks round.*] Wait a moment, someone might come in or overhear us. I think Waffles is looking through the window.

THEODORE. There's nobody there.

JULIA [*throws her arms round his neck*]. Theo!

[SONYA *laughs*. ORLOVSKY, DYADIN *and* KHRUSHCHOV *laugh, clap their hands and shout*, 'Hurrah! Well done!']

THEODORE. Gosh! You frightened us. Where have you sprung from?

SONYA. Congratulations, Julia. And you can say the same to me.

[*Laughter, kisses, noise.*]

DYADIN. Charming, charming!

CURTAIN

PLATONOV

(?1880–1881)

CHARACTERS

ANNA VOYNITSEV, a general's young widow

SERGEY VOYNITSEV, General Voynitsev's son by his first marriage

SONYA, his wife

PORFIRY GLAGOLYEV ⎫
CYRIL, his son ⎪ landowners,
GERASIM PETRIN ⎬ neighbours of the
PAUL SHCHERBUK ⎭ Voynitsevs

MARY GREKOV, a girl of 20

IVAN TRILETSKY, a retired colonel

NICHOLAS, his son, a young doctor

ABRAHAM VENGEROVICH, a rich Jew

ISAAC, his son, a student

TIMOTHY BUGROV, a businessman

MICHAEL PLATONOV, a village schoolmaster

SASHA, his wife, daughter of Ivan Triletsky

OSIP, a horse thief, aged about 30

MARKO, a court messenger, a little old man

VASILY ⎫
JACOB ⎬ servants of the Voynitsevs
KATYA ⎭

Guests and servants

The action takes place on the Voynitsevs' estate in the south of European Russia

ACT ONE

The VOYNITSEVS' *drawing-room. A french window opening on the garden and two doors leading to other rooms. Mixed modern and antique furniture. A grand piano. Near it a music-stand with a violin and some music. A harmonium. Pictures (oleographs) in gilt frames.*

SCENE I

[ANNA *sits at the piano, head bent over the keys.* NICHOLAS *comes in.*]

NICHOLAS [*goes up to* ANNA]. Well?

ANNA [*raises her head*]. Nothing. I'm rather bored.

NICHOLAS. How about a smoke, my pet? I'm dying for a cigarette. Haven't had one since this morning, don't know why.

ANNA [*hands him cigarettes*]. Take plenty, so you needn't bother me later. [*They light up.*] I'm bored, Nicholas, bored and fed up, with nothing to do.

[NICHOLAS *takes her hand.*]

ANNA. Feeling my pulse? I'm quite well.

NICHOLAS. Not your pulse—a little kiss. [*Kisses her hand.*] I like kissing your hand, it's like satin. What soap do you use, they're so white? Wonderful hands. I'll have another, actually. [*Kisses her hand.*] Like a game of chess?

ANNA. All right. [*Looks at the clock.*] Quarter past twelve, our guests must be ravenous.

NICHOLAS [*sets the chess-board*]. No doubt. I'm starving myself.

ANNA. I don't care about you—you always are starving, though you keep stuffing yourself. [*They sit down to play chess.*] Your move— oh, he already has moved. You should think first. I'm going here. You always are starving.

NICHOLAS. You've moved? I see. Yes, I'm starving. Is dinner soon?

ANNA. I don't think so. The chef celebrated our arrival by having a drop too much, and now he's out cold. But we'll get lunch before very long. Really, Nicholas, when will you have had enough? Stuffing yourself like that, it's ghastly. What a big stomach for such a little man.

NICHOLAS. Pretty remarkable, I agree.

ANNA. Barges in here and scoffs half a pie without asking. You know it's not my pie, don't you? You're a pig, dear. Your move.

NICHOLAS. I don't know, I only know the pie would go bad if I didn't eat it. Have you moved? Quite good. Here's mine. I eat a lot because I'm healthy—you don't mind that, do you? *Mens sana in corpore sano*. Why think? Move without thinking, dear. [*Sings.*] 'I could a tale unfold——'

ANNA. Be quiet, I can't think.

NICHOLAS. It's a pity—a clever girl like you, and no idea of gastronomy! A poor eater is a monster, a moral freak, because—. Hey, you can't go there, what do you think you're at? Oh, that's different. Now taste's a natural function like sight and hearing, in fact it's one of the five senses, old girl, and thus an integral branch of psychology. Psychology, I said.

ANNA. You're about to be witty, I do believe. Don't, dear, it bores me and it doesn't go with your face. I never laugh at your jokes, you may have noticed that—if not, it's time you did.

NICHOLAS. Your ladyship's move, and look out for your knight. You don't laugh because you always miss the point, see?

ANNA. What are you goggling at? Your move. Will your young woman come today, do you think?

NICHOLAS. She did say she would.

ANNA. Then it's time she was here, it's gone twelve. Are you—I'm sorry if I'm being indiscreet, but are you just friends or is there more to it?

NICHOLAS. Meaning what?

ANNA. Be frank, Nicholas. I ask as your friend, not so I can gossip about it. What are Mary Grekov and you to each other? Be frank, and please don't be funny about it. Come on, it's just a friendly inquiry, honestly.

NICHOLAS. What we are to each other no one yet knows.

ANNA. At least——

NICHOLAS. I visit her, talk to her, bore her, put her mother to the expense of serving coffee, and that's all. Your move. I go there every day or two, I might add, and stroll along their shady garden paths. I talk about my interests, and she talks about hers, holding me by this button and taking the fluff off my collar. I'm always covered with fluff, aren't I?

ANNA. Go on.

NICHOLAS. That's all. It's hard to say what attracts me about her. Am I bored, am I in love, or is it something else? I've no idea. I know I miss her terribly in the afternoons, and from a few random inquiries I know she misses me.

ANNA. It's love then?

NICHOLAS [*shrugs*]. Very likely. Do I love her or don't I? What do you think?

ANNA. A charming thing to say! You should know best.

NICHOLAS. Oh, you don't understand. Your move.

ANNA. There. No, I don't—few women would understand such behaviour. [*Pause.*]

NICHOLAS. She's a nice child.

ANNA. I like her—a bright little thing. Only mind you don't get her into any trouble, my friend, because that's a failing of yours. You'll hang around, talk a lot of hot air, promise the earth, get her a bad name—and then simply drop her. I'd be sorry for her. What's she doing these days?

NICHOLAS. Reading.

ANNA. And studying chemistry? [*Laughs.*]

NICHOLAS. I think so.

ANNA. Good for her. Steady on, mind your sleeve. I like her and her sharp little nose, she might make quite a decent scientist.

NICHOLAS. She doesn't know what to do, poor thing.

ANNA. Tell you what, Nicholas—ask Mary to come and see me some time. I'll make friends with her and—anyway I shan't try to act as a go-between or anything. We'll see what she's made of and either get rid of her or take her seriously. Let's hope—. [*Pause.*] To me you're just a baby, you're an awful lightweight—that's why I meddle in your affairs. Your move. My advice is—leave her alone or marry her. Marriage or nothing, mind. If you do spring a surprise and choose marriage, look before you leap. Mind you have a real look at her from every angle. Think, consider, weigh it up—then you won't be sorry afterwards, do you hear?

NICHOLAS. Of course, I'm all ears.

ANNA. I know you. You're so impulsive and you'll marry on impulse. A woman can twist you round her finger. Consult your friends, in fact don't trust your own feeble brain. [*Bangs the table.*] That's what your head's made of. [*Whistles.*] The wind whistles through your ears, man—you're all brain and no sense.

NICHOLAS. Whistles like a peasant. Amazing woman! [*Pause.*] Mary won't visit you.

ANNA. Why not?

NICHOLAS. Because Platonov's always hanging round here. She just can't stand him since he started pitching into her. The man decided she was silly—he got that idea in his great shaggy head and it damn well can't be budged. He thinks it's his job to annoy silly girls, I don't know why, and he's always playing tricks on them. Your move. But she's no fool. A fat lot he knows about people!

ANNA. Don't worry, we'll keep him in line. Tell her she has nothing to fear. But why is Platonov so late? It's high time he was here. [*Looks at the clock.*] It's very bad manners, we haven't met for six months.

NICHOLAS. I passed the schoolhouse on my way here, and the shutters were all closed. He must still be asleep. The man's a swine. I haven't seen him for ages myself.

ANNA. Is he well?

NICHOLAS. He always is, there's life in the old dog yet.

[PORFIRY *and* SERGEY *come in.*]

SCENE II

[*The above,* PORFIRY *and* SERGEY.]

PORFIRY [*coming in*]. Yes, my dear Sergey, we old stagers are a bit better at this business—and a bit luckier—than you young hopefuls. Men lost nothing, you see, and women gained. [*They sit down.*] Let's sit down, I'm tired. We loved women chivalrously, believed in them, worshipped them—because we thought they were superior. Woman's a superior being, Sergey.

ANNA. Hey, stop cheating!

NICHOLAS. Cheating?

ANNA. Who put this piece here?

NICHOLAS. *You* did.

ANNA. Oh yes. Sorry.

NICHOLAS. So I should jolly well think.

PORFIRY. Then we also had our friends. Friendship went deeper when I was young—was less of a luxury. We had literary circles and clubs too. By the way, any of us would have gone through hell-fire and high water for our friends.

SERGEY [*yawns*]. Yes, those were the days.

NICHOLAS. In these dreadful times we employ the fire brigade to go through fire for our friends.

ANNA. Don't be silly, Nicholas. [*Pause.*]

PORFIRY. At the Moscow opera last winter I saw a young man reduced to tears by good music. Now wasn't that nice?

SERGEY. Very much so, I should say.

PORFIRY. So should I. But why did women and their escorts, sitting near by, have to smile at him—eh? What was there to grin at? When he realized they could all see him crying, he squirmed in his seat, blushed, produced a ghastly grin of his own, and left the theatre. People weren't ashamed of honest tears in our day, and no one laughed at them.

NICHOLAS [*to* ANNA]. I wish this sentimental old ninny would die of melancholia—I hate such talk, it gets on my nerves.

ANNA. Shush!

PORFIRY. We were luckier than you. Music-lovers didn't have to leave the theatre in our day, they'd stay till the opera was over. You're yawning, Sergey, I must be getting you down——

SERGEY. No, but do wind up, Glagolyev. It's time——

PORFIRY. Ah well, and so on and so forth. To sum up, people loved and hated in our day, that's what it comes to, so they could feel indignation and scorn——

SERGEY. I see, and nowadays they can't, eh?

PORFIRY. That's what I think.

[SERGEY *gets up and goes to the window*.]

PORFIRY. You don't find that sort any more—that's what's wrong with us these days. [*Pause*.]

SERGEY. Bit sweeping, aren't you?

ANNA. Oh, I say—! He stinks of cheap scent, I feel quite sick. [*Coughs*.] Move back a bit, please.

NICHOLAS [*moving away*]. She's losing—so blame the wretched scent. What a woman.

SERGEY. You should be ashamed to bandy accusations based on pure guesswork and a bias in favour of your own long-vanished youth.

PORFIRY. I may be mistaken.

SERGEY. May be. Forget the 'may be'. Your accusation's not particularly funny.

PORFIRY [*laughs*]. But you're getting annoyed, old boy, and that proves you're unsporting and don't know how to respect your opponent's views.

SERGEY. It's enough to prove I can feel indignation, isn't it?

PORFIRY. I'm not condemning everyone out of hand, of course—there are exceptions.

SERGEY. Of course. [*Bows*.] Thank you for those kind words, such admissions are the secret of your charm. But what if you ran across some booby who didn't know you, and who thought you knew what you were talking about? You'd have him believe that all of us —me, Nicholas, Mother and anyone else more or less young—are incapable of indignation or scorn.

PORFIRY. Look here, I didn't say——

ANNA. I want to listen to Mr. Glagolyev. Let's stop, I've had enough.

NICHOLAS. No, no. You can play and listen at the same time.

ANNA. I've had enough. [*Gets up*.] I'm fed up, we can finish the game later.

NICHOLAS. When I'm losing she's glued to her chair, but let me start winning and she wants to hear Glagolyev. [*To* PORFIRY.] Who wants to hear you, you nuisance? [*To* ANNA.] Kindly sit down and get on with the game, or I shall say you've lost.

ANNA. Do, for all I care. [*Sits opposite* PORFIRY.]

SCENE III

[The above and ABRAHAM.]

ABRAHAM [*comes in*]. Isn't it hot? It's so hot—reminds me of Palestine, seeing I'm a Jew. [*Sits at the piano and strums.*] I'm told it's very hot there.

NICHOLAS [*stands up*]. I'll note it down. [*Takes a notebook from his pocket.*] I'll make a note of it, dear lady. [*Makes a note.*] Mrs. Anna Voynitsev, the widow of General Voynitsev—three roubles. That makes ten all told. Now when do I see the colour of my money?

PORFIRY. You never saw the old days, ladies and gentlemen, you'd sing a different tune if you had. You'd understand—. [*Sighs.*] But how can you?

SERGEY. I think we could trust literature and history more. We haven't seen the past, but we feel it. That feel often comes from here. [*Hits the back of his neck.*] Now you don't see the present day, you've no feel for that.

NICHOLAS. Shall I chalk it up to your ladyship, or will you pay now?

ANNA. Stop, I can't hear what they're saying.

NICHOLAS. Why listen, they'll be on all afternoon?

ANNA. Sergey, give this lunatic ten roubles.

SERGEY. Ten? [*Takes out his pocket-book, to* PORFIRY.] Let's change the subject.

PORFIRY. All right, if you don't like it.

SERGEY. I like listening to you, but I don't want to hear what sounds like slander. [*Gives* NICHOLAS *ten roubles.*]

NICHOLAS. Thanks. [*Slaps* ABRAHAM *on the shoulder.*] That's how to get on in the world. Sit a defenceless woman at the chess-board and take ten smackers off her without a pang of conscience. Pretty good, eh?

ABRAHAM. I agree. You'd do quite well in Jerusalem, Doctor.

ANNA. Stop it, Triletsky. [*To* PORFIRY.] So you think woman's a superior being, Mr. Glagolyev.

PORFIRY. Yes.

ANNA. I see. You must be a great ladies' man.

PORFIRY. Yes, I adore women, dote on them. One reason is, I see in them everything I like, generosity and——

ANNA. You adore them, but are they worth it?

PORFIRY. Yes.

ANNA. Are you sure? Quite sure, or have you just talked yourself into it?

[NICHOLAS *picks up the violin and bows it.*]

PORFIRY. I'm quite sure, I only need to know you to be so.

ANNA. Really? You're certainly quite a character.

SERGEY. He's a romantic.

PORFIRY. Perhaps. Why not? Is romanticism such a bad thing? You people have thrown it out. A good idea, but perhaps you've got rid of the baby with the bath-water.

ANNA. Well, don't let's quarrel over it, my friend, I'm no debater. We may have got rid of this or that, but we're certainly cleverer, thank God. Aren't we? And that's the main thing. [*Laughs.*] As long as you have clever people getting cleverer, the rest can look after itself. Oh, stop that awful noise, Nicholas. Put that fiddle down.

NICHOLAS [*hanging up the violin*]. A fine instrument.

PORFIRY. Platonov once put it rather well. 'We've learnt sense about women,' he said. 'But that's only meant dragging both ourselves and women through the mud.'

NICHOLAS [*laughs*]. It must have been his birthday, he'd had a drop too much.

ANNA. Did he say that? [*Laughs.*] Yes, he likes to make these utterances sometimes, but he only said it for effect, surely? And talking of friend Platonov, what's he really like, do you think? Is he really such a knight in shining armour?

PORFIRY. Well—I think Platonov's a superb example of modern vagueness. He's the hero of our best modern novel, one that hasn't yet been written, I'm sorry to say. [*Laughs.*] Vagueness seems to me typical of modern society, and your Russian novelist senses it. He's baffled and bewildered, he has nothing to hold on to, he doesn't understand. And these people aren't easy to understand. [*Points to* SERGEY.] Our novels are abominable, affected and trivial and no wonder. Everything's so vague and blurred—it's one great chaotic mess. And it's this vagueness which the sagacious Platonov typifies, I think. Is he well?

ANNA. He's said to be well. [*Pause.*] Such a nice little man.

PORFIRY. Yes, you can't help looking up to him. I went to see him several times last winter and I'll never forget the few hours I was lucky to spend with him.

ANNA [*looks at the clock*]. It's time he was here. Did you send for him, Sergey?

SERGEY. Yes, twice.

ANNA. You're all talking nonsense. Triletsky, quickly—send Jacob for him.

NICHOLAS [*stretches*]. Shall I tell them to lay the table?

ANNA. No, I'll do that.

NICHOLAS [*moves off and knocks into* BUGROV *by the door*]. Our grocer man's puffing like a steam engine. [*Pats him on the stomach and goes out.*]

SCENE IV

[ANNA, PORFIRY, ABRAHAM, SERGEY *and* BUGROV.]

BUGROV [*coming in*]. Gosh! Frightfully hot, isn't it? Must be going to rain.

SERGEY. Did you come through the garden?

BUGROV. Yes.

SERGEY. Is Sonya there?

BUGROV. Which Sonya?

SERGEY. My wife.

ABRAHAM. Back in a minute. [*Goes into the garden.*]

SCENE V

[ANNA, PORFIRY, SERGEY, BUGROV, PLATONOV *and* SASHA, *who wears Russian national dress.*]

PLATONOV [*in the doorway, to* SASHA]. After you, young woman. [*Comes in after* SASHA.] Well, we got away at last. Say hallo to everyone, Sasha. Good morning to your ladyship. [*Goes up to* ANNA, *kisses one hand and then the other.*]

ANNA. You cruel, horrid man. How could you keep us waiting all this time? You know how impatient I am. Dearest Sasha. [*Kisses* SASHA.]

PLATONOV. Well, we got away at last, thank God. We haven't seen a parquet floor for six months—or armchairs, high ceilings or human beings even. We've hibernated in our den like bears. We've only just crawled out into the light. Sergey, my dear fellow. [*Embraces* SERGEY.]

SERGEY. You've grown, you've put on weight and—damn it, how you've filled out, Sasha. [*Shakes her hand.*] Are you well? Plumper and prettier than ever!

PLATONOV [*shakes hands with* PORFIRY]. Glad to meet you.

ANNA. How are things, Sasha, how are you keeping? Please sit down, all of you. Now tell us all about it. Let's sit.

PLATONOV [*laughs*]. Heavens, can that be Sergey? Where's the long hair, the fancy shirt and that nice tenor voice? Come on, speak!

SERGEY. Oh, what an ass I am. [*Laughs.*]

PLATONOV. That's a bass voice—a true bass. Shall we sit down then? Come and sit near me, Mr. Glagolyev. I sit. [*Sits.*] Sit down, everyone. Phew, isn't it hot? Smell anything, Sasha? [*They sit.*]

SASHA. Yes. [*Laughter.*]

PLATONOV. Human flesh—delightful smell! It's as if we hadn't met for ages. Winter seems to drag on for ever, hang it. There's my chair—see, Sasha? I used to sit there day in day out six months ago, seeking the meaning of life with her ladyship and gambling away your shiny ten-copeck pieces. Isn't it hot?

ANNA. I've been dying to see you. Are you well?

PLATONOV. Very much so. Your ladyship, I report that you've put on weight and are looking somewhat prettier. It's hot and stuffy today, I miss the cold weather already.

ANNA. Yes, they've both filled out madly, lucky people. How was life, Michael?

PLATONOV. Rotten as usual. I slept all winter, didn't see the sky for six months. I ate, drank, slept, read Mayne Reid to my wife. Rotten!

SASHA. It was all right, but of course we were bored.

PLATONOV. Not just bored, dear—paralysed. I missed you awfully, you're a sight for sore eyes. To see you, Anna, after seeing no one or only crashing bores all this dreary while—it's the height of luxury.

ANNA. That earns you a cigarette. [*Gives him one.*]

PLATONOV. Thanks. [*They light up.*]

SASHA. Did you get here yesterday?

ANNA. Yes, at ten o'clock.

PLATONOV. I saw your lights on at eleven, but I was afraid to call. I bet you were tired.

ANNA. You should have popped over, we sat up talking till two.

[SASHA *whispers in* PLATONOV's *ear.*]

PLATONOV. Damnation! [*Slaps his forehead.*] What a memory—why didn't you tell me before? Sergey!

SERGEY. Yes?

PLATONOV. He's struck dumb too. Gets married and doesn't breathe a word. [*Gets up.*] I forget and they don't mention it.

SASHA. I forgot too, what with all his talk. [*To* SERGEY.] Congratulations and all the best.

PLATONOV. I have the honour—. [*Bows.*] I wish you every happiness, man. It's marvellous, I never thought you'd take the plunge. What speed off the mark. Who'd have expected anything so odd?

SERGEY. Good for me, eh? Quick off the mark! [*Laughs.*] I never contemplated anything so odd myself—it was fixed in a jiffy, old boy. I fall in love. I marry.

PLATONOV. This love business went on every winter, it's the marrying that's new. You'll have to watch your step now, as our priest says.

A wife's the worst and fussiest kind of busybody. If she's stupid you're done for. Have you got a job?

SERGEY. I was offered one at a school, but I don't know. I don't really want it, the pay's poor, and anyway——

PLATONOV. Will you take it?

SERGEY. I haven't the foggiest yet—probably not.

PLATONOV. I see, so we're going to take things easy. Three years, isn't it, since we left college?

SERGEY. Yes.

PLATONOV. I see. [*Sighs.*] You need a good hiding. I'll have to speak to your wife—wasting three good years!

ANNA. It's too hot for all this palaver, I feel like yawning. Why didn't you come over before, Sasha?

SASHA. We were busy. Michael was mending the bird-cage and I was at church. The cage broke and we couldn't leave our nightingale just like that.

PORFIRY. What's on in church today—saint's day or something?

SASHA. No. I went to ask Father Constantine to hold a requiem. Today was Michael's old father's name-day, and I couldn't very well miss church. I had a mass said for him. [*Pause.*]

PORFIRY. How long since your father died, Platonov?

PLATONOV. Three, four years.

SASHA. Three years eight months.

PORFIRY. Lord, how time flies. Three years eight months. It must be some while since we last met. [*Sighs.*] It was at Ivanovka, we were both on jury service, and something happened utterly typical of the old boy. A surveyor, a wretched boozy little man, was being tried for taking bribes and [*laughs*] we found him not guilty—on your poor father's insistence. He kept on at us for two or three hours, arguing away and getting quite hot under the collar. 'I shan't find against him,' he shouts, 'till you all swear you don't take bribes either.' Illogical, but—we could do nothing with him. Quite wore us out, he did. Old General Voynitsev was with us at the time— your husband, Anna. He too was quite somebody.

ANNA. You wouldn't catch *him* letting anyone off!

PORFIRY. No, he was all set on 'guilty'. I remember them both—red in the face, fair gibbering with rage. The villagers on the jury backed the general, and the rest of us, people of our class, were for old Mr. Platonov. We won, of course. [*Laughs.*] Your father challenged the general to a duel and the general called him—sorry!—a thorough-going swine. What a lark. Later we got them drunk and they made it up—there's nothing easier than reconciling Russians. He was so kind, your father—most kind-hearted.

PLATONOV. Not kind—just feckless.

PORFIRY. A great man in his way. I thought a lot of him, we were on the best of terms.

PLATONOV. That's more than I can claim. We parted company when I was a mere boy and for the last three years we were at daggers drawn. I didn't think much of him and he thought I was no good—and we were both right. I disliked the man, I still do—for dying peacefully. He died like an honest man. To refuse to admit what a swine you are—that's the awful thing about your Russian scoundrel.

PORFIRY. *De mortuis aut bene, aut nihil.*

PLATONOV. No, that's a Latin heresy. My view is—*de omnibus aut nihil, aut veritas.* I prefer the truth to keeping quiet, though—at least you learn more. I don't think the dead need these concessions.

[IVAN *comes in.*]

SCENE VI

[*The above and* IVAN.]

IVAN. Well, well, well—my son-in-law and daughter. Stars from the Constellation Triletsky. Morning, my dears, and a salvo of greetings to you. God, it's hot. Michael, old boy——

PLATONOV [*stands up*]. Morning, Colonel. [*Embraces him.*] Fit?

IVAN. I always am. The Lord's kind and doesn't punish me. Sasha. [*Kisses* SASHA's *head.*] Haven't clapped eyes on you for ages. Are you all right?

SASHA. Yes. And you?

IVAN [*sits down by* SASHA]. I'm always fit, not a day's illness in my life. Haven't seen you for ages. Not a day but I mean to go over, see my grandson and criticize the universe with my son-in-law, but I never manage it, I'm so busy, my dears. I wanted to go over two days ago and show you my new double-barrelled shot-gun, Michael, but I was waylaid by the police inspector who made me play cards. That shot-gun's terrific. English and lethal at five hundred feet. Is baby well?

SASHA. Yes, he sends his regards.

IVAN. Is he old enough for that?

SERGEY. Metaphorically speaking, you know.

IVAN. I see. Metaphorically. Tell him to grow up quickly, Sasha, I'll take him shooting. Got a little gun lined up for him already. I'll make a sportsman of the boy so I've someone I can leave my hunting stuff to when I die.

ANNA. Isn't the colonel a darling? I'm going quail-shooting with him on St. Peter's Day.

IVAN. Oho! We'll mount an anti-snipe campaign, Anna, we'll launch a polar expedition to Satan's Bog.

ANNA. And we'll try out your new gun.

IVAN. That we will, divine Diana. [*Kisses her hand.*] Remember last year, dear? Ha ha! I like your sort, God help me, I don't like softies. This is women's emancipation with a vengeance. Sniff her shoulder and you smell gunpowder, she's a regular Amazon, a fighter, a real warrior chief. Give her a pair of epaulettes and she'd wreck the world. So let's go. And we'll take Sasha along, we'll take everyone. We'll show them what stuff the army's made of, divine Diana, your ladyship, Alexandra of Macedon.

PLATONOV. Been at the bottle, eh, Colonel?

IVAN. Of course, stands to reason.

PLATONOV. Hence all the blah, blah, blah.

IVAN. I got here about eight, old boy, when everyone was still asleep and I had nothing to do but kick my heels. I saw her come out and laugh, so we knocked back a bottle of good old madeira. Diana here drank three glasses and I dealt with the rest.

ANNA. Trust you to shout it from the roof-tops!

[NICHOLAS *runs in.*]

SCENE VII

[*The above and* NICHOLAS.]

NICHOLAS. Hallo, relatives.

PLATONOV. Aha, her ladyship's personal physician grade three. *Argentum nitricum aquae destillatae.* Glad to see you, old man. All healthy glow and shine and scent!

NICHOLAS [*kisses* SASHA'*s head*]. Old Michael's filled out, damn it, he's like a ruddy great ox.

SASHA. What a stink of scent. How are you?

NICHOLAS. Fit as a fiddle. It was a bright idea to come. [*Sits down.*] How's things, Mike?

PLATONOV. Things?

NICHOLAS. With you, of course.

PLATONOV. Oh. Who knows? It's a long story, old man, and a dull one. Where did you get that natty hair cut? Pretty stylish! Cost you a rouble?

NICHOLAS. I won't have barbers do my hair, I use women for that and if I pay them roubles, it's not for hair-dos! [*Eats fruit drops.*] You know, my dear fellow, I——

PLATONOV. Trying to be funny? Well, don't. Don't put yourself out. Spare us, please.

SCENE VIII

[*The above,* PETRIN *and* ABRAHAM. PETRIN *comes in with a news-paper and sits down.* ABRAHAM *sits in a corner.*]

NICHOLAS [*to his father*]. How about a good cry, revered parent?

IVAN. Why should I?

NICHOLAS. For joy—why not? Look at me. I'm your son. [*Points to* SASHA.] Here's your daughter. [*Points to* PLATONOV.] This young fellow's your son-in-law. Your daughter alone is a pearl beyond price, Father. Only you could have fathered such a fascinating daughter. And what about your son-in-law?

IVAN. Why cry, though, my boy? I don't see the need.

NICHOLAS. And your son-in-law? What a man! You might go to the ends of the earth and not find his like. Honest, decent, generous, fair. And take your grandson. He's no end of a lad, the little bounder. Waves his hands, holds his arms out like this. 'Where's grandpa?' he squeals. 'Bring the old pirate here. Let me pull those ruddy great whiskers!'

IVAN [*takes a handkerchief from his pocket*]. But why should I cry? Oh well, thank God. [*Cries.*] No need to cry.

NICHOLAS. Blubbing, Colonel, eh?

IVAN. No, why should I? Ah well, the Lord be praised.

PLATONOV. Stop it, Nicholas.

NICHOLAS [*stands up and sits by* BUGROV]. There's a lot of heat being generated today, Bugrov.

BUGROV. Very true, it's as hot as an oven. Ninety in the shade, I reckon.

NICHOLAS. What does it mean? Why all the heat, Bugrov?

BUGROV. You should know.

NICHOLAS. I don't, I only studied medicine.

BUGROV. I think it's hot because a cold June would strike us both as pretty funny. [*Laughter.*]

NICHOLAS. I see. Which is better for the grass, Bugrov—the climate or the atmosphere?

BUGROV. Everything's good for it, but for crops a spot of rain's more the thing. What use is a climate with no rain? It isn't worth a row of beans.

NICHOLAS. Quite, very true. Words of purest wisdom, I shouldn't wonder. What's your view of things in general, Mr. Grocer?

BUGROV [*laughs*]. I have none.

NICHOLAS. As if that needed proving! You have your head screwed on, sir. Now, how about Anna doing the impossible and giving us some food?

ANNA. Why can't you wait like everyone else?

NICHOLAS. She doesn't know how hungry we are. She doesn't know what a frightful thirst you and I have, especially the former. We'll put away the food and drink all right! To start with—. [*Whispers in* BUGROV's *ear.*] Not bad, eh? Down the hatch—it's the same in any language. There's everything out there, to be consumed on or off the premises. Caviare, sturgeon, salmon, sardines. Then there's a six- or seven-decker pie, this big—and stuffed with sundry grotesque flora and fauna of the Old World and the New. If we could only get at it! Pretty ravenous, are you, Bugrov? Frankly——

SASHA [*to* NICHOLAS]. You're not all that hungry, you just want to make a scene. You can't bear people sitting quietly.

NICHOLAS. I can't bear people starving to death, you little dumpling.

PLATONOV. If that's meant to be funny, why is no one laughing?

ANNA. What a bore, isn't he? And what awful, ghastly cheek. You wait, you wretch. I'll give you something to eat. [*Goes out.*]

NICHOLAS. And not a moment too soon.

SCENE IX

[*The above except* ANNA.]

PLATONOV. It's not a bad idea, actually. What's the time? I'm starving too.

SERGEY. Where's my wife? Platonov hasn't seen her yet, I must introduce him. [*Gets up.*] I'll go and look for her. She likes the garden so much, you can't get her out of it.

PLATONOV. By the way, Sergey, I'd rather you didn't introduce me to your wife, I'd like to see if she recognizes me. I once knew her slightly and——

SERGEY. You knew Sonya?

PLATONOV. Once upon a time—in my student days, I think. Don't introduce me, please, and don't say anything. Not a word about me.

SERGEY. All right. The man knows everyone. When does he find time to meet them all? [*Goes in the garden.*]

NICHOLAS. What price my piece in the *Russian Courier*! Have you read the great work, everyone? Have you, Mr. Vengerovich?

ABRAHAM. Yes.

NICHOLAS. Splendid, wasn't it? I put you over as a regular vampire, didn't I? The things I wrote—why, all Europe will be shocked.

PETRIN [*guffaws*]. So that's who you meant—the one you call 'V'. But who's 'B', pray?

BUGROV [*laughs*]. That's me. [*Mops his brow.*] Confound him.

ABRAHAM. Never mind, it's all very praiseworthy. If I could write I'd certainly write for the papers. You get paid, for a start, and then in Russia writers are thought to be terribly clever, I don't know why. Only you didn't write that article, Doctor—Mr. Glagolyev did.

PORFIRY. How do you know?

ABRAHAM. I just do.

PORFIRY. That's funny. It's true I wrote it, but how did you know?

ABRAHAM. You can always find things out if you want. You sent it by registered post and—well, our post-office clerk has a good memory, that's all. It's no mystery, my Hebrew cunning has nothing to do with it. [*Laughs.*] Don't worry, I'm not going to try and get my own back.

PORFIRY. I'm not worried, but—it is odd.

[MARY *comes in.*]

SCENE X

[*The above and* MARY.]

NICHOLAS [*jumps up*]. Mary, how nice—this *is* a surprise.

MARY [*shaking hands*]. Hallo, Nicholas. [*Nods to all.*] Good morning, all.

NICHOLAS [*helps her off with her cape*]. Let me take your cape. Fit and keen? Good morning once again. [*Kisses her hand.*] How are you?

MARY. Same as usual. [*Is embarrassed and sits on the first available chair.*] Is Anna in?

NICHOLAS. Yes. [*Sits by her.*]

PORFIRY. Good morning, Mary.

IVAN. This the Grekov girl? Why, I hardly knew you. [*Goes up to* MARY *and kisses her hand.*] Nice to see you.

MARY. How do you do, Colonel? [*Coughs.*] It's terribly hot. Please don't kiss my hand, it embarrasses me—I don't like it.

PLATONOV [*goes up to* MARY]. How do you do? [*Tries to kiss her hand.*] How are you? Hey, give me your hand.

MARY [*snatches her hand away*]. No.

PLATONOV. Why? Not worthy, eh?

MARY. I don't know how worthy you are, but—you were being insincere, weren't you?

PLATONOV. Insincere? How can you tell?

MARY. You wouldn't have tried to kiss my hand if I hadn't said I disliked it. You always do like annoying me.

PLATONOV. Aren't you rather jumping to conclusions?

NICHOLAS [*to* PLATONOV]. Go away.

PLATONOV. In a minute. How's your essence of bed-bugs, Miss Grekov?

MARY. What essence?

PLATONOV. I hear you're distilling something out of bed-bugs—a contribution to science. A good idea.

MARY. You're always joking.

NICHOLAS. Yes, he's quite the funny man. Well, here you are, Mary. How's your mother keeping?

PLATONOV. Now isn't she nice and pink! Must be feeling the heat.

MARY [*stands up*]. Why are you saying all this?

PLATONOV. I want a word with you, it's ages since our last talk. But why so annoyed? Isn't it time you stopped being angry with me?

MARY. I've noticed you're never quite yourself when we meet. I don't know what bothers you about me, but—I humour you by keeping out of your way. If Nicholas hadn't sworn you wouldn't be here I'd have stayed away. [*To* NICHOLAS.] Aren't you ashamed to tell lies?

PLATONOV. Shame on you for lying, Nicholas. [*To* MARY.] You're about to cry. Carry on—tears can be a great relief.

[MARY *hurries towards the door, where she meets* ANNA.]

SCENE XI

[*The above and* ANNA.]

NICHOLAS [*to* PLATONOV]. This is downright stupid, do you hear? Any more of this and you'll answer to me.

PLATONOV. What business is it of yours?

NICHOLAS. This is silly, you don't know what you're doing.

PORFIRY. It's also rather cruel, Platonov.

ANNA. Mary, I'm so glad. [*Shakes* MARY's *hand.*] You come here so seldom, but now you are here I love you for it. Let's sit down. [*They sit down.*] So glad. It's all Nicholas's doing—he managed to get you away from your village.

NICHOLAS [*to* PLATONOV]. What if I love her?

PLATONOV. Then go ahead. Get on with it.

NICHOLAS. You don't know what you're saying.

ANNA. How are you, dear?

MARY. All right, thanks.

ANNA. You're worn out. [*Looks into her face.*] Driving fifteen miles is quite a business when you're not used to it.

MARY. No—. [*Puts her handkerchief to her eyes and cries.*] That's not it——

ANNA. What is it, Mary? [*Pause.*]

MARY. Nothing——

[NICHOLAS *walks up and down the stage.*]

PORFIRY [*to* PLATONOV]. You should apologize, Platonov.

PLATONOV. Whatever for?

PORFIRY. How can you ask? You were most unkind.

SASHA [*goes up to* PLATONOV]. Apologize, or I'm leaving. Say you're sorry.

ANNA. I often cry after a journey myself, one gets so much on edge.

PORFIRY. Now come on, I insist. You've been most unkind, I'm surprised at you.

SASHA. Apologize when you're told. Have you no shame?

ANNA. Oh, I see. [*Looks at* PLATONOV.] He's already managed to—. Sorry, Mary. I forgot to talk to this—this—. It's my fault.

PLATONOV [*goes up to* MARY]. Mary!

MARY [*raises her head*]. What do you want?

PLATONOV. I'm sorry. I apologize publicly, I'm consumed with shame, positively incinerated. Give me your hand. I mean it, I give you my word. [*Takes her hand.*] Let's be friends and stop snivelling. Are we friends? [*Kisses her hand.*]

MARY. Yes.

[*Covers her face with her handkerchief and runs out.* NICHOLAS *follows her.*]

SCENE XII

[*The above except* MARY *and* NICHOLAS.]

ANNA. I never thought you'd go so far. Really!

PORFIRY. Go easy, Michael, for God's sake.

PLATONOV. That'll do. [*Sits on the sofa.*] Wretched girl. I was silly to talk to her, but it isn't worth wasting words on silliness.

ANNA. Why did Triletsky go after her? Not all women like to be seen crying.

PORFIRY. I respect women's sensitivity. You didn't say anything much, did you? But—. One word, one little hint——

ANNA. It was very wrong of you.

PLATONOV. I've apologized, haven't I?

[*Enter* SERGEY, SONYA *and* ISAAC.]

SCENE XIII

[*The above,* SERGEY, SONYA, ISAAC *and, later,* NICHOLAS.]

SERGEY [*runs in*]. She's coming. [*Sings.*] Here she is.

[ISAAC *stands by the door, his arms folded on his chest.*]

ANNA. The heat's got Sonya down at last. Do come in.

PLATONOV [*aside*]. Sonya! God Almighty, hasn't she changed!

SONYA. I was so interested talking to Mr. Vengerovich, I quite forgot the heat. [*Sits on the sofa about a yard away from* PLATONOV.] I love your garden, Sergey.

PORFIRY [*sits down near* SONYA]. Sergey——

SERGEY. Yes?

PORFIRY. Sonya promised you'd all come over to my place on Thursday, old friend.

PLATONOV [*aside*]. She looked at me.

SERGEY. We'll be as good as our word and drive over *en masse*.

NICHOLAS [*comes in*]. 'Oh, women, women,' said Shakespeare. But he was wrong, he should have said 'Oh, wretched women!'

ANNA. Where's Mary?

NICHOLAS. I took her in the garden to walk it off.

PORFIRY. You've never called on me, Sonya, but you'll like my place, I hope. I've a better garden than you, a deep river and some decent horses. [*Pause.*]

ANNA. Silence. One more idiot's been born. [*Laughter.*]

SONYA [*quietly to* PORFIRY, *nodding towards* PLATONOV]. Who's this— the man sitting next to me.

PORFIRY [*laughs*]. Our schoolmaster—don't know his name.

BUGROV [*to* NICHOLAS]. Doctor, can you cure all diseases or only some?

NICHOLAS. All.

BUGROV. Anthrax included?

NICHOLAS. Yes.

BUGROV. If a mad dog bit me, could you cure that?

NICHOLAS. Why, has one bitten you? [*Moves away.*]

BUGROV [*taken aback*]. God, I hope not. Really, Doctor, draw it mild! [*Laughter.*]

ANNA. How do we reach your place, Mr. Glagolyev? Through Yusnovka?

PORFIRY. No, that's the long way round. Go straight to Platonovka. I live quite near, just over a mile away.

SONYA. I know Platonovka. It still exists then?

PORFIRY. But of course.

SONYA. I knew the owner once—name of Platonov. Any idea of his whereabouts, Sergey?

PLATONOV [*aside*]. She might ask me.

SERGEY. I think so. Can you remember his first name? [*Laughs.*]

PLATONOV. I used to know him myself, I think it's Michael. [*Laughter.*]

SONYA. That's right. Michael Platonov. I knew him as a student, almost a boy. You all laugh, but I'm afraid I don't see anything funny about it.

ANNA [*laughs and points at* PLATONOV]. Do recognize him for goodness' sake, the suspense is killing him.

[PLATONOV *gets up.*]

SONYA [*gets up and looks at* PLATONOV]. Yes, it's him. Why don't you speak, Michael? Is it really you?

PLATONOV. Don't you know me. Sonya? No wonder. Four and a half years, in fact nearly five, have passed, and they've made inroads on my face—worse than if the rats had got at it.

SONYA [*gives him her hand*]. I'm just beginning to recognize you. How you have changed.

SERGEY [*takes* SASHA *to* SONYA]. This is his wife Sasha—sister of that great wit Nicholas Triletsky.

SONYA [*shakes hands with* SASHA]. How do you do? [*Sits down.*] So you're married—doesn't time fly? Still, five years is five years.

ANNA. Good for Platonov—never goes anywhere, but knows everyone. I commend him as one of our best friends.

PLATONOV. This flowery introduction entitles me to ask you how things are, Sonya. How are you keeping?

SONYA. Things aren't too bad, but I'm keeping none too well. And you? What are you up to these days?

PLATONOV. Fate's played me a trick I never expected at the time when you thought me a second Byron, and I saw myself as a Christopher Columbus and Cabinet Minister rolled into one. I'm just a schoolmaster.

SONYA. What—you!

PLATONOV. Yes, me. [*Pause.*] I suppose it is a bit funny.

SONYA. It's grotesque. But why—couldn't you have done better?

PLATONOV. I can't answer that in one sentence. [*Pause.*]

SONYA. You at least got your degree, didn't you?

PLATONOV. No, I gave it up.

SONYA. But you're still human aren't you?

PLATONOV. Sorry, I don't quite understand.

SONYA. I put it badly. You're still a man, you can still work, I mean to say, in the field of—freedom, say, or women's emancipation. There's nothing to stop you serving an ideal, is there?

NICHOLAS [*aside*]. The girl's talking through her hat.

PLATONOV [*aside*]. I see. [*To her.*] How can I put it? Perhaps there is nothing to stop me, but then how could there be? [*Laughs.*] How can anything stop me when I'm not in motion anyway? I'm like a great rock—a stumbling block, in fact.

[SHCHERBUK *comes in.*]

SCENE XIV

[*The above and* SHCHERBUK.]

SHCHERBUK [*in the doorway*]. Don't give my horses any oats, they pulled so badly.

ANNA. Oh good, my boy friend's here.

ALL. Paul. Mr. Shcherbuk.

SHCHERBUK [*silently kisses* ANNA's *and* SASHA's *hands, silently bows to the men in turn, then bows to the whole company*]. Friends, will anyone tell an unworthy specimen where the person is that he yearns to see? I strongly suspect that it's she. [*Points at* SONYA. *To* ANNA.] Will you introduce me to the lady—give her some idea what I'm like?

ANNA [*takes his arm and leads him to* SONYA]. Paul Shcherbuk, retired cornet of guards.

SHCHERBUK. Can't you put more feeling in it?

ANNA. Sorry—friend, neighbour, escort, guest and creditor.

SHCHERBUK. Quite right, I was the old general's bosom friend. Used to make conquests under his supervision—lead the ladies a dance, in other words. [*Bows.*] May I kiss your hand?

SONYA [*holds out her hand and snatches it back*]. Very charming, but—no.

SHCHERBUK. I'm hurt. I held your husband in my arms when he was no higher than this table, and he left a mark on me that I'll carry till my dying day. [*Opens his mouth.*] See? Tooth missing, isn't there? [*Laughter.*] I held him in my arms, but he knocked out my tooth with a pistol he happened to be playing with. That put me in my place, ha, ha, ha! Oh, he was quite a handful. You must keep him in hand, ma'am—don't know your name. Your beauty reminds me of some picture, but the nose is different. Can't I kiss your hand?

[PETRIN *sits by* ABRAHAM *and reads him something from the newspaper.*]

SONYA [*holds out her hand*]. If you insist then——

SHCHERBUK [*kisses her hand*]. Thanking you kindly. [*To* PLATONOV.] How are you, Michael? Quite a lad you've grown into! [*Sits down.*] When I knew you, you were still the wide-eyed innocent. But he does keep growing, doesn't he? I won't go on or I'll bring bad luck. You're one hell of a good-looking fellow, though. Why not join the army, boy?

PLATONOV. I've a weak chest.

SHCHERBUK [*points at* NICHOLAS]. Is that what he says? Trust that ass and you'll find yourself minus a head.

NICHOLAS. Don't be rude, Shcherbuk.

SHCHERBUK. He treated me for back trouble. It was 'don't eat this, don't eat that, don't sleep on the floor'. And then he never cured me. 'Why take my money when you didn't cure me?' I ask him. 'It was one thing or the other,' says he—'either cure you or take your money.' Isn't he priceless?

NICHOLAS. Don't talk such nonsense, monster. What did you pay me, may I ask? Six times I visited you, remember, and got one rouble— a torn note too. I offered it to a beggar, but he wouldn't take it, said it was torn and the number was missing.

SHCHERBUK. My illness didn't bring him over six times, it was my tenant's daughter, who's quite something.

NICHOLAS. Platonov, you're sitting near him—bang that hairless pate with my compliments, be a good fellow.

SHCHERBUK. Oh, pack it in, let sleeping dogs lie. Children should be seen and not heard. [*To* PLATONOV.] Your father was a bit of a lad too. We were great friends, the old boy and I. He loved his little joke—you don't find jokers like him and me these days. Those were the days. [*To* PETRIN.] Hey, Petrin, for heaven's sake! Read the paper while we're talking, would you? Where are your manners?

[PETRIN *goes on reading.*]

SASHA [*jogs* IVAN's *shoulder*]. Don't go to sleep here, Father, aren't you ashamed?

[IVAN *wakes up, but falls asleep again a minute later.*]

SHCHERBUK. No, I can't go on. [*Stands up.*] Better listen to him, he's reading.

PETRIN [*stands up and goes over to* PLATONOV]. What did you say, sir?

PLATONOV. Nothing whatever.

PETRIN. Yes, you did, you mentioned me.

PLATONOV. You must have imagined it.

PETRIN. A bit censorious, aren't you?

PLATONOV. I didn't speak. You imagined it, I tell you.

PETRIN. Oh, talk away for all I care. Petrin this, Petrin that. What about Petrin? [*Puts the newspaper in his pocket.*] Perhaps Petrin was at university, perhaps he took a law degree. Or didn't you know? I shall carry my degree to my grave with me. Yes sir. And I'm quite high up in the civil service, I'd have you know. I've been around a bit longer than you—I'll soon be sixty, praise God.

PLATONOV. Very nice too, but where does it get us?

PETRIN. When you're as old as me, boy, you'll know. It's no joke, life isn't, it can turn nasty on you.

PLATONOV [*shrugs*]. I really don't know what you mean, Petrin, can't make you out. First you're on about yourself, then you get on to life. What has being alive to do with you? I don't see any connection.

PETRIN. When life's shaken you up and broken you, you'll start giving young people a wide berth. Life, sir—well, what is it? Man takes one of three roads at birth—there are only three. Turn right and be eaten by wolves. Or turn left and eat them. Or else carry straight on and eat yourself.

PLATONOV. Amazing. I see. Did you reach this conclusion empirically?

PETRIN. I did.

PLATONOV. Oh, did you? [*Laughs.*] Tell that to the marines, my dear Petrin. In fact you'll spare me this high-minded chat if you take my advice. It makes me laugh and I honestly don't believe it. I distrust your senile, home-spun wisdom. You're old friends of my father, but I profoundly distrust—and I mean what I say—your homely talk of complex things and all the various bees in your bonnets.

PETRIN. Oh, indeed. You **can** make anything out of a young sapling,

I suppose—a house, a ship and so on. But an old tree's too tall and wide to be any use, of course.

PLATONOV. I'm not talking about just any old men, I mean my father's old friends.

PORFIRY. I was one too, you know.

PLATONOV. He had any amount of them, sometimes our whole yard was jammed with carriages.

PORFIRY. But—you mean you don't trust me either? [*Laughs.*]

PLATONOV. How can I put it? No, I don't trust you much either.

PORFIRY. Oh? [*Holds out his hand.*] Thanks for being so blunt, boy, it makes me like you more than ever.

PLATONOV. You're a good sort. I think a lot of you actually, but——

PORFIRY. Come on, out with it.

PLATONOV. But—. One would have to be frightfully gullible to believe in these absurd characters from eighteenth-century Russian plays—these respectable fuddy-duddies and smarmy worthies from Fonvizin who've spent their lives hobnobbing with the scum of the earth, not to mention various tyrants who are thought saintly because they do neither good nor harm. Please don't be annoyed.

ANNA. I don't like this kind of talk, especially from Platonov. It always ends badly. Michael, meet our new friend. [*Points to* ISAAC.] Isaac Vengerovich, student.

PLATONOV. Oh. [*Gets up and goes towards* ISAAC.] Delighted indeed. [*Holds out his hand.*] What I'd give to be a student again. [*Pause.*] I'm trying to shake hands, so either take mine or give me yours.

ISAAC. I won't do either.

PLATONOV. What!

ISAAC. I won't shake hands with you.

PLATONOV. This is highly mysterious. And why not?

ANNA [*aside*]. What the blazes——

ISAAC. I know what I'm doing. I despise your sort.

PLATONOV. Loud cheers. [*Looks him over.*] Awfully good, all this. Or so I'd say, but I don't want to tickle your ego—you want to look after that, you may need it later. [*Pause.*] You look down at me from a great height. No doubt you're some kind of giant.

ISAAC. I'm an honest man, not a cheap mediocrity.

PLATONOV. Oh, congratulations. Of course one hardly expects dishonesty in a young student, but it happens that your honesty isn't under discussion. So you won't shake hands, boy?

ISAAC. I don't feel all that charitable.

[NICHOLAS *hisses.*]

PLATONOV. So you won't shake hands? Have it your own way. I was talking about good manners, not about your views on charity. Do you despise me very much?

ISAAC. As much as any man who heartily loathes scroungers, phoneys and mediocrities.

PLATONOV [*sighs*]. I haven't heard this sort of thing for ages, it's quite like the old days. At one time I was pretty good at dishing it out myself. Unfortunately it's all just talk—all very nice, but a lot of hot air. Oh for one grain of sincerity! False notes jar terribly when one's not used to them.

ISAAC. How about changing the subject?

PLATONOV. Why? The audience is enjoying it and we're not yet utterly sick of each other. Let's carry on in the same vein.

[VASILY *runs in, followed by* OSIP.]

SCENE XV

[*The above and* OSIP.]

OSIP [*comes in*]. Hurrumph! Honoured and delighted to congratulate your ladyship on your safe arrival. [*Pause.*] May all your prayers be granted. [*Laughter.*]

PLATONOV. Who's this I see? The devil's bosom pal? The scourge of the neighbourhood? The fiend in human shape?

ANNA. Really, this is the last straw! What brought you here?

OSIP. I came to pay my respects.

ANNA. You needn't have bothered. Now go and lose yourself.

PLATONOV. So it's you, the man who strikes terror by day and night. Haven't seen you for ages, you apocalyptic beast. Aren't you going to hold forth, my murderous friend? Pray silence for great Osip!

OSIP [*bows*]. Glad to see your ladyship. Best wishes to you, Mr. Voynitsev, on the occasion of your marriage. Best of luck on the family side—all the best of everything.

SERGEY. Thank you. [*To* SONYA.] This is the family bogyman.

ANNA. Don't let him stay, Platonov, he must leave. I'm very annoyed with him. [*To* OSIP.] Tell them to give you a meal in the kitchen. Look at his eyes, like a wild beast. How much of our timber did you steal this winter?

OSIP [*laughs*]. Only three or four trees. [*Laughter.*]

ANNA [*laughs*]. Rubbish, you stole more. Why, he's got a watch chain! I really believe it's gold. May I ask what time it is?

OSIP [*looks at the clock on the wall*]. Twenty-two minutes past one. May I kiss your hand?

ANNA [*lifts her hand to his lips*]. All right then.

OSIP [*kisses her hand*]. Thank you for your kindness, ma'am. [*Bows.*] Why are you holding me, Mr. Platonov?

PLATONOV. I don't want you to go. I like you, old man, you're a hell of a fellow, damn you! But what possessed you to call here, O sage?

OSIP. I was chasing that ass Vasily and took the chance to drop in.

PLATONOV. A wise man chasing a fool—shouldn't it be the other way round? Ladies and gentlemen, I have the honour to present a fascinating specimen. One of the most intriguing carnivores from the contemporary circus. [*Turns* OSIP *in all directions.*] Known to one and all as Osip—horse-thief, parasite, murderer, burglar. Born in Voynitsevka, he's done his murders and burglaries in that village and it's there he's finishing his rake's progress. [*Laughter.*]

OSIP [*laughs*]. You are a funny one, Mr. Platonov.

NICHOLAS [*looks* OSIP *over*]. What's your job, my man?

OSIP. Thieving, sir.

NICHOLAS. I see. A nice sort of job. You're pretty cynical, I must say.

OSIP. What's cynical?

NICHOLAS. Cynic's a Greek word. Translated into your language it means someone who's a filthy swine and doesn't care ho knows it.

PLATONOV. Ye gods, he grins! And what a grin! And look at his face —solid concrete, they don't come any tougher. [*Takes him to a mirror.*] Look, monster. See? Aren't you amazed?

OSIP. I'm no better than the next man. Worse perhaps.

PLATONOV. Think so? But you're a hero, you're quite fabulous. [*Claps him on the shoulder.*] O bold, conquering Russian! You put us all in the shade, us miserable little parasites, with our fidgeting and mooning around. We ought to go into the desert with you and the knights of old. We should have a go at some of those giants with two-ton heads and all their hissing and whistling. I believe you'd take on the devil himself.

OSIP. Don't rightly know, sir.

PLATONOV. You'd soon settle his hash, you're tough enough, with those muscles like steel cables. Why aren't you in prison, by the way?

ANNA. Platonov, stop it, this is a bore.

PLATONOV. Done time, haven't you, Osip?

OSIP. I've been inside—every winter, actually.

PLATONOV. Very right and proper. It's cold in the woods, so go to prison. But why aren't you there now?

OSIP. I don't know. Can I go now, sir?

PLATONOV. A bit out of this world, aren't you? Outside time and space? Above custom and the law?

OSIP. Look, sir. The law says you can only be sent to Siberia if you're caught red-handed or there's proof against you. Everyone knows I'm a thief and a villain, granted [*laughs*], but not everyone can prove it. People are so feeble these days, they're stupid, haven't any sense. They're always afraid, so they're afraid to give evidence. They could get me deported, but they don't know their law. They're afraid of everything. In fact your peasant's an ass, sir. They gang up and do things behind your back, oh, they're a rotten, miserable lot. Shocking ignorant they are. They deserve what they get, that bunch.

PLATONOV. What pompous talk, you swine. Got it all worked out, haven't you? Repulsive animal! All based on theory! [*Sighs.*] What rotten things can still happen in Russia.

OSIP. I'm not the only one, sir, everyone's this way nowadays—take Mr. Vengerovich here——

PLATONOV. Yes, but he's outside the law too. We all know it, no one can prove it.

ABRAHAM. Can't you leave me out of it?

PLATONOV [*to* OSIP]. No point bringing him in, he's the same as you, except for having more sense and being happy as a sandboy. And one can't quite tell him what one thinks of him—unlike you. You're both tarred with the same brush, but—. He owns sixty taverns, man —sixty! You don't own sixty copecks.

ABRAHAM. Sixty-three, actually.

PLATONOV. It'll be seventy-three by next year. He gives to charity, holds dinner parties. People respect him, take their hats off to him, while you—you may be a great man, but you don't know how to live, boy. You haven't the art, you rascal.

ABRAHAM. This is getting a bit fanciful, Platonov. [*Gets up and sits on another chair.*]

PLATONOV. He's better insured against sudden storms. He'll live in peace to twice his present age, if not longer, and he'll die a peaceful death, won't he?

ANNA. Stop it, Platonov.

SERGEY. Take it easy, Michael. Osip, please leave, you only bring out the worst in Platonov.

ABRAHAM. He'd like to get rid of me too, but he won't.

PLATONOV. I will—or else I'll leave myself.

ANNA. Will you stop, Platonov? Don't beat about the bush—will you give over or not?

SASHA. For heaven's sake be quiet. [*Quietly.*] This isn't very nice, you're letting me down.

PLATONOV [*to* OSIP]. Buzz off! I heartily wish you may get lost double quick.

OSIP. A friend of mine called Martha has a parrot that calls everyone 'you fool'—dogs too. But when it sees a hawk or Mr. Vengerovich, it shouts, 'Damn you!' [*Laughs.*] Good-bye. [*Goes.*]

SCENE XVI

[*The above except* OSIP.]

ABRAHAM. Don't lecture me, boy, or adopt that line—you're the last person who should take such a liberty. I'm a citizen and, I can truthfully say, a useful one. I'm a father. But what are you, boy? A popinjay, sir, a bankrupt squire too corrupt to parade as a crusader.

PLATONOV. If you're a citizen, that makes citizen a very dirty word indeed.

ANNA. Won't he stop? Must you wreck our day with your harangues? Why talk so much, what right have you?

NICHOLAS. These paragons of justice and honesty are uncomfortable to live with, they must have a finger in every pie.

PORFIRY. I say, isn't this getting rather out of hand?

ANNA [*to* PLATONOV]. Quarrelsome guests embarrass their hosts, remember?

SERGEY. True, so let's all simmer down this instant. Let's have peace, harmony and silence.

ABRAHAM. He's always badgering me. What have I done to him? The man's a mountebank!

SERGEY. Shush!

NICHOLAS. Let them quarrel, it's more amusing. [*Pause.*]

PLATONOV. When you look around and really think, you feel ready to faint. Anyone at all decent and tolerable holds his tongue and just looks on, that's what's so awful. They all stand in awe of this bloated upstart and kow-tow to him. Everyone's in his clutches. Decency's flown out of the window.

ANNA. Take it easy, Platonov. This is last year's business all over again, and that I can't stand.

PLATONOV [*drinks water*]. All right. [*Sits down.*]

ABRAHAM. All right. [*Pause.*]

SHCHERBUK. I'm in agony, friends—agony.

ANNA. What is it now?

SHCHERBUK. I'm so unhappy, everyone. Better be dead and buried than live with a bad wife. There's been another to-do. Last week she and that blasted, red-haired lover-boy of hers practically murdered me. I'm sleeping out of doors under the apple-tree enjoying my dreams and looking enviously on scenes from my past life. [*Sighs.*] Then all of a sudden there's a great blow on my head. Help! My last hour's come, thinks I. Is it an earthquake? The elements in conflict, a flood, a rain of fire? I open my eyes and there's friend Ginger. Catches me round the middle in a ruddy great bear hug, then hurls me on the ground. Up jumps that evil woman, grips me by my innocent beard. [*Clutches his beard.*] It was no joke. [*Hits his bald head.*] They nearly killed me, I thought my hour had come.

ANNA. You're exaggerating.

SHCHERBUK. She's an old woman. She's as old as they come, all skin and bone, the old hag—and she has to have a lover. Old bitch! That suits Ginger down to the ground, of course. It's my money, not her love, he's after.

[JACOB *comes in and hands* ANNA *a visiting card.*]

SERGEY. Who's that from?

ANNA. Oh, do be quiet, Mr. Shcherbuk. [*Reads.*] 'Le Comte Glagolyev.' Why so much ceremony? Please ask him in. [*To* PORFIRY.] Your son.

PORFIRY. My son? Where's he sprung from? He's abroad.

[CYRIL *comes in.*]

SCENE XVII

[*The above and* CYRIL.]

ANNA. My dear Cyril, this is nice.

PORFIRY [*stands up*]. So you're here? [*Sits down.*]

CYRIL. Morning, ladies, Platonov, Vengerovich, Triletsky. So the eccentric Mr. Platonov's here. Best wishes, all. It's fearfully hot in Russia. I'm straight from Paris, straight from French soil. Phew! You don't believe me? My word of honour. I just took my suitcase home. Well, everyone, Paris is quite a town!

SERGEY. Sit down, Frenchman.

CYRIL. No, no, no. I'm not staying, just dropped in. I only need a word with Father. [*To his father.*] Now look here, what does this mean?

PORFIRY. What does what mean?

CYRIL. Trying to pick a quarrel? Why didn't you send me the money I asked for?

PORFIRY. We can talk about that at home.

CYRIL. Why didn't you send me the money? Laughing, are you, think it's just a joke? Oh, very funny! Ladies and gentlemen, can a man live abroad without money?

ANNA. How did you get on in Paris? Do sit down, Cyril.

CYRIL. Thanks to him I came back with only a toothbrush. Thirty-five telegrams I sent him from Paris. Why didn't you send me money, eh? Red in the face, are you? Feeling ashamed of yourself?

NICHOLAS. Don't shout, your lordship. If you won't stop I'll send your visiting card to the police and prosecute you for passing yourself off as a count. It's not decent.

PORFIRY. Don't make a scene, Cyril. I thought six thousand was enough. Do calm down.

CYRIL. Give me some money so I can go back again. Give it me right away. I'm just leaving, so hurry up. No time to waste.

ANNA. Why the great rush? You've plenty of time. Tell us about your travels instead.

JACOB [*comes in*]. Lunch is served, madam.

ANNA. Oh, in that case let's go and eat.

NICHOLAS. Lunch, eh? Loud cheers! [*Takes* SASHA'S *arm with one hand and* CYRIL'S *with the other and starts to run off.*]

SASHA. Let me go, you lunatic. I can get there without your help.

CYRIL. Let go, you lout. I don't like jokes. [*Breaks away.*]

[SASHA *and* NICHOLAS *run out.*]

ANNA [*takes* CYRIL'S *arm*]. Come, Mr. Parisian, don't get hot under the collar. [*To* ABRAHAM *and* BUGROV.] Lunch, gentlemen. [*Goes out with* CYRIL.]

BUGROV [*stands up and stretches*]. You could starve to death waiting for lunch here. [*Goes out.*]

PLATONOV [*offers* SONYA *his arm*]. May I? Don't look so surprised. This is an unknown world to you—a world [*in a quieter voice*] of idiots, Sonya, complete, utter, hopeless idiots. [*Goes out with* SONYA.]

ABRAHAM [*to his son*]. See what I mean?

ISAAC. A most original scoundrel. [*Goes out with his father.*]

SERGEY [*nudges* IVAN]. Lunch, Colonel.

IVAN [*jumps up*]. Eh? Who's that?

SERGEY. No one. Come and have lunch.

IVAN. Splendid, old boy. [*Goes out with* SERGEY *and* SHCHERBUK.]

SCENE XVIII

[PETRIN *and* PORFIRY.]

PETRIN. Are you game then?

PORFIRY. I don't mind, as I said before.

PETRIN. So you'll really marry her, old man?

PORFIRY. I don't know, old boy. Is she at all keen?

PETRIN. You bet your life she is.

PORFIRY. I don't know, one mustn't take things for granted. You never know what's at the back of people's minds. But where do you come in?

PETRIN. My concern for you, old boy. You're a good man, she's a fine woman. Shall I put in a word?

PORFIRY. No, I'll do that. Keep it to yourself, please try not to fuss, I'm quite capable of marrying without assistance. [*Goes out.*]

PETRIN [*alone*]. If only he were! Holy Moses, put yourselves in my place. If Anna Voynitsev marries him, I'm rich, I'll get back all the money I lent her, by God! The idea's so marvellous, I don't think I can eat my lunch. Dost thou, Anna, take this man Porfiry to be thy wedded husband? Or should it be the other way round?

[ANNA *comes in.*]

SCENE XIX

[PETRIN *and* ANNA.]

ANNA. Why don't you come and have lunch?

PETRIN. Can you take a hint, Anna dear?

ANNA. Yes, but be quick about it, I'm busy.

PETRIN. I see. How about giving me a spot of cash, dear?

ANNA. Hint! I don't call that a hint. How much? One rouble? Two?

PETRIN. Can't you do something about that money you owe me? I'm fed up with IOUs—they're a great fraud, a mirage. The money's yours on paper, but in practice it isn't.

ANNA. You're not still on about that sixty thousand? Aren't you ashamed? I don't know how you have the nerve to bother me about it—scandalous! What can an old bachelor like you want with the wretched stuff?

PETRIN. It just happens to be mine, dear lady.

ANNA. You wangled those IOUs out of my husband when he was drunk and ill, remember?

PETRIN. What do you mean? That's what IOUs are for, so you can present them for payment. Accounts should be settled.

ANNA. All right, that will do. I've no money and never shall have for your sort. Run along and sue me, Mr. Legal Eagle. All this jiggery-pokery when you've already got one foot in the grave! You *are* funny.

PETRIN. May I drop a hint, dear?

ANNA. You may not. [*Moves towards the door.*] Come and have some grub.

PETRIN. One moment, dear lady. Do you like friend Porfiry?

ANNA. Mind your own business and keep your nose out of mine, even if you do have a law degree.

PETRIN. Mind my own business! [*Beats his chest.*] And who, might I ask, was the late Major-General's best friend? Who closed his eyes when he died?

ANNA. You, you, you—and much good may it do you.

PETRIN. I'll go and drink to his memory. [*Sighs.*] And to you too. You're proud and arrogant, madam. Pride's a vice. [*Goes out.*]

[PLATONOV *comes in.*]

SCENE XX

[ANNA *and* PLATONOV.]

PLATONOV. What damned cheek! You tell him to go and he blandly stays put—a self-centred, money-grubbing oaf if ever I saw one. What are you thinking about, madam?

ANNA. Have you calmed down?

PLATONOV. Yes, but don't let's be annoyed. [*Kisses her hand.*] Your guests all deserve to be sent packing, dearest lady.

ANNA. I'd love to throw them out myself, you awful man. You were holding forth about decency and making some digs at me. But it's easy enough to be decent in theory, the trouble comes when you try to put it into practice. Neither you nor I have the right to chuck them out, my eloquent friend. They're our patrons and creditors, you see. I've only to look at them the wrong way and we'll be put off this estate tomorrow. It's my honour or my estate, you see. I've chosen the estate. Make what you like of it, my talkative friend, and unless you want me to leave this delightful neighbourhood, don't talk to me about decency and don't interfere. Someone's calling me. Let's go for a ride this afternoon, and don't you dare go away! [*Claps him on the shoulder.*] We'll have some fun. Come and eat. [*Goes out.*]

PLATONOV [*after a pause*]. I'll boot him out none the less, I'll have them all out. Stupid and bad-mannered it may be, but I'll do it. I swore I'd leave these swine alone, but I can't help it. You can't keep a good man down—still less a weakling.

[ISAAC *comes in.*]

SCENE XXI

[PLATONOV *and* ISAAC.]

ISAAC. Look here, Mr. Schoolmaster, I'd advise you to leave my father alone.

PLATONOV. I'm grateful for your advice.

ISAAC. I'm not joking. My father has a lot of friends, so he can easily get you sacked. I'm warning you.

PLATONOV. Very decent of you, boy. What's your first name?

ISAAC. Isaac.

PLATONOV. So Abraham begat Isaac, did he? Thank you, my noble young friend. Now, will you in turn kindly give your dear daddy this message? For all I care he and his many friends can go and boil their heads. Now get some food, boy, or you'll find it's all gone.

ISAAC [*shrugs his shoulders and moves towards the door*]. This is funny, if not downright silly. [*Stops.*] Don't think I'm annoyed with you for bothering my father because I'm not. I'm not annoyed, I'm simply observing—studying you as a typical modern square peg in a round hole. I understand you all too well. If you were happy, if you weren't so bored and idle, you'd leave my father alone, believe me. You aren't seeking the meaning of life, my dear misfit, you're just indulging yourself, having a good time. There are no serfs these days, so you have to find someone else to take it out of, which is why you pitch into every Tom, Dick and Harry.

PLATONOV [*laughs*]. This is really good, honestly. You know, you actually have some degree of imagination.

ISAAC. You never pick on my father in private—that sticks out a mile, that's what's so disgusting. You stage your little entertainment in the drawing-room where fools can see you in all your glory. Quite the showman, aren't you?

PLATONOV. I'd like a word with you in about ten years, or even five. I wonder how you'll last. Will the tone of voice and flashing eyes still be intact? But I fear you'll go down the drain, boy. How are your studies? Not well, I see from your face. You'll come to no good. Anyway, go and get your lunch. I shan't talk to you any more, I dont like that bad-tempered face.

ISAAC [*laughs*]. You're quite the sensitive plant! [*Goes towards the door.*] I'd rather seem bad-tempered than look as if I wanted a good punch on the jaw.

PLATONOV. No doubt, but run along and eat.

ISAAC. We're not on speaking terms, and don't you forget it. [*Goes out.*]

PLATONOV [*alone*]. That young fool thinks a lot and talks a lot—behind people's backs. [*Looks through the door of the dining-room.*] She's looking round, looking for me with those lovely, soft eyes. How pretty she still is, how beautiful her face is. Her hair's the same, same colour and style. How often I've kissed that hair and what wonderful memories that little head brings back. [*Pause.*] Can I really be so old that I must live on memories? [*Pause.*] Memories are all right in a way, but—is my day really over? God, I hope not, I'd rather be dead. I must live, must go on living. I'm still young.

[SERGEY *comes in.*]

SCENE XXII

[PLATONOV, SERGEY *and, later,* NICHOLAS.]

SERGEY [*comes in and wipes his mouth with a napkin*]. Come and drink Sonya's health, don't hide in here. Well?

PLATONOV. I've been admiring your wife—magnificent woman.

[SERGEY *laughs.*]

PLATONOV. You're a lucky man.

SERGEY. Quite true. Well, actually, er—one can't call me always lucky, but I suppose I usually am.

PLATONOV [*looks through the dining-room door*]. I've known her for ages, Sergey, I know her pretty well in fact. She's very good-looking, but not a patch on what she used to be. Pity you didn't know her then —what a lovely woman!

SERGEY. Yes.

PLATONOV. What eyes.

SERGEY. And what hair.

PLATONOV. She was a splendid girl. [*Laughs.*] But what about my Sasha! There's a real peasant for you. There she is, you can just see her behind the vodka decanter. All hot and bothered about my behaviour. In agony, poor thing, because I'm in bad odour over my slanging match with Vengerovich.

SERGEY. Excuse my asking, but are you happy together?

PLATONOV. She's my wife, man. If I lost her, I think I'd go to seed completely. Good old family life—you'll learn in good time. It's a pity you haven't knocked around enough and don't know what a good thing a family is. I wouldn't take a million roubles for dear old Sasha. She's a fool and I'm a dead loss, so we get on like a house on fire.

[NICHOLAS *comes in.*]

PLATONOV [*to* NICHOLAS]. Been tanking up?

NICHOLAS. Not half. [*Slaps his stomach.*] Good solid stuff. Come on, boys and girls, have a drink! Little welcome-home celebration! Good old pals! [*Embraces both together.*] Come and have a drink. Ah well. [*Stretches.*] Ah well, such is life. Happy the man who doth not visit the congregation of the unrighteous. [*Stretches.*] Good old pals! Lot of dirty scoundrels!

PLATONOV Seen your patients to-day?

NICHOLAS. Tell you later. Look here, Michael, once and for all, will you leave me alone? I'm sick and tired of you and your lectures. Have a heart! You'll get no change out of me, I can tell you that. If you can't help coming out with these things, let me have your stuff in

writing—I'll learn it by heart. Or lecture me at some definite time of
day. You can have one hour a day, say four to five in the afternoon,
eh? I'll even pay you a rouble an hour. [*Stretches.*] The whole day
long——

PLATONOV [*to* SERGEY]. I say, what's the idea of that advertisement in
the *Gazette*? Has it really come to that?

SERGEY. No, don't worry. [*Laughs.*] It's a little business deal. There'll be
an auction and Glagolyev will buy the estate. He'll get the bank off
our necks and we'll pay him the interest instead. It's his idea.

PLATONOV. I don't get it. What's in it for him? Or is he just being
generous? I don't understand such generosity, and I can't see that
you—well, need it.

SERGEY. No. Actually, I don't quite see it either. Better ask Mother,
she'll explain. I only know that we'll keep the estate after the sale
and we'll pay Glagolyev for it. Mother's giving him a down payment of five thousand straight away. He's easier to deal with than the
bank, anyway. God, am I fed up with that bank! I'm even more
sick of it than Triletsky is of you. Don't let's talk business. [*Takes*
PLATONOV *by the arm.*] Come on, we'll drink and be friends.
Nicholas, come on, old man. [*Takes* NICHOLAS *by the arm.*] Let's
drink and be friends, friends. I don't care if I lose all I possess, and to
hell with these commercial transactions, as long as those I love are
alive and well—you, my Sonya and my mother-in-law. You're my
whole life. Come on.

PLATONOV. Coming. I'll drink to all that, so I'll probably drink you
dry. I haven't been drunk for ages and I feel like really pushing the
boat out.

ANNA [*through the door*]. So this is what friendship means. A fine team
you three make. [*Sings.*] 'When I harness three fleet horses——'

NICHOLAS. 'Yes, a team of nut-brown horses.' Let's start on the brandy,
boys.

ANNA [*through the door*]. Come and eat, you scroungers, it's all cold.

PLATONOV. So this is friendship. I've always been lucky in love but
never in friendship. I'm afraid you too may all come to regret my
friendship. Let's drink to the happy ending of all friendships, our
own included. May it end as quietly and peacefully as its beginning.
[*Goes into the dining-room.*]

END OF ACT ONE

ACT TWO

PART ONE

The garden. In the foreground a flowerbed which has a path round it and a statue in the middle with a lampion on top. Benches, chairs, small tables. On the right, the front of the house with porch. Open windows through which comes the sound of laughter, conversation, and of a piano and violin playing quadrilles, waltzes and so on. At the back of the garden, a Chinese summer-house festooned with lanterns, and with the monogram 'S.V.' over the entrance. Beyond that a game of skittles is in progress, the rolling of balls is heard and shouts: 'Five down, four up' and so on. The garden and house are lit up. Guests and servants dart about the garden. VASILY *and* JACOB (*drunk and in tails*) *hang up lanterns and light lampions.*

SCENE I

[BUGROV *and* NICHOLAS, *who wears a peaked cap with a cockade.*]

NICHOLAS [*comes out of doors arm-in-arm with* BUGROV]. Come on, it's nothing to you—I'm only asking for a loan.

BUGROV. Don't be hard on me, sir, I honestly can't.

NICHOLAS. But you can, Bugrov, you can afford anything. You could buy the universe twice over, but you can't be bothered. I only want a loan, man, don't you see? I swear I'll never pay it back.

BUGROV. You see! Let the cat out of the bag there, didn't you?

NICHOLAS. I see nothing except how callous you are. Come on, great man, hand over. Come on, man. I ask you—beg you then. Are you really so unfeeling? Have a heart.

BUGROV [*sighs*]. Well, Doctor, you may not cure your patients, but you certainly know how to present your bill.

NICHOLAS. Well said. [*Sighs.*] You're right.

BUGROV [*takes out his wallet*]. You're always making fun of people, always ready with your sniggers. You shouldn't, you know, you really shouldn't. I haven't much book-learning, but I am a Christian, same as you brainy fellows. If I say something silly, put me right—

don't just laugh. No sir. We're only peasants, we're a rough, thick-skinned lot, so don't expect too much—make allowances. [*Opens his wallet.*] For the last time. [*Counts.*] One, six, twelve.

NICHOLAS [*looks into the wallet*]. Ye gods! And Russians are always said to be broke! Where did you pick up that lot?

BUGROV. Fifty. [*Gives him the money.*] For the last time.

NICHOLAS. What's that little note? Hand that over too, it's looking at me with tears in its eyes. [*Takes the money.*] Come on, hand over.

BUGROV [*gives it to him*]. Take it. You are greedy, though.

NICHOLAS. What, all in one-rouble notes? Been going round begging or something? Not forgeries, are they?

BUGROV. Give them back if they're forgeries.

NICHOLAS. I would if you needed them. Thanks, and may you put on still more weight and get a medal. But tell me, why do you lead such an odd life? You drink a lot, you talk in that deep voice, you sweat, and you don't sleep at the right times. Why aren't you asleep now, for instance? You're a bilious, bad-tempered little grocer with high blood pressure and you ought to go to bed early. And you have more veins than ordinary people. How can you kill yourself like this?

BUGROV. I say——

NICHOLAS. Oh, you do, do you? Anyway, don't be frightened, I'm only joking. You're not ready to die yet, you'll survive. Pretty well-heeled, aren't you, Bugrov?

BUGROV. I've enough to last my day.

NICHOLAS. You're a nice, clever fellow, but a great rogue. Excuse me, I'm speaking as a friend. We are friends, aren't we? A great rogue. Why are you buying up Voynitsev's debts and lending him money?

BUGROV. That's a bit out of your depth, sir.

NICHOLAS. So you want to get your paws on Anna Voynitsev's mine, you and Vengerovich? She's to take pity on her stepson and give him the mine to save him from going bankrupt, is that the idea? You're a great man, but a rogue—a real shark.

BUGROV. Now I'm going to have a nap somewhere near the summer-house. Will you wake me up when supper's ready?

NICHOLAS. Splendid. Go and have your nap.

BUGROV [*moves off*]. If they don't serve supper, wake me at half past ten. [*Goes off to the summer-house.*]

SCENE II

[NICHOLAS *and, later,* SERGEY.]

NICHOLAS [*examines the money*]. Smells of peasant! The swine's certainly lined his pockets! What shall I do with it? [*To* VASILY *and* JACOB.] Hey, flunkeys! Vasily, tell Jacob to come here. Jacob, tell Vasily to come here. Come on, this way and look slippy.

[JACOB *and* VASILY *come up to* NICHOLAS.]

NICHOLAS. In tails too, damn it! Quite the gentlemen of leisure. [*Gives* JACOB *a rouble*.] One for you. [*To* VASILY.] And one for you. That's for having long noses.

JACOB *and* VASILY [*bow*]. Many thanks, sir.

NICHOLAS. Unsteady on your pins, lads? Drunk, eh? Both feeling a bit ropy? You'll catch it if the mistress finds out, you'll get your ears boxed. [*Gives them another rouble*.] Another rouble for you. That's because you're Jacob and he's Vasily, and not the other way round. Now bow.

[JACOB *and* VASILY *bow*.]

NICHOLAS. Very nice. And here's another rouble because I'm Nicholas and not Ivan. [*Gives them another*.] Bow. That's right. And mind you don't spend it all on drink, or I'll prescribe you something nasty. Quite the gentlemen, aren't you? Now go and light lanterns. Quick march, I've had enough of you.

[JACOB *and* VASILY *go out.* SERGEY *crosses the stage*.]

NICHOLAS [*to* SERGEY]. Here's three roubles for you.

[SERGEY *takes the money, puts it in his pocket automatically and goes to the back of the garden.*]

NICHOLAS. You might say thanks.

[IVAN *and* SASHA *come out of the house.*]

SCENE III

[NICHOLAS, IVAN *and* SASHA.]

SASHA [*coming in*]. Oh, when will all this end? Dear God, why have you punished me so? Here's Father drunk, and so are Nicholas and Michael. Have you no shame? Have you no fear of God, even if you don't care what men think? They're all looking at you. And I— how do you think I feel with them all pointing at you?

IVAN. That's all wrong. Stop, you've got me mixed up. Stop it.

SASHA. You're not fit to be let inside a decent house—hardly through the front door and already drunk. You're quite revolting! And at your age! You should set an example, not join in.

IVAN. Stop it, you've got mé mixed up. What was I on about? Oh yes. I'm not lying, girl. Another five years in the army, and I'd have been a general, take it from me. Don't you think so? Faugh! [*Laughs.*] What, not a general—a man of my calibre! With my education? You've precious little sense if that's your idea, precious little.

SASHA. Let's go. Generals don't drink so much.

IVAN. Everyone drinks when he's happy. I'd be a general. And kindly shut up, you're just like your mother—fuss, fuss, fuss, God help us. She kept at it day and night, nothing was ever right. Fuss, fuss, fuss! Now what was I on about? Yes, you're your mother's image, my pet, absolutely. Eyes and hair—. She waddled like a goose too. [*Kisses her.*] Darling, you're just like your dear mother, I loved her terribly.

SASHA. That'll do. Let's go on. Seriously, Father, it's time you gave up drinking and making scenes. Leave it to these hearty types. They're young, and it really doesn't suit an old man like you.

IVAN. Very well, dear, I see what you mean. I'll stop then. All right, I take the point. Now what was I on about?

NICHOLAS [*to* IVAN]. A hundred copecks, Colonel. [*Gives him a rouble.*]

IVAN. Just so. I accept, son. Thanks. I wouldn't take it from just anyone, but from my son—with great pleasure, always. I don't like other people's money, children, God I don't. I'm an honest man, your father's honest. Never robbed my country or my family in my life, though I only had to help myself here and there to be rich and famous.

NICHOLAS. Good for you, Father, but don't boast.

IVAN. I'm not, I'm giving you children a few tips, showing you the ropes. I'll answer for you to the Almighty.

NICHOLAS. Where are you going?

IVAN. Home. I'm taking this little creature home too. She's been on and on about it, really pitched into me—so I'm seeing her home. She's afraid to go alone, so I'll see her there and come back again.

NICHOLAS. Come back, of course. [*To* SASHA.] Would you like some too? Here you are then, three roubles for you.

SASHA. Give me two more while you're about it, so Michael can have some summer trousers—he only has one pair. It's awful only having one pair, he has to wear woollen ones when they're being washed.

NICHOLAS. If I had my way he'd get none, light or heavy. Let him make do. But how can I refuse you? Here's two more. [*Gives her the money.*]

IVAN. What was I on about? Oh yes, it all comes back to me—I was on the general staff once, thinking of ways to kill Turks. I was an armchair warrior—never one for cold steel, no sir. Ah, well.

SASHA. Why are we hanging about? Let's go. Good-bye, Nicholas. Come on, Father.

IVAN. One moment. For God's sake shut up. Chatter, chatter, chatter, like a ruddy bird-cage. Now this is how to live, children—with decency, honesty, integrity. Yes indeed. I got the Order of St. Vladimir, third class.

SASHA. That'll do, Father. Come on.

NICHOLAS. We know you already—no need to make speeches. Now run along and see her home.

IVAN. You're a smart lad, Nicholas, you might turn out like Pirogov— a great doctor.

NICHOLAS. Oh, run along.

IVAN. What was I on about? Oh yes. I once met Pirogov, when he was still in Kiev. Yes indeed—very smart boy, Pirogov, pretty good. All right, I'm off. Come on, Sasha. I'm so weak, I feel as if I'm on my last legs. Lord, forgive us sinners. I have sinned, yea I have sinned.

Yes indeed. I'm a sinner, children, I serve Mammon. Never said my prayers as a boy, always had my eye on the main chance. I've been a real materialist, I have. Yes indeed. You must pray for me not to die, children. Have you gone, Sasha? Where are you? Oh, there you are. Come on.

[ANNA *looks out of the window.*]

NICHOLAS. He still hasn't budged. The old chap's raving. Run along then, and don't go past the mill or the dogs'll get you.

SASHA. You've got his cap on, Nicholas. Give it him or he'll catch cold.

NICHOLAS [*takes the cap and puts it on his father*]. On your way, revered parent. Left turn and quick march!

IVAN. Left incline! Yes indeed. You're quite right, Nicholas, God knows. And so's Michael. He's a free-thinker, but he has the right ideas. All right, I'm going. [*They move off.*] Come on, Sasha. Are you coming or shall I carry you?

SASHA. Don't be silly.

IVAN. Let me carry you. I always used to carry your mother—made me a bit unsteady on my pins, though. Once came a cropper carrying her over a little hill. She just laughed, dear woman—wasn't a bit angry. Let me carry you.

SASHA. Don't make things up. And put your cap on properly. [*Adjusts his cap.*] You're still quite one of the boys, Father.

IVAN. Yes indeed.

[*They go out.* PETRIN *and* SHCHERBUK *come in.*]

SCENE IV

[NICHOLAS, PETRIN *and* SHCHERBUK.]

PETRIN [*comes out of doors arm-in-arm with* SHCHERBUK]. Put fifty thousand in front of me and I'd steal it. On my word of honour. As long as I knew I wouldn't be caught. I'd steal it, and you'd do the same.

SHCHERBUK. No, I would not.

PETRIN. Put down one rouble and I'd steal that. Honesty! You make me sick. Who wants your honesty? Show me an honest man and you show me a fool.

SHCHERBUK. I'm a fool then.

NICHOLAS. Here's a rouble each, reverend sirs. [*Gives them each a rouble.*]

PETRIN [*takes the money*]. Let's have it.

SHCHERBUK [*laughs loudly and takes the money*]. Thanks, Doctor.

NICHOLAS. A bit pickled, eh, gentlemen?

PETRIN. A bit.

NICHOLAS. And here's another rouble to have prayers said for your souls. You're sinful, aren't you? So take it. I should tell you both to go to hell, but as it's a holiday—I'll be generous, damn it.

ANNA [*at the window*]. Triletsky, give me a rouble. [*Disappears.*]

NICHOLAS. What, one rouble for a major-general's widow! You get five. Coming. [*Goes indoors.*]

PETRIN [*looks at the window*]. Has our fairy princess disappeared?

SHCHERBUK [*looks at the window*]. Yes.

PETRIN. I can't stand her. She's a bad woman, too proud. Women should be quiet and respectful. [*Shakes his head.*] Have you seen Glagolyev? What a stuffed shirt. Squats there like a toadstool, doesn't move or speak—just goggles at you. Is that how to win a lady's heart?

SHCHERBUK. He'll marry her.

PETRIN. Yes, but when? In a hundred years? A hundred years is no good to me, thank you.

SHCHERBUK. Why should the old boy marry, Gerasim? If he really must, he should marry some ordinary woman. He's no good for Anna. She's a girl of spirit, a true European, educated——

PETRIN. Oh, I do wish he would—I'm so keen on it, words fail me. You see, they haven't had a bean since the old general died, may he rest in peace. She owns a mine, but Vengerovich has his eye on that, and who am I to cross swords with Vengerovich? And what can I get on their IOUs as things stand? If I present them now, what'll I get?

SHCHERBUK. Not a thing.

PETRIN. But if she marries Glagolyev, I'll know how to get my money. I'll send in my bills at once and put the bailiffs in. She won't let her stepson go bankrupt, she'll pay up. Oh Lord, may all my dreams come true. Sixteen thousand roubles, Paul my boy.

SHCHERBUK. They owe me three thousand. My old woman tells me to get it back, but I don't know how to. We're not dealing with peasants, they're our friends. Just let *her* try and get it out of them! Shall we go over to the lodge, Gerasim?

PETRIN. What for?

SHCHERBUK. We'll whisper sweet ballads while the ladies dance.

PETRIN. Is Dunyasha there?

SHCHERBUK. Yes. [*They move off.*] It's more fun there. [*Sings.*] 'I've been so unhappy since I stopped living there.'

PETRIN. Tick tock, tick tock. [*Shouts.*] Yes indeed. [*Sings.*]
　　　'We greet the New Year with delight
　　　Among our very dearest friends.'

[*Goes out.*]

SCENE V

[SERGEY *and* SONYA, *emerging from the back of the garden.*]

SERGEY. What are you thinking about?

SONYA. I really don't know.

SERGEY. Why won't you let me help you—don't you think I can? Why all the mysteries, Sonya—secrets from your husband? [*They sit down.*]

SONYA. What secrets? I don't know what's the matter with me either. Don't torment yourself for no reason, and pay no attention to my bad moods. [*Pause.*] Let's go away from here.

SERGEY. What, leave?

SONYA. Yes.

SERGEY. Why?

SONYA. I want to, I want to go abroad. How about it?

SERGEY. You want to—. But why?

SONYA. This life is good, healthy and lots of fun, but it's all too much for me. Everything in the garden's lovely, only—we must go away. You promised you wouldn't ask questions.

SERGEY. We'll go tomorrow then, get away from here. [*Kisses her hands.*] You're bored here and no wonder, I know how you feel. What a damn awful lot! These Petrins and Shcherbuks——

SONYA. It's not their fault, let's leave them out of it. [*Pause.*]

SERGEY. How do you women manage to get so depressed. Why so downhearted? [*Kisses her cheek.*] That'll do, now cheer up. Make the most of life. Can't you pack up your troubles, as Platonov says? Oh yes—talking of Platonov, why do you avoid him? He's quite a big noise—cultured chap, anything but a bore. Why not have a heart-to-heart with him and unbend a bit? That should chase the cobwebs away. And you should talk to Mother and Triletsky more. [*Laughs.*] Talk to them, don't look down on them, you don't know what they're like yet. I want you to know them better because they're my type, I'm fond of them. You'll like them too when you know them better.

ANNA [*at the window*]. Sergey, Sergey! Who's there? Will someone tell Sergey I want him?

SERGEY. What for?

ANNA. Oh, there you are. Come in for a moment.

SERGEY. Coming. [*To* SONYA.] We'll leave tomorrow then unless you change your mind. [*Goes indoors.*]

SONYA [*after a pause*]. It's really almost tragic. Already I can forget my husband for days on end, I ignore him, don't listen to him—it's all getting me down. What can I do? [*Reflects.*] It's awful, we've been married such a short time, and already—. It's all his—Platonov's—doing. I'm helpless, I've no moral fibre, I can't resist the man. He pursues me morning, noon and night, seeks me out, doesn't give me a moment's peace with his meaning glances. It's dreadful—and so stupid. I can't even answer for myself. He only has to lift a finger and anything could happen.

SCENE VI

[SONYA *and* PLATONOV. PLATONOV *comes out of the house.*]

SONYA. Here he is, looking for someone. Who? I can tell who he wants by his walk. It's a rotten trick to pester me.

PLATONOV. Isn't it hot? I shouldn't have drunk so much. [*Seeing* SONYA.] You here, Sonya? All on your own? [*Laughs.*]

SONYA. Yes.

PLATONOV. Avoiding mere mortals, eh?

SONYA. Why should I? I've nothing against them and they don't bother me.

PLATONOV. Really? [*Sits down by her.*] May I? [*Pause.*] Then if you're not avoiding people, Sonya, why avoid me? Eh? No, let me finish. I'm glad to get a word in at last. You avoid me, keep out of my way, don't look at me. What is it? A joke, or do you mean it?

SONYA. I never meant to avoid you, what gave you that idea?

PLATONOV. You seemed pleased to see me at first and favoured me with your attention, but now you can't stand me. If I go into one room, you go in another. If I go in the garden, you leave it. If I speak to you, you fob me off or give me a dry, stuffy 'yes' and go away. Our relations are in a sort of mess. Is it my fault? Am I so repulsive? [*Stands up.*] I don't feel particularly guilty. Do you mind ending this absurd, childish business here and now? I won't have any more of it.

SONYA. I admit I do, er, avoid you a bit. If I'd known you disliked it so much I'd have managed it differently.

PLATONOV. You avoid me? [*Sits down.*] And admit it? But why, why?

SONYA. Don't shout, I mean don't talk so loud. You don't think you're reprimanding me, I hope. I don't like being shouted at. It's not you, it's your conversation I've been avoiding. You're a good man as far as I know. Everyone here likes you and thinks highly of you, while some people actually worship you, and are flattered to speak to you.

PLATONOV. Oh come, come.

SONYA. When I came here I joined your audience after our first talk, but things turned out badly, I was out of luck. I soon found you almost unbearable—I can't think of a milder word, sorry. You told me nearly every day how you once loved me, how I loved you and so on. The student loved the girl, the girl loved the student— the story's too old and commonplace to waste many words on or to be thought important to us now. Anyway, the point is, when you spoke about the past, you—you spoke as if you wanted something, something that you failed to get in the past and would like to lay your hands on now. Your tone never changed, which was a bore, and every day I felt you were hinting at alleged obligations imposed on us both by a common experience. And I thought you attached too much importance to—that, to put it more clearly, you were reading too much into a relationship which was just that of two good friends. You have this odd way of looking, and there are your outbursts and shouting, and you clutch my hand and follow me about —as if you were spying on me. What's it all in aid of? You won't leave me alone, in fact. But why the supervision? What am I to you? Really, one might think you were up to something and playing a kind of waiting game. [*Pause.*]

PLATONOV. Finished? [*Gets up.*] Thanks for being frank. [*Moves towards the door.*]

SONYA. Annoyed? [*Gets up.*] Don't go, don't be so touchy. I didn't mean——

PLATONOV [*stops*]. Oh, really! [*Pause.*] So you're not bored with me, you're afraid, you're a coward—aren't you, Sonya? [*Goes up to her.*]

SONYA. Stop it, Platonov. That's an absolute lie. I never was afraid and I don't intend to be now.

PLATONOV. Where are your will-power and common sense—if any man in the least bit unusual can seem a danger to your Sergey? I used to come here every day before you arrived and I spoke to you because I thought you an intelligent, sensible woman. What frightful depravity! In fact—. I'm sorry, I was carried away. I had no right to talk to you like that, you must excuse the unseemly outburst.

SONYA. Indeed you have no right to talk like that. People may listen to you, but that doesn't mean you can say the first thing that comes into your head. Go away and leave me alone.

PLATONOV [*laughs*]. Persecuted, are we, much in demand? Our hand is clutched, is it? Poor little girl, does someone want to take her away from her husband? Platonov loves you, does he? The eccentric Mr. Platonov! Oh joy, oh bliss! I've never known such a quantity of humbug outside a sweet shop. What a joke! No educated woman should feed her vanity on that scale! [*Goes indoors.*]

SONYA. You're rude and impertinent, Platonov. You must be crazy. [*Goes after him and stops by the door.*] It's awful, why did he say all that? He wanted to shock me. Well, I'm not having it. I'll go and tell him——

[*Goes indoors,* OSIP *comes out from behind the summer-house.*]

SCENE VII

[OSIP, JACOB *and* VASILY.]

OSIP [*comes in*]. 'Five down, six up.' What the hell do they think they're playing? Cards would suit them better, some card game or other. [*To* JACOB.] Hallo, Jacob. Is what's-his-name, er, Vengerovich here?

JACOB. Yes.

OSIP. Go and call him. Bring him out here quietly, say it's important.

JACOB. All right. [*Goes indoors.*]

OSIP [*tears down a lantern, puts it out and sticks it in his pocket*]. Last year I played cards in town at Darya's place—the one who buys stolen goods and runs the licensed premises complete with young ladies. The lowest stake was three copecks, but the forfeits went up to two roubles. I won eight roubles. [*Tears down another lantern.*] It's fun in town.

VASILY. Those lanterns weren't put up for your benefit. Why take them down?

OSIP. I can't even see you. Hallo, old donkey. How's things? [*Goes up to him.*] How's everything, old horse? [*Pause.*] You swineherd, you! [*Takes* VASILY'S *cap off.*] God, you are funny, you haven't an ounce of sense. [*Throws the cap at a tree.*] Slap my face for being a bad man.

VASILY. Someone else can, I shan't.

OSIP. Then murder me. If you've any sense you'll do it on your own, not in a gang. Spit in my face for being a bad man.

VASILY. No. Leave me alone.

OSIP. Won't spit? Afraid of me, eh? Down on your knees! [*Pause.*] Kneel! Who am I talking to, a live man or thin air? [*Pause.*] Well?

VASILY [*kneels*]. It ain't right, Mr. Osip.

OSIP. Ashamed to kneel, eh? That's good—a gent in tails kneeling to a thief. Now give three cheers at the top of your voice. Come on.

[ABRAHAM *comes in.*]

SCENE VIII

[OSIP *and* ABRAHAM.]

ABRAHAM [*comes out of the house*]. Does someone want me?

OSIP [*quickly takes off his cap*]. Me, sir.

[VASILY *stands up, sits on the bench and cries.*]

ABRAHAM. What is it?

OSIP. You were asking for me at the inn, sir, so I came along.

ABRAHAM. Oh. But couldn't you have picked another place?

OSIP. One place is as good as another for honest men, sir.

ABRAHAM. I need you slightly. Come over to that bench. [*They go to a bench at the back of the stage.*] Stand a bit further away and look as if you weren't talking to me—that's right. Was it the innkeeper Lev Solomonovich who sent you?

OSIP. Yes sir.

ABRAHAM. He shouldn't have, it wasn't you I wanted, but—it can't be helped. You're past praying for, I should have no truck with you. You're a real wrong 'un.

OSIP. Very bad, sir, they don't come no worse.

ABRAHAM. Keep your voice down. You've had lots of cash from me, but you don't seem interested—my money might be so much waste paper. You're rude, you steal. Turning away? Don't like the truth? Hurts a bit, doesn't it?

OSIP. Yes sir, but not coming from you, sir. Is that why you sent for me, to read me a lecture?

ABRAHAM. Not so loud. Do you know—Platonov?

OSIP. The schoolteacher? Of course.

ABRAHAM. Yes, the teacher. A teacher of bad language, more like— that's about all he does teach. What would you take to cripple him?

OSIP. Cripple him?

ABRAHAM. Not kill him—maim him. Murder's wrong, and what's the point of it? It's a thing I, er—. I want him damaged, given a beating he'll remember all his life.

OSIP. That can be arranged.

ABRAHAM. Break him up a bit, spoil his looks. How much do you want? Shush! Someone's coming, let's move off a bit.

[*They go to the back of the stage.* PLATONOV *and* MARY *come out of the house.*]

SCENE IX

[ABRAHAM VENGEROVICH *and* OSIP *at the back of the stage.* PLATONOV *and* MARY.]

PLATONOV [*laughs*]. What did you say? [*Laughs loudly.*] I didn't quite catch——

MARY. Oh. Then I'll say it again—put it even more bluntly. You won't take offence, of course. You're so used to all kinds of rudeness, I doubt if what I say will surprise you at all.

PLATONOV. Come on, out with it, my beauty.

MARY. I'm not beautiful, anyone who thinks that has no taste. I'm ugly, aren't I? Be honest, what do you think?

PLATONOV. I'll tell you later, you speak first.

MARY. Well, listen then. You're either an outstanding man or a scoundrel, one or the other.

[PLATONOV *laughs.*]

MARY. You laugh—actually, it is funny. [*Laughs.*]

PLATONOV [*laughs*]. She actually said it. Good for Miss Stupid. Well, well, well. [*Takes her by the waist.*]

MARY [*sits down*]. But let me——

PLATONOV. So she wants a go at me as well. Holds forth, studies chemistry, issues weighty pronouncements. Get away with you, you awful girl. [*Kisses her.*] You pretty, funny little beast.

MARY. One moment, what is this? I, er, I didn't say anything. [*Gets up and sits down again.*] Why did you kiss me? I'm not that sort of——

PLATONOV. You've quite flabbergasted me. 'I'll come out with something striking,' thinks she. 'Show him how clever I am.' [*Kisses her.*] Baffled, eh? And with that silly stare. Ah me.

MARY. You—do you love me? Do you?

PLATONOV [*shrieks*]. Do you love me?

MARY. If, if—er, yes. [*Cries.*] You do love me, don't you, or you wouldn't have behaved like this. Do you?

PLATONOV. Not at all, darling. I don't like half-wits, I can't help it. I do love one silly creature, but that's only because I've nothing else to do. Aha, we blench, our eyes flash! 'I'll show him who he's dealing with,' thinks she!

MARY [*stands up*]. Are you being funny or something? [*Pause.*]

PLATONOV. We'll be slapping his face any minute.

MARY. I'm too proud, I won't soil my hands, sir. I told you you were an outstanding man or a scoundrel. Now I say you're an outstanding scoundrel. I despise you. [*Moves off towards the house.*] I shan't cry, I'm only glad to have learnt what you're like at last.

[NICHOLAS *comes in.*]

SCENE X

[*The above and* NICHOLAS, *who wears a top hat.*]

NICHOLAS [*coming in*]. The cranes are crying. Where have they sprung from? [*Looks up.*] It's so early.

MARY. Nicholas, if you've any respect for me or yourself, have nothing to do with this person. [*Points to* PLATONOV.]

NICHOLAS [*laughs*]. Have a heart, he's one of my revered relatives.

MARY. A friend too?

NICHOLAS. Yes.

MARY. I can't say I envy you. Or him either, I think. You're not a bad sort, but—you're so jocular. Sometimes your jokes make me sick. I don't want to be unkind, but I've just been insulted, and you're joking. [*Cries.*] I've been insulted. Anyway, I shan't cry, I'm too proud. Go on seeing this person, be fond of him, worship his intellect, fear him. You all think he's like Hamlet. Admire him if you must. I don't care, I want nothing from you. Joke with him to your heart's content, the scoundrel. [*Goes indoors.*]

NICHOLAS [*after a pause*]. Did you take that in, old boy?

PLATONOV. Not really.

NICHOLAS. Can't you have the decency to leave her alone, Michael? Aren't you ashamed? An intelligent, capable man like you going in for this damned hanky-panky! No wonder you've been called a scoundrel. [*Pause.*] I can't very well split in two and respect you with one half, while the other takes the side of the girl who just called you a scoundrel.

PLATONOV. Don't respect me then, and you won't need to tear yourself apart.

NICHOLAS. I can't help respecting you. You don't know what you're saying.

PLATONOV. Then all you can do is not take her side. I don't understand you, Nicholas—how can a clever man like you find good in such a silly girl?

NICHOLAS. Well, Anna Voynitsev's always saying I'm no gentleman. She points to you as a model of the proprieties. But I think her reproach applies just as much to you, the model gentleman. Everyone round here, you more than anyone, is shouting from the rooftops that I'm in love with her. You laugh at me, make fun of me, suspect me, spy on me.

PLATONOV. Be a bit clearer.

NICHOLAS. I'm being quite clear already, I think. You also have the nerve to call her a silly little ninny in front of me. You're no gentleman. Gentlemen know that lovers have their pride. She's no fool, take it from me, she's just a scapegoat. There are times when you're ready to hate someone, aren't there? You want to pitch into them and vent your spite. So why not try her? She fits the bill. She's weak and defenceless, she looks on you with such foolish trustfulness. Oh, it's all very clear. [*Stands up.*] Come and have a drink.

OSIP [*to* ABRAHAM]. If you don't pay me the rest after the job I'll steal my hundred roubles' worth, make no mistake about that!

ABRAHAM [*to* OSIP]. Not so loud. As you beat him, don't forget to say it's with the innkeeper's compliments. Shush! Run along.

[*Goes towards the house.* OSIP *goes out.*]

NICHOLAS. Vengerovich, damn it! [*To* ABRAHAM.] Not ill, are you?

ABRAHAM. Don't worry, I'm all right.

NICHOLAS. A pity, seeing I'm so short of money—honestly, I'm really cut up about it.

ABRAHAM. It sounds more as though you need a few patients to 'cut up', Doctor. [*Laughs.*]

NICHOLAS. Very funny! Brilliant—if a bit on the heavy side. Ha ha ha. I repeat, ha ha ha. Laugh, Platonov. [*To* ABRAHAM.] Hand over, old chap—see what you can do.

ABRAHAM. But you owe me so much already.

NICHOLAS. No need to mention it, it's no secret. How much is it, anyway?

ABRAHAM. About, er, two hundred and forty-five roubles, I think.

NICHOLAS. Come on, big-wig, do me a favour—I'll do as much for you one day. Be kind, generous and brave. The bravest Jew is the one who lends money without receipt, so act accordingly.

ABRAHAM. Jews, Jews—always Jews! I never met a Russian in my life who lent money without an IOU, believe me. And nowhere is the loan of money without security so much in vogue as amongst us dishonest Jews. Lord strike me, I'm not lying. [*Sighs.*] You young men could learn a lot from Jews, especially us older ones, and that's a fact. [*Takes his wallet out of his pocket.*] We're glad to make you a loan, but you will laugh and joke about it. It's not right, though. I'm an old man with children. You may think I'm a low hound, but treat me as human. That's what university education's for.

NICHOLAS. Well put, Abe old man.

ABRAHAM. This won't do. You educated people seem no better than my shop-assistants. Who said you could call me by my first name? How much do you want? It won't do, young sirs. How much?

NICHOLAS. What you like. [*Pause.*]

ABRAHAM. I can let you have, er, fifty. [*Gives him the money.*]

NICHOLAS. Munificent! [*Takes it.*] You're a great man.

ABRAHAM. You've got my hat on, Doctor.

NICHOLAS. Have I? Oh. [*Takes the top hat off.*] Here. Why not send it to the cleaners, they're quite cheap. What's the Yiddish for hat?

ABRAHAM. Whatever you like. [*Puts on the hat.*]

NICHOLAS. A top hat really suits you, you're a regular baron. Why not buy a title?

ABRAHAM. I've no idea, please leave me alone.

NICHOLAS. You're a great man. Why can't people understand you?

ABRAHAM. I'd rather hear why people can't leave me in peace. [*Goes indoors.*]

SCENE XI

[PLATONOV *and* NICHOLAS.]

PLATONOV. Why did you borrow that money?

NICHOLAS. I just did. [*Sits down.*]

PLATONOV. What does that mean?

NICHOLAS. I took it, and that's that. Not sorry for him are you?

PLATONOV. That's not the point, man.

NICHOLAS. Then what is?

PLATONOV. Don't you know?

NICHOLAS. No.

PLATONOV. Rubbish, of course you do. [*Pause.*] I might really take to you, old boy, if you could only live by some sort of code, however pathetic, for one week, even one day. Your type needs rules as much as their daily bread. [*Pause.*]

NICHOLAS. I don't know, we can't change our nature, old boy—can't crush the flesh. I knew that when we both used to get nought out of ten for Latin at school. So let's stop this silly talk before we're struck dumb. [*Pause.*] Two days ago I was visiting a lady friend's house and saw some portraits called Public Figures of Our Day, and read their biographies. And do you know, they hadn't got you and me there! I couldn't find us, however hard I tried. *Lasciate ogni speranza*, as the Italians say. Neither you nor me is a Public Figure and, do you know, I don't care. Now Sonya somehow does care.

PLATONOV. Where does Sonya come in?

NICHOLAS. She's hurt because she's not a Public Figure either. She thinks, if she lifts a finger the earth should gape and men throw their hats in the air. She thinks—there's more tommy-rot in her head than in the most pretentious modern novel. Actually, she's no good, she's an iceberg, a stone, a statue. You long to go and chip a bit of plaster off her nose. Always ready with her hysterics, sighs and lamentations, and so feeble, a sort of clever doll. She looks down on me, thinks I'm

the scum of the earth, but is her Sergey any better than you and me?
Is he? The only good thing about him is, he doesn't drink vodka, has
all sorts of airy ideas and has the nerve to call himself a go-ahead
person. Anyway, judge not that ye be not judged. [*Stands up.*]
Let's go and have a drink.

PLATONOV. No thanks, it's too close in there.

NICHOLAS. Then I'll go. [*Stretches.*] By the way, what's the meaning of
this S and V in the monogram? Sonya Voynitsev or Sergey Voynitsev? Whom did our scholarly friend wish to honour—himself or
his wife?

PLATONOV. I think it stands for 'Salute to Vengerovich'. He's paying
for this orgy.

NICHOLAS. True. What's up with Anna Voynitsev today—laughing,
groaning, kissing people? Not in love, is she?

PLATONOV. Who can she love here? Herself? Don't trust her laughter.
When an intelligent woman never cries you can't take her laughter
as genuine—she laughs when she wants to cry. But our Anna doesn't
want to cry—feels more like shooting herself, you can see it in her
eyes.

NICHOLAS. Women don't shoot themselves, they take poison. But
don't let's generalize, I talk such rot when I do that. Anna's a fine
woman. When I see a woman I usually feel frightfully lecherous, but
my evil designs slide off her like water off a duck's back, and I can't
say that of anyone else. Looking at that matter-of-fact face, I start
believing in platonic love. Coming?

PLATONOV. No.

NICHOLAS. Then I'll go and have a drink with the priest. [*Moves off and
bumps into* CYRIL *near the door.*] Ah, your Lordship, the self-appointed
count! Have three roubles. [*Shoves three roubles in his hand and goes out.*]

SCENE XII

[PLATONOV *and* CYRIL.]

CYRIL. What an odd person, with his 'have three roubles' right out of
the blue. [*Shouts.*] I can afford to give you three roubles. Idiot.
[*To* PLATONOV.] I'm most impressed by his stupidity. [*Laughs.*]
Hideously stupid, he is.

PLATONOV. You dance, don't you? Then why aren't you dancing?

CYRIL. Dance? Here? Who with, pray? [*Sits down next to him.*]

PLATONOV. No lack of partners, is there?

CYRIL. What specimens they all are with their ugly mugs, hooked noses and the airs they put on. And the women! [*Laughs loudly.*] Hell! Give me the bar, in such company, not the dance floor. [*Pause.*] Isn't Russian air stale—so dank and stuffy, somehow. I can't stand Russia, stinking, barbarous place! Ugh! How different in—ever been to Paris?

PLATONOV. No.

CYRIL. Pity. Anyway, you may still get around to it. Let me know when you do, I'll initiate you. I'll give you three hundred letters of introduction and that'll put three hundred of the smartest little fillies in Paris at your disposal.

PLATONOV. No thanks, I've been well catered for in that direction. I say, is it true your father wants to buy my estate?

CYRIL. I don't know, I don't dabble in trade. Have you noticed *mon père* making up to Anna Voynitsev? [*Laughs.*] Another odd specimen! The old stoat wants to get married—more fool him. Your Anna's charming, and not bad looking. [*Pause.*] Delightful, she is —those curves! Quite shocking! [*Claps* PLATONOV *on the shoulder.*] You lucky man, you. Does she wear corsets, eh? Tight ones?

PLATONOV. I've no idea, I don't watch her dressing.

CYRIL. But from what I heard—. Mean to say you don't——?

PLATONOV. Count, you're an idiot.

CYRIL. I was only joking. Why so annoyed? You are a funny chap. [*Quietly.*] Is it true she—er, a slightly ticklish question, but it need go no further, I hope. Is it true that she goes mad about money every so often?

PLATONOV. Better ask her, I don't know.

CYRIL. What, straight out? [*Laughs.*] What an idea! You don't know what you're saying, Platonov.

PLATONOV [*sits down on another bench*]. You're a prize bore.

CYRIL [*guffaws*]. Perhaps I will ask—why not, anyway?

PLATONOV. Yes, why not? [*Aside.*] Carry on, she'll smack your silly face. [*To* CYRIL.] Go on then.

CYRIL [*jumps up*]. My word, a splendid idea! Hell and damnation! I'll ask her, Platonov, and I swear she'll be mine, I can feel it. I'll ask her at once and I bet you she'll be mine. [*Runs towards the house and meets* ANNA *and* NICHOLAS *in the doorway.*] My humblest apologies, madam.

[*Scrapes his feet and goes off.* PLATONOV *sits down in his previous place.*]

SCENE XIII

[PLATONOV, ANNA *and* NICHOLAS.]

NICHOLAS [*sitting on the front steps*]. There's our great pundit, all agog and eagerly awaiting a victim for one of his bed-time harangues.

ANNA. He's not rising.

NICHOLAS. That's bad. Somehow he's not taking the bait today. Wretched moralizer! I'm sorry for you, Platonov. Still, I'm drunk and—the priest's waiting for me. Good-bye. [*Goes off.*]

ANNA [*goes towards* PLATONOV]. What are you doing out here?

PLATONOV. It's stuffy indoors and this lovely sky's better than your ceiling whitewashed by village women.

ANNA [*sits down*]. What marvellous weather. Cool, clear air, a starry sky and the moon. It's a pity ladies can't sleep out of doors. As a little girl I always slept in the garden in summer. [*Pause.*] Is that a new tie?

PLATONOV. Yes. [*Pause.*]

ANNA. I'm in a funny mood today. I like everything, I'm having a good time. Do say something, Platonov. Why won't you speak? I only came out to hear you talk, you wretch.

PLATONOV. What am I to tell you?

ANNA. Some nice, spicy bit of news. You're such a good, pretty little boy this evening, I think I'm more in love with you than ever. You're a darling—and not so naughty as usual.

PLATONOV. And you're really beautiful this evening—you always are, as a matter of fact.

ANNA. Are we friends, Platonov?

PLATONOV. Probably, I suppose so. What else can you call it?

ANNA. Anyway, we're friends?

PLATONOV. Great friends, I should think. I'm fond of you, devoted. I shan't forget you in a hurry.

ANNA. Great friends?

PLATONOV. Why all the questions? Pack it in, dear. 'Friends, friends.' You're like an old maid.

ANNA. Very well, we're friends, but do you know, sir, that friendship between a man and a woman's only one step removed from love? [*Laughs.*]

PLATONOV. So that's it! [*Laughs.*] What are you leading up to? However far we may get, we're not likely to go the whole hog, are we?

ANNA. Love—whole hog! What a juxtaposition. It's a good job your wife can't hear you, Michael. Sorry, I used your Christian name, I honestly didn't mean to. But why shouldn't we go all the way? We're human, aren't we? Love's a wonderful thing. So why blush?

PLATONOV [*stares at her*]. I see you're either making a nice little joke or want to—come to some arrangement. Let's go and waltz.

ANNA. You can't dance. [*Pause.*] And it's time we had a proper talk. [*Looks round.*] Listen, dear, and please don't make speeches.

PLATONOV. Come and dance.

ANNA. Let's sit a bit further off. Come here. [*Sits on another bench.*] Only I don't know how to start. You're such an awkward, slippery brute.

PLATONOV. Shall I start then?

ANNA. You'll only talk a lot of rot if you do. Good grief, the man's embarrassed. Only I wouldn't be too sure of it! [*Claps* PLATONOV *on the shoulder.*] You like your little joke, don't you? Speak then. But be brief.

PLATONOV. I will. What's the point? That's all I have to say. [*Pause.*] It's honestly not worth it.

ANNA. Why not? Listen. You don't understand me. If you were free I'd marry you without a second thought, and give you the title deeds of this valuable property, but as it is—. Well? No answer—does that mean you agree, eh? [*Pause.*] Look, Platonov, it's not decent to remain silent at a time like this.

PLATONOV [*jumps up*]. Let's forget what's been said, Anna. Let's pretend our talk never took place, for God's sake. It never happened.

ANNA [*shrugs her shoulders*]. But why, you funny man?

PLATONOV. Because I respect you. And my own feelings for you also inspire me with respect—I'd rather die than lose it. I'm free, dear, I don't mind having a good time, I'm not against affairs with women, I don't even object to the odd high-minded intrigue. But to start some back-stairs liaison with *you*, to make *you* the target of my idle designs—you, an intelligent, beautiful, free woman! No! It's asking too much, I'd rather you told me to go and bury myself. To spend a stupid month or two together and part feeling thoroughly ashamed of it!

ANNA. We're talking about love.

PLATONOV. Do you think I don't love you? I do—you're so good, intelligent, gracious. I love you desperately, madly. I'll give my life for you if you want, I love you as a woman and as a person. Don't try and tell me that love must always involve a certain relationship, because my love's a thousand times dearer to me than the sort you have in mind.

ANNA [*stands up*]. Go away, dear, and wake up. Then we'll talk.

PLATONOV. Let's forget what's been said. [*Kisses her hand.*] We'll be friends, but we won't play games together, our friendship deserves a better fate. Another point—I am slightly married, you know. So let's drop the subject and let everything be as it was.

ANNA. Go away, dear, do. A married man—. But you love me, don't you? Why drag in your wife? Quick march! We'll talk again in a couple of hours. At the moment you've got a bad attack of lying.

PLATONOV. I couldn't lie to you. [*Quietly, into her ear.*] If I could, I'd have been your lover long ago.

ANNA [*brusquely*]. Oh, go away!

PLATONOV. Nonsense, you're not really annoyed—you're just pretending——. [*Goes indoors.*]

ANNA. What a funny man. [*Sits down.*] He has no idea what he's saying. 'Love must always involve a certain relationship.' Poppycock! He might be discussing the love of a male and female novelist. [*Pause.*] The wretch! This way we shan't be done chattering till doomsday. Well, if I can't get my way by fair means, I'll use foul. Tonight! It's

time we escaped from this absurd state of suspense, I'm fed up with it.
I shall use force. Who's there? Porfiry Glagolyev, and looking for
me.

[PORFIRY *comes in.*]

SCENE XIV

[ANNA *and* PORFIRY.]

PORFIRY. What a bore, their conversation's a year out of date and they
think as I thought as a child, all old, stale stuff. I'll have a word with
her and go.

ANNA. What are you muttering, may I ask?

PORFIRY. You here? [*Goes towards her.*] I was blaming myself for
being odd man out here.

ANNA. Because you're not like us? Come, come—if people can get
used to black-beetles, you can get used to us. Sit down and let's talk.

PORFIRY [*sits by her*]. I was looking for you, I want a word with you.

ANNA. Carry on.

PORFIRY. I want to talk to you, want an answer to my—letter.

ANNA. I see. Why did you pick on me?

PORFIRY. Look, I'll give up my, er, conjugal rights, never mind them.
I need a friend, a good housekeeper. I have a paradise, but no angels
in it.

ANNA [*aside*]. What a lot of soft soap. [*To* PORFIRY.] Being a woman
and no angel, I often wonder what I'd do in paradise if I ever got
there.

PORFIRY. How can you know what you'll do in paradise if you don't
know what you're doing tomorrow. A sensible woman can always
find something to do, both on earth and in heaven.

ANNA. That's all very well, but would it be worth my while to live
with you? It's all so odd, Mr. Glagolyev. Sorry, but your proposal
does seem so very peculiar. Why should you marry? What do you
need with a little bit of skirt? Sorry, it's not my business, but as we've
got this far I'll finish. If I was your age and as rich, clever and fair-
minded as you, I'd seek nothing on this earth but the common good.
I mean I'd look only for the reward of loving my neighbour, if I
can put it like that.

PORFIRY. I'm no champion of human welfare, that needs ability and will-power such as God didn't give me. I was born to admire great deeds and do lots of trivial, worthless ones. I'm only an admirer. Won't you come to me?

ANNA. No, and don't mention it again. Don't attach too much significance to my refusal. It's such a waste of time, man. If we all owned everything we admire, we'd have no room for our possessions. So it's not always stupid or unkind to say no. [*Laughs.*] There's a bit of philosophy to get your teeth in. What's that noise? Hear anything? I bet it's Platonov kicking up a row again. What a man!

[MARY *and* NICHOLAS *come in.*]

SCENE XV

[ANNA, PORFIRY, MARY *and* NICHOLAS.]

MARY [*coming in*]. I was never so insulted in my life. [*Cries.*] Never! Only someone thoroughly depraved could keep silent in face of such a thing.

NICHOLAS. All right, I believe you, but where do I come in? I can hardly go and beat him up, can I?

MARY. Yes, you can, if you've no better idea. Go away. I'm only a woman, but I wouldn't keep quiet if I saw you insulted in that rotten, beastly, uncalled-for way.

NICHOLAS. But I, er—. Do be sensible. What have I done wrong?

MARY. You're a coward, that's what you are. Now go and prop up that repulsive bar. Good-bye. And don't bother to come and see me again, we don't need one another. Good-bye.

NICHOLAS. All right, good-bye, if that's the way you want it. I'm sick and tired of the whole thing. Tears, tears, tears. God, now my head's going round— a case of *coenurus cerebralis*. Oh dear. [*Makes a gesture of resignation and goes out.*]

MARY. *Coenurus cerebralis.* [*Moves off.*] What an insult. Why? What have I done?

ANNA [*comes up to her*]. I won't try and stop you, Mary, I'd leave myself in your place. [*Kisses her.*] Don't cry, dear, most women were created just for men to use as door-mats.

MARY. But not me, I'll—have him dismissed. I won't have him as schoolmaster here, he has no right to teach. I'll go and see the education officer tomorrow.

ANNA. That will do. I'll come and see you in a day or two and we'll find fault with Platonov together, but meanwhile you calm down. Stop crying, you shall have satisfaction. And don't be annoyed with Triletsky, dear. He's too kind and gentle, that's why he didn't stick up for you—such people can't stick up for anyone. What did Platonov do?

MARY. Kissed me in public, called me a fool and pushed me into the table. Don't think he'll get away with it! Either he's mad or—. I'll show him a thing or two. [*Goes out.*]

ANNA [*calls after her*]. Good-bye, we'll meet soon. [*To* JACOB.] Have Miss Grekov's carriage brought round, Jacob. Oh, Platonov, Platonov—his quarrelling will get him into hot water one day.

PORFIRY. What a lovely girl. But the worthy Platonov's taken against her—he insulted her.

ANNA. And for no reason at all—insults her today, apologizes tomorrow. Isn't that your upper-class Russian all over?

[CYRIL *comes in.*]

SCENE XVI

[*The above and* CYRIL.]

CYRIL [*aside*]. He's with her again! Hell, what can this mean? [*Glares at his father.*]

PORFIRY [*after a pause*]. What do you want?

CYRIL. While you sit here you're wanted in there. Go in, they're asking for you.

PORFIRY. Who wants me?

CYRIL. Some people.

PORFIRY. So I should think. [*Gets up.*] Say what you like, Anna, I shan't give you up. When you get to know me you may change your tune. I'll be seeing you. [*Goes indoors.*]

SCENE XVII

[ANNA *and* CYRIL.]

CYRIL [*sits by her*]. The old stoat! What an ass! No one's asking for him, I was just pretending.

ANNA. When you grow wiser you'll be sorry you treated your father like that.

CYRIL. You're joking. What I came for was a couple of words. Yes or no?

ANNA. Meaning?

CYRIL [*laughs*]. As if you didn't know! Yes or no?

ANNA. You have me baffled.

CYRIL. You'll soon catch on. A spot of lucre is a great help to under-standing. If it's yes, captain of my soul, then please feel in my pocket and pull out my wallet full of Daddy's money. [*Turns his side pocket towards her.*]

ANNA. You're very frank, but don't be too clever or you might get your face slapped.

CYRIL. To have your face slapped by an attractive woman—that's quite an agreeable prospect. She starts by slapping your face, but ends up saying yes a bit later.

ANNA [*gets up*]. Take your hat and clear out this instant.

CYRIL [*gets up*]. Where to?

ANNA. Wherever you like. Get out and don't dare show your face in here again.

CYRIL. But why so angry? I won't go.

ANNA. Then I'll have you thrown out. [*Goes indoors.*]

CYRIL. Aren't you angry! I never said anything, did I? No need to be angry. [*Follows her out.*]

SCENE XVIII

[PLATONOV *and* SONYA *coming out of the house.*]

PLATONOV. I'm still only an ordinary schoolteacher, a thing I'm not really cut out for—that's all that's happened since we met last. [*They sit down.*] Evil pullulates around me, contaminating the earth and swallowing up my countrymen and brothers in Christ, while I sit idle as if I'd just done a job of work. I sit, watch and say nothing. I'm twenty-seven and I'll be no different when I'm thirty, I don't expect to change. I'll be just as fat, lazy, dull and totally indifferent to everything except the flesh. Then there's death to be thought of. My life's ruined. My hair stands on end when I think of dying. [*Pause.*] How can I lift myself up, Sonya? [*Pause.*] You don't speak, you don't know—and how could you? I'm not sorry for myself, but to hell with me, anyway. What's happened to you? Where's your high-mindedness, your sincerity, your sense of fair play, your courage? What's become of your health? What have you done with it? To spend years on end in idleness while others wear their fingers to the bone for you, to watch others' sufferings, and still feel able to look people in the face—that's real depravity, Sonya.

[SONYA *stands up, but* PLATONOV *makes her sit down again.*]

PLATONOV. Just a moment, this is my last word. What turned you into an affected, idle chatterbox? And who taught you to lie? You used to be so different. All right, I'll let you go in a moment, but please may I finish? What a fine, generous woman you were. Perhaps you can still rise again, Sonya dear, it may not be too late. Think, pull yourself together and lift yourself up, for God's sake. [*Clutches her hand.*] Tell me frankly, dear, in the name of all we used to have in common, what made you marry that man? What could that marriage offer?

SONYA. He's a fine person.

PLATONOV. Don't say things you don't believe.

SONYA [*stands up*]. He happens to be my husband, and I must ask you——

PLATONOV. I don't care who he is, I'll still tell the truth. Sit down. [*Helps her to sit down.*] Why didn't you pick a man who could work and suffer? Why not marry someone else, not this little man sunk in debt and sloth?

SONYA. Let me alone. Don't shout, someone's coming.

[*Some guests pass across the stage.*]

PLATONOV. Let them hear, blast them. [*Quietly.*] I'm sorry to be so blunt, but I did love you. I loved you more than anything in the world, so you're still dear to me. How I loved this hair, these hands, this face. Why are you powdering your face, Sonya? Stop it. Oh, if only someone else had come along, you'd soon have been on your feet, but here you'll only sink deeper and deeper, poor thing. If my wretched strength would run to it, I'd get us both out of this dump. [*Pause.*] Such is life, but why can't we live it as we ought?

SONYA [*stands up and covers her face with her hands*]. Leave me alone. [*Noises are heard in the house.*] Go away. [*Moves towards the house.*]

PLATONOV [*follows her*]. Take your hands away, that's right. You're not going away, are you? Let's be friends, Sonya. You won't go, will you? We'll have another talk, eh?

[*More noise comes from the house and there is the sound of people running downstairs.*]

SONYA. Yes.

PLATONOV. Let's be friends, dear—why should we be enemies? Just a moment, I've a couple more things to say.

[SERGEY *runs out of the house, followed by some guests.*]

SCENE XIX

[*The above,* SERGEY *and guests. Later,* ANNA *and* NICHOLAS.]

SERGEY [*running in*]. Ah, here are the people we want. Come and let off some fireworks. [*Shouts.*] Jacob, to the river—quick march! [*To* SONYA.] Not changed your mind, have you?

PLATONOV. She won't go, she'll stay here.

SERGEY. Oh? Good for you in that case. Shake hands, Michael. [*Shakes* PLATONOV's *hand.*] I always believed in your eloquence. Let's go and let off fireworks. [*Moves into the back of the garden with the guests.*]

PLATONOV [*after a pause*]. Yes, that's the way of it, Sonya. Ah well.

SERGEY [*off-stage*]. Where are you, Mother? Platonov? [*Pause.*]

PLATONOV. I'd better go too, damn it. [*Shouts.*] Just a moment, Sergey, don't start without me. I say, old man, will you send Jacob back here for the balloon. [*Runs into the garden.*]

ANNA [*runs out of the house*]. Wait, Sergey, we're not all here yet. Just fire the cannon for the moment. [*To* SONYA.] Come on, Sonya—why so downhearted?

PLATONOV [*off-stage*]. This way, my lady. We'll keep up the old song and not start a new one.

ANNA. Coming, dear. [*Runs off.*]

PLATONOV [*off-stage*]. Who's coming in the boat with me? Come on the river, Sonya?

SONYA. To go or not to go? [*Reflects.*]

NICHOLAS [*comes in*]. Hey, where are you? [*Sings.*] I'm coming, coming! [*Glares at* SONYA.]

SONYA. What do you want?

NICHOLAS. Nothing.

SONYA. Then go away, I'm in no mood to talk or listen this evening.

NICHOLAS. All right, all right. [*Pause.*] Somehow I'm terribly keen to run my finger over your forehead and see what it's made of. Not to insult you, just as a sort of gesture.

SONYA. You clown! [*Turns away.*] You're not a true humorist, you're just a clown, a buffoon.

NICHOLAS. Yes, a buffoon. That's why I get board and lodging here, as a kind of court jester. Pocket money too. When they tire of me I'll be kicked out in disgrace. True, isn't it? Anyway, I'm not the only one who says so. You said the same on a visit to Glagolyev, that up-to-date freemason.

SONYA. All right, all right, I'm glad you were told. Now you know I can tell the difference between clowning and true wit. If you were an actor you'd be a hit with the gallery, but the stalls would give you the bird. I favour the stalls.

NICHOLAS. A most felicitous witticism. Well done. And now I'll take my leave. [*Bows.*] Till our next pleasant meeting. I'd go on talking to you, but I'm scared, struck dumb. [*Goes to the back of the garden.*]

SONYA [*stamps her foot*]. Useless man! He doesn't know what I really think of him, futile little creature!

PLATONOV [*off-stage*]. Who's coming on the river?

SONYA. Oh well, it must be fate. [*Shouts.*] Coming. [*Runs off.*]

SCENE XX

[PORFIRY *and* CYRIL *come out of the house.*]

PORFIRY. You're lying, you loathsome little brat.

CYRIL. Don't be silly, why on earth should I? Ask *her* if you don't believe me. Just after you'd gone I whispered a few words to her on this very bench, put my arms round her and gave her a whacking great kiss. She began by asking three thousand roubles and I, er, did a spot of bargaining and we settled for one. So give me a thousand.

PORFIRY. This concerns a woman's honour, Cyril. Don't defile that, it's holy. Say no more.

CYRIL. But I swear! Don't you believe me? I swear by all I hold most sacred. So give me that thousand roubles, I'll take them along straight away and——

PORFIRY. This is dreadful. You're lying. She was just having you on, stupid.

CYRIL. But I embraced her, I tell you. What's surprising about that? Women are all the same these days, they're not all that innocent— don't you believe it, I know them! And you were actually thinking of marriage! [*Guffaws.*]

PORFIRY. For God's sake, Cyril, don't you know what slander is?

CYRIL. Give me a thousand, I'll hand it to her in your presence. I embraced her on this very bench, kissed her and struck my bargain. I swear it, what more do you want? That's why I got rid of you—so we could discuss terms. He doesn't believe I can dominate women. Offer her two thousand, and she's yours. I know women, man.

PORFIRY [*takes his wallet out of his pocket and throws it on the ground*]. Take it.

[CYRIL *picks it up and counts the money.*]

SERGEY [*off-stage*]. I'm starting. Fire away, Mother. Triletsky, climb on the summer-house. Who trod on that box? You?

NICHOLAS [*off-stage*]. I'm climbing, damn me. [*Laughs.*] Who's that? Someone's squashed Bugrov, I trod on Bugrov's head. Where are the matches?

CYRIL [*aside*]. I am avenged. [*Shouts.*] Hip, hip, hooray! [*Runs off.*]

NICHOLAS. Who's that yelling? Let him have it in the neck.

SERGEY [*off-stage*]. Shall we start?

PORFIRY [*clutches his head*]. God, how depraved. A rotten business. I worshipped her, God forgive her. [*Sits on the bench and buries his face in his hands.*]

SERGEY [*off-stage*]. Who took the string? Aren't you ashamed, Mother? Where's my string that was lying here?

ANNA [*off-stage*]. There it is. You've got eyes, haven't you?

[PORFIRY *falls off the bench.*]

ANNA [*off-stage*]. You! Who are you? Don't hang around here. [*Shouts.*] Give it here, give it to me.

[SONYA *runs in.*]

SCENE XXI

[SONYA, *alone.*]

SONYA [*pale, with ruffled hair*]. This is all much too much for me. [*Clutches her breast.*] Does this mean my ruin? Or my happiness? It's close out here. He'll either ruin me or show me how to lead a new life. I welcome and bless you, my new life. So that's settled.

SERGEY [*off-stage, shouting*]. Look out!

[*Fireworks.*]

PART TWO

A forest clearing. To the left, where the clearing begins, a school-house. Through the clearing, which stretches as far as the eye can see, runs a railway-line, turning right near the school. A row of telegraph poles. Night.

SCENE I

[SASHA *sits by an open window.* OSIP *stands in front of it with a gun slung over his shoulder.*]

OSIP. How did it happen? Quite simply. I'm walking in the woods near here and she's standing in a little gully with her dress tucked up, scooping water from the stream with a burdock leaf—keeps scooping and drinking, and then wetting her head. I climb down, go up and look at her. She pays no attention, as if to say 'Another country bumpkin, so why bother?' 'Wanted a nice drink of cold water, did you, ma'am?' says I. 'None of your business,' says she. 'Run off back where you came from.' She doesn't look at me as she says it, and I get a bit frightened, and ashamed and hurt, being only an ordinary peasant like. 'Why goggle at me, you fool?' she asks. 'Never seen human beings before?' She stares at me. 'Taken a fancy to me?' she asks. 'That I have,' says I. 'You're a fine woman, ma'am—kind-hearted and beautiful too. Never saw anything lovelier.' And I tell her about Manka the policeman's daughter, prettiest girl in our village. 'But put her beside you,' says I, 'and she ain't no more than a horse or camel. You're so delicate like. If I kissed you, I think I'd drop dead.' She bursts out laughing. 'All right,' says she, 'kiss me if you want.' I go hot all over when she says them words, I go up to her, take her gently by the shoulder and give her a whacking great kiss between check and neck, right here.

SASHA [*laughs*]. What did she do?

OSIP. 'Now clear out,' says she. 'Wash more often,' says she, 'and mind you clean your finger-nails.' So I go away.

SASHA. Bit forward, isn't she? [*Gives* OSIP *a bowl of soup.*] Eat that. Sit down somewhere.

OSIP. I don't matter, I can stand. Grateful for your kindness, ma'am, I'll pay you back one day.

SASHA. Take your cap off, you shouldn't eat with it on. And say grace first.

OSIP [*takes his cap off*]. I haven't been that pious in years. [*Eats.*] I seem to have gone clean off my head since then—can't eat, can't sleep, can you believe it? I keep thinking I see her. If I close my eyes, there she is. I get so soft-hearted, I'm ready to burst. I was so low I nearly drowned myself, I felt like taking a pot shot at the general. When she was widowed I started doing errands for her. Shot partridges, snared quail, painted her summer-house various colours. I once brought her a live wolf. Did lots of things to please her, whatever she told me. If she'd told me to go away and eat myself, I would have. The tender passion—you can't help it, can you?

SASHA. I know. When I fell in love with Michael—before I knew he loved me—I was terribly miserable too. I sometimes prayed I might die, sinful as it was.

OSIP. There you are, you see—that's what feelings can do. [*Drinks soup straight from the bowl.*] No more soup, is there? [*Gives her his bowl.*]

SASHA [*goes away and appears by the window half a minute later with a saucepan*]. There's no soup, would you like potatoes? Fried in goose fat.

OSIP. Thank you kindly. [*Takes the saucepan and eats.*] I've made a thorough pig of myself. Well, there was I dashing round like a lunatic, to go back to what we were just talking about. Kept visiting her, I did. After last Easter I brought her a hare. 'Here you are, ma'am,' I says. 'I've brought this cross-eyed creature.' She takes it in her hands, strokes it. 'Is it true you're a robber, Osip?' she asks. 'True,' says I. 'Otherwise people wouldn't say so.' So I came out with the whole story. 'Turn over a new leaf,' says she. 'Go on a pilgrimage— walk to Kiev,' she says. 'From Kiev go to Moscow, then to the Monastery of the Trinity and St. Sergius, on to New Jerusalem Monastery and back home. That'll make a new man of you in a year.' So I got myself up as a poor man, put on a knapsack and started for Kiev. But it didn't work out. I did reform, but not all that much. Fine potatoes! Near Kharkov I got in with a fast set, spent all my money on drink, got in a fight and came home. Even lost my identity papers. [*Pause.*] Now she won't take anything from me, she's annoyed.

SASHA. Why don't you go to church?

OSIP. I would, but, er, it would make people laugh. 'Look at him, come to confess his sins!' And I'm scared to go near the church in daytime. There are lots of people about, they might kill me.

SASHA. Well, why do you harm poor people?

OSIP. Why not? You wouldn't understand, ma'am, you can't judge such low things or make sense of them. Doesn't your husband ever hurt people?

SASHA. No. Or if he does, he never means to. He's kind.

OSIP. I look up to him more than anyone, I must say. The general's boy, Mr. Voynitsev, is a fool, hasn't any sense. Your brother has no sense either, even if he is a doctor. But Mr. Platonov's very brainy like. Does he hold any rank in the service?

SASHA. Of course he does.

OSIP. Does he? [*Pause.*] He does, does he? Good for him. Only he is a bit hard like. Calls everyone a fool or a lackey, it's not right. I wouldn't do that, if I was a good man—I'd be nice to all these lackeys, fools and swindlers. They're a wretched lot, you know— they need pity. He's a hard man, he is. True, he's not stuck up and he's matey with everyone, but there ain't no kindness in him. You wouldn't understand. Thanking you most kindly, I could eat potatoes like this till the cows come home. [*Gives her the saucepan.*] Thanks.

SASHA. Don't mention it.

OSIP [*sighs*]. You're a fine woman, ma'am. Why do you always feed me? You've not a drop of feminine malice in you, have you? You're real saintly. [*Laughs.*] I've never seen your like before. Saint Sasha, pray for us sinners. [*Bows.*] Rejoice, Saint Sasha.

SASHA. My husband's coming.

OSIP. You can't fool me. Just now he's discussing the tender passion with the young mistress. Handsome fellow, isn't he? He could have the whole female sex running after him if he liked. Has the gift of the gab too. [*Laughs.*] He's always making up to Mrs. Voynitsev, but she'll settle his hash—won't care how handsome he is. He might be quite keen, but she——

SASHA. That's going too far, I don't like it. You'd better be off.

OSIP. At once. You should have been in bed long ago. Waiting up for your husband, I reckon?

SASHA. Yes.

OSIP. You're a good wife. It must have taken Platonov ten years' hard looking to find you. He managed it, though. [*Bows.*] Good-bye, Mrs. Platonov. Good night.

SASHA [*yawns*]. Do go.

OSIP. All right. [*Moves off.*] I'll go home—to where my floor's the ground, my ceiling the sky. Where walls and roof are, goodness only knows. Such is the home of a man cursed by God—plenty of room, but nowhere to lay your head. One good thing—you pay no rates. [*Stops.*] Good night, ma'am, come and see me in the woods some time. Ask for Osip, the birds and lizards all know the way. See that tree stump glowing? Like a ghost? And that other one? My mother told me that tree-stumps shine like that where a sinner's buried, so people will pray for him. I'll have one shining over my grave, I'm no angel. Look, there's another. There's lots of sinners in this world. [*Goes off and can be heard whistling every minute or two.*]

SCENE II

[SASHA, *alone*.]

SASHA [*comes out of the schoolhouse with a candle and book*]. Michael's a long time. [*Sits.*] I hope he won't ruin his health. That's all these walks do—make you ill—and I want to go to bed. Where did I get to? [*Reads.*] 'Finally, it's time to proclaim anew those great, eternal ideals of humanity, those immortal principles of freedom—our fathers' guiding stars which we have unfortunately betrayed.' What does it mean? [*Reflects.*] I can't understand. Why don't they write so it's clear to anyone? It goes on—. I'll leave out the preface. [*Reads.*] 'Sacher-Masoch', what a funny name—can't be Russian. I'll read on—Michael said I must, so I must. [*Yawns and reads.*] 'One gay winter's evening.' I can skip that, it's only a description. [*Turns the leaves and reads.*] 'It was hard to tell who was playing what instrument. The majestic power of an organ played by a man's iron hand suddenly gave way to a tender flute, seemingly played by a lovely woman's lips. Then the sounds died away.' Shush, someone's coming. [*Pause.*] It's Michael. [*Puts out the candle.*] At last. [*Stands up and shouts.*] Hallo, quick march! Left, right, left, left!

[PLATONOV *comes on.*]

SCENE III

[SASHA *and* PLATONOV.]

PLATONOV [*coming in*]. Right, right, I'm walking out of step just to annoy you. Actually, dear, it's neither left nor right. A drunk man knows no left or right. All he knows is forwards, backwards, sideways and downwards.

SASHA. Come and sit here, you old soak, I'll teach you to walk sideways and downwards. Sit. [*Flings herself on* PLATONOV's *neck.*]

PLATONOV. Let's. [*Sits.*] Why aren't you in bed, microbe?

SASHA. I don't feel like it. [*Sits by him.*] They kept you late.

PLATONOV. True. Has the express gone by?

SASHA. No. The goods train went through about an hour ago.

PLATONOV. So it can't be two yet. Been back long?

SASHA. I reached home at ten. Little Nicholas was yelling his head off when I got in. I left without saying good-bye, I hope they won't mind. Was there dancing after I left?

PLATONOV. Dancing, supper and a few rows. By the way, do you know—did it happen while you were there? Old Glagolyev had a stroke.

SASHA. What!

PLATONOV. Yes. Your brother bled him and generally presided.

SASHA. But why? What was the matter? He looks so well.

PLATONOV. It was only a slight stroke—lucky for him, but bad luck on that little ass he's fool enough to call his son. They've taken him home. Not an evening passes without some scene, we must be fated.

SASHA. How scared Anna and Sonya must have been! What a fine woman Sonya is, I don't often see such pretty women. There's something about her. [*Pause.*]

PLATONOV. Oh, how stupid and nasty.

SASHA. What?

PLATONOV. What have I done! [*Buries his face in his hands.*] How shameful.

SASHA. What is it?

PLATONOV. Well may you ask. Nothing good. When did I ever do anything I wasn't ashamed of later?

SASHA [*aside*]. The poor boy's drunk. [*To* PLATONOV.] Come to bed.

PLATONOV. I've never sunk so low. How can I respect myself after that? There's nothing worse than losing your self-respect. God, there's nothing solid about me, nothing to respect or love. [*Pause.*] You love me, that's what I don't understand. You must have found something lovable in me then? Do you love me?

SASHA. What a question! How can I help it?

PLATONOV. I know, but what makes you love me? What's good about me that you love? Name it.

SASHA. Why do I love you—? You are funny tonight. Why shouldn't I, when you're my husband?

PLATONOV. So you only love me because I'm your husband?

SASHA. I don't understand.

PLATONOV. Oh, don't you? [*Laughs.*] You hopeless idiot, you should have been a housefly. With that brain you'd have been the smartest fly on record. [*Kisses her forehead.*] What would happen if you could understand me and lost that admirable innocence? Would you be such a happy woman if that pure little mind could grasp how unlovable I am? If you want to love me, my pet, don't try and find out about me. [*Kisses her hand.*] My little female! Thanks to your innocence I'm happy too and have a family like anyone else.

SASHA [*laughs*]. You're funny.

PLATONOV. My treasure, my dear, silly little woman—you shouldn't be my wife, I should keep you in a glass case on my desk. How did we contrive to produce young Nicholas? You're of an age to make little pastry soldiers, my dearest better half, not to give birth to baby Nicholases.

SASHA. This is silly talk.

PLATONOV. God grant you don't understand me. And don't try to either. Let the earth continue to rest on whales and those whales on pitchforks. Where should we find faithful wives if it wasn't for the Sashas of this world? [*Tries to kiss her.*]

SASHA [*not giving in*]. Go away. [*Angrily.*] Why marry me if I'm so stupid, why not choose someone cleverer? I didn't force you to.

PLATONOV [*laughs*]. Even get angry, can you? Damn it, that's a discovery in the field of—. In what field? It's quite a discovery, anyway, dear. So you're capable of anger, eh? Not joking, are you?

SASHA [*stands up*]. Go to bed, man. You wouldn't make these discoveries if you didn't drink. You drunkard. Call yourself a schoolmaster? You're no schoolmaster, you're a pig. Go to bed. [*Claps him on the back and goes into the schoolhouse.*]

SCENE IV

[PLATONOV, *alone.*]

PLATONOV. Am I really drunk? I can't be, I didn't have that much. Still I do feel a bit queer in the head. [*Pause.*] When I talked to Sonya—was I drunk then? [*Thinks.*] No, I wasn't, that's just the

trouble, ye gods! I was sober, damn me. [*Jumps up.*] What harm did
her wretched husband do me? Why did I have to drag him through
the mire in front of her? I'll never forgive myself. I spouted away
like some wretched posturing boy, showing off and boasting. [*Mimics
himself.*] 'Why didn't you marry a man who works and suffers?'
What the blazes does she want with a hard-working sufferer?
Why say things you don't mean, you fool? But God, she believed it,
listened to those idiot ravings, dropped her little eyes—felt all
sloppy and sentimental, poor girl. How stupid, sordid and inept!
I'm sick of it all. [*Laughs.*] Opinionated fool! Complacent business-
men are figures of fun, though people don't know whether to
laugh or cry at them. But when will someone laugh at me, that's
what I'd like to know? It's funny enough—he doesn't take bribes
or steal, doesn't beat his wife, his ideas are quite respectable, but he's
no good, that's the funny thing, no damn good at all. [*Pause.*] I must
be off. I'll ask the school inspector for a new job, I'll write to town
today.

[ISAAC *comes in.*]

SCENE V

[PLATONOV *and* ISAAC.]

ISAAC [*coming in*]. Ah, there's the schoolhouse where that half-baked
philosopher does his sleeping. Is he asleep as usual? Or is he quarrelling
—also as usual? [*Seeing* PLATONOV.] There he is, the empty windbag,
neither sleeping nor quarrelling, an abnormal state. [*To* PLATONOV.]
Not in bed yet?

PLATONOV. You've got eyes, haven't you? Why stop here? May I
wish you good night?

ISAAC. I'm going in a moment. Enjoying a little solitude? [*Looks
round.*] Monarch of all you survey, eh? On a lovely night like this.

PLATONOV. Going home?

ISAAC. Yes. Father took the carriage, so I've got to walk. Enjoying
yourself? Nice, isn't it, to drink champagne and observe yourself
under the influence? Can I sit by you?

PLATONOV. Yes.

ISAAC. Thanks. [*Sits.*] I always like saying thanks. It must be nice to
sit on these steps and feel you're a lord of creation. Where's the lady

friend, Platonov? What with nature rustling and grasshoppers chirping, we only need a little amorous chit-chat to turn this place into a paradise. This flirtatious, timid breeze only wants your sweetheart's warm breath to make your cheeks glow with happiness. Mother Nature's whispers need setting off with words of love. I want a woman! You look surprised. Ha ha! Yes, it's not how I usually talk—not my normal lingo. When I'm sober I'll blush at what I've said, but why shouldn't I do some romantic babbling anyway? Who's to stop me?

PLATONOV. No one.

ISAAC. So the language of the Gods doesn't suit my station, perhaps, or my appearance? You think I don't look romantic?

PLATONOV. Exactly.

ISAAC. Unromantic—. I see. I'm glad. Jews don't look romantic. Nature played a joke on us—issued us with unromantic faces. People usually judge by appearances, so they deny us romantic feelings on the strength of our looks. It's said there are no Jewish poets.

PLATONOV. Who says so?

ISAAC. Everyone, and it's a rotten slander.

PLATONOV. Stop quibbling. Who says so?

ISAAC. Everyone. Yet how many true poets we have—not Pushkins or Lermontovs, but real ones—Auerbach, Heine, Goethe.

PLATONOV. Goethe was a German.

ISAAC. He was a Jew!

PLATONOV. He was a German!

ISAAC. He was a Jew! I know what I'm saying.

PLATONOV. I know what I'm saying too, but have it your own way. It's hard to get the better of a half-educated Jew.

ISAAC. Very hard. [*Pause.*] But suppose there were no Jewish poets, what matter? If we have some, fine—but if we haven't, even better. As a sensual man a poet is usually a parasite and egoist. Did Goethe as a poet ever give a crust of bread to one German working man?

PLATONOV. That'll do, boy, it's been said before. He never took a crust of bread off a German working man either, that's what matters. And it's a million times better to be a poet than a nobody. But let's stop this. You haven't the faintest idea what you're talking about, so leave us all alone—the crust of bread, the poets who are beyond your desiccated understanding, and me whom you're for ever pestering.

ISAAC. All right, I won't try to stir your generous heart, you effervescent fellow. I won't try to pull the blanket of illusions off you. Go to sleep. [*Pause.*] Look at the sky. Yes, it's nice and quiet here, with nothing but trees around. There are none of those sleek, self-satisfied faces. No indeed. The trees don't whisper to me, and the moon doesn't look down as favourably on me as it does on this fellow Platonov. It tries to look coldly. 'You're not one of us,' it seems to say. 'So leave paradise. Run along to your dirty Jewish shop.' But what nonsense, I'm raving—I must stop.

PLATONOV. Quite so. Go home, boy. The longer you stay, the more nonsense you'll talk. And, as you said, you'll blush for all this rubbish later. Go.

ISAAC. But I want to talk. [*Laughs.*] Now I'm a poet.

PLATONOV. You can't be a poet if you're ashamed to be young. You are young, so make the most of it—that may be funny and stupid, but it's at least human.

ISAAC. If you say so, but what nonsense it all is. You're a funny fellow, Platonov, like everyone else round here. You should have lived before the flood. Anna Voynitsev's funny too, and so's Sergey. She's not bad-looking actually, anatomically speaking, with those clever eyes and fine fingers. She's not bad in parts. Splendid breast and neck—. [*Pause.*] Why not? Aren't I as good a man as you? It's only once in a lifetime. If thoughts can have such a powerful attraction for, er, the marrow of my spine, what would happen if she appeared among those trees and beckoned me with her ethereal fingers? I'd melt away in sheer ecstasy! Don't look at me like that. All right, so I'm a silly young fool. But who dares tell me I can't be foolish once in my life? Just as a scientific experiment I want to play the fool—or be happy, as you'd call it. And happy I am. What has that to do with anyone else, eh?

PLATONOV. But—. [*Looks at* ISAAC's *watch-chain.*]

ISAAC. Individual happiness is a form of selfishness, anyway.

PLATONOV. Oh yes! Individual happiness is selfishness, individual misery is virtue—what ghastly poppycock you talk! And what a watch-chain! What wonderful seals. How it shines!

ISAAC. It interests you, eh? [*Laughs.*] Tinsel and glitter fascinate you. [*Shakes his head.*] You preach at me, practically break into verse— yet you can admire gold at the same time! Take the chain. Throw it away. [*Tears off the chain and throws it aside.*]

PLATONOV. What a splendid sound—you can tell it's heavy from the noise it makes.

ISAAC. Gold's a burden in more ways than weight. You're lucky you can sit on these filthy steps where the full weight of filthy lucre isn't felt. Oh, my golden chains—golden fetters, more like.

PLATONOV. Fetters can be broken! Our fathers managed to waste theirs on drink.

ISAAC. There are so many wretched, hungry, drunken people in this world. These millions who sow much, but eat not—when will they starve no more? When? I asked you a question, Platonov—why don't you answer?

PLATONOV. Leave me alone, do you mind? I don't like bells that go on and on ringing to no purpose. You must leave me, sorry, I want to go to bed.

ISAAC. Me a bell? You, more like.

PLATONOV. We're both bells, the difference being that I ring myself and you're rung by others. Good night. [*Gets up.*]

ISAAC. Good night. [*The school clock strikes two.*] Two already. I should be asleep by now, but I can't—what with insomnia, champagne and excitement. It's an unhealthy life, it's ruining my system. [*Gets up.*] I already have a pain in my chest, I think. Good night. I shan't shake hands, I'm proud to say. You've no right to shake hands with me.

PLATONOV. Don't be silly, what do I care?

ISAAC. I hope no one overheard what we said and my, er, chatter, and I hope it won't be passed on. [*Goes to the back of the stage and comes back.*]

PLATONOV. What do you want?

ISAAC. My chain was here somewhere.

PLATONOV. There's your chain. [*Kicks it.*] So you didn't forget it. Look, do me a favour—donate this chain to a friend of mine who's one of those who sow much, but eat not. This chain will keep his family for years. May I give him it?

ISAAC. No. I'd be glad to, but I honestly can't. It's a gift, a souvenir.

PLATONOV. I see. Then get out!

ISAAC [*picks up the chain*]. Leave me alone, please. [*Moves off, wearily sits down on the railway track at the back of the stage and buries his face in his hands.*]

PLATONOV. How vulgar—if you're young you should be an idealist. What frightful depravity. [*Sits down.*] Aren't people disgusting when they remind you of your own murky past? I was a bit like that once. Ah me!

[*The sound of horses' hooves.*]

SCENE VI

[PLATONOV *and* ANNA, *who comes in wearing a riding-habit and carrying a hunting-crop.*]

PLATONOV. It's Anna.

ANNA. How can I see him? Shall I knock? [*Seeing* PLATONOV.] You here? That's lucky. I knew you wouldn't be asleep. How can people sleep at such a time? God gave us the winter to sleep in. Good evening, you great oaf. [*Holds out her hand.*] Well? What are you doing, where's your hand?

[PLATONOV *holds out his hand.*]

ANNA. Not drunk, are you?

PLATONOV. Damned if I know—I'm either sober or completely sozzled. But what are you doing? Going for a walk? Have you nothing better to do, dear sleep-walker?

ANNA [*sits by him*]. Yes. [*Pause.*] Yes, Michael. [*Sings.*] 'Such happiness, such torture.' [*Laughs.*] What huge, astonished eyes! Come on, don't be scared, old friend.

PLATONOV. I'm not—not for myself, anyway. [*Pause.*] I can see you're in a silly mood.

ANNA. In my old age——

PLATONOV. Old women can be excused, they *are* silly. But who says you're old? You're as young as a June morning, your whole life lies ahead of you.

ANNA. I want a bit of life now, not ahead of me. I am young, Platonov, terribly young. I feel it, it seems to blow through me like a wind. I'm hellishly young. It's cold. [*Pause.*]

PLATONOV [*jumps up*]. I refuse to understand or guess or have ideas. I don't want anything! Go away. Tell me what a lout I am and go away, go on! Don't look like that! You just—think what you're doing.

ANNA. I already have.

PLATONOV. Think again, you proud, intelligent, lovely woman. What turned your steps in this direction? Oh——

ANNA. I didn't step, I drove, dear.

PLATONOV. Such a clever, lovely young woman—and comes to me? I can't believe my eyes or ears. She came to conquer, to storm the fortress, only I'm no fortress and you'll make no conquests. I'm so weak, so terribly weak, you must see that.

ANNA [*gets up and goes to him*]. Humility can be worse than pride. What will happen, Michael? This thing must end somehow, you must see that——

PLATONOV. I can't end something I haven't even begun.

ANNA. What a foul way to argue! And aren't you ashamed to lie? On such a night, under such a sky—and telling lies! Lie in autumn if you want, with mud and slush everywhere—but not now, not here. You can be heard, you're being watched. Look up, silly. [*Pause.*] Look, your lies have made the very stars twinkle. You've said quite enough, dear. Now be good—like the sky and the stars. Don't break this harmony with your petty selfishness. Drive your devils away. [*Puts one arm round him.*] We're made for each other. Let's enjoy this love and let others settle all the problems that torment you. [*Kisses him.*] Let's enjoy our love.

PLATONOV. Ulysses deserved the Sirens' song, but I'm no Ulysses, Siren. [*Embraces her.*] If only I could make you happy! You're so lovely. But I shan't make you happy, I'll make you what I've made all the women who've thrown themselves at me—miserable.

ANNA. You've a pretty high opinion of yourself. Are you really such a lady-killer? [*Laughs.*] You do look nice by moonlight—charming.

PLATONOV. I know what I'm like. Love affairs only end happily when I'm not involved.

ANNA. Let's sit. Over here. [*They sit on the railway track.*] Any more to say, O sage?

PLATONOV. If I was an honourable man I'd leave you. I knew this would happen, I had a feeling earlier today. I'm such a cad, why didn't I leave?

ANNA. Chase those devils away, Michael. Don't poison yourself. Your visitor's a woman, isn't she, not a wild beast. What a long face! Tears in his eyes! Really! If you don't want me, I'll go. Well? I'll go and everything will be as it was. All right? [*Laughs.*] Take it, you fool, snatch it, grab it! What more do you want? Smoke me like a cigarette, press me out, smash me, be a man! [*Shakes him.*] You silly boy.

PLATONOV. But are you really meant for me? Really? [*Kisses her hands.*] Run along, dear, and find someone worthy of you.

ANNA. That's enough silly talk. It's all very simple, surely. You love a woman. She loves you. And here she is. It's a fine night. What could be simpler? So why all the clever talk? Trying to show off, or what?

PLATONOV. I see. [*Gets up.*] But what if you only want a bit of hanky-panky, fun and games and all that? Eh? I'm not cut out for anything casual. You shan't trifle with me. You won't get rid of me with just a pat on the back as you have of so many others. I'm too expensive for a cheap affair. [*Clutches his head.*] To respect and love you in the middle of all this pettiness, mediocrity, provincialism and vulgar frivolity——

ANNA [*comes up to him*]. You do love and respect me, so why all the fuss, why bargain with me, why say such nasty things? Why all the ifs? I love you. I've told you so, you know it's true. What else do you want? I need peace. [*Puts her head on his chest.*] Peace and quiet. I need a rest, Platonov, so get that into your head. I want to forget everything, that's all. You just don't know—what a trial my life is. I want some real life for a change.

PLATONOV. You'll get no peace from me.

ANNA. Then at least cut out the clever talk. Live! Everything lives and moves, life's all around us, so let's have some life too. We'll solve our problems tomorrow, but today—tonight—let's live! Live, I tell you. [*Pause.*] Really, why do I carry on like this? [*Laughs.*] Oh, for heaven's sake! I grow lyrical and he can only squirm.

PLATONOV [*grips her arm*]. Listen. For the last time. I speak as an honourable man. Go away. It's my last word. Go!

ANNA. Oh yes? [*Laughs.*] Not trying to be funny, are you? Don't be silly, man. Now I'll never leave you. [*Throws her arms round his neck.*]

Do you hear? For the last time, I won't let you go, come what may. Ruin me, destroy yourself, but I'll have you! Let's live! Whoopee! Don't try and get away, silly. You're mine. *Now* churn out your clever talk!

PLATONOV. Once more, as an honourable man——

ANNA. If I can't get you honourably, I'll take you by force. If you love me—love me, don't fool around. Hurrah, hurrah! 'Ring out, ye peals of victory.' Come, come to me. [*Throws a black kerchief over his head.*] Come to me.

PLATONOV. To you? [*Laughs.*] You're no good. You're asking for trouble, you'll be sorry for this. I shan't be your husband, because you're not my type and I won't let you monkey with me. We'll see who laughs last. You'll be sorry. Shall we go?

ANNA [*laughs*]. Allons! [*Takes his arm.*] Wait, someone's coming, let's hide behind a tree. [*They hide behind a tree.*] It's someone in a frock-coat, not a peasant. Why don't you write leading articles for the papers? You'd do it well, seriously.

[NICHOLAS *comes in.*]

SCENE VII

[*The above and* NICHOLAS.]

NICHOLAS [*goes to the schoolhouse and bangs on a window*]. Sasha! My dear sister!

SASHA [*opens the window*]. Who's there? You, is it, Nicholas? What do you want?

NICHOLAS. Not asleep yet? Let me stay the night, dear.

SASHA. Come on then.

NICHOLAS. Put me in a classroom, but please don't let Michael know I'm staying, or he'll keep me awake talking. I feel terribly dizzy, I'm seeing double. I stand in front of one window, but there seem to be two, so which shall I climb through? What a business! It's a good job I'm not married, I'd think I'd committed bigamy. Everything's double, I see two heads on your two necks. By the way, dear, I blew my nose near that felled oak by the stream—you know the one— and forty roubles must have fallen out of my handkerchief. Pick them up early tomorrow, darling, you can keep them.

SASHA. The carpenters will get them at dawn. You are careless, Nicholas. Oh, I nearly forgot. The shopkeeper's wife called—wants you to go over as soon as possible, she was most urgent. Her husband's been taken ill, a stroke or something. Better be quick.

NICHOLAS. Confound the man, I can't bother. I have a splitting head myself and a belly-ache too. [*Climbs through the window.*] Out of my way.

SASHA. Hurry up, you're treading on my dress. [*Shuts the window.*]

PLATONOV. Hell, there's someone else coming.

ANNA. Stay where you are.

PLATONOV. Let me go, I'll leave if I want. Who's there?

ANNA. Petrin and Shcherbuk.

[PETRIN *and* SHCHERBUK *come in without their frock-coats, tottering.* PETRIN *wears a black top hat,* SHCHERBUK *a grey one.*]

SCENE VIII

[ISAAC, *at the back of the stage,* PLATONOV, ANNA, PETRIN *and* SHCHERBUK.]

PETRIN. Long live Petrin! Hurrah for our learned lawyer! Which is the way? Where have we got to? What's that? [*Laughs.*] Aha, a branch of the Ministry of Education, Paul, where they teach fools to forget God and swindle man. So that's where we are. Well, well, well. It's where that—what the hell's his name?—Platonov lives, the man of culture. But where's the fellow now? Speak out, don't be ashamed. Is he singing a duet with our general's widow? Thy will be done, O Lord. [*Shouts.*] Glagolyev's a fool. She told him to take a running jump at himself, and he went and had a stroke.

SHCHERBUK. I want to go home—must get to bed. Blast them all.

PETRIN. Where are our coats, Paul? We're staying at the station-master's—and with no coats! [*Laughs.*] Did the girls take them off? You gay dog, you! The girls took our coats. [*Sighs.*] Get any champagne, Paul? I bet you're drunk now? And whose did you drink? Mine. You took my drink and ate my food. Anna Voynitsev's clothes belong to me, and so do Sergey's stockings—it's all mine, I gave them the lot. And my old boots need mending, the heels are crooked. I give them everything, squander it on them, and what do I get, eh? A lot of damn rudeness. Their servant misses me out at table, manages to jog me with his elbow. She treats me like a swine.

PLATONOV. I'm fed up with this.

ANNA. Wait, they'll go in a minute. What an animal Petrin is, what lies he tells! And that old sissy believes him.

PETRIN. They treat that Jew better than us. The Jew's on top and we're at his feet. Why? Because the Jew lends more money.

> 'And on his brow are writ the words:
> "For sale by public auction".'

SHCHERBUK. That's from Nekrasov, they say he's dead.

PETRIN. All right, not a penny more do they get, do you hear? Not one. The old man can turn over in his grave and curse the grave-diggers! I've had enough, I'll sue her. Tomorrow! I'll make her name mud, ungrateful hussy.

SHCHERBUK. She's a real aristocrat, every inch the general's lady, while I'm a complete outsider and must make do with some village wench. What a bumpy road, there should be a highway with telegraph poles and jingling bells.

[*They go out.*]

SCENE IX

[*The above without* PETRIN *and* SHCHERBUK.]

ANNA [*comes out from behind a tree*]. Have they gone?

PLATONOV. Yes.

ANNA [*takes him by the shoulders*]. Shall we proceed?

PLATONOV. All right, I'll come, but if you only knew how unwilling I am. It's not me coming to you, it's the devil who keeps on at me and says I've got to. It's not me you'll get, it's my weak body. I'd have booted you out if I hadn't such a badly behaved body.

ANNA. What a foul thing to say. [*Hits* PLATONOV *with her riding-crop*.] Talk away—but don't talk rot. [*Moves away from* PLATONOV.] You want, you don't want—to hell with that! I'm not going down on my bended knees to you, that's asking too much.

PLATONOV. It's a bit late to take umbrage.

[*Goes after her and takes her hand. She snatches it away.*]

PLATONOV. I'll come anyway, the devil inside me can't be stopped now. Turn away, would you? It's a bit late to take umbrage, as I say. We're both so placed, we can't part however much we insult each other. And get this clear. If I can't accept your love in my heart, it's just that I'm quite sure you're making a fatal mistake.

SASHA [*at the window*]. Michael, where are you?

PLATONOV. Blast!

SASHA [*at the window*]. Ah, there you are. Who are you with? [*Laughs.*] Anna! I hardly recognized you, you look so black. What are you wearing? Hallo there.

ANNA. Hallo, Sasha.

SASHA. Wearing your riding-habit? You're out riding then? That's a good idea, it's such a lovely night. Let's join her, Michael.

ANNA. I've ridden far enough, I'm going home now.

SASHA. Well, in that case, of course—. Come inside, Michael. I really don't know what to do—Nicholas isn't well.

PLATONOV. Which Nicholas?

SASHA. My brother. He must have had too much to drink. Come in, please, and you come too, Anna. I'll just fetch some milk from the cellar. We'll have a glass each, it's nice and cold.

ANNA. No thanks, I'm on my way home. [*To* PLATONOV.] You go in, I'll wait.

SASHA. I'm only going to run down to the cellar. Come in, Michael. [*Disappears.*]

PLATONOV. I'd quite forgotten she existed. She trusts me so. You run along, I'll put her to bed and come after you.

ANNA. Be quick about it.

PLATONOV. We just missed having a flaming row! Good-bye for now. [*Goes into the schoolhouse.*]

SCENE X

[ANNA *and* ISAAC, *followed by* OSIP.]

ANNA. A nice surprise—I'd forgotten she existed myself. [*Pause.*] How cruel. Still, it's not the first time he's deceived the poor child. Ah well, may as well be hung for a sheep as a lamb. Only God will know, and it's happened before. How ghastly—now I have to wait till he's put her to bed, an hour or more.

ISAAC [*goes up to her*]. Mrs. Voynitsev. [*Falls on his knees.*] Mrs. Voynitsev. [*Clutches her hand.*] Anna.

ANNA. Who's this? Who are you? [*Bends down to him.*] Who is it? You, Mr. Vengerovich, is it? What's the matter?

ISAAC. Anna. [*Kisses her hand.*]

ANNA. Go away, this is all wrong. Call yourself a man?

ISAAC. Anna.

ANNA. Take your hands off me. Go away. [*Pushes his shoulder.*]

ISAAC [*falls flat on the ground*]. Oh, how stupid!

OSIP [*comes in*]. Hallo, you funny people. Not you, is it, ma'am? [*Bows.*] What brought you to our sanctum?

ANNA. Is it you, Osip? Hallo! Seeing what you can pick up? Spying out the land? [*Takes him by the chin.*] Did you see it all?

OSIP. Yes.

ANNA. Why so pale, though? [*Laughs.*] Are you in love with me, Osip?

OSIP. As you wish, ma'am.

ANNA. Are you?

OSIP. I can't make you out. [*Weeps.*] I thought you were a saint. If you'd asked me to go through fire, I'd have been glad to.

ANNA. Why didn't you go to Kiev?

OSIP. What do I want in Kiev? I thought you were a saint, I worshipped you.

ANNA. That'll do, you fool. Bring me some more hares, I'll take them again. All right, good-bye. Come and see me tomorrow, I'll give you some money and you can go to Kiev by rail. All right? Good-bye. And don't dare lay your hands on Platonov, do you hear?

OSIP. I'll take no more orders from you.

ANNA. Good grief, he'll tell me to get myself to a nunnery next. What business is it of his? Well, well, well. Crying? Not a child, are you? Stop it. When he comes out, you fire a shot.

OSIP. At him?

ANNA. No, in the air. Good-bye, Osip. Fire a loud shot, all right?

OSIP. Yes.

ANNA. There's a good boy.

OSIP. Only he won't come, he's with his wife now.

ANNA. Oh, won't he? Good-bye, assassin. [*Runs out.*]

SCENE XI

[OSIP *and* ISAAC.]

OSIP [*bangs his hat on the ground and cries*]. It's all over. Everything can go to hell.

ISAAC [*lying on the ground*]. What does he say?

OSIP. I saw and heard the whole business. My eyes were ready to pop and there was a ruddy great banging in my ears. I heard it all. What else can I do but kill him, if I feel ready to tear him up and swallow him alive. [*Sits on the embankment with his back to the school.*] I must kill him.

ISAAC. What's that? Kill who?

SCENE XII

[*The above,* PLATONOV *and* NICHOLAS.]

PLATONOV [*pushes* NICHOLAS *out of the schoolhouse*]. Get out! Off with you to the shopkeeper's this instant—at the double!

NICHOLAS [*stretches*]. Better have hit me with a stick tomorrow than woken me up today.

PLATONOV. You're a real stinker, do you hear?

NICHOLAS. It can't be helped, it must be the way I'm built.

PLATONOV. What if the shopkeeper's already dead?

NICHOLAS. May he rest in peace in that case, and if he's still battling for life, there's no point in putting the wind up me. I'm not going to see any shopkeeper, I want to go to bed.

PLATONOV. You damn well shall go, you hound. [*Shoves him.*] I won't let you sleep. Who do you think you are, I'd like to know? Why do you never do anything? Why are you fooling around here, idling away the best years of your life?

NICHOLAS. Don't be a nuisance. You are a little tick, old man.

PLATONOV. What order of being are you, may one ask? This is ghastly. What do you live for? Why don't you study, continue your education? Why don't you study, animal?

NICHOLAS. Let's discuss this fascinating topic some time when I'm not sleepy. Now let me get back to bed. [*Scratches himself.*] It's a bit steep, all this 'Arise, you stinker' stuff, coming clean out of the blue. Professional ethics? Damn and blast professional ethics.

PLATONOV. What God do you serve, you odd creature? What sort of man are you? We'll never be any good, I can tell you that.

NICHOLAS. Look here, Michael, who gave you the right to lay your ruddy great frozen paws on people's hearts? You're so rude, old boy, it takes one's breath away.

PLATONOV. We'll never be more than the scum of the earth. We're done for, we're no damn good. [*Weeps.*] There's nobody one can bear to contemplate. How dirty, second-rate and second-hand everything is. Clear out, Nicholas, go!

NICHOLAS [*shrugs*]. Crying? [*Pause.*] I'll go and see the shopkeeper. I'm going, do you hear?

PLATONOV. Do what you like.

NICHOLAS. I'm going, look.

PLATONOV [*stamps*]. Buzz off!

NICHOLAS. All right. Go to bed, Michael—no need to get het up. Good-bye! [*Moves off and stops.*] One last word. You can tell all moralizers, yourself included, to practise what they preach. You can't bear to contemplate yourself, but I'm no sight for sore eyes either. Your eyes look very good in the moonlight, by the way, glittering like green glass. Another thing, I shouldn't be talking to you. You need a really good hiding, you should be torn to pieces. I should have nothing more to do with you because of that little girl. Shall I tell you something you've never heard in all your born days? No I can't, I'm no good at duelling, luckily for you. [*Pause.*] Good-bye. [*Goes.*]

SCENE XIII

[PLATONOV, ISAAC *and* OSIP.]

PLATONOV [*clutches his head*]. It's not just me, they're all that way, the whole lot. God, where are there any real people? But who am I to talk? 'Don't visit her, she's not yours, she belongs to someone else, you'll ruin her life, do her permanent harm.' Shall I leave? I shall not. I shall visit her, I shall live here as a drunken scapegrace. Depraved, drunken fools—always drunk, the mother a fool, the father a drunk. Father, mother—. Father—. Rot in your graves for the rotten mess you made of my poor life with your drunken folly. [*Pause.*] No—. What have I said? God forgive me, may they rest in peace. [*Bumps into* ISAAC *who is lying on the ground.*] Who's this?

ISAAC [*gets on his knees*]. What a wild, ugly, disgraceful night.

PLATONOV. Oh, go and write it all down in your stupid diary in the ink of your father's conscience. Clear out!

ISAAC. All right, I'll make a note of it. [*Goes out.*]

PLATONOV. What was he doing here? Eavesdropping? [*To* OSIP.] Who are you? What do you want, pirate? Eavesdropping too? Clear out! No, wait. Run after Vengerovich and take his chain.

OSIP [*gets up*]. What chain?

PLATONOV. He has a large gold chain on his chest. Catch him up and take it. Look slippy. [*Stamps.*] Hurry up or you'll miss him, he's rushing to the village like a maniac.

OSIP. And you to Anna Voynitsev, I suppose?

PLATONOV. Hurry up, you rogue. Don't beat him up, just take his chain. Off with you. Don't stand around. Run!

[OSIP *runs off.*]

PLATONOV [*after a pause*]. To go or not? [*Sighs.*] I'll go, and a long, fundamentally boring and ugly episode will begin. I thought I was proof against this sort of thing, and what happens? A woman says one word and all hell breaks loose inside me. Others have problems of world significance, my problem's a woman. All life's a woman. Caesar had the Rubicon, I have—woman. I'm always chasing a bit of skirt. It would be less pitiful if I didn't fight against it, but I do fight. I'm weak, utterly weak.

SASHA [*at the window*]. You there, Michael?

PLATONOV. Yes, my poor treasure.

SASHA. Come indoors.

PLATONOV. No, Sasha. I want a spell outside. I've got a splitting headache. Go to sleep, angel.

SASHA. Good night. [*Shuts window.*]

PLATONOV. It hurts to deceive someone who trusts you blindly. It made me sweat and blush. Coming!

[*Moves off.* KATYA *and* JACOB *come towards him.*]

SCENE XIV

[PLATONOV, KATYA *and* JACOB.]

KATYA [*to* JACOB]. Wait here, I shan't be long. I'll get a book. Mind you don't go away. [*Goes to meet* PLATONOV.]

PLATONOV [*seeing* KATYA]. You? What do you want?

KATYA [*terrified*]. Oh, it's you, sir. I was looking for you.

PLATONOV. You, Katya? You're all night-birds, from the mistress to the maid. What do you want?

KATYA [*quietly*]. I've a letter for you from my mistress, sir.

PLATONOV. What?

KATYA. A letter from my mistress.

PLATONOV. What's this nonsense? Which mistress?

KATYA [*more quietly*]. Miss Sonya, sir.

PLATONOV. What? Are you mad? You'd better put your head in cold water. Get out.

KATYA [*hands over a letter*]. This is it, sir.

PLATONOV [*snatches the letter off her*]. A letter—a letter. What letter? Couldn't you have brought it in the morning? [*Opens it.*] How can I read in this light.

KATYA. She said please be quick.

PLATONOV [*strikes a match*]. What the hell brought you here? [*Reads.*] 'Am taking first step. Come and take it with me. Am new woman. Come and take me. Am yours.' What the blazes! A sort of telegram. 'Shall wait till four in summer-house near four pillars. Husband drunk, gone hunting with young Glagolyev. All yours, S.' God, this is the giddy limit! [*To* KATYA.] What are you looking at?

KATYA. How can I help looking? I've got eyes, sir.

PLATONOV. Then put them out. Is that letter really for me?

KATYA. Yes.

PLATONOV. Nonsense. Get out!

KATYA. Very good, sir. [*Goes off with* JACOB.]

SCENE XV

[PLATONOV, *alone.*]

PLATONOV [*after a pause*]. So that's how it turned out. You have landed in a mess, old boy, you've ruined a woman, a living creature. What was the point, where was the need? Damn my idle tongue, look where it's got me. What can I do now? Come on, head—think, if you're so clever. Curse yourself, tear your hair. [*Thinks.*] I must go away, go away at once and not dare show my face again here this side of doomsday. I'll make myself scarce double quick and buckle down to a life of poverty and hard work. Better live badly than get entangled like this. [*Pause.*] I'll go away, but—does Sonya really love me? [*Laughs.*] But why? What a dark, strange world it is. [*Pause.*] Strange. That lovely, magnificent woman with her wonderful hair—can she really love a penniless eccentric? I don't believe it. [*Lights a match and scans the letter.*] Yes. Me? Sonya? [*Laughs.*] Love? [*Clutches his chest.*] Happiness—that's what this means! Me—happy! A new life, new people, new scenery! I'm coming. Quick march to the summer-house near the four pillars! Wait for me, Sonya, you have been mine, you shall be again. [*Moves off and stops.*] No, I can't. [*Moves back.*] How can I destroy my family? [*Shouts.*] Sasha, I'm coming in, open up. [*Clutches his head.*] I won't, I shan't, I will not go! [*Pause.*] I will! [*Moves off.*] I'll go, I'll destroy, trample, defile. [*Bumps into* SERGEY *and* CYRIL.]

SCENE XVI

[PLATONOV, SERGEY *and* CYRIL. SERGEY *and* CYRIL *run in with guns slung across their backs.*]

SERGEY. Here he is! [*Embraces* PLATONOV.] Well? Coming shooting?

PLATONOV. No, just a minute.

SERGEY. Trying to shake me off, old man? [*Laughs.*] Drunk. I'm drunk. For the first time in my life. God, I'm so happy, old boy. [*Embraces* PLATONOV.] Shall we go? She sent me—told me to bag some game for her.

CYRIL. Hurry, it's getting light.

SERGEY. Heard of our idea? A stroke of genius, eh? We want to put on *Hamlet*—honestly. It'll be one hell of a performance. [*Laughs.*] You are pale. Drunk too, are you?

PLATONOV. Drunk. Let me go.

SERGEY. Wait. It's my idea. We start painting the scenery tomorrow. I'll take Hamlet, Sonya will be Ophelia, you can be Claudius and Triletsky will be Horatio. I'm so happy, really pleased. Shakespeare, Sonya, you and Mother—what more could a man want? Oh yes, a spot of Glinka, that's all. I'm Hamlet.

> 'O shame! where is thy blush? Rebellious hell,
> If thou canst mutine in a matron's bones,
> To flaming youth let virtue be as wax,
> And melt in her own fire.'

[*Laughs.*] Quite a Hamlet, eh?

PLATONOV [*breaks away and runs off*]. You swine. [*Runs out.*]

SERGEY. I say, he *is* drunk! Oh, who cares? [*Laughs.*] What do you think of our friend?

CYRIL. Pretty well loaded. Come on.

SERGEY. Come on then. You'd be my friend too if—. 'Ophelia, nymph, in thy orisons be all my sins remembered.' [*Goes out. Sound of an approaching train.*]

SCENE XVII

[OSIP, *followed by* SASHA.]

OSIP [*runs in carrying the chain*]. Where is he? [*Looks round.*] Where is he? Gone? Not here? [*Whistles.*] Platonov! Michael! Hallo there!

[*Pause.*] Not here? [*Runs up to the window and knocks.*] Mr. Platonov! [*Smashes the pane.*]

SASHA [*at the window*]. Who's that?

OSIP. Call Platonov. Hurry up.

SASHA. What's happened? He's not in here.

OSIP [*shouts*]. Isn't he? Then he must be with Anna Voynitsev, she was here asking him to come to her. All is lost. He's gone to her, blast him.

SASHA. That's a lie.

OSIP. He's gone to her, so help me God. I heard and saw it all, they were embracing and kissing here.

SASHA. That's a lie.

OSIP. It isn't, or may my father and mother never go to heaven. He's gone to Anna Voynitsev. Left his wife. Go after him, ma'am. No, no, it's too late. Now you're unhappy too. [*Takes the gun off his shoulders.*] She gave me her final order and I'm carrying it out— finally. [*Shoots into the air.*] Just let them meet. [*Flings his gun on the ground.*] I'll cut his throat, ma'am. [*Jumps across the embankment and sits on a tree stump.*] Don't worry, ma'am, I'll cut his throat, never doubt. [*Lights appear.*]

SASHA [*comes out in her nightdress with her hair down*]. He's gone, betrayed me. [*Sobs.*] I'm done for. God, kill me after this! [*A whistle.*] I'll throw myself under the train, I don't want to live. [*Lies on the rails.*] He betrayed me. Kill me, Mother of God! [*Pause.*] Forgive me, Lord, forgive me. [*Shrieks.*] Nicholas! [*Rises to her knees.*] My son! Save me, save me! The train's coming! Save me!

[OSIP *jumps towards* SASHA.]

SASHA [*falls on the rails*]. Oh——

OSIP [*picks her up and carries her into the schoolhouse*]. I'll cut his throat, don't worry.

[*The train passes.*]

END OF ACT TWO

ACT THREE

A room in the schoolhouse. Doors, right and left. A cupboard containing crockery, a chest of drawers, an old upright piano, chairs, a sofa upholstered in oilcloth, a guitar and so on. All very untidy.

SCENE I

[SONYA *and* PLATONOV. PLATONOV *is asleep on the sofa by the window with a straw hat over his face.*]

SONYA [*wakes* PLATONOV *up*]. Platonov! Michael! [*Gives him a shove.*] Wake up. [*Takes the hat off his face.*] Why put this dirty old hat over your face? Ugh, what a slovenly fellow! What a pigsty! He's lost his studs and sleeps with his chest bare, unwashed, in a dirty nightshirt. Michael, I'm talking to you. Get up.

PLATONOV. What?

SONYA. Wake up.

PLATONOV. In a moment. All right.

SONYA. That's enough of that. Get up, will you?

PLATONOV. Who is it? [*Sits up.*] Is it you, Sonya?

SONYA [*holds a watch near his eyes*]. Look.

PLATONOV. All right. [*Lies down again.*]

SONYA. Platonov!

PLATONOV. What do you want? [*Sits up.*] Eh?

SONYA. Look at the time.

PLATONOV. What is this? Another of your tricks, Sonya?

SONYA. Exactly. Kindly look at the watch. What time is it?

PLATONOV. Half past seven.

SONYA. Exactly. Have you forgotten our arrangement?

PLATONOV. What arrangement? Say what you mean, Sonya, I'm in no mood for jokes or nonsensical riddles.

SONYA. 'What arrangement'! Have you forgotten? What's wrong with you? Your eyes are bloodshot and you look an awful mess. Are you ill? [*Pause.*] We arranged to be at the hut at six o'clock this morning. Have you forgotten? It's long past six.

PLATONOV. Anything else?

SONYA [*sits by him*]. Aren't you ashamed? Why didn't you come? You did promise.

PLATONOV. I'd have kept my promise too, if I hadn't fallen asleep. You can see I've been sleeping, can't you? Don't pester me.

SONYA [*shakes her head*]. You are unreliable. Don't look so angry, you're unreliable towards me, anyway. Think. Have you ever been on time at any of our meetings? How often you've broken your promises to me!

PLATONOV. I'm glad to hear it.

SONYA. That's not very clever, Platonov, you should be ashamed. Why have you stopped being decent, intelligent and sincere when I'm with you? Why these vulgar outbursts unworthy of the man I owe my salvation to? You always treat me like an ogre—no kind looks, no tender words, not one word of love. I come and see you and you smell of drink, you're dressed horribly, you haven't done your hair and you answer rudely and at random.

PLATONOV [*jumps up and strides about the stage*]. At it again!

SONYA. Drunk, are you?

PLATONOV. Mind your own business.

SONYA. What a charming remark. [*Weeps.*]

PLATONOV. Women!

SONYA. Don't talk to me about women. You go on about women a thousand times a day and I'm fed up. [*Gets up.*] What are you doing to me? Do you want to kill me? You've made me ill, my chest aches day and night, thanks to you. Can't you see, aren't you interested? You hate me. You wouldn't dare treat me like this if you loved me. I'm not an ordinary village girl without manners or refinement, and I shan't let someone like you—. [*Sits down.*] For God's sake! [*Weeps.*]

PLATONOV. That will do.

SONYA. Why are you killing me? It's not three weeks since that night and I'm already as thin as a rake. Where's the happiness you promised? Where will your antics end? Think, if you're so clever, noble and decent—give thought, Platonov, before it's too late. Think now. Sit on this chair, make your mind a blank and concentrate on what you're doing to me.

PLATONOV. I'm no good at thinking. [*Pause.*] You think. [*Goes up to her.*] Come on. I've taken away your family, your well-being and your future. Why? What for? I've robbed you as if I was your worst enemy. What can I give you? How can I repay your sacrifices? This sordid affair is your misfortune, downfall and ruin. [*Sits down.*]

SONYA. I give myself to him and he has the nerve to call our relationship a sordid affair.

PLATONOV. This is hardly the time to quibble. You have your view of this affair and I have mine. I've ruined you and that's that—you're not the only one either. Wait and see what your husband has to say when he finds out.

SONYA. Are you afraid he may make things unpleasant for you?

PLATONOV. No, I'm not, I'm afraid we may kill him.

SONYA. Then why did you come to me that day, you miserable coward, if you knew we were going to kill him?

PLATONOV. Oh, don't be so emotional. This heart-rending stuff leaves me cold. But why did you—? Anyway—. [*Makes a gesture of resignation.*] Speaking to you means bringing on floods of tears.

SONYA. Yes, I never cried before our affair. It's time you started shivering with fear because he knows already.

PLATONOV. What?

SONYA. He knows already.

PLATONOV [*sits up*]. What!

SONYA. He knows. I told him this morning.

PLATONOV. You're joking.

SONYA. You've turned pale. I should hate you, not love you. I must be mad. I don't know why—why I do love you. Yes, he knows. [*Plucks his sleeve.*] So tremble in your boots. He knows everything, I tell you. Go on, tremble.

PLATONOV. Impossible. I don't believe it. [*Pause.*]

SONYA. He knows. He had to be told some day, didn't he?

PLATONOV. But why are *you* trembling? How did you put it? What did you say?

SONYA. I told him I—I couldn't——

PLATONOV. And he?

SONYA. He was just like you—scared. You look quite insufferable at the moment.

PLATONOV. What did he say?

SONYA. He thought I was joking at first, but when he saw I wasn't he blenched, staggered, burst into tears and crawled on all fours. He looked as disgusting as you do now.

PLATONOV. What have you done, you loathsome woman! [*Clutches his head.*] You've killed him. Can you—dare you—say all this so cold-bloodedly? You've killed him. Did you name me?

SONYA. Yes, what do you think?

PLATONOV. What did he say?

SONYA [*jumps up*]. You really should be ashamed, Platonov, you don't know what you're saying. You think I shouldn't have told him, I suppose?

PLATONOV. You certainly shouldn't. [*Lies on the sofa, face downwards.*]

SONYA. Is that the way for a decent man to talk?

PLATONOV. It would have been more decent to say nothing than to kill him, because that's what we've done. He cried and crawled on all fours. Oh dear! [*Jumps up.*] Poor wretch—if it wasn't for you he'd never have known about us till the day he died.

SONYA. I had to tell him as an honest woman.

PLATONOV. You know what you've done by telling him, I take it? You can never go back to your husband now.

SONYA. Yes, never. What else do you think? You're beginning to talk like a thorough cad, Platonov.

PLATONOV. 'Never—.' But what will happen to you when we part—as we soon shall? You'll be the first to realize the error of your ways and see the light. You'll leave me first. [*Makes a gesture of resignation.*] Anyway, do as you like, Sonya. You're cleverer and more honest than I, so you'd better take charge. This is a fine kettle of fish—you'd better deal with it. Bring me back to life if you can and set me on my feet. Only hurry up, for God's sake, or I'll go mad.

SONYA. We leave here tomorrow.

PLATONOV. Yes, yes, we'll go. But let's hurry.

SONYA. I must get you away. I wrote to Mother about you, we'll go and see her.

PLATONOV. Anywhere you like, do as you wish.

SONYA. This means a new life, dear, can't you see? Do as I say, let me have my way. My head's clearer than yours. Trust me, darling, I'll put you back on your feet. I'll take you to a brighter place with no dust, grime, idleness or dirty nightshirts. I'll make a man of you— I'll make you happy, can't you see? [*Pause.*] I'll make you work. We'll be real people, Michael, we'll eat our own bread, sweat, get blisters. [*Lays her head on his chest.*] I shall work.

PLATONOV. Where will you work? Other women, stronger than you, lie around idle because they've nothing to do. You don't know how to work and what job will you do? The way we're fixed, Sonya, we'd do better to think straight—not take comfort in illusions. But have it your own way.

SONYA. You'll see. I'm stronger than these other women. I'll light the way for you, believe me, Michael. You've brought me back to life and I shall always be grateful. Shall we leave tomorrow then? I'll go and start packing, and you do the same. Come to the hut at ten o'clock and bring your things. All right?

PLATONOV. Yes.

SONYA. Promise?

PLATONOV. Look, I've said I will, haven't I?

SONYA. Promise.

PLATONOV. All right, we'll go. I swear.

SONYA [*laughs*]. I believe you. Come a bit earlier if you like, I'll be ready before ten. We'll drive off tonight. We'll have lots of fun, Michael. You don't know your own luck, silly boy. Why, this is our happiness, our life. Tomorrow you'll be a different man, new and fresh. We'll breathe a new air, new blood will flow through our veins. [*Laughs.*] Farewell, our decrepit old selves. Here's my hand. Hold it tight.

[*Gives him her hand.* PLATONOV *kisses it.*]

SONYA. Mind you're there, you old porpoise. I'll be waiting. Good-bye for the moment and cheer up. I'll be packed in a jiffy. [*Kisses him.*]

PLATONOV. Good-bye. Did you say ten or eleven?

SONYA. Ten. Or come a bit earlier. Good-bye. Put on some decent clothes for the journey. [*Laughs.*] I have some money, we can get supper on the way. Good-bye. I'll go and get ready. Cheer up, I expect you at ten. [*Runs off.*]

SCENE II

[PLATONOV, *alone.*]

PLATONOV [*after a pause*]. Tell me the old, old story—I've heard all that hundreds of times. [*Pause.*] I'll write to him and Sasha. They can have a bit of a cry, and forgive and forget. Good-bye, Voynit-sevka. Good-bye, Sasha, Anna and all. [*Opens the cupboard.*] I'll be a new man tomorrow, terribly new. What shall I put my clothes in? I've no suitcase. [*Pours some wine.*] Good-bye, school. [*Drinks.*] Good-bye, children, you won't see your Mr. Platonov again—that bad, but kind teacher. Was I drinking just now? Why? I'm going to give it up, this is the last time. I'll sit down and write to Sasha. [*Lies on the sofa.*] Sonya truly believes—and blessed are those who have faith. Laugh away, Anna, because laugh you will, and pretty loud at that. Oh yes, I think I had a letter from her. Where is it? [*Gets a letter from the window-sill.*] It's the hundredth, if not the two hundredth, since that wild night. [*Reads.*] 'Platonov, you who don't answer my letters, you tactless, cruel, stupid lout. If you don't answer this one either and don't come and see me—then I'll come and see *you*, damn you. I've been waiting all day. It's silly, Platonov—anyone would think you were ashamed of that night. Oh, forget it then. Sergey and Sonya are behaving abominably—their wild honey-moon is over and all because they haven't their talkative idiot with them, meaning you. Good-bye.' [*Pause.*] What handwriting—neat and bold, with commas and full stops, and no spelling mistakes. A literate woman's a pretty rare thing. [MARKO *comes in.*] I must write her a letter or she may turn up here. [*Seeing* MARKO.] A pretty rare thing——

SCENE III

[PLATONOV *and* MARKO.]

PLATONOV. Come in. Who do you want? [*Gets up.*]

MARKO. You, sir. [*Takes a document out of his bag.*] A summons for you, sir.

PLATONOV. Oh. Very nice too. What summons? Who sent you?

MARKO. The magistrate, sir.

PLATONOV. I see. And what does he want? Give it here. [*Takes the summons.*] I don't understand, is he inviting me to a christening? The old so-and-so breeds like a rabbit. [*Reads.*] ' . . . as defendant charged with assault on the person of Mary, daughter of Councillor Grekov.' [*Laughs.*] Oh hell! Loud cheers! Damn it all! Good old distilled bed-bugs! When's the case on? The day after tomorrow? I'll be there. Tell them I'm coming, reverend sir. Good for her, I must say. What a girl, she should have done it long ago.

MARKO. Would you mind signing, sir?

PLATONOV. Signing? All right. You look awfully like a dying duck, old boy.

MARKO. Permission to disagree, sir.

PLATONOV [*sits at the table*]. Then what do you look like?

MARKO. The image and likeness of God, sir.

PLATONOV. An old soldier, eh?

MARKO. Yes sir. Discharged after Sevastopol, sir. Had four years in hospital on top of my service. Sergeant of artillery, sir.

PLATONOV. I see. Were your guns any good?

MARKO. Ordinary ones—with a round barrel, like.

PLATONOV. Pencil all right?

MARKO. Yes sir. To say you duly received this summons. Put your full name, sir.

PLATONOV [*gets up*]. There. I've signed five times. How's the magistrate? Still gambling?

MARKO. Yes sir.

PLATONOV. Round the clock from five in the afternoon?

MARKO. Just so, sir.

PLATONOV. Has he lost his chain of office yet?

MARKO. No sir.

PLATONOV. Tell him—no, don't tell him anything. He doesn't pay his gambling debts, of course. Silly fool gambles, runs up debts and has a horde of children. What a clever little girl, honestly I never expected it. Who are the witnesses then? Who's being subpoenaed?

MARKO [*fingers through the summonses and reads*]. 'To Dr. Nicholas Triletsky', sir——

PLATONOV. Triletsky? [*Laughs.*] That should be quite amusing. Anyone else?

MARKO [*reads*]. 'To Mr. Cyril Glagolyev; to Mr. Alphonse Schrifter; to Mr. Maxim Aleutov, retired cornet of the guards; to Master Ivan Talye, son of Councillor Talye; to Mr. Sergey Voynitsev, graduate of St. Petersburg Nonversity——'

PLATONOV. Is that how it's spelt—'nonversity'?

MARKO. No sir.

PLATONOV. Then why read it out that way?

MARKO. Sheer ignorance, sir. [*Reads.*] 'Uni-uni-nonversity; to his wife, Mrs. Sonya Voynitsev; to Mr. Isaac Vengerovich, student of Kharkov Nonversity.' That's all.

PLATONOV. This is for the day after tomorrow, and I must leave tomorrow. What a pity. It would have been quite a case, I imagine. Well. What a nuisance, I'd have given her a run for her money. [*Walks up and down the stage.*] A great pity.

MARKO. Matter of a tip, sir.

PLATONOV. Eh?

MARKO. A tip. I had to walk four miles.

PLATONOV. A tip? I don't need one. But what am I saying? All right, old man, but I won't give you money, I'll give you tea instead to save my pocket and keep you sober. [*Takes a caddy from the cupboard.*] Come here. It's good strong tea—not seventy degrees proof, but strong. How would you like it?

MARKO [*holds out his pocket*]. In here, sir.

PLATONOV. What, straight in your pocket? Won't it smell?

MARKO. Pour away, sir, do. Don't hesitate.

PLATONOV [*pours tea leaves into his pocket*]. Enough?

MARKO. Thanking you kindly, sir.

PLATONOV. I say, aren't you old! I like old sweats like you—grand chaps. You sometimes meet a really awful one, though.

MARKO. It takes all sorts, sir. Only God's perfect. Good luck, sir.

PLATONOV. Wait a moment. [*Sits down and writes on the summons.*]

'I kissed you because—because I was annoyed and didn't know what I wanted, but I'd kiss you now with the greatest respect. I was rotten to you, I admit, just as I am to everyone. We shan't meet in court, I fear—tomorrow I leave for good. Good luck, and do at least be fair to me by not forgiving me.' [*To* MARKO.] Do you know where Miss Grekov lives?

MARKO. Yes, sir. About eight miles away if you cross by the ford.

PLATONOV. Oh, yes—in Zhilkovo. Take her this letter and you'll earn three roubles. Give it to the young lady in person. No answer's needed, and if she tries to give you one, don't accept it. Take it today, this instant. Take it first, and deliver the summonses later. [*Walks up and down the stage.*]

MARKO. I understand, sir.

PLATONOV. What else? Oh, yes. Tell everyone I apologized to Miss Grekov, but she wouldn't accept my apology.

MARKO. I see. Good luck, sir.

PLATONOV. Good-bye, old boy, and look after yourself.

[MARKO *goes out.*]

SCENE IV

[PLATONOV, *alone.*]

PLATONOV. So the Grekov and I are quits. She'll drag my name through the mud all over the county, and serve me right. It'll be the first time I've been punished by a woman. [*Lies on the sofa.*] Treat them like dirt and they only cling harder. Take Sonya. [*Covers his face with a handkerchief.*] I used to be free as the wind, but now I lie here, dreaming. Love—*amo, amas, amat.* Why did I get involved? I've wrecked her life and a fat lot of good I've done myself! [*Sighs.*] Poor Voynitsevs. And there's Sasha, poor kid—how will she get on without me? She'll pine away and die. She went away, she could sense what was happening and left with the child without a single word. She left after that night. I ought to say good-bye to her.

ANNA [*at the window*]. Can I come in? Hey, anyone there?

PLATONOV. Anna! [*Jumps up.*] Anna Voynitsev! What can I say to her? Why should she come here, anyway, I wonder? [*Straightens his clothes.*]

ANNA [*at the window*]. Can I come in? I'm coming, do you hear?

PLATONOV. She's here! How can I keep her out? [*Does his hair.*] How can I get rid of her? I'll have a drink before she comes in. [*Quickly opens the cupboard.*] What the hell is she after? I've no idea. [*Takes a quick drink.*] I'm all right if she doesn't know anything, but what if she does? I shall look such a fool.

SCENE V

[PLATONOV *and* ANNA. ANNA *comes in.* PLATONOV *slowly closes the cupboard.*]

ANNA. Hallo there. How are you?

PLATONOV. It won't shut. [*Pause.*]

ANNA. I say—hallo there.

PLATONOV. Ah, you, Anna, is it? Sorry, I didn't notice. Wretched door won't shut. Odd. [*Drops the key and picks it up.*]

ANNA. Come a bit nearer and leave that cupboard alone, do.

PLATONOV [*goes up to her*]. Hallo.

ANNA. Why don't you look at me?

PLATONOV. I'm too ashamed. [*Kisses her hand.*]

ANNA. What of?

PLATONOV. Everything.

ANNA. I see. Seduced someone, have you?

PLATONOV. Something of the sort.

ANNA. Same old Platonov! Who's the girl?

PLATONOV. I shan't tell you.

ANNA. Let's sit down. [*Sits on the sofa.*] We'll find out, young man, we'll find out. Why so ashamed? I've long known your sinful nature, haven't I?

PLATONOV. Don't ask questions, Anna. I'm not inclined to participate in an inquisition. Speak if you want, but don't ask questions.

ANNA. All right. Did you get my letters?

PLATONOV. Yes.

ANNA. Then why didn't you come?

PLATONOV. Oh, this is too much.

ANNA. Why is it too much?

PLATONOV. Because it is.

ANNA. Are you sulking?

PLATONOV. No, why should I? For God's sake don't ask questions.

ANNA. Kindly answer me, sir. Sit down properly. Why haven't you been to see us in the last three weeks?

PLATONOV. I've been ill.

ANNA. That's a lie.

PLATONOV. All right, it's a lie. Don't question me, Anna.

ANNA. You smell of booze. What's the meaning of this, Platonov? What's up? You look like nothing on earth—eyes bloodshot, ghastly face. You're filthy, so's your house. Take a good look round, the place is like a pigsty. What's the trouble—been drinking?

PLATONOV. Heavily.

ANNA. It's last year's business all over again. Last year you seduced some girl and went round till autumn looking the most awful drip—just as you look now, great lover and cringing worm all rolled into one. How dare you drink!

PLATONOV. I'll stop.

ANNA. Promise? But why should I bother you with promises? [*Gets up.*] Where's your drink?

[PLATONOV *points to the cupboard.*]

ANNA. Aren't you ashamed to be such a worm? Where's your backbone? [*Opens the cupboard.*] What a mess. Sasha will give you what for when she gets back. Do you want her back?

PLATONOV. Don't ask questions and don't stare at me, that's all I ask.

ANNA. Which bottle has liquor in it?

PLATONOV. All of them.

ANNA. What, all five? You old soak, you. A regular grog-shop in his cupboard! It's high time Sasha came back. You must explain things to her somehow. I'm not a very terrible rival. I'm ready to compromise—it's not my plan to keep you two apart. [*Sips from a bottle.*] Very tasty. Come on, how about a little drink? Eh? We'll just have one and then give it up.

[PLATONOV *goes to the cupboard.*]

ANNA. Hold your glass. [*Pours.*] Down the hatch. That's all you're getting.

[PLATONOV *drinks.*]

ANNA. Now I'll have one. [*Pours.*] To bad men everywhere. [*Drinks.*] You're one of them. Quite decent liquor, you have some taste. [*Hands him the bottles.*] Catch! Bring them here. [*They go to the window.*] Now say good-bye to your nice drinks. [*Looks through the window.*] Pity to pour it away, though—how about another, eh?

PLATONOV. As you like.

ANNA [*pours*]. Drink up, be quick about it.

PLATONOV [*drinks*]. Your health! And good luck.

ANNA [*pours and drinks*]. Have you missed me? Let's sit, and put the bottles down for a moment. [*They sit.*] Miss me?

PLATONOV. Every moment.

ANNA. Then why didn't you come?

PLATONOV. Don't ask. I shan't tell you, not because I have any secrets from you, I just want to spare your ears. I'm going completely to the dogs, darling, what with my pangs of conscience, misery, depressions—it's sheer torture in fact. You came, and that cheered me up.

ANNA. You look thin and ugly. I loathe these romantic heroes. What are you trying to pose as? Someone in a magazine story? Depression, misery, the battleground of passions, love complete with trimmings. Come off it, be a man. Can't you live like ordinary people, you idiot? Who do you think you are—God Almighty? Can't you live, sit and breathe like a mere mortal?

PLATONOV. It's easy to talk. What can I do?

ANNA. A living man—and doesn't know what to do! Most peculiar. What can he do? All right, I'll answer as well as I can, though the question's too idle to need an answer.

PLATONOV. You can't answer.

ANNA. Firstly, live like a human being. Don't drink, don't loll about, wash a bit more often and come and see me. Secondly, be content with what you have. You're being silly, my good sir. Isn't it enough to have gone in for this schoolmastering caper? [*Stands up.*] Come over to my place at once.

PLATONOV. What? [*Stands up.*] Go to your house? Oh dear me no.

ANNA. Come on. You'll meet a few people, talk, listen, argue a bit.

PLATONOV. No, no, no. And don't order me about.

ANNA. Why not?

PLATONOV. I can't go, and that's that.

ANNA. Oh yes you can, put on your hat and come.

PLATONOV. I can't, Anna, nothing would induce me. I won't move one step from this house.

ANNA. Oh yes you can. [*Puts his hat on his head.*] You're just fooling around, my dear man, don't try this funny stuff with me. [*Takes his arm.*] Left, right! Come on, Platonov. Quick march. [*Pause.*] Come along, Michael.

PLATONOV. I can't.

ANNA. He's stubborn as a mule. Put your best foot forward. Come on. Left, right—. Michael, darling, my dearest precious one.

PLATONOV [*breaking away*]. I'm not going, Anna.

ANNA. Then let's stroll round outside the school.

PLATONOV. Why must you pester me? Didn't I say I wasn't coming? I want to stay here, so leave me alone. [*Pause.*] I'm not going.

ANNA. I tell you what, I'll lend you some money and you go away for a month or two.

PLATONOV. Where to?

ANNA. Moscow, St. Petersburg—. How about it? Do go, Michael. You badly need a change. You can go for drives, look at the people, visit the theatres, tune yourself up and give yourself an airing. I'll give you money and letters. Like me to come with you? Eh? We'll drive around, have fun and come back refreshed and radiant.

PLATONOV. A fine idea, but it can't be done, sorry. I leave here tomorrow, but not with you.

ANNA. As you wish. Where are you going?

PLATONOV. Where I'm going. [*Pause.*] I'm leaving here for good.

ANNA. Don't be silly. [*Drinks from the bottle.*] Rubbish!

PLATONOV. It's not rubbish, dear, I'm going for good.

ANNA. But why on earth, you funny man?

PLATONOV. Don't ask me, but I'm not coming back, really. I'm leaving and—. Good-bye, that's all. Don't ask questions, you'll learn nothing from me now.

ANNA. Rubbish.

PLATONOV. This is our last meeting. I shall disappear for good. [*Takes her by the sleeve, then by the shoulder.*] Forget that idiot, ass, scoundrel and blackguard Platonov. He'll be swallowed up into the earth and vanish. We may meet in a few dozen years when we'll both be able to laugh and shed senile tears over these days, but now to hell with it! [*Kisses her hand.*]

ANNA. Come on, have a drink. [*Pours him some.*] A drunk can be excused for drivelling.

PLATONOV [*takes a drink*]. I won't get drunk. I'll remember you, fairy godmother, I'll never forget. All right, laugh, my emancipated blonde! Tomorrow I escape—from this place and from myself. Don't know where I'm going. I'm running away to a new life. I've a fair idea how it'll turn out!

ANNA. This is all very well, but what's come over you?

PLATONOV. What? I—. You'll find out later. My dear, when you shudder at what I'm going to do, don't curse me. I've been pretty well punished already, remember. Isn't it punishment enough to part from you for ever? Why do you smile? Believe me, you must believe me. I feel so beastly rotten and foul, I could strangle myself.

ANNA [*through tears*]. I can't think you could do anything awful. Will you write to me at least?

PLATONOV. I shan't dare to, and you won't want my letters anyway. Once and for all, unconditionally—farewell!

ANNA. You'll go to the dogs without me, Platonov. [*Rubs her forehead.*] I'm a bit drunk. Let's go together.

PLATONOV. No. Tomorrow you'll learn all and——. [*Turns to the window.*]

ANNA. Need money?

PLATONOV. No.

ANNA. Quite sure I can't help?

PLATONOV. I don't know. Send me a picture of yourself today. [*Turns back.*] Go away, Anna, or I don't know what the hell I'll do. I'll burst into tears, beat my breast and—. Go away. I can't stay, I tell you straight. So what are you waiting for? I must go, get that in your head. Why look at me like that and pull such faces?

ANNA. Good-bye. [*Gives him her hand.*] We'll meet again.

PLATONOV. No. [*Kisses her hand.*] That's enough—go away, dear. [*Kisses her hand.*] Good-bye. Leave me. [*Covers his face with her hand.*]

ANNA. He's all sloppy and sentimental, dear boy. Well? Let go my hand. Good-bye. How about a farewell drink? [*Pours.*] Drink up! Happy journey to you and good luck on arrival.

[PLATONOV *drinks.*]

ANNA. Couldn't you stay, though? [*Pours and drinks.*] We could have some fun. That's not a crime, is it? Can such a thing be imagined at Voynitsevka? [*Pause.*] Another one? To drown our sorrows?

PLATONOV. Yes.

ANNA [*pours*]. Drink up, darling. To hell with everything!

PLATONOV [*drinks*]. Good luck. Live here and—. You don't need me.

ANNA. If we're to drink, let's make a good job of it. [*Pours.*] You die if you drink and you die if you don't, so it's better to drink and to die. [*Drinks.*] I'm a drunkard, eh, Platonov? Want some more? I suppose we shouldn't. We'll get tongue-tied and then what shall we talk with? [*Sits down.*] There's nothing worse than being an educated woman, one with nothing to do. What's the point of me? Why do I live? [*Pause.*] I can't help being immoral. I'm an immoral woman, Platonov. [*Laughs.*] Eh? Perhaps that's why I love you, because I'm immoral. [*Rubs her forehead.*] I'll come to a bad end, my sort always do. I should be a professor, a headmistress or something. If I'd been a diplomat I'd have given the world a pretty thorough shake-up. An educated woman with nothing to do. I'm not needed, you see. Horses, cows and dogs are needed but not me—I'm just no use. Well? Why don't you speak?

PLATONOV. We're both in a bad way.

ANNA. If only I had children. Do you like children? [*Gets up.*] Stay behind, darling. Will you? We'd have lots of fun together. What will happen to me if you leave? I want a holiday, need a good rest. I want to be—a wife and mother. [*Pause.*] Say something. Speak. Won't you stay? You do love me, don't you, silly?

PLATONOV [*looks out of the window*]. I'll kill myself if I stay here.

ANNA. You love me, don't you?

PLATONOV. Who doesn't?

ANNA. You love me, I love you—what more do you want? You must be going crazy. What more do you want? Why didn't you come and see me that night? [*Pause.*] Are you staying?

PLATONOV. For God's sake go. You're torturing me.

ANNA [*gives him her hand*]. Well, in that case—good luck.

PLATONOV. Go away, or I shall tell everything and if I do I'll kill myself.

ANNA. I'm giving you my hand, can't you see? I'll pop over for a minute this evening.

PLATONOV. Don't, I'll come over and say good-bye myself. I'll come over—no, I will not! We've seen the last of each other. You won't want to see me, you won't want any more to do with me. A new life—. [*Embraces and kisses her.*] For the last time. [*Pushes her through the door.*] Good-bye. Run along, and good luck to you. [*Bolts the door.*]

ANNA [*behind the door*]. I swear we'll meet again.

PLATONOV. Never! Good-bye! [*Stuffs his fingers in his ears.*] I can't hear. Shut up and go away, I've blocked my ears.

ANNA. I'm going. I'll send Sergey over, and I guarantee you won't leave, unless it's with me. Good-bye. [*Pause.*]

SCENE VI

[PLATONOV, *alone.*]

PLATONOV. Has she gone? [*Goes to the door and listens.*] Yes. Perhaps not. [*Opens the door.*] She is rather a handful, isn't she? [*Looks out through the door.*] Gone. [*Lies on the sofa.*] Good-bye, my dear. [*Sighs.*] That's the last I'll see of you. Gone. She might have stayed five minutes longer. [*Pause.*] It wouldn't have been a bad idea. I'll ask Sonya to put off our departure by a couple of weeks, and go off with Anna. Only two weeks. Sonya will agree, she can stay with her mother for the time being. Shall I ask her, eh? While I'm away with Anna, Sonya can have a rest—pull herself together in fact. I shan't be away for ever, after all. [*A knock on the door.*] I'm leaving, it's settled. Excellent. [*Another knock.*] Who's knocking? Is it Anna? Who's there? [*Another knock.*] Is that you? [*Stands up.*] I won't let you in. [*Goes to the door.*] Is it her? [*Another knock.*] I think she's giggling. [*Laughs.*] It's her, I must let her in. [*Opens the door.*] Oh!

[*Enter* OSIP.]

SCENE VII

[PLATONOV *and* OSIP.]

PLATONOV. What on earth? You, damn you? What brings you here?

OSIP. Good evening, Mr. Platonov.

PLATONOV. What have you to say for yourself? To what and to whom do I owe the honour of so important a visit? Say your piece quickly and get to hell out of here.

OSIP. I'll sit. [*Sits.*]

PLATONOV. Oh, carry on. [*Pause.*] Is this you, Osip? What's wrong? You look as if you'd suffered all ten plagues of Egypt. What's wrong with you—pale, thin, worn? Are you ill?

OSIP. You've a pretty plaguy look yourself. What's happened to you? I'm in the hell of a state—how about you?

PLATONOV. Me? I'm not in touch with hell, I provide my own. [*Touches* OSIP's *shoulder.*] All skin and bones.

OSIP. You're not so plump yourself? Not ill, are you, sir? Been behaving too well, is that it?

PLATONOV [*sits down by him*]. What are you doing here?

OSIP. I want to say good-bye.

PLATONOV. Oh? Going somewhere?

OSIP. I'm not—*you* are.

PLATONOV. Oh, I see. How do you know?

OSIP. It's pretty obvious.

PLATONOV. You needn't have bothered, because I'm not going.

OSIP. Oh yes you are, sir.

PLATONOV. You seem to be quite a know-all and busybody. You're a magician, Osip. I am going, my dear fellow, you're quite right.

OSIP. So I did know, you see. I even know where you're going.

PLATONOV. Oh? What a man! I don't know that myself. You must be a real pundit—all right, where am I going?

OSIP. Want to know?

PLATONOV. Please, I'm interested. Where?

OSIP. To the next world, sir.

PLATONOV. That's a long way. [*Pause.*] Most mysterious—you wouldn't be going to dispatch me, would you?

OSIP. Just so, sir. I've brought you your ticket.

PLATONOV. Very nice of you. Well, well. So you've come to murder me?

OSIP. Yes sir.

PLATONOV [*imitating him*]. 'Yes sir.' What damned cheek! He's come to dispatch me to the next world. Is this your idea, or are you someone's agent?

OSIP [*shows him a twenty-five rouble note*]. Vengerovich gave me this to break your lordship's bones. [*Tears up the note.*]

PLATONOV. Old Vengerovich, eh?

OSIP. Yes.

PLATONOV. Then why tear it up? To show how noble you are, or what?

OSIP. That's a bit beyond me. I tore it up so you won't think I killed you for money when you get to the next world.

[PLATONOV *stands up and walks up and down the stage.*]

OSIP. Afraid, sir? Scared? [*Laughs.*] Run, shout if you want. I'm not standing by the door or holding it—you can get away. Go and call someone, tell them Osip came to kill you. Because I did. Don't you believe me? [*Pause.*]

PLATONOV [*goes up to* OSIP *and looks at him*]. Remarkable. [*Pause.*] What are you grinning at, idiot? [*Hits his arm.*] Stop grinning when I'm talking to you. And shut up. I'll hang you. I'll knock you into a cocked hat, you crook. [*Goes quickly away from him.*] Anyway— don't annoy me, I'm not supposed to get angry. I don't feel well.

OSIP. I'm a bad man, sir, so slap my face.

PLATONOV. By all means. [*Goes up to* OSIP *and slaps his face.*] Staggered you a bit? You wait, you'll stagger a sight more than that when hundreds of sticks smash in your empty skull. Remember how pock-marked Filka died?

OSIP. He lived like a dog and died like a dog.

PLATONOV. Ugh, you vile rat! I've a good mind to break a few bones, you blackguard. Why do you hurt people, you mean wretch, like some plague or conflagration? What have they done to you? Ugh, you horror! [*Slaps his face.*] Filthy swine. I'll show you, I'll—. [*Quickly goes away from* OSIP.] Now get out.

OSIP. Spit in my eyes, sir, for being such a bad man.

PLATONOV. I wouldn't waste good saliva.

OSIP [*stands up*]. How dare you talk like that?

PLATONOV. Get out of here before I really sort you out.

OSIP. You wouldn't dare, you're a bad man too.

PLATONOV. Bandy words with me, would you? [*Goes up to him.*] You came to kill me, I think? Well then, carry on. Here I am, go ahead.

OSIP. I used to think a lot of you, sir, used to think you were quite somebody. But now—. I'm sorry to kill you, but I must, you do too much damage. Why did the young lady come to see you today?

PLATONOV [*ruffles* OSIP's *chest*]. Go on, kill me.

OSIP. Why did Mrs. Voynitsev come here after her? You're deceiving her too, are you? And where's your wife? Which of the three do you really care for? Still think you're not a bad man? [*Swiftly trips* PLATONOV *and falls on the floor with him.*]

PLATONOV. Get out. I'll do the killing, not you. I'm stronger. [*They struggle.*] Less noise!

OSIP. Now on to your stomach. And keep your arm still—it hasn't done anything wrong, so why twist it? There you go again! My regards to General Voynitsev in the next world.

PLATONOV. Let go.

OSIP [*takes a knife from his belt*]. Less noise, I shall kill you anyway. Oh, aren't we big and strong, sir? Don't want to die, eh? Then keep your hands off what ain't yours.

PLATONOV [*shouts*]. My arm! Wait, wait! My arm!

OSIP. Don't feel up to dying, sir? You'll be in paradise in two ticks.

PLATONOV. Don't stab me in the back, monster. Stab me in the chest. My arm! Let go, Osip! I have a wife and son. Is that your knife shining, you vicious brute?

[SASHA *runs in.*]

SCENE VIII

[*The above and* SASHA.]

SASHA [*runs in*]. What's the matter? [*Shrieks.*] Michael! [*Runs towards the struggling pair and falls on them.*] What are you doing?

OSIP. Who's this? You, ma'am? [*Jumps up.*] I'll let him off. [*To* SASHA.] Here—my knife. [*Gives her the knife.*] I won't cut his throat while you're here, I'll let him off and do it later—he won't get away. [*Jumps out of the window.*]

PLATONOV [*after a pause*]. Blast the man. Hallo, Sasha—it's you, is it? [*Groans.*]

SASHA. Did he hurt you? Can you stand up? Quick.

PLATONOV. I don't know, he's a pretty tough customer. Give me your hand. [*Gets up.*] Don't worry, dear, I'm right as rain—he only roughed me up a bit.

SASHA. Vile creature! I told you to keep clear of him.

PLATONOV. Where's the sofa? What are you staring at? Your faithless husband's alive, can't you see? [*Lies on the sofa.*] Thank goodness you came, or I'd be dead and you a widow.

SASHA. Put your head on this pillow. [*Puts a pillow under his head.*] That's right. [*Sits on his leg.*] Feel any pain? [*Pause.*] Why have you closed your eyes?

PLATONOV. Oh, it's nothing. So you're here, Sasha? Back home, eh, precious? [*Kisses her hand.*]

SASHA. Little Nicholas is ill.

PLATONOV. Why, what's the matter?

SASHA. A sort of cough, a rash, and his temperature's up. He hasn't slept for two nights and he keeps crying. He won't eat or drink. [*Weeps.*] He's seriously ill, Michael, I'm so afraid. I had a bad dream too.

PLATONOV. What's your dear brother playing at? He's a doctor, isn't he?

SASHA. Well may you ask—you get no sympathy from him. He did look in three or four days ago, kicked his heels a bit and left. I tell him about Nicholas's illness and he just pinches himself and yawns. He said I was being silly.

PLATONOV. He can't talk, the fathead! He'll forget his own name next. He'd run away from his own sickbed, let alone anyone else's.

SASHA. What can we do?

PLATONOV. Hope for the best. Are you living at your father's?

SASHA. Yes.

PLATONOV. How is he?

SASHA. All right. He walks up and down his room, smokes his pipe and means to come and see you. I went to him in a bit of a state and, well, he guessed that I, er, that you and I—. What can we do about Nicholas?

PLATONOV. Don't worry, dear.

SASHA. I can't help it. If he dies, God forbid, what will happen to us?

PLATONOV. God won't take our little boy from you—why punish you? Not for having a no-good husband, surely? [*Pause.*] Look after the little chap, Sasha. Take care of him for me and I swear I'll make a man of him. Everything he does will please you. He is a Platonov after all, poor boy. But he should change his name. I don't add up to much as a man, but I'll make a great father. He'll be all right, don't worry. Oh, my poor arm! [*Groans.*] It aches, that bandit really hurt it. What's the matter with it? [*Examines his arm.*] It's red. Oh, to hell with it! Yes, Sasha—you'll be happy in your son. You laugh. Laugh away, darling. Crying now, eh? Why? Don't cry. [*Embraces her head.*] You came here—but why did you ever leave? Don't cry, my pet. Why all the tears? I do love you, child— very, very much. It's all my fault, but that can't be helped. You must forgive me. There, there.

SASHA. Is that affair over then?

PLATONOV. 'Affair?' What a word, my little suburban housewife.

SASHA. You mean it's still going on?

PLATONOV. How can I put it? There is no 'affair', only a frightful mix-up. Don't let it upset you too much—if it's not over yet it soon will be.

SASHA. But when?

PLATONOV. Quite soon, I should think. We'll go back to our old ways and to hell with everything new. I'm utterly fed up and worn out. The thing won't last, don't you believe it—I don't, it's all pretty casual. She'll cool off first, and be the first to laugh at it and regret it. Sonya's not my type. She's going through a phase I've been through already, and she's all starry-eyed about things that just make me laugh. Not my type at all. [*Pause.*] She won't be your rival much longer, take it from me. What's the matter, Sasha? [SASHA *stands up and stumbles.*]

PLATONOV [*gets up*]. Sasha!

SASHA. So it's—Sonya is it? Not Anna?

PLATONOV. Don't tell me that's news to you.

SASHA. Sonya? What a dirty, rotten business.

PLATONOV. What's the matter? You're pale, you're unsteady on your feet. [*Groans.*] Must you torture me as well? I've got a bad arm, isn't that enough? This isn't the first you've heard of it, surely? Why did you go away then? Not because of Sonya?

SASHA. Anna didn't matter so much. But another man's wife! What a rotten, dirty business. I never thought you could sink so low. God will punish you, you heartless man. [*Goes to the door.*]

PLATONOV [*after a pause*]. Bit shocked, eh? But where are you going?

SASHA [*stops by the door*]. The best of luck——

PLATONOV. Who to?

SASHA. You and Sonya.

PLATONOV. You've read too many trashy novels, Sasha. We're still very close to each other. We have a son, and I'm your husband after all. And I don't need happiness anyway. Don't go, Sasha. You're leaving—for good, I suppose?

SASHA. I can't cope. Oh God, God!

PLATONOV. Can't you?

SASHA. God, can it be true? [*Clutches her temples and sits down.*] I—I don't know what to do.

PLATONOV. Don't you? [*Goes up to her.*] Have it your own way. I'd rather you stayed, though. Don't cry, silly. [*Pause.*] I've done wrong, Sasha, but you can forgive me, surely?

SASHA. Have you forgiven yourself?

PLATONOV. A very questionable question. [*Kisses her head.*] Oh, do stay. Look, I'm sorry. Apart from you there's nothing but vodka, squalor, Osips. I'm fed up. Stay on as a nurse, if not as a wife. Women are queer cattle. You're so funny. If you don't mind feeding that rogue Osip, mollycoddling cats and dogs and staying up half the night to pray for various supposed enemies—can't you toss a crust to your guilty, repentant husband? Why must you hound me too? Don't go away, dear. [*Embraces her.*] I need a nanny. I'm a swine, I've run off with a friend's wife, I'm Sonya's lover, Anna's too perhaps, and I'm promiscuous. Haven't played the game by the family at all. So be as shocked and outraged as you like. But who'll love you, who'll appreciate the little woman as much as me? Who will you cook for? Whose soup will you put too much salt in? You're entitled to go, it's only fair you should, but—. [*Lifts her to her feet.*] Who will set you on your feet like this? Can you do without me, darling?

SASHA. Oh, this is too much—let me go. I'm done for. My life's in ruins—and you make jokes! [*Tears herself away.*] It's not funny, you know. Good-bye, I can't live with you. Now everybody will think you're a rotten swine. How do you think I'll feel? [*Sobs.*]

PLATONOV. All right, go. [*Kisses her head and lies on the sofa.*] I understand.

SASHA. You've wrecked our family. We were happy and contented. I was the happiest woman in the world. [*Sits down.*] How could you, Michael? [*Stands up.*] How could you? We can't put the clock back now. I'm done for. [*Sobs.*]

PLATONOV. All right then, go.

SASHA. Good-bye. You won't see me again. Don't come and see us. Father will bring Nicholas over. May God forgive you as I forgive you. You've wrecked our lives.

PLATONOV. Still here?

SASHA. No. Oh, all right! [*Looks at* PLATONOV *for some time and goes out.*]

SCENE IX

[PLATONOV *alone, followed by* SERGEY.]

PLATONOV. Look who's starting a new life now. That hurts! I'm losing everything, going crazy! God, that Sasha, that insect—that microbe!—should *dare*, and think she's so saintly that she can sling mud at me, damn it all!

[*Lies on the sofa.* SERGEY *comes in and stands by the door.*]

PLATONOV [*after a pause*]. Is this the epilogue or is the farce still going on? [*Seeing* SERGEY, *closes his eyes and snores gently.*]

SERGEY [*goes up to* PLATONOV]. Platonov! [*Pause.*] You're not asleep, I can tell from your face. [*Sits near him.*] I shouldn't have thought this was the time for sleep——

[PLATONOV *sits up.*]

SERGEY [*stands up and looks through the window*]. You've killed me, do you know that? [*Pause.*] Thank you very much. Oh, what do I care, confound you? Let it go, it must be fate.

[*Weeps.* PLATONOV *stands up and walks slowly to the opposite corner of the room.*]

SERGEY. I once had a stroke of luck, but I had to lose even that. He's clever, good-looking, great-hearted. But that wasn't enough—he had to have my happiness as well. He took it and I—. What of me? I don't count, it's all right. I'm ill, I'm not quite all there, I'm a sentimental, godforsaken weakling with leanings towards idleness, mysticism and superstition. And a friend gave me the *coup de grâce*.

PLATONOV. Get out!

SERGEY. In a moment. I came to challenge you to a duel, but now I'm here I'm in tears. I'll go. [*Pause.*] Have I lost her for ever?

PLATONOV. Yes.

SERGEY [*whistles*]. I see. Of course——

PLATONOV. Get out, please! Go!

SERGEY. In a moment. What can I do here? [*Goes towards the door.*] Nothing. [*Pause.*] Give her back, Platonov, be decent. She is mine, isn't she? Platonov! You can be happy without her. Save me, old boy, eh? Give her back. [*Sobs.*] She is mine. Mine, is that clear?

PLATONOV [*goes towards the sofa*]. Do go, or I swear I'll shoot myself.

SERGEY. Don't do that, damn you. [*Makes a gesture of despair and goes out.*]

PLATONOV [*clutches his head*]. Miserable wretch. Oh God, a curse upon my godforsaken head! [*Sobs.*] Leave people alone, you snake! I've made others unhappy, and they've done the same to me. So keep away from them. They're always doing me harm, but they can't quite do me in. Under every chair and piece of wood squats an assassin, staring at me, wanting to kill me. Then strike! [*Beats his chest.*] Strike before I kill myself. [*Runs to the door.*] But don't strike my breast, that's already torn to shreds! [*Shouts.*] Sasha! Sasha, for God's sake!

[*Opens the door.* PORFIRY *comes in.*]

SCENE X

[PLATONOV *and* PORFIRY, *followed by* CYRIL.]

PORFIRY [*comes in well wrapped up and carrying a crutch*]. You in, Platonov? Delighted. I'm intruding, but I won't keep you, I'll leave directly. I just want to ask one thing and I'll go away when I get an answer. What's the matter? You're pale, unsteady on your feet, shuddering. What's up?

PLATONOV. What, me? Eh? I must be drunk, or—I'm going mad. I'm drunk, drunk. My head's spinning.

PORFIRY [*aside*]. I'll ask my question. The sober hide what drunks confide. [*To* PLATONOV.] It's an odd—perhaps even stupid— question, but for God's sake answer, the matter's vital to me. I'll believe you, knowing you're a decent sort. If you think the question odd, absurd, silly—insulting, even—never mind. Just answer, for God's sake. I'm in an awful spot. Someone we both know—you know her well—. I thought she was beyond reproach. I mean Anna Voynitsev. [*Supports* PLATONOV.] Don't fall down, for God's sake.

PLATONOV. Go away, Porfiry—Mr. Glagolyev, I mean. I always thought you were a stupid old man.

PORFIRY. You're a friend of hers, you know her pretty well. She's either been misrepresented to me or—my eyes have been opened. She's a virtuous woman, isn't she? She—she—. Has she the right to be the wife of an honourable man? [*Pause.*] I don't know how to put my question. Try to understand, for God's sake. I've been told she——

PLATONOV. Everything in this world is rotten, vile and dirty. Everything——. Rotten, filthy——. [*Faints on* GLAGOLYEV *and collapses on the ground.*]

CYRIL [*comes in*]. Why hang round here? I'm not waiting any longer.

PORFIRY. 'Everything is rotten, vile and dirty.' Everything—that must include her.

CYRIL [*looks at* PLATONOV]. Father, what's wrong with Platonov?

PORFIRY. He's disgustingly drunk. Yes, rotten and filthy. The full, cruel, bitter truth. [*Pause.*] We're off to Paris.

CYRIL. What? Pa—Paris? What do you want to do in Paris? [*Laughs.*]

PORFIRY. Wallow, like that swine. [*Points to* PLATONOV.]

CYRIL. Wallow? In Paris?

PORFIRY. We'll try our luck in new surroundings. I've had enough. I'm tired of acting a farce for my own benefit and worrying my head with ideals. There's no more trust, no love, no decent people. Let's go.

CYRIL. To Paris?

PORFIRY. Yes. If sin we must, let's sin abroad, not in Russia. Let's have a good time before we rot. You can show me the ropes, Cyril. Paris, here we come!

CYRIL. This *is* nice, Father. You taught me to read, I'll teach you to live. Let's go.

[*They go.*]

END OF ACT THREE

ACT FOUR

The study of the late General Voynitsev. Two doors. Antique furniture, Persian rugs, flowers. The walls are hung with guns, pistols, Caucasian daggers and so on. Family portraits. Busts of Krylov, Pushkin and Gogol. A cabinet with stuffed birds in it. A bookcase. On it are cigarette-holders, boxes, sticks, gun-barrels and so on. A desk piled with papers, portraits, statuettes and firearms. Morning.

SCENE I

[SONYA *and* KATYA *come in.*]

SONYA. Don't be upset. Tell me what you mean.

KATYA. Something awful's going on, ma'am. The doors and windows are all wide open. Everything indoors has been turned upside down and broken. The door's been pulled off its hinges. Something awful's happened, ma'am. No wonder our hen started crowing like a cock.

SONYA. What do you think happened?

KATYA. I don't know, ma'am—what can I think? I only know it must be something. Either Mr. Platonov's left or he's done away with himself. He's very hot-tempered, he is. I've known him these two years.

SONYA. I don't believe it. Have you been down to the village?

KATYA. Yes, but he's not about. I was looking for three or four hours.

SONYA [*sits down*]. What, oh what can I do? [*Pause.*] Quite sure he's nowhere round here, are you?

KATYA. I don't know, ma'am. Something awful must have happened —no wonder I've got this pain in my heart. Give it up, ma'am, it's a sin. [*Cries.*] I'm so sorry for the master. Such a handsome man he was, and now look at him. Two days, and he's turned into a proper wreck, poor fellow. Goes round in a daze. That's the end of a kind gentleman. I'm sorry for Mr. Platonov too. A most cheerful gentleman, he was—he was a proper scream, but now he looks like death. Give it up, ma'am.

SONYA. Give what up?

KATYA. Love. What good is it? It only brings disgrace. I'm sorry for you too, you look like nothing on earth. You've grown thin, you don't eat, drink or sleep—all you do is cough.

SONYA. Katya, would you mind trying the schoolhouse again—he may be back.

KATYA. All right, ma'am. [*Pause.*] You ought to go to bed.

SONYA. Go over again, Katya. Not gone yet?

KATYA [*aside*]. It's all very well for you, you're not a servant. [*Brusquely and tearfully.*] Where am I to go then, ma'am?

SONYA. I want to go to bed, I got no sleep all night. Don't shout so, and be off with you.

KATYA. Very well, ma'am, but you shouldn't torture yourself like this. You should go to your room and lie down. [*Goes out.*]

SCENE II

[SONYA, *followed by* SERGEY.]

SONYA. This is terrible. He promised me yesterday to be at the hut by ten, but he didn't turn up. I waited till daybreak. So much for his promises. And so much for our love and going away together. He doesn't love me.

SERGEY [*comes in*]. I'll go to bed, might get a bit of sleep. [*Seeing* SONYA.] You—here? In my study?

SONYA. Me—here? [*Looks round.*] Yes, I just happened to come in without noticing. [*Goes towards the door.*]

SERGEY. One moment.

SONYA [*stops*]. Yes?

SERGEY. Can you give me a few minutes? Are you capable of staying here for two or three minutes?

SONYA. If you've something to say, say it.

SERGEY. Yes. [*Pause.*] There was a time when we could meet in here not as strangers.

SONYA. There was.

SERGEY. Sorry, I don't know what I'm talking about. Are you going away?

SONYA. Yes.

SERGEY. I see. Soon?

SONYA. Today.

SERGEY. With him?

SONYA. Yes.

SERGEY. I hope you'll both be happy. [*Pause.*] You've a solid base to build on—rampant lust, plus a third party's unhappiness! One man's meat is another man's poison. That's been said before, anyway. And it's nicer to hear a new lie than an old truth. Do what you like, confound you both.

SONYA. You had something to say.

SERGEY. I'm not exactly silent, am I? All right then, this is it. I want to do the right thing by you and not be in your debt, so I'd like to apologize for the way I behaved last night. I was nasty to you, I was rude and spiteful. Please forgive me, will you?

SONYA. Yes. [*Makes to go out.*]

SERGEY. Wait, wait, I've something else to say. [*Sighs.*] I'm crazy, Sonya. I simply can't bear this terrible blow. I'm mad, but I can still understand. In the vast fog of my brain—a sort of grey, leaden, heavy cloud—there's a gleam of light by which I see everything. If I lose that, it means I'm lost—completely. But I see all this clearly enough. [*Pause.*] Here am I in my own study, once used by my father, Major-General Voynitsev of His Majesty's suite, who held the Order of St. George—a great and famous man. People saw only his bad side. They saw him hitting out and trampling on people, but when he was beaten and trampled himself, no one cared. [*Points to* SONYA.] May I introduce my ex-wife?

[SONYA *makes to go out.*]

SERGEY. Wait, let me finish. I may be talking stupidly, but please hear me out—it's the last time, isn't it?

SONYA. You've said it all before. What can you add? We must separate—what else is there to say? Do you want to prove it's my fault? Don't bother, I know what to think of myself.

SERGEY. What can I say? Oh, Sonya, you don't know anything, or you wouldn't look at me so arrogantly. Something ghastly's happening to me. [*Kneels before her.*] What are you doing, where are you pushing us both? For God's sake have pity. I'm dying, I'm going off my head. Don't leave me. I'll forget—I already have forgiven. I'll be your slave, I'll love you, love you more than ever. I'll make you happy as the day is long, which is more than he'll do. You'll only wreck your life and his, you'll destroy Platonov. I know I can't make you love me, but don't leave me. You'll be happy again, you won't be so deathly pale and wretched. I'll be a man again, and Platonov can come and see us. This may be a mere pipe-dream, but don't go. Let's put back the clock while there's still time. Platonov will agree, I know him. He doesn't love you, it's just that—you gave yourself to him and he took you. [*Gets up.*] Are you crying?

SONYA [*gets up*]. Don't think I'm crying on your account. Platonov may agree, I don't care. [*Harshly.*] You're a rotten lot. Where is Platonov?

SERGEY. I don't know.

SONYA. Don't pester me, leave me alone—I hate you. Clear out! Where's Platonov? You're all rotten! Where is he? I hate you.

SERGEY. Why?

SONYA. Where is he?

SERGEY. I paid him some money and he promised to leave. If he's kept his word he must have gone by now.

SONYA. You bribed him? Why do you lie?

SERGEY. I gave him a thousand roubles and he said he'd give you up. I'm lying, actually—it's all a lie. For God's sake don't believe me. Friend Platonov's still alive and kicking, blast him. Go and get him, slobber over him, I didn't bribe him. But will you—will he—really be happy? Is this my wife, my Sonya? What does it all mean, though? I still can't believe it. The whole thing's platonic, isn't it? You haven't gone, er, the whole way?

SONYA. I'm his wife, his mistress—call it what you like. [*Makes to go out.*] Why keep me here? I haven't time to listen to all sorts of——

SERGEY. Wait, Sonya. You—his mistress! How could you? And brazen it out like this! [*Clutches her hand.*] How could you, oh, how could you?

[ANNA *comes in.*]

SONYA. Leave me alone. [*Goes out.*]

SCENE III

[SERGEY *and* ANNA.]

[ANNA *comes in and looks out of the window*.]

SERGEY [*with a gesture of despair*]. This is the absolute end! [*Pause*.] What's going on out there?

ANNA. Osip's been lynched by the villagers.

SERGEY. Already?

ANNA. Yes, near the well. Do you see? There he is.

SERGEY [*looks out of the window*]. Well, it serves him right. [*Pause*.]

ANNA. Heard the news, dear? They say Platonov's made himself scarce and—. Have you read his letter?

SERGEY. Yes.

ANNA. What price our estate! How do you like that? Gone with the wind! The Lord gave and the Lord taketh away. So much for our famous deal! It was all because we believed Glagolyev—he said he'd buy it, but didn't show up at the auction. The servants say he's gone to Paris. He's turned funny in his old age, the swine. But for him we'd have quietly paid off the interest and stayed on here. [*Sighs*.] Never trust your enemies in this world—or your friends either!

SERGEY. Yes, never trust your friends.

ANNA. Well, what will you do now, Squire? Where will you go? What the Lord gave your ancestors, he took from you—you've nothing left.

SERGEY. I don't care.

ANNA. Oh yes you do. How will you eat? Let's sit. [*They sit*.] Don't be so gloomy, it can't be helped. It hurts to say good-bye to your nice little home, but what can you do, dear? You can't put the clock back now. So that's the way of things. Be a good boy, Sergey, and the great thing is, do keep cool.

SERGEY. Don't bother about me, Mother, leave me out of it. You're not exactly calm either, so comfort yourself first and attend to me later.

ANNA. Well—. This isn't women's business, we must always stay in the background. The great thing is, keep cool. You've lost what you had, but it's the future that matters, not the past. You have your whole life ahead, a man's life with lots of good hard work in it, so why mope? Get a job in some school and start work. You're no end of a fellow—a scholar, a solid citizen. You never dabble in anything shady, you have your principles and you're a staid married man. You can go far if you want to, you're a very good little boy. Only don't quarrel with your wife—hardly married and already quarrelling! Why don't you speak, dear? You're upset, but you won't say why. What's happening between you two?

SERGEY. It's not happening, it *has* happened.

ANNA. What has? Or is it a secret?

SERGEY [*sighs*]. A ghastly calamity has struck our house, Mother. I don't know why I didn't tell you before—I kept hoping, and besides, I was ashamed to talk of it. And I myself only found out about it yesterday morning. As for the estate, I don't give a damn.

ANNA [*laughs*]. I'm quaking in my shoes! I suppose she's a bit annoyed with you or something.

SERGEY. Well may you laugh—you wait, you'll find yourself laughing on the other side of your face. [*Pause.*] She's been unfaithful to me. May I introduce myself—the well-known cuckold!

ANNA. Oh, don't be so silly. Whatever next! This is quite outrageous— you should think before you speak. You're fantastic, you do come out with the most shocking remarks. Cuckold my foot! You can't know the meaning of the word.

SERGEY. Oh yes I do, and not in theory either—I've found out the hard way.

ANNA. You are funny, you shouldn't insult your wife. Oh——

SERGEY. I swear it's true. [*Pause.*]

ANNA. How odd. What you say is quite impossible. It's slander too, and it can't be true. What—here in our village!

SERGEY. Yes, here in your blasted village.

ANNA. I see. But who in our blasted village can have had the grotesque idea of planting a pair of horns on your patrician brow? There just isn't anyone. You can't mean Cyril Glagolyev? Hardly—he's stopped coming here. There's no one here to interest your Sonya, it's just stupid jealousy, dear.

SERGEY. It's Platonov.

ANNA. What's Platonov?

SERGEY. He's the one.

ANNA [*jumps up*]. You can talk nonsense, but the sort of nonsense you're talking now—. Look, it's sheer poppycock. There are limits. You're being unforgivably stupid.

SERGEY. Then ask her. Or go and ask him if you don't believe me. I didn't want to believe it myself, I still don't, but she's leaving today—deserting me—so I have no choice. He's going with her. Look—I'm about as full of life as a dead cat, can't you see? I'm done for.

ANNA. It can't be true, Sergey—it's a figment of your childish imagination, I tell you. There's nothing in it.

SERGEY. She is leaving today, I tell you. I can also tell you that she's been on about being his mistress for the last couple of days. She told me herself. Incredible as it may seem, and however much it goes against the grain, one's just got to believe it.

ANNA. I remember, it's all clear to me now. Give me a chair, Sergey. No, don't bother. So that's it! I see. Wait, let me remember properly.

[*Pause.* BUGROV *comes in.*]

SCENE IV

[ANNA, SERGEY *and* BUGROV.]

BUGROV [*comes in*]. Hallo there. A happy Sunday morning to you. Alive and kicking, eh?

ANNA. Yes, yes, yes. This is awful.

BUGROV. There's a spot of rain, but it's hot. [*Mops his brow.*] Phew! Drive or walk, it's like an oven. Are you well? [*Pause.*] I really called because, as you know, the auction was held yesterday. Now the point is, er, and [*laughs*] a bit of a sore point it is to you, of course, a mite painful. So I, er—. Don't hold it against me, please. I didn't buy your estate. Abraham Vengerovich bought it, only in my name.

SERGEY [*rings the bell violently*]. To hell with them!

BUGROV. Precisely. Now don't think I—. It wasn't me—. So you see, it was only in my name.

[*Sits down.* JACOB *comes in.*]

SERGEY [*to* JACOB]. How many times have I asked you rotten filthy [*coughs*] swine not to let anyone in unannounced. You all deserve a good thrashing. Brutes! [*Throws the bell under the table.*] Get out, you swine.

[*Walks up and down the stage.* JACOB *shrugs his shoulders and goes out.*]

BUGROV [*coughs*]. It's only in my name. Mr. Vengerovich told me to say you can live here as long as you like—till Christmas, even. There will be one or two changes round here, but they won't bother you. Or if they do you can move into the lodge, where there's lots of room and it's warm. He also told me to ask if you'll sell me the mine—I mean sell it to him in my name. It's your mine, ma'am, so how about it? We'll pay a good price.

ANNA. No, I'm not damn well selling. What are you offering? Chicken-feed, I suppose? You can put that where the monkey put the nuts.

BUGROV. Vengerovich told me to say that if you don't agree to sell him the mine, ma'am, deducting what Mr. Voynitsev and the late general owe him—he's going to sue. And so shall I, ma'am, te he he! We're all friends here, but business is business. A little matter of commerce. Trouble is, damn it, I, er, bought your IOUs from Petrin.

SERGEY. I won't let anyone trade on my stepmother's estate paying my debts. The estate's hers, not mine.

BUGROV. Perhaps the lady will have pity on us.

SERGEY. I won't bandy words with you. Oh, really! [*Makes a gesture of despair.*] Do what you like.

ANNA. Please leave us, Mr. Bugrov. Sorry, but please go.

BUGROV. Very well. [*Gets up.*] Now don't worry, you can stay on, till Christmas even. I'll drop in tomorrow or the next day. The very best to you. [*Goes out.*]

ANNA. We'll leave tomorrow. Yes, now I remember—Platonov! So that's why he's skedaddling.

SERGEY. Let them do what they like, let them take the lot. I've lost my wife, so nothing else matters. My wife's left me, Mother.

ANNA. Yes, so she has. But what on earth did he see in that ninny Sonya, what did he—what *could* he—find in the girl? How blind men are, how stupid, swept off their feet by any—. But what were you playing at? Call yourself a husband? Where were your eyes, you awful drip? Snivelling while someone whips his wife from under his very nose! Call yourself a man! You're just a baby. Fancy marrying a brat like you, a silly little donkey—what a farce! You're both no good—you and your precious Platonov. This is quite ghastly.

SERGEY. Nothing will help now, and it's no use blaming me either. I've lost her and you've lost him, there's no more to be said. Leave me alone, Mother. You can't bear my stupid face, can you?

ANNA. What am I to do? Something must be done, we must save them.

SERGEY. Save who? I'm the one who needs saving. They're happy for the moment. [*Sighs.*]

ANNA. Oh, you and your reasoning! They need saving, not you. Platonov doesn't love her, you know. He seduced her, as you once seduced that silly German girl. He doesn't love her, I tell you. What did she say? Why don't you speak?

SERGEY. She said she was his mistress.

ANNA. She's more of a fool than a mistress. Now shut up! Perhaps it's not too late to mend things. Platonov's capable of making a great song and dance if a girl so much as kisses him or holds his hand. It hasn't gone all that far yet, I'll be bound.

SERGEY. Oh yes it has.

ANNA. You're a bit out of your depth.

[MARY *comes in.*]

SCENE V

[SERGEY, ANNA *and* MARY.]

MARY [*comes in*]. So there you are. Good morning. [*Shakes hands with* ANNA.] Good morning, Sergey. Sorry, I seem to be in the way. An uninvited visitor's worse than, worse than—what's the saying— worse than the plague, that's it. I've only looked in for a moment. You'll never believe this! [*Laughs.*] I must show it you, Anna. I'm sorry, Sergey, we must keep this between the two of us. [*Takes* ANNA *to one side.*] Just read that. [*Gives her a note.*] It came yesterday. Read it.

ANNA [*scans the note*]. Oh.

MARY. I'm having him prosecuted, you know. [*Puts her head on* ANNA's *breast.*] Will you send for him, please? He must come here.

ANNA. What's all this in aid of?

MARY. I want to see the look on his face now. Send for him, please, I've a word or two to say to him. You don't know what I've been up to. Don't listen, Sergey. [*In a whisper.*] I went to see the school inspector, and Platonov's being given a job somewhere else at my request. Oh, what have I done! [*Weeps.*] Send for him. Who'd have thought he would write a letter like this. Oh, if only I'd known! God, it's agony.

ANNA. Go to the library, dear, I'll join you in a minute and we can discuss it. I must talk to Sergey in private.

MARY. The library? All right. But you will send for him, won't you? What he must look like now after this letter! You did read it? Let me put it away. [*Puts the letter away.*] My dear, my darling—please! I'll go—but you send for him. Don't listen, Sergey. We'll talk German, Anna. *Schicken Sie, meine Liebe!*

ANNA. All right. Now run along.

MARY. Very well. [*Quickly kisses her.*] Don't be angry, dear, you just can't think what agony this is. I'm going, Sergey, you can carry on your talk. [*Goes out.*]

ANNA. I'm going to get at the truth. Now don't you go off the deep end, perhaps your marriage can still be patched up. What a frightful business—who'd have thought it? I'll have a word with Sonya at once, I'll really put her through it. You're making a silly mistake. Perhaps I'm wrong, though. [*Buries her face in her hands.*] No, no, no.

SERGEY. No, I'm not mistaken.

ANNA. Still, I'll have a word with her. And with him too.

SERGEY. Oh, go and have your words! But you might as well save your breath. [*Sits at the table.*] Let's get out of here. There's no hope, not even a straw to clutch at.

ANNA. I'm going to get at the facts. You can stay here and cry. Go to bed, you great baby. Where's Sonya?

SERGEY. She must be in her room.

[ANNA *goes out.*]

SCENE VI

[SERGEY, *followed by* PLATONOV.]

SERGEY. What a ghastly business. How long will it drag on—a day or two, a week, a month, a year? There's no end to this anguish. I ought to shoot myself.

PLATONOV [*comes in with his arm in a sling*]. There he is—I think he's crying. [*Pause.*] Peace be on you, my poor friend. [*Goes up to* SERGEY.] For God's sake, listen. I haven't come to make excuses. I'm not to be judged by you—or by myself. I've come to ask a favour for your sake, not my own, and I ask it as a good friend. Hate me, despise me, think what you like of me—but don't kill yourself. I'm not thinking of bullets, but of your all-round situation. You're not all that strong and unhappiness will finish you. My life will end, so let me be the suicide—not you. Do you want me to die? Do you? [*Pause.*]

SERGEY. I don't want anything.

[ANNA *comes in.*]

SCENE VII

[SERGEY, PLATONOV *and* ANNA.]

ANNA. Is he here? [*Goes slowly up to* PLATONOV.] Platonov, is it true?

PLATONOV. Yes.

ANNA. And he dares, dares to speak so casually. So it's true. You low swine, you knew you were playing a dirty game, didn't you?

PLATONOV. Low swine—can't we be a bit more civil? I knew nothing. All I knew or know about this business is that I've never wished him a thousandth part of his present sufferings.

ANNA. You might also note that one friend's wife shouldn't be another's plaything. [*Shouts.*] You don't love her, you were just bored.

SERGEY. Ask him what he came for, Mother.

ANNA. What a rotten thing to do—to toy with people. They're flesh and blood like you. Think you're awfully clever, don't you?

SERGEY [*jumps up*]. And he has the nerve to come here! What for? I know what you're after, but you won't surprise or shock us with a lot of hot air.

PLATONOV. Who's 'us'?

SERGEY. Now I know what your pompous talk's worth. You leave me alone. If you came here to atone by speechifying, your fine phrases won't work, believe you me.

PLATONOV. Angry screams don't prove a man's guilt, any more than fine phrases condone it. I think I did mention that I mean to shoot myself?

SERGEY. That's not the way to atone—in words I no longer trust. I despise your words. That's how a Russian atones. [*Points at the window.*]

PLATONOV. What is it?

SERGEY. Out there by the well lies a man who's atoned for his misdeeds.

PLATONOV. I saw him. But why all the eloquence, Sergey? You're unhappy, I believe, overwhelmed with grief—so why show off? What's the reason—insincerity or stupidity?

SERGEY [*sits down*]. Ask him why he came, Mother.

ANNA. What do you want here, Platonov?

PLATONOV. Ask your own questions—why trouble your stepmother? The game's up, your wife's left you and you're done for, you've nothing left. Sonya's as lovely as a spring morning—she's perfection itself. A man without a woman's like a steam-engine with no steam. You've lost your steam and your life's ruined. All is lost—your honour, your human dignity and your aristocratic pretensions—the whole thing! It's all over.

SERGEY. I'm not listening, you may as well leave me alone.

PLATONOV. Oh, naturally! Don't try and insult me, Voynitsev—I didn't come here to be insulted. Your unhappiness doesn't give you the right to ride roughshod over me. I'm a human being, so treat me as one. You're unhappy, but you and your unhappiness are nothing to the anguish I've felt since you left. That was a terrible night after you left, Voynitsev. I can tell you lovers of humanity that your unhappiness is nothing to my agony.

ANNA. Very possibly, but who cares about your agony or what happened that night?

PLATONOV. Don't you care either?

ANNA. I'm quite sure I don't.

PLATONOV. Oh? Don't lie, Anna. [*Sighs.*] Perhaps you're right in your way. Perhaps. But where can I find decent people, where can I turn? [*Buries his face in his hands.*] Where are there such people? They don't understand me, so who will? They're stupid, cruel, heartless.

SERGEY. I understand you all right, I've taken your measure. This grovelling doesn't suit you, my dear sir and ex-friend. I know what you are—you're a slippery customer, that's what.

PLATONOV. I'll overlook that remark, you fool, but you watch your step—don't say it again. [*To* ANNA.] Why are you hanging around? You like a good scene, don't you? Interesting, isn't it? This is none of your business, we don't need witnesses.

ANNA. It's none of your business either. And you can clear off. Damn cheek! Behaves like a filthy rotten cad, then comes here feeling sorry for himself. That's what I call being tactful! Anyway—sorry, but you'd please better go or you'll learn a few more home truths.

SERGEY [*jumps up*]. What more does he want from me? What do you want, what do you expect? That's what I don't see.

PLATONOV. I can see you don't. The thing is to drown your sorrows when you're unhappy, not go looking for company—that's been proved thousands of times. [*Goes to the door.*] I'm sorry I lowered myself by talking to you, I was foolish enough to think you were decent. But you're all the same—a lot of wild, uncouth provincial clod-hoppers. [*Goes out and slams the door.*]

ANNA [*wrings her hands*]. How revolting. Run after him at once and say—. Tell him——

SERGEY. What can I say?

ANNA. You'll find something to say. Anything. Hurry, please. He meant well, as you should have seen, but you were so cruel. Hurry, darling.

SERGEY. I can't, leave me alone.

ANNA. He's not the only one to blame, you know, we all are—we all have passions, we're all weak. So run along and say something nice. Show you're human, for goodness' sake. Go on—run!

SERGEY. I'm going mad.

ANNA. Then go mad, but don't dare insult people. Run, for God's sake. [*Cries.*] Sergey!

SERGEY. Leave me alone, Mother.

ANNA. I'll go myself. Why don't I go? I'll——

PLATONOV [*comes in*]. Oh!

[*Sits on the sofa.* SERGEY *gets up.*]

ANNA [*aside*]. What's the matter with him? [*Pause.*]

PLATONOV. My arm aches, I'm nearly starved to death. I'm cold, feverish, in pain. I'm suffering, can't you see? My life's over. What do you want from me, what more do you need? Wasn't that blasted night enough?

SERGEY [*goes up to* PLATONOV]. Let's forgive each other, Michael. I—. You can understand my feelings. Let's part friends. [*Pause.*] I forgive you—honestly, I do. If I could forget too, I'd be happier than I ever was. Let's leave each other in peace.

PLATONOV. Let's. [*Pause.*] But I've really come unstuck, the machine's broken. I'm terribly sleepy and my eyes won't stay open, but I can't sleep. I prostrate myself, I apologize, I'm sorry, I'm silent. Do and think what you like.

[SERGEY *goes away from* PLATONOV *and sits at the table.*]

PLATONOV. I'm not quitting this house if you set fire to it. If I'm annoying anyone they can leave the room. [*Makes to lie down.*] Give me something warm—not to eat, to put over myself. I'm not going home, it's raining. I'll lie here.

ANNA [*goes up to* PLATONOV]. Go home, Michael, I'll send over what you need or bring it. [*Touches his shoulder.*] Go on, go home.

PLATONOV. If anyone doesn't want me in here they can leave. Give me a drink of water, I'm thirsty.

[ANNA *hands him a carafe.*]

PLATONOV [*drinks from the carafe*]. I'm ill, really ill, dear.

ANNA. Go home. [*Puts her hand on his brow.*] Your head's hot. Go home and I'll send for Triletsky.

PLATONOV [*quietly*]. I'm in a bad way, madam, a very bad way.

ANNA. Well, how do you think I feel? You go. Please, you *must* go, do you hear?

[SONYA *comes in.*]

SCENE VIII

[*The above and* SONYA.]

SONYA [*comes in*]. Will you kindly take your money back? Very generous! I think I've told you once—. [*Seeing* PLATONOV.] You—here! Why? [*Pause.*] Odd. What are you doing here?

PLATONOV. Me?

SONYA. Yes, you.

ANNA. Let's go out, Sergey. [*Goes out and comes in on tiptoe a minute later and sits in the corner.*]

PLATONOV. It's all over, Sonya.

SONYA. Meaning what?

PLATONOV. What it means. We'll talk later.

SONYA. What do you mean by 'all', Michael?

PLATONOV. I need nothing, neither love nor hate—just a bit of peace. Please. I don't even want to talk. What's happened is good enough for me. So please——

SONYA. What's he saying?

PLATONOV. I'm saying I've had enough. I don't want any new life. I don't know what to do with the old one, I don't want anything.

SONYA [*shrugs*]. This makes no sense.

PLATONOV. Oh? The affair's finished, that's all.

SONYA. You mean you're not coming away with me?

PLATONOV. There's no point in going pale, Sonya—Mrs. Voynitsev, rather.

SONYA. Is this some caddish trick?

PLATONOV. Probably.

SONYA. You rotten swine! [*Weeps.*]

PLATONOV. I know, I've been told hundreds of times. We should have talked later, without witnesses.

[SONYA *sobs.*]

PLATONOV. You'd better go to your room, there's nothing more useless than tears when you're unhappy. It had to happen and it has. There are laws in nature and there's a logic in our lives. It's all been logical. [*Pause.*]

SONYA [*sobs*]. What has this to do with me or with my life which you took over till you were tired of it? Where do I come in? Don't you love me any more?

PLATONOV. You'll console yourself somehow, if only by letting this scene be a lesson to you in future.

SONYA. It won't be a lesson, it'll finish me off. How dare you talk like this? What a rotten thing to do.

PLATONOV. Why cry? I'm so sick of all this. [*Shouts.*] I'm ill.

SONYA. He swore oaths, begged me, he began it—and now he comes here! I make you sick, do I? You wanted me, but only for a couple of weeks. I loathe you. I can't stand the sight of him. Clear out! [*Sobs more violently.*]

ANNA. Platonov.

PLATONOV. Yes?

ANNA. Go away.

[PLATONOV *gets up and slowly goes towards the door.*]

SONYA. Wait, don't go. You—is this true? Are you sure you're quite sober? Sit down and think. [*Clutches his shoulder.*]

PLATONOV. I have sat down and thought. Get free of me, Sonya, I'm not meant for you. I rotted and fossilized so long ago, there's no reviving me now. Better to bury me a good way off, so I shan't pollute the air. For the last time, will you believe me?

SONYA [*wrings her hands*]. Tell me, what shall I—what *can* I—do? I shall die, I can't put up with this rotten behaviour. I shan't live five minutes, I'll kill myself. [*Sits in an armchair in the corner.*] What are you doing to me? [*Becomes hysterical.*]

SERGEY [*goes up to* SONYA]. Sonya!

ANNA. Oh good heavens, do calm down, Sonya. Give her some water, Sergey.

SERGEY. Sonya! Don't take on so, stop it. [*To* PLATONOV.] What are you hanging round for? For God's sake, go.

ANNA. That'll do, Sonya. Stop it.

PLATONOV [*goes up to* SONYA]. Well, what is it? Eh? [*Quickly moves away.*] This is idiotic.

SONYA. Leave me, all of you, I don't need your help. [*To* ANNA.] Go away, I hate you. I know who I have to thank for all this. You won't get away with it.

ANNA. Shush! We mustn't quarrel.

SONYA. He wouldn't have ruined me if it hadn't been for your corrupting influence. [*Sobs.*] Go away. [*To* SERGEY.] You go too.

[SERGEY *moves away, sits at the table and puts his head in his hands.*]

ANNA [*to* PLATONOV]. Clear out, I tell you. You're a complete nit-wit today. What more do you want?

PLATONOV [*stops his ears*]. Where can I go? I'm chilled to the bone. [*Goes to the door.*] Let me go to hell, the sooner the better.

[NICHOLAS *comes in.*]

SCENE IX

[*The above and* NICHOLAS.]

NICHOLAS [*in the doorway*]. If you say any more about 'announcing' me, you won't know what's hit you.

JACOB [*off-stage*]. Master's orders.

NICHOLAS. To hell with you and your master, he's as big a fool as you are. [*Comes in.*] He must surely be here. [*Falls on the sofa.*] Oh this is terrible, this, this, this—. [*Jumps up.*] Oh! [*To* PLATONOV.] The tragedy's reached its last act, Mr. Play-actor, it's nearly over now.

PLATONOV. What do you want?

NICHOLAS. Why waste your time hanging round here, you wretch? Aren't you ashamed, don't you feel guilty? Been laying down the law, eh? Preaching sermons?

PLATONOV. Talk sense, Nicholas. What do you want?

NICHOLAS. It's disgusting. [*Sits down and covers his face with his hands.*] It's an utter disaster—and so unexpected.

PLATONOV. What is?

NICHOLAS. 'What is?' Don't you know? Or care? Too busy, I suppose!

ANNA. Nicholas!

PLATONOV. It's about Sasha, is it? Tell me, Nicholas. Oh, this is the limit! What's happened to her?

NICHOLAS. She's poisoned herself by eating matches.

PLATONOV. What!

NICHOLAS [*shouts*]. Poisoned herself with matches. [*Jumps up.*] Here, read this. [*Holds a note before his eyes.*] Read it, my philosophical friend.

PLATONOV [*reads*]. 'It's sinful to commemorate suicides, but pray for me. I'm taking my life because I'm ill. Michael, love little Nicholas and my brother as I love you. Don't abandon Father. Live a good life. Nicholas, my son, may God bless you, even as I bless you with a mother's blessing. Forgive a sinful woman. The key to Michael's chest-of-drawers is in my woollen dress.' My darling! Sinful! Sasha— sinful? This is more than I can take. [*Clutches his head.*] She's poisoned herself. [*Pause.*] Sasha's poisoned herself. Where is she? Look—I must go to her. [*Tears the bandage off his arm.*] I—I'll bring her back to life.

NICHOLAS [*lies on the sofa face downwards*]. Bring her back to life! You shouldn't have killed her in the first place.

PLATONOV. Killed? How can you say such a thing, you lunatic? You can't think I killed her. Did I—did I want her to die? [*Weeps.*] She poisoned herself. That's all I needed to crush me like a squashed worm. If it was done to punish me, then—. [*Shakes his fist.*] It's a cruel, immoral punishment. Oh, it's more than I can bear. How could she? All right, I'm in the wrong, granted, I'm rotten—but I'm still alive, aren't I? [*Pause.*] Look at me, all of you, look at me—. Isn't it a pretty sight?

NICHOLAS [*jumps up*]. Yes, yes, yes. Now we're going to cry—we've always been one for turning on the waterworks, haven't we? You want a good hiding! Put on your cap and come. Call yourself a husband! A fine husband—ruining a woman's life for no reason. Look what you drove her to. And these people want to keep him here, they like him. He's an original type, an interesting case—his fading good looks etched with tragic lines! Come and see what you've done, you original and interesting case.

PLATONOV. Talk less, there's nothing to be said.

NICHOLAS. You're lucky I called in at home at dawn today, you hound. What if I hadn't, if I hadn't caught her? She'd have died. Get that into your head, since you're so good at seeing everything except what's under your nose. And I'd have made you pay, for all your tragic looks. Less goddam blethering from you, a bit more readiness to listen—and this disaster needn't have happened. She's worth ten of you clever people. Let's go.

SERGEY. Don't shout. Oh, I'm so fed up with all of them.

NICHOLAS. Come on.

PLATONOV. Wait. She—isn't dead, you say?

NICHOLAS. You mean you wish she were?

PLATONOV [*shrieks*]. She didn't die! I'll never understand it. She's not dead then? [*Embraces* NICHOLAS.] She's alive! [*Laughs.*] Alive!

ANNA. This makes no sense to me. Do explain, Triletsky. They all seem so stupid today. What does this letter mean?

NICHOLAS. She wrote it. But for me she'd have died, and she's still terribly ill—I don't know that she'll get over it. Just let her die and—. [*To* PLATONOV.] Would you mind keeping away from me?

PLATONOV. You gave me such a scare. God, still alive! So you didn't let her die, you splendid fellow. [*Kisses* NICHOLAS.] My dear fellow! [*Laughs.*] I never believed in medicine, but now I even believe in you. How is she—weak, unwell? We'll have her up and about again.

NICHOLAS. But will she recover?

PLATONOV. She will, I'll make sure of that. Why didn't you say she was alive in the first place? Anna dear, give me a glass of cold water and I'll be happy. Forgive me, all of you. I'm going mad, Anna. [*Kisses* ANNA's *hand.*] Sasha's alive. Water, dear.

[ANNA *goes out with an empty carafe and comes back a minute later with some water.*]

PLATONOV [*to* NICHOLAS]. Let's go and see her, we'll soon have her up and about. We'll turn the whole of medicine upside down from Hippocrates to Triletsky, we'll stir things up a bit! Who has more right to life than Sasha? Come on then. No, wait, my head's swimming, I'm terribly ill. One moment. [*Sits on the sofa.*] I'll rest a bit first. Is she very weak?

NICHOLAS. He's very pleased, but what he's got to be pleased at, I can't see.

ANNA. You gave me a fright too, you should take care what you say. Drink. [*Gives* PLATONOV *some water.*]

PLATONOV [*drinks greedily*]. Thank you, dear. I'm such a frightful hound. [*To* NICHOLAS.] Sit by me. [NICHOLAS *sits down*.] You're dead beat too. Thank you, my friend. Did she take much?

NICHOLAS. Enough to finish her off.

PLATONOV. Sasha of all people! Thank God it's all right. My arm hurts. More water, please. I'm terribly ill myself, Nicholas. Can hardly keep going, I'm on the point of collapse. Must be getting a chill. I keep seeing toy soldiers in cotton uniforms with pointed caps. The background's green and yellow. I want some quinine.

NICHOLAS. You want a damn good hiding.

PLATONOV [*laughs*]. Oh, very funny. You see, I do laugh at some of your jokes. Are you my brother-in-law? God, I'm so ill, you'd never believe it.

[NICHOLAS *feels his pulse*.]

ANNA [*quietly, to* NICHOLAS]. Take him along, Nicholas. I'll come over this evening and see Sasha. What made her give us such a fright? She's not still in danger, is she?

NICHOLAS. I can't say yet. She didn't kill herself, but she's in a pretty bad way.

PLATONOV. What did you give her?

NICHOLAS. What she needed. [*Gets up*.] Come on.

PLATONOV. And what have you just given Anna?

NICHOLAS. You're seeing things. Come on.

PLATONOV. All right. [*Gets up*.] Do give over, Sergey. [*Sits down*.] Pack it in. Why are you so cut up? As if someone had stolen the sun and left us in darkness—and you a former philosophy student! Be a Socrates, go on. [*Quietly*.] I don't know what I'm talking about, actually.

NICHOLAS [*puts his hand on* PLATONOV's *head*]. Now you have to fall ill! It might do you good, though—clear your conscience.

ANNA. Off with you, Platonov. Send for another doctor in town— a consultation might help. I'll send for one, though, don't bother. And do set Sasha's mind at rest.

PLATONOV. There's a tiny piano crawling over your breast, Anna. What a scream! [*Laughs*.] Very funny. Sit down and play us

something, Nicholas. [*Laughs.*] How priceless. I'm ill, Nicholas. I'm
quite serious, it's no joke. Come on.

[IVAN *comes in.*]

SCENE X

[*The above and* IVAN.]

IVAN [*dishevelled, in his dressing-gown*]. My poor Sasha! [*Weeps.*]

NICHOLAS. This is the limit—you and your tears. Clear out. What
brought you here anyway?

IVAN. She's dying, she's asking for a priest. I'm so frightened. [*Goes up
to* PLATONOV.] In God's name, Michael, you dear, clever, fine,
honourable fellow—go and tell her you love her. Please! Give up
your sordid love affairs, I beg you on my knees. She's dying, you see.
She's all I have, if she dies it will finish me—I'll be dead before you
can get me a priest. Tell her you love her, that she's still your wife—
put her mind at rest, for Christ's sake. A lie can be the means to
salvation. You're an upright man, God knows, but tell a lie to save a
life. Come on, please. Do me this kindness for Christ's sake, for an
old man, and God will reward you a hundredfold. I'm shaking with
fear.

PLATONOV. Been at the bottle already, Colonel? [*Laughs.*] We'll cure
Sasha and have a drink together. I'm so thirsty.

IVAN. Come on, it really is most awfully decent of you. Just say a
couple of words and she's saved. Medicine won't save her if her
trouble's in the psychology department.

NICHOLAS. Please leave us for a moment, Father. [*Takes his father by
the sleeve.*] Who says she's dying, what gave you that idea? She's not
in danger. You wait in that room and we'll go over and see her at
once with Platonov. Aren't you ashamed, bursting into a strange
house in that condition?

IVAN [*to* ANNA]. You should be ashamed, Diana, God won't forgive
you. He's a young man, inexperienced.

NICHOLAS [*pushes him into another room*]. Wait there. [*To* PLATONOV.]
Ready to go?

PLATONOV. I'm terribly ill.

NICHOLAS. Will you come or won't you?

PLATONOV [*gets up*]. Don't talk so much. What's the cure for a dry mouth? Let's go. I don't think I brought my cap in here. [*Sits down.*] Would you mind looking for my cap?

SONYA. He should have known this would happen. I gave myself to him without hesitation, knowing I was killing my husband, but I—I stopped at nothing for his sake. [*Gets up and goes over to* PLATONOV.] What have you done to me? [*Sobs.*]

NICHOLAS [*clutches his head*]. What a business! [*Walks up and down the stage.*]

ANNA. Calm down, Sonya, this isn't the time. He's ill.

SONYA. How can you be so inhuman—treat someone else's life as a plaything? [*Sits down by* PLATONOV.] My life's ruined, I'm not really alive any more. Save me, Platonov, it's not too late. [*Pause.*]

ANNA [*cries*]. What do you want, Sonya? There's time for this later— what can he say now? Haven't you heard? Weren't you listening?

SONYA. Platonov, I ask you again. [*Sobs.*] Is it no?

[PLATONOV *moves away from her.*]

SONYA. You don't want me? All right then. [*Falls on her knees.*] Platonov!

ANNA. That's rather overdoing it, Sonya. How dare you? No one's worth grovelling to—. [*Picks her up and helps her to sit down.*] Remember you're a woman.

SONYA [*sobs*]. Tell him—. Persuade him——

ANNA. Pull yourself together. Be firm, you're not a child. Oh, come off it. Go to your room. [*Pause.*] Go and lie down. [*To* NICHOLAS.] What can we do with her?

NICHOLAS. Better ask friend Platonov about that. [*Walks up and down the stage.*]

ANNA. Let's put her to bed. Sergey, Nicholas—well, make yourselves useful!

[SERGEY *gets up and goes over to* SONYA.]

NICHOLAS. Come on then, I must give her a sedative.

ANNA. I wouldn't mind a spot of chloroform myself. [*To* SERGEY.] Be a man, Sergey. You at least must keep your head. I feel no better than you do, but I'm standing on my two feet. Come on,

Sonya. What a ghastly day! [*They lead* SONYA *off.*] Buck up, Sergey. Let's be sensible.

SERGEY. I'll try, Mother, I'm doing my best.

NICHOLAS. Don't mope, Sergey old horse. You'll pull through, don't worry. You're not the first it's happened to and you won't be the last.

SERGEY. I'll do my best, I'll try. [*They go out.*]

SCENE XI

[PLATONOV, *followed by* MARY.]

PLATONOV [*alone*]. A cigarette, Nicholas, and some water. [*Looks round.*] Have they gone? I must leave too. [*Pause.*] I've hounded and ruined weak, innocent women. If I'd destroyed them in some other way—in a fantastic gust of passion, Spanish style—I wouldn't mind. But I just destroyed them so—stupidly. Murder *à la russe* or something. [*Whips his hand in front of his eyes.*] Keep seeing things. Little clouds. It looks as if I'm in for a bout of delirium. I feel a complete and utter wreck. And not so long ago I seemed on top of the world. [*Buries his face in his hands.*] I'm so bitterly, painfully ashamed. [*Gets up.*] I was hungry, cold, worn out. I was going to the dogs, I'd become a complete charlatan and I turned up here, where they took me in, warmed me, clothed me, and cherished me as the apple of their eye. A fine way I've paid them out! But I'm ill. Feel awful. Must kill myself. [*Goes to the table.*] Take your choice, there's a regular arsenal. [*Takes a revolver.*] Hamlet feared dreams, I fear life. What would happen if I went on living? I'd die of shame. [*Puts the revolver to his temple.*] The farce is over. This means one intelligent ape the less. Christ, forgive me. [*Pause.*] Well? So now I can die, and my arm can ache as much as it likes. [*Pause.*] I can't do it! [*Puts the revolver on the table.*] I want to live. [*Sits on the sofa.*] I want to live. [MARY *comes in.*] I'd like some water. Where's Triletsky? [*Seeing* MARY.] Who's that? Aha! [*Laughs.*] My worst enemy. Do we meet in court tomorrow? [*Pause.*]

MARY. Of course we can't be enemies after your letter.

PLATONOV. I don't care. Isn't there any water?

MARY. Water? What's wrong with you?

PLATONOV. I'm ill, I'm going to run a temperature. Yes, I liked that letter, it was rather clever. What would be even cleverer would be if people had nothing to do with me. I wanted to shoot myself. [*Laughs.*] Didn't bring it off, couldn't do it—mind and instinct pulling different ways. You've a smart look about you, are you a clever little girl? [*Kisses her hand.*] Your hand's cold. Listen. Shall I go on?

MARY. Yes, yes, yes.

PLATONOV. Then take me home with you. I'm ill, thirsty. I'm in frightful agony. I want to sleep, but I've nowhere to lie down. Let me sleep in a barn or somewhere, give me some water and a bit of quinine. Please! [*Holds out his hand.*]

MARY. Come on then, I'll be delighted. You can stay as long as you like. You still don't know what I've been up to. Come on.

PLATONOV. Thanks, clever little girl. A cigarette, some water and a bed. Is it raining?

MARY. Yes.

PLATONOV. We'll have to drive in the rain. We won't go to court, we're friends now. [*Looks at her.*] Am I raving?

MARY. Not at all. Let's go. I've a covered carriage.

PLATONOV. You're a pretty little thing. Why are you blushing? I shan't touch you, I'll just kiss your cold little hand. [*Kisses her hand and draws her to him.*]

MARY [*sits on his lap*]. No, this won't do. [*Gets up.*] Come on. You look a bit odd. Let go of my hand.

PLATONOV. I'm ill. [*Gets up.*] Come on. I'll kiss your cheek. [*Kisses her cheek.*] No ulterior motive! This is all beyond me anyway, it's all silly. Come on, Mary, and let's be quick about it. I was going to shoot myself with this revolver. In the cheek. [*Kisses her cheek.*] I'm raving, but I see your face. I love everyone—yes, you too. I've always treasured people. Never wanted to hurt anyone, but I did. I hurt them all. [*Kisses her hand.*]

MARY. Now I see it all, I understand your position. You mean Sonya, don't you?

PLATONOV. Sonya, Zizi, Mimi, Masha—there are enough of you. I love you all. When I was at the university I used to say a few kind words to the street-walkers in Theatre Square. Everyone was in the

theatre, but I was out on the square. I bought out one called Raisa.
Then I collected three hundred roubles with some other students and
we bought another one her freedom. Want to see her letters?

MARY. What's wrong with you?

PLATONOV. Think I'm mad, eh? No, it's just fever and delirium—ask
Triletsky. [*Takes her by the shoulders.*] They all love me, all. You
insult them—but they still love you. For instance, I insulted the
Grekov girl and banged her against the table, but still she loves me.
You are the Grekov girl, actually, aren't you? Sorry.

MARY. Where does it hurt?

PLATONOV. Being Platonov hurts. You love me, don't you? Be
frank. I don't want anything, just say if you love me.

MARY. Yes. [*Puts her head on his chest.*] Yes.

PLATONOV [*kisses her head*]. They all love me. When I get better I'll
seduce you. I used to help prostitutes, now I help to recruit them.

MARY. I don't care. I don't want anything else, you're the only man I
care for. I don't want to know anyone else. Do what you like with
me, you're the only man for me. [*Weeps.*]

PLATONOV. Now I understand Oedipus putting out his eyes. How low
I've fallen and how well I know it. Leave me alone, it's not worth it.
I'm ill. [*Frees himself.*] I'm leaving now. Sorry, Mary, I'm going mad.
Where's Triletsky?

[SONYA *comes in.*]

SCENE XII

[*The above and* SONYA. SONYA *goes up to the table and rummages
on it.*]

MARY [*clutches* PLATONOV's *hand*]. Shush!

[*Pause.* SONYA *takes the revolver, fires at* PLATONOV *and misses.*]

MARY [*stands between* PLATONOV *and* SONYA]. What are you doing?
[*Shouts.*] Help! In here, quick!

SONYA. Out of my way! [*Runs round* MARY *and shoots* PLATONOV
point-blank in the chest.]

PLATONOV. Wait, just a moment—. What is this?

[*Falls.* ANNA, IVAN, NICHOLAS *and* SERGEY *run in.*]

SCENE XIII

[*The above,* ANNA, IVAN, NICHOLAS *and* SERGEY, *followed by servants and* MARKO.]

ANNA [*snatches the revolver off* SONYA *and hurls her on the sofa*]. Platonov!

[*Bends over* PLATONOV. SERGEY *covers his face and turns to the door.*]

NICHOLAS [*bends over* PLATONOV *and quickly unbuttons his frock-coat. Pause.*] Michael, can you hear me? [*Pause.*]

ANNA. For God's sake, Platonov! Michael, Michael! Hurry up, Triletsky.

NICHOLAS [*shouts*]. Water!

MARY [*gives him a carafe*]. Save him, you'll save him, won't you?

[*Walks up and down the stage.* NICHOLAS *drinks the water and throws the carafe to one side.*]

IVAN [*clutches his head*]. Didn't he say I was done for. Well, I am. [*Kneels.*] God Almighty, I'm done for, finished.

[JACOB, VASILY, KATYA *and the* CHEF *run in.*]

MARKO [*comes in*]. A message from the magistrate, sir. [*Pause.*]

ANNA. Platonov!

[PLATONOV *raises himself a little and looks round at everyone.*]

ANNA. Platonov, it's all right—drink some water.

PLATONOV [*points to* MARKO]. Give him three roubles. [*Falls and dies.*]

ANNA. Buck up, Sergey. This will soon be over, Nicholas, it won't last for ever. So pull yourselves together.

KATYA [*bows low to* ANNA]. It's my fault, I delivered the note. It was the money tempted me. I'm sorry, it was unforgivable, ma'am.

ANNA. Pull yourselves together, don't go off the deep end. He's only just—. He'll be all right.

NICHOLAS [*shouts*]. He's dead!

ANNA. No, no.

[MARY *sits at the table, looks at the note and weeps bitterly.*]

IVAN. May he rest in peace. He's gone, done for.

NICHOLAS. Life's only worth a copeck. Good-bye, Michael, you've lost your copeck. What are you all goggling at? He shot himself. The party's over. [*Weeps.*] Who can I celebrate your funeral with? Fools! You couldn't look after Platonov. [*Stands up.*] Father, go and tell Sasha she may as well die. [*Swaying, goes up to* SERGEY.] What about you, eh? [*Embraces* SERGEY.] Poor old Platonov's dead. [*Sobs.*]

SERGEY. What are we to do, Nicholas?

NICHOLAS. Bury the dead and do our best for the living.

ANNA [*slowly gets up and walks towards* SONYA]. Calm yourself, Sonya. [*Sobs.*] What have you done! But, but—calm yourself. [*To* NICHOLAS.] Don't say anything to Sasha, I'll tell her myself. [*Goes to* PLATONOV *and kneels before him.*] Platonov! My darling! I can't believe it. You can't be dead. [*Takes his hand.*] My life!

NICHOLAS. There's work to do, Sergey. We must help your wife, and then——

SERGEY. Yes, yes, yes. [*Goes to* SONYA.]

IVAN. God has forsaken me for my sins. Why did you sin, you silly old clown? I killed God's creatures, got drunk, swore and condemned people. The Lord could put up with no more, and struck me.

END OF ACT FOUR

THE PRONUNCIATION OF RUSSIAN PROPER NAMES

English-speaking actors do not usually attempt a phonetically accurate reproduction of Russian proper names on the stage. But where the less familiar proper names are concerned it is probably worth trying at least to preserve the Russian stress accent, and so an alphabetical list is appended of the proper names in the text, the stress being indicated by an acute accent over the relevant vowel.

Aleksándrovich
Alekséyevskoye
Altukhóv
Aplómbov
Ayvazóvsky

Babelmandébsky
Bátyushkov
Berezhnítsky
Borís
Bortsóv
Bortsóvka
Bugróv

Cheprakóv
Chubukóv

Dásha
Dmítry
Dunyásha
Dyádin
Dýmba

Fédya
Feódorovna
Fínberg
Fonvísin
Fyódor

Gánzen
Gerásim
Glagólyev
Glínka
Gógol
Grékov
Grendilévsky
Grúzdev
Gúsev

Iván
Ivánov

Kashkinázi
Kátya
Khamónyev
Khárkov
Kharlámpy
Khírin
Khrápov
Khrushchóv
Kíev
Kokóshkin
Korchágin
Kotélnikov
Krylóv
Kubán
Kúritsyn
Kuzmá
Kuznetsóv

Lénsky
Leoníd
Lérmontov
Lomonósov
Lómov
Lyudmíla

Maríya
Márko
Másha
Matvéyev
Matvéyevich
Mazútov
Merchútkin
Mérik
Mikíshkin

Mirónov
Mísha
Mozgovóy
Muráshkin

Nastásya
Natálya
Natásha
Nazárovna
Nekrásov
Nikíta
Novo–Petróvskoye
Nyúkhin
Nyúnin

Odéssa
Olénin
Ólga
Onégin
Orlóvsky
Ósip

Patrónnikov
Pelagéya
Pétrin
Pirogóv
Platónov
Platónovka
Polikárpov
Poltáva
Popóv
Porfíry
Púshkin

Répin
Revunóv–Karaúlov
Rýblovo

Sabínin
Samára
Sásha
Sávva
Serebryakóv
Sergéy

Sevastópol
Shcherbúk
Shervetsóv
Shipúchin
Smirnóv
Solomónovich
Sónnenstein
Sónya
Svetlovídov

Tatyána
Telibéyev
Tíkhon
Tolkachóv
Trilétsky
Turgénev

Varsonófyevo
Vasíly
Vengeróvich
Víkhrin
Vladímir
Vlásin
Vlásov
Vólgin
Volódya
Voynítsev
Voynítsevka
Voynítsky

Yefímovna
Yegór
Yergóv
Yevdokím
Yevstignéyev

Záytsev
Zheltúkhin
Zhigálov
Zína
Zipunóv
Zmeyúkin

EXPLANATORY NOTES

The following notes, which have been kept as brief as possible, are designed to explain references in the text which might be obscure to English-speaking readers and to point out certain difficulties which have occurred in the translation.

SHORT PLAYS

4. 'Vologda.' Town about three hundred miles north of Moscow.

4. 'St. Tikhon.' Reference is to the Zadonsk Monastery in the Voronezh Province of central Russia, founded in the seventeenth century and famous for its association with St. Tikhon Zadonsky (1724–83).

4. 'Holy Mountains.' A monastery in the Kharkov Province of the Ukraine, said to date from the fifteenth century.

9. 'The Kuban District.' The area of the River Kuban, north of the Caucasus.

18. 'Poltava.' Town in the Ukraine, 70 miles south-west of Kharkov.

18. '. . . as the man says in the play.' Literally, 'as Shchastlivtsev says'. Shchastlivtsev is a character in the play The Forest (1871) by A. N. Ostrovsky (1823–86).

27. 'Calchas.' Though Chekhov does not state the name of the play in which his hero has been acting, this was presumably Shakespeare's Troilus and Cressida, the dramatis personae of which include: 'CALCHAS, a Trojan priest taking part with the Greeks.'

31. 'Boris Godunov.' The passage comes from the verse play Boris Godunov (published 1831) by A. S. Pushkin (1799–1837).

31. 'Blow, winds . . .' From Shakespeare's King Lear, Act Three, Scene ii.

31. 'O! the recorders . . .' From Shakespeare's Hamlet, Act Three Scene ii.

32. 'O silent night . . .' The passage comes from the second canto of Pushkin's narrative poem Poltava (1829).

33. 'Farewell the tranquil mind . . .' From Shakespeare's Othello, Act Three, Scene iii.

33. 'Away from Moscow! . . .' These are Chatsky's famous exit lines from Act Four, Scene xiv of Woe from Wit (written 1822–4) by A. S. Griboyedov (1795–1829).

35. 'N. N. Solovtsov.' The famous actor (1856–1902) and childhood friend of Chekhov.

44. 'Whispers, passion's bated breathing.' The first lines of a well-known lyric by A. A. Fet (1820–92).

45. 'Tamara.' A reference to the heroine of the poem *Tamara* (1841) by M. Yu. Lermontov (1814–41).

56. '. . . the government land settlement.' Reference is to the statutes issued in connection with the Emancipation of the Serfs in 1861.

61. 'My fate, ye gods . . .' Famusov's exit lines from the end of Act One of Griboyedov's *Woe from Wit*.

84. 'It's talk like this . . .' A near-quotation from Famusov's opening speech in Act Two, Scene i of Griboyedov's *Woe from Wit*.

92. 'Oh, tell me not . . .' From the poem *A Heavy Cross Became her Lot in Life* (1855) by N. A. Nekrasov (1821–78).

96. 'Volunteer Fleet.' This consisted of merchant ships and their crews which could be mobilized in an emergency.

99. 'I loved you once, and love perhaps might still—.' The opening line of a well-known lyric by Pushkin.

100. 'Restless, he seeks the raging storm . . .' These are the last two lines of Lermontov's well-known lyric *The Sail* (1832).

115. 'Jack the Ripper.' The famous murderer, believed responsible for killing six or more women in London in late 1888. He was never caught, but was believed by some to be a mad Russian doctor.

118. 'Onegin, how can I deny . . .' From the aria 'To love all ages must submit', sung by Tatyana's husband in the last act of the opera *Eugene Onegin* (1877–88) by P. I. Tchaikovsky (1840–93), based on Pushkin's verse novel with the same title.

125. 'Two friends one night . . .' From the fable *The Passers-by and the Geese* by I. A. Krylov (1769–1844).

125. 'Oh, tell me not . . .' See note on p. 112, above.

129. '. . . good old Keating's powder.' Literally, 'Persian powder', a common measure of protection against insects.

136. 'Turgenev.' I. S. Turgenev (1818–83), the well-known Russian novelist.

136. 'Samara.' Town on the middle Volga, now called Kuybyshev.

THE WOOD—DEMON

156 and 162. 'Thou shalt of all the universe . . .' The lines are from Lermontov's poem *The Demon* (1839). Chekhov has substituted the word 'faithful' for the word 'first', which occurs in the original.

179. '*Lensky's aria* . . . Eugene Onegin.' The reference is to the opera

Eugene Onegin (1877–8) by P. I. Tchaikovsky (1840–93), based on Pushkin's verse novel with the same title.

179. '. . . the volunteers in Serbia . . .' When Serbia declared war on Turkey in 1876, many Russians sympathaized with the Serbs as fellow-Slavs and volunteered to fight in the Serbian army. In the following year Russia declared war on Turkey, thus beginning the Russo–Turkish War of 1877–8.

196. 'Lomonosov.' M. V. Lomonosov (1711–65) was the son of a fisherman in the north Russian port of Archangel. He ran away to Moscow at the age of 17 and became famous as a scientist, educationist, poet, and grammarian.

198. 'Ayvazovsky.' See note to p. 58, above.

201. 'Against my will to these sad shores . . .' This couplet comes from Pushkin's dramatic poem *The Mermaid* (1832).

204. 'Scatter the seed . . .' From Nekrasov's poem *To the Sowers* (1876–7).

213. 'O wondrous spot, wood-demons' haunt . . .' The lines occur near the beginning of Pushkin's poem *Ruslan and Lyudmila* (1820).

213. '. . . lieutenant in the Serbian army . . .' See note to p. 237, above.

PLATONOV

226. '*Russian national dress.*' See note to p. 104 of *The Oxford Chekhov*, vol. viii, p. 318.

227. 'Mayne Reid.' Thomas Mayne Reid (1818–83), of Irish origin, author of children's adventure stories written in English and popular in Russia in Russian translation.

233. 'the *Russian Courier.*' *Russky kuryer*, a Moscow daily paper (1879–91).

243. 'Fonvizin.' D. I. Fonvizin (1745–92), the leading Russian eighteenth-century playwright.

261. 'Pirogov.' N. I. Pirogov (1810–81), the famous surgeon.

261. 'Kiev.' Large city in the Ukraine and site of the well-known Monastery of the Caves.

290. 'Monastery of the Trinity and St. Sergius.' At modern Zagorsk, about 50 miles north of Moscow. One of the best-known Russian monasteries.

290. 'New Jerusalem Monastery.' In the Zvenigorod District of Moscow Province, founded in 1656.

290. 'Kharkov.' Large city in the Ukraine.

290. 'Of course he does.' Literally: 'Of course—he's a Collegiate Registrar.' This was the fourteenth and lowest grade in the 'table of ranks'—the hierarchy to which all Russian officials, including schoolmasters in state schools, belonged.

292. 'Sacher-Masoch.' The Austrian writer L. Sacher-Masoch (1836–95), from whose name the word 'masochism' is derived.

296. 'Pushkins or Lermontovs.' Reference is to the poets. A. S. Pushkin (1799–1837) and M. Yu. Lermontov (1814–41).

296. 'Auerbach, Heine, Goethe.' Reference is to Bertolt Auerbach (1812–82), the German novelist; and to the German poets Heinrich Heine (1797–1856) and Johann Wolfgang Goethe (1749–1832).

302. 'Ring out, ye peals of victory.' From a poem by G. R. Derzhavin (1743–1816). A misquotation—the original has 'thunder' in place of 'ye peals'.

304. 'Nekrasov.' N. A. Nekrasov (1821–78), the Russian poet.

312. 'Glinka.' M. I. Glinka (1804–57), the Russian composer.

312. 'O shame! where is thy blush?' etc. *Hamlet*, Act Three, Scene iv. The Russian original is a paraphrase of these lines of *Hamlet*, or of others from the same speech.

320. 'Sevastopol.' Reference is to the siege of Sevastopol (1854–5), the Crimean naval base, during the Crimean War.

340. 'Krylov.' I. A. Krylov (c. 1769–1844), the best known Russian writer of fables.

340. 'Gogol.' N. V. Gogol (1809–52), the Russian writer.

363. 'Theatre Square.' Large square in front of the Bolshoy Theatre in the centre of Moscow, now Sverdlov Square.

GEORGE ELIOT	**Adam Bede**
	Daniel Deronda
	Middlemarch
	The Mill on the Floss
	Silas Marner
ELIZABETH GASKELL	**Cranford**
	The Life of Charlotte Brontë
	Mary Barton
	North and South
	Wives and Daughters
THOMAS HARDY	**Far from the Madding Crowd**
	Jude the Obscure
	The Mayor of Casterbridge
	A Pair of Blue Eyes
	The Return of the Native
	Tess of the d'Urbervilles
	The Woodlanders
WALTER SCOTT	**Ivanhoe**
	Rob Roy
	Waverley
MARY SHELLEY	**Frankenstein**
	The Last Man
ROBERT LOUIS STEVENSON	**Kidnapped** and **Catriona**
	The Strange Case of Dr Jekyll and Mr Hyde and **Weir of Hermiston**
	Treasure Island
BRAM STOKER	**Dracula**
WILLIAM MAKEPEACE THACKERAY	**Barry Lyndon**
	Vanity Fair
OSCAR WILDE	**Complete Shorter Fiction**
	The Picture of Dorian Gray

The Oxford World's Classics Website

www.worldsclassics.co.uk

- Information about new titles
- Explore the full range of Oxford World's Classics
- Links to other literary sites and the main OUP webpage
- Imaginative competitions, with bookish prizes
- Peruse *Compass*, the Oxford World's Classics magazine
- Articles by editors
- Extracts from Introductions
- A forum for discussion and feedback on the series
- Special information for teachers and lecturers

www.worldsclassics.co.uk

American Literature

British and Irish Literature

Children's Literature

Classics and Ancient Literature

Colonial Literature

Eastern Literature

European Literature

History

Medieval Literature

Oxford English Drama

Poetry

Philosophy

Politics

Religion

The Oxford Shakespeare

A complete list of Oxford Paperbacks, including Oxford World's Classics, OPUS, Past Masters, Oxford Authors, Oxford Shakespeare, Oxford Drama, and Oxford Paperback Reference, is available in the UK from the Academic Division Publicity Department, Oxford University Press, Great Clarendon Street, Oxford OX2 6DP.

In the USA, complete lists are available from the Paperbacks Marketing Manager, Oxford University Press, 198 Madison Avenue, New York, NY 10016.

Oxford Paperbacks are available from all good bookshops. In case of difficulty, customers in the UK can order direct from Oxford University Press Bookshop, Freepost, 116 High Street, Oxford OX1 4BR, enclosing full payment. Please add 10 per cent of published price for postage and packing.